PEARSON

ALWAYS LEARNING

Financial Risk Manager (FRM®) Part I
Financial Markets and Products

Fourth Custom Edition for
Global Association of Risk Professionals
2014

GARP | Global Association
of Risk Professionals

Excerpts taken from:

Options, Futures, and Other Derivatives, Eighth Edition, by John C. Hull

Derivatives Markets, Third Edition, by Robert McDonald

Pearson Learning Solutions, 501 Boylston Street, Suite 900, Boston, MA 02116
A Pearson Education Company
www.pearsoned.com

Printed in the United States of America

1 2 3 4 5 6 7 8 9 10 V011 17 16 15 14 13

000200010271841524

JH/LC

PEARSON   ISBN 10: 1-269-59108-8
ISBN 13: 978-1-269-59108-9

Contents

2014 FRM Committee Members

Introduction: Futures and Options Markets

1

■ Learning Objectives

Candidates, after completing this reading, should be able to:

- Describe the risks in the commodities business that are addressed by the use of futures contracts.
- Describe the key features and terms of a futures contract.

- Differentiate between equity securities and futures contracts.
- Define and interpret volume and open interest.
- Explain the requisites for a successful futures market.

Excerpt is Chapter 1 of Futures and Options, *The Institute for Financial Markets.*

Management of commodity and asset price risk has preoccupied businessmen for as long as organized marketplaces have existed. Medieval merchants and traders faced the same problem as today's producers, distributors, dealers and investors: they all have had to find ways of managing the uncertainty of prices over time.

Special contractual arrangements between individuals were the answer for many centuries. But as the markets grew, organized futures exchanges became established as a key tool in risk management. Today, the efficiency of the futures markets makes it possible for farmers, international trading corporations, manufacturers, securities dealers, banks, commercial distributors, and many others to manage their price risks. Futures markets also allow speculators and investors to participate in the price discovery process, making the entire marketplace more efficient.

Although modern futures markets developed from the need to manage risk in an agriculturally-driven economy, the mechanism proved so effective and flexible that it was readily adaptable to a changing economy, with futures markets developing for industrial raw materials such as copper and, eventually, oil, natural gas, and electricity. In recent decades, this same futures model has been applied to the raw materials of finance: interest rates, currency exchange rates and the value of corporate equities.

This book provides a comprehensive introduction to the futures and futures options markets: a basic understanding of what the markets are, how they work, who uses them and why.

THE DEVELOPMENT OF FUTURES MARKETS

The first attempt to cope with the risks of commodity price changes was the use of a "to-arrive" contract, in which buyer and seller would agree privately and in advance to the terms of a sale that would be consummated when the goods "arrived." Contracts of sale on a to-arrive basis were made as early as 1780 in the Liverpool cotton trade.

In the United States, buyers and sellers began meeting in the street to transact commodity business. As volume increased, the need for a more permanent central marketplace became apparent. In 1848, the Chicago Board of Trade became the nation's first organized commodity market. Although the to-arrive contract was an important innovation, several additional changes in commercial practices were necessary before futures would become a useful tool in the marketing, hedging and trading of commodities.

Lack of Adequate Storage

The relationship of a buyer and seller, as all business relationships, is founded on trust: the buyer has to believe the seller can deliver the promised goods; the seller has to believe the buyer can pay for them. Advances in warehouse capacities helped guarantee that there would be adequate supplies of commodities to match outstanding contracts. Other problems, such as spoilage and fraud in the handling of commodities in store, required the development of an organized system of dealing with the quality of stored commodities. Today, in addition to laws and regulations governing the proper handling of commodities in storage, futures exchanges have developed systems for licensing and inspection of warehouses from which deliveries can be made on futures contracts.

Standardization of Quality

Commodities grown or produced in different areas can vary widely in grade, weight per unit of volume or other important characteristics, differences that discourage sight-unseen trading. During the mid-nineteenth century the Chicago Board of Trade introduced grading, weighing and measurement standards for grains that have evolved into the standardization of deliverable grades that is central to futures trading today. The principles of standardization developed in the context of agricultural commodities have been adapted to the broad range of items underlying contemporary futures contracts, including energy products and financial instruments.

Variation in Terms of Payment

To cope with a plethora of terms of payment, commodity exchanges required all payment terms be cash on delivery. Moreover, all trades on futures exchanges must clear, or be booked, through members of the exchange who meet exchange-approved standards of financial responsibility.

Price Dissemination

Because there was no central location for price information, traders were never sure they were buying at the lowest available offer or selling at the highest available bid. In addition, the private nature of to-arrive contracts meant that information on other trades was often not available to help make a determination about the current market. Commodity exchanges met the need for accurate and rapid price dissemination in two ways: first, by requiring that all trading take place in a single location (physical or electronic), where buyers and sellers communicate competitive bids and offers; and, second, by requiring that all completed transactions be given immediate and widespread publicity.

The Problem of Resale

Most speculators have no interest in actually making or taking delivery when they buy or sell a futures contract. Similarly, the hedger attempting to protect against adverse price movements by buying or selling futures is not always interested in the grade and quality of the commodity or financial instrument specified in the futures contract. Most hedgers engage in futures trading because they are seeking to transfer risk, not because they are interested in delivering or receiving the specific item underlying the futures contract. Thus, it is necessary to allow participants to buy and sell futures contracts as easily as possible.

One way to accomplish this is to permit the offsetting of trades, that is, allowing a sale to liquidate the obligations of an earlier buy, and vice versa. The development of the futures clearinghouse made contract offset possible by guaranteeing that the buyer (holder of a long position) could liquidate his or her obligation entirely by selling to any willing buyer in the futures market, not necessarily the original counterparty. The clearinghouse is one of the most important innovations of the futures exchanges; its existence solves many problems that might otherwise interfere with maintaining a liquid market with low transaction costs. The operation of the clearinghouse is explained fully in Chapter 2.

Guaranteed Contract Performance

For trading markets to flourish, there can be no question as to the reliability of either party. Everyone in the market must know in advance that he or she can expect performance by the opposite party on any contract. This is particularly true in futures trading, since it is rare for a contract buyer to know the identity of the actual seller at the time of purchase. This is another function met by the clearinghouse. In its role as master bookkeeper and guarantor, the clearinghouse acts as a financial intermediary on each cleared trade, guaranteeing the financial integrity of every futures contract.

Standardization of Trading Practices

All trading in futures is conducted via standardized contracts under published exchange rules that detail methods of operation and permitted trading procedures. Trading rules perform a dual function: they are an essential part of the efficient functioning of the markets and they serve to lessen trading risks by inhibiting fraud.

WHAT IS A FUTURES CONTRACT?

A futures contract is an agreement between two parties, one to buy and the other to sell a fixed quantity and grade of a commodity, security, currency, index or other specified item at an agreed-upon price on or before a given date in the future.

Futures have several key features:

- The buyer of a futures contract, the "long," contracts to receive delivery.
- The seller of a futures contract, the "short," contracts to make delivery.
- Futures contracts can be extinguished by an offsetting, *i.e.*, opposite, transaction made on the exchange where the contract was initiated at any time prior to the contract's maturity.
- Futures contracts can be settled by physical delivery or cash, depending on the contract's specifications as determined by the exchange.
- Futures on the same or similar commodities can be traded on more than one exchange.

The terms of futures contracts are standardized by the exchange on which the contract trades. This means that the futures contract specifies the following elements:

- *Underlying, or spot, instrument:* the commodity, security, currency or index the futures contract covers. (The spot instrument is also known as the physical commodity, the actual commodity or the cash commodity—physicals, actuals or cash, for short.)

- *Contract size:* how much of the underlying commodity is contracted for.

- *Settlement mechanism:* whether the futures contract will be settled by delivery of the underlying item or by cash settlement, and, in the case of actual delivery, the delivery location(s) and specific requirements. (In cash settlement, on the final trading day all existing contracts are valued against a specified cash, *i.e.*, non-futures, price. Cash settlement is discussed in Chapter 2.)

- *Delivery, or maturity, date(s):* the date by which the buyer is contractually obligated to pay the seller and the seller is contractually obligated to deliver to the buyer or the date upon which cash settlement takes place.

- *Specific grade or quality of the contract:* in some cases, contract terms permit delivery of a grade higher or lower in quality than the specified grade at a premium or discount to the futures contract grade.

Futures contracts may be traded in any delivery month established by the exchange, in some cases five or more years into the future. However, not all delivery months have the same levels of activity, particularly those that have a long time until they mature, and some futures contracts historically record the greatest activity in certain delivery months. Many newspapers carry futures price quotations, and a quick glance will show which delivery months trade and which are the most active.

It is important to remember that a futures contract that is not cash settled and that is held to maturity will result in delivery of the actual commodity. If the trader is long, he must accept any deliverable grade of the commodity that is tendered, irrespective of whether he wants that particular grade, and at any location permitted by the contract, whether or not he wants to receive delivery at that location.

For many physical commodities, *e.g.*, grains, cotton, coffee, and metals, data on inventories of commodities that have been inspected and approved for delivery on futures contracts can be obtained from the exchange where the futures contract is traded. The amount of such inventory in position and inspected for delivery is known generally as the "certificated stock." Increases or reductions in the certificated stock of a particular commodity can produce

an immediate market response, particularly if the change is a sizable one when measured against the preceding day's total.

To emphasize some of the unique features of futures, it is useful to compare futures with forward contracts and equity securities (stocks) and to note the important differences.

Forwards vs. Futures

A forward contract (or "forward") is an agreement between two parties to make and accept delivery of a commodity or asset at a certain future time and for a certain price. Typically, the contract is between an agricultural producer and a grain elevator, between two financial institutions, or between a bank and one of its clients. The terms of a forward contract are negotiated each time a transaction is made; these include items such as the delivery date, the grade and/or location of the commodity or asset to be delivered, the delivery location, credit arrangements and conditions in the event of default. Forwards can be customized to meet the exact specifications of the contracting parties, which makes them particularly effective for parties interested in actual delivery. On the other hand, the cost of this customization can be significant.

The two most important characteristics that distinguish a forward from a futures contract are:

- Forwards are not traded on an exchange. As a result, forwards cannot be liquidated easily with an offsetting trade.

- Forwards are not guaranteed by a centralized clearinghouse. The absence of a clearinghouse means that the creditworthiness of each party to the forward contract must be considered by the other party. As such, only "good" or "known" parties are generally eligible to use forwards.

Equity Securities (Stocks) vs. Futures

Important differences between futures contracts and equities include:

- Futures markets exist to facilitate risk shifting and price discovery; the principal purpose of securities markets is to assist in capital formation.

- In futures trading there is a short for every long. It is no more difficult to take a short position in the futures markets than it is to take a long position. Unlike shorting stock, no previous price "up tick" is required, no inventory must exist to be borrowed against and there is no concern over dividends to be paid if declared during the tenure of the short position.

- The life of each futures contract is limited; most stocks do not expire.

- The margin put up to carry a futures position is earnest money, securing the promise to fulfill the contract's obligations. In stock purchases, margin acts as a down payment, and the balance of the purchase cost over margin is borrowed with interest paid on the loan.

- Price and position limits exist in many futures markets. A price limit establishes the maximum range of trading prices for a futures or related options contract on a given day. A position limit establishes the maximum position one market participant may assume in any market. Individual stocks (although not necessarily stock indexes) typically have no limits on either price movements or the size of positions.

- While the outstanding supply of shares of an issuer's stock is fixed at any point in time, there is no limit on the total number of futures or futures options contracts (known as open interest, discussed below) that may be created and exist at any time in a given market.

- Unlike equities, for which a customer can ask a broker for a stock certificate, there is no futures or futures options contract certificate of ownership. The only written record of a futures position is the trade confirmation received from the brokerage house through which the trades are made.

- In open-outcry futures markets members representing customers and themselves compete on an exchange floor for the best prices. Many non-electronic stock markets operate with a specialist system, which requires that a single individual be responsible for maintaining an orderly market in a particular stock. Privileges and obligations differ between the two systems, and these can, at times, have an impact on transaction prices. (Currently, electronic trading of both futures and stocks has become the predominate form of trading for most European as well as many other futures and stock markets outside the United States and increasingly important in the U.S.)

- Trading in U.S. futures and futures options is regulated by the Commodity Futures Trading Commission, futures exchanges, and the National Futures Association; securities transactions in the U.S. are regulated by the Securities and Exchange Commission, stock exchanges, state regulatory agencies, and FINRA.

FUTURES VOLUME AND OPEN INTEREST

Considerable importance is attached by futures market analysts to the daily trading volume and open interest statistics for each market. These figures are computed and published each day by the clearinghouse of each exchange from the trade data submitted by members.

Volume is defined as the total of purchases or sales during a trading session, not the total of purchases and sales combined. Since there is a buyer and a seller for each contract traded, the total of all purchases must equal the total of all sales each day, once any out-trade discrepancies have been resolved by the exchange or clearinghouse. (An out-trade is a futures buy or sell that the clearinghouse cannot match with a corresponding sell or buy.) For example, if Ms. B buys one contract of February heating oil and Mr. S sells one contract of February heating oil, the volume of trading between them is one contract, not two.

Open interest represents a tabulation of the total number of futures contracts in a market that remain "open" at the end of a trading session, that is, those contracts not yet liquidated either by an offsetting futures market transaction or by delivery. When a new futures (or futures options) contract is first listed for trading, there is, of course, no open interest. As trading proceeds, however, open interest is created. For example, if trader A buys one futures contract (for a specific contract month) from trader B and neither trader A nor B started with any position in that specific contract, one new futures contract has been created. That is, open interest in that contract has increased by one. This is illustrated in Figure 1-1, which reflects the case in which the FCMs are clearing members of the exchanges on which the trades are executed.

What happens to open interest when an existing holder of a long position liquidates that position? The answer depends on whether the sale is to a new buyer or to someone covering or offsetting an existing short position. If trader A in the example above liquidates his long position by making an offsetting sale to a new buyer, say trader C, there is no change in open interest, as illustrated in Figure 1-2. In this case, trader C has simply replaced

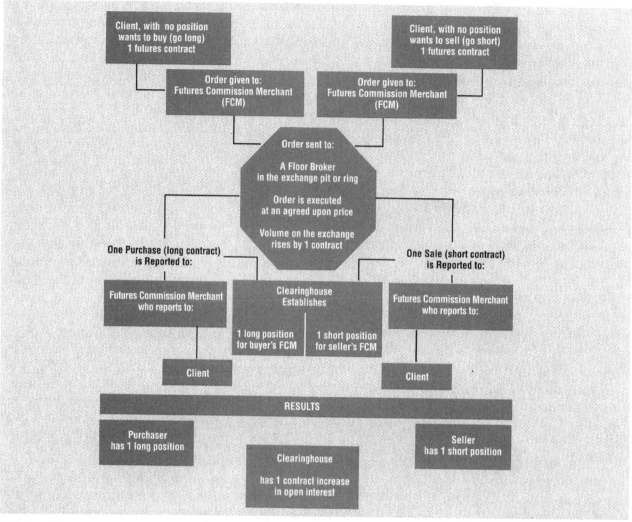

FIGURE 1-1 Creation of a futures contract: Neither buyer nor seller has a futures position, and FCMs are clearing members.

trader A as the holder of a long position, and the open interest remains the same. On the other hand, suppose that trader A sold to a fourth person, trader D, who had held a short position in the particular futures contract. In such a situation, one long position and one short position would be extinguished by offset, reducing the number of open contracts (and thus open interest) by one. This latter case is illustrated in Figure 1-3. Remember, the number of open short positions always equals the number of open long positions.

The effects of trading on open interest may be summarized as follows:

- Open interest increases when the buyer and seller is each taking on a new position (long and short, respectively).
- Open interest remains the same when only one party, the buyer or seller, is taking on a new position and the other is offsetting an existing long or short position.
- Open interest decreases when both parties, the buyer and seller, are offsetting existing long and short positions.
- Open interest also declines when an existing short makes delivery to an existing long.

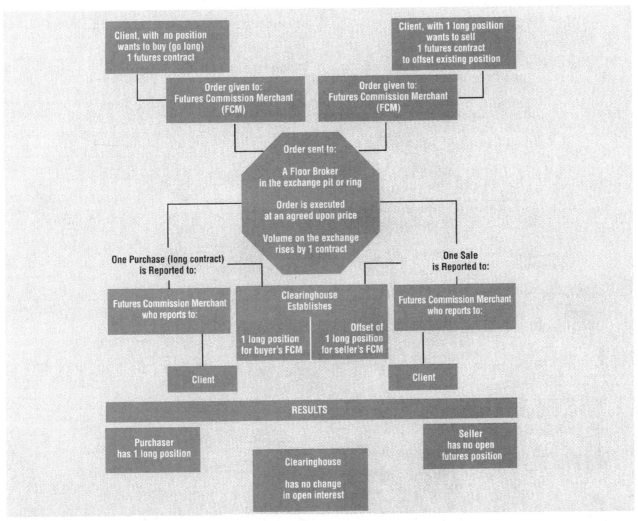

FIGURE 1-2 Creation and extinguishing (offset) of a futures contract: One trader has a futures position and one trader does not, and FCMs are clearing members.

REQUISITES OF A FUTURES MARKET

Over the years, trading in futures contracts has been inaugurated in a wide variety of basic commodities, or raw materials, ranging from wheat and electricity to currencies, insurance and financial instruments, including equity securities and indexes of them. And each year the many competing exchanges attempt to start trading in a number of new futures and options contracts. Some succeed; others do not. The question naturally arises, "Why is futures trading a success in some commodities and not in others?"

The paramount requisite for a successful futures contract is that there exist real economic risks that producers and users need to manage. With little or no volatility in the price of the underlying instrument, there is little incentive to trade or manage risk. When such price volatility and associated risk exist, a successful futures contract requires that those who have such exposures are willing to use the futures market for their risk management activities.

Further, a futures contract cannot exist in a vacuum; it must be based on an active underlying cash market. Whether the stock market or the stockyards, gas pipelines or grain elevators, a viable cash market permits the type of commercial activities that keep futures market prices and cash market prices in a relationship that reflects the supply and demand environment. In addition, information

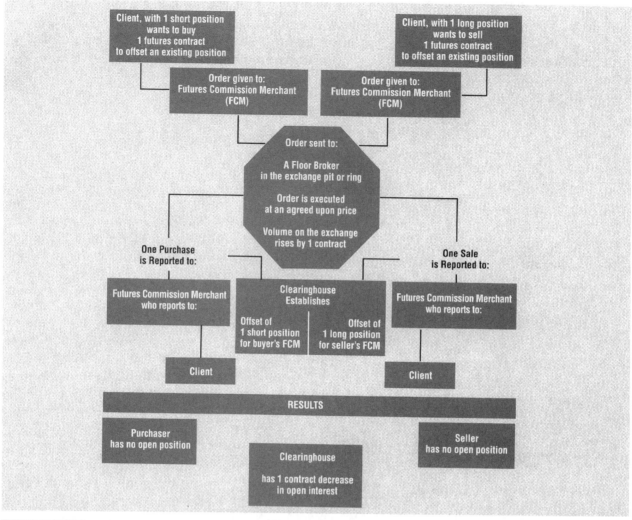

FIGURE 1-3 Extinguishing (offset) of a futures contract: Buyer and seller have opposite futures positions, and FCMs are clearing members.

on the cash market must be widely available to interested parties; if price data and information about supply and demand are not widely available, traders and others are unlikely to trade, and the market will fail.

A related issue is government policy; futures are not useful if there are rigid government controls over prices, production and the marketing of commodities. During World War II, when the U.S. Office of Price Administration established ceiling prices for most commodities in short supply, many futures markets ceased to function, because, when a government sets the buying and selling price of a commodity, there is no need for hedging and, therefore, no need for a futures market.

Still another consideration is that there be diversity among those with exposure to the underlying instrument. Both production and consumption of the commodity or, alternately, exposure to price risk, must be widely distributed among a large number of participants under competitive market conditions. This assures that no individual or small group acting in concert can manipulate the supply or demand of the underlying instrument.

It is also important that the underlying instrument be standardized. That is, there must be at least one grade or type of the commodity or instrument that represents a major portion of the supply of the commodity or other item. This facilitates adherence to delivery standards and an efficient pricing function. Because buying and selling futures contracts involve trading an item sight-unseen, there must be assurance that the item delivered against a short futures position will meet the quality standards called for in the contract.

Another requirement is that there be an efficient delivery infrastructure. This is made simpler if the underlying instrument is storable and transportable, such as oil, metals, and government bonds. Exchanges have addressed this problem (and the related problem of having commodities that are not deliverable without undue expense or inconvenience) by establishing cash-settled contracts, which call for delivery by paying the difference between the futures price when the contract was initiated (bought or sold) and a cash price at maturity of the contract.

A final factor affecting the viability of a futures contract is that there be no other liquid futures contract that can be used to hedge the same or similar risks. If a portfolio of 1,000 stocks can be hedged adequately with the S&P 500 futures or futures options, there likely will be little demand for a contract on the 1,000 stocks. Generally, an exchange will not fragment its existing futures markets by listing contracts that are close substitutes, because doing so often divides the same contract volume among multiple contracts and may discourage existing users from further trading.

THE USES OF FUTURES AND OPTIONS

Uses of futures and options fall into two broad categories: hedging and speculating. Although the futures industry's definitions of these activities are consistent with dictionary definitions, it is important to understand these terms within their specific industry context.

Hedging is the use of futures for the purpose of risk management. By this definition, a hedger has some risk or risks associated with the price or supply availability of the actual underlying commodity or financial instrument. Futures transactions and positions have the express purpose of mitigating those risks.

Speculating is the use of futures for risk-taking. Clearly, profit is the motive for the speculator to take these risks. By this definition, the speculator, before entering the futures market, has no risk associated with the actual underlying item. The speculator's risk exists only by virtue of the futures position.

Both of these categories of futures activity can take on various forms. These include "pure" or "inventory" hedging, carrying physical positions, arbitrage, position-taking, pricing and outright speculation.

Hedging

A hedger's principal economic activity consists of producing, distributing, processing, storing, or investing in the actual commodity or financial instrument in some form. The hedger's activity in the futures markets would not happen were it not for the need to minimize the risks of loss inherent in these activities over a period of time.

Hedging involves taking a position in the futures market opposite to an exposure in the cash market. The concept is that the futures position counterbalances the risks faced in the cash market. For example, if you are a producer of oil, you are ordinarily at risk for price declines. If you sell oil futures in the right amount, you can diminish your exposure to changes in the price of spot crude oil. Thus, a hedge makes you neutral, or indifferent, to changes in the cash market price of a commodity, despite the fact that you still hold the actual commodity.

This is also true for a situation in which you are short the cash commodity, for instance, a utility that buys crude oil. The utility could buy crude oil futures to lock in its energy cost. After placing the hedge, the utility would be indifferent to the direction of cash crude oil prices, because it had already locked in its cost of buying oil.

Prudent hedging may result in lowering other business costs as well. For example, when the risk of loss due to an adverse price change is reduced by hedging, banks and other lending institutions are often more willing to lend and, frequently, at lower interest rates.

Hedging reduces exposure to price risk by shifting that risk to others with opposite risk profiles, or to speculators who are willing to accept the risk in exchange for profit opportunity. An interesting corollary to reducing risks by hedging with futures is that a hedger may miss out on greater profits that may accrue should there be favorable price changes.

Carrying of Commodity Positions

Futures markets can be used to defray the costs of carrying an inventory of a commodity. A farm commodity such as wheat, for example, is harvested during a few weeks of the year, while the use of wheat is distributed throughout the entire year. After a farm crop is harvested it still must be owned or "carried" by someone until it is consumed. Storage of the commodity, however, is costly, and the owner of the stored commodity may suffer losses from adverse price changes before the commodity is sold.

Futures prices of storable commodities often reflect all or part of the cost of storage, insurance and interest payments to carry the commodity until expiration of the futures contract. In such cases, the holder of an inventory can initiate a short hedge in the expectation that all or part of the cost of carrying the cash position will be defrayed by holding the short futures position. Alternately, a user of a commodity who needs it sometime in the future can establish a long futures position and expect to pay no more, and possibly less, for carrying the commodity position via the futures market than if the commodity were held in physical inventory.

Arbitrage

Arbitrage, or the simultaneous purchase and resale of the same underlying commodity, currency or security in different markets, also plays a major role in futures markets. When futures and cash prices move temporarily out of line with each other, professional traders and others will buy in the (relatively) cheaper market and simultaneously sell in the (relatively) more expensive market to generate a riskless profit. This kind of activity guarantees that futures and cash prices will stay in proper alignment. Thus, if either cash or futures move away from a fair market value, arbitrage will quickly pull prices back into line. Arbitrage, therefore, also guarantees that futures provide an effective hedge for cash positions.

Position-Taking

Position-taking involves assuming a futures position without an offsetting cash position. Position-taking may he considered a form of speculation, just as holding unsold inventory could be considered speculation. Many companies, however, use position-taking as a means of hedging anticipated risks. For instance, a company that will be issuing debt in the future may want to lock in today's prevailing interest rates, thereby hedging the interest-rate risk inherent in the company's future debt issuance. Alternatively, an international trading firm may want to hedge the foreign exchange risk of foreign currency revenues that will be received several months hence. Thus, not all

position-taking is speculative. Some can be classified as "anticipatory" hedging and may take place on either the long or short side of the market.

Price Discovery

Futures markets help establish a publicly known, single price for a commodity. Although prices in most commodities change rapidly, the interplay of buyers and sellers on a worldwide scale, in an open, competitive market, quickly establishes what a commodity is "worth" at any given moment. Because prices are quickly disseminated electronically, the smallest user of the market is no longer at a significant information disadvantage to the largest user with regard to the current value of a commodity.

Futures markets are some of the most efficient price discovery markets available. In many industries, futures are the only price reference available. In these and other businesses, participants often link the price of a cash market transaction to the futures market price at a specified time, or use current futures prices as a guide to cash prices.

A related, though little recognized, benefit of futures trading is that it facilitates distribution of statistical information in addition to prices. An organized futures exchange acts as a focal point for the dissemination of supply and demand statistics, weather reports and other information vital to the industries it serves. Ultimately, this makes it easier for all parties to assess their risks and plan for the future.

Speculation

Futures markets provide for the orderly transfer of price risk from the hedger to the speculator. The speculator willingly accepts this risk in return for the prospect of dramatic gains. Speculators generally have no practical use for the commodities in which they trade.

The futures markets could not function effectively without speculators, because their trading serves to provide liquidity, making possible the execution of large orders with a minimum of price disturbance. Over the longer term, speculators help to smooth price fluctuations, rather than intensify them, by making their risk-taking capital available to the market.

FOR YOUR CONSIDERATION

With changing needs and technology, various industrial and agricultural materials change in importance, and financial markets introduce new products. Perhaps a raw material or agricultural product will rise in importance, world trade patterns will change to make a particular currency more prominent, or new securities or credit instruments will emerge. In your opinion, what futures contracts might develop in the future? What conditions might have to change to make your forecast a reality?

Study Questions

1. A futures contract is a legal agreement between a buyer and seller governing the future delivery of the specified commodity, financial instrument, index or other underlying instrument.
   - A. True
   - B. False

2. The buyer of a futures contract is called the:
   - A. Short.
   - B. Long.
   - C. Hedger.
   - D. Speculator.

3. The process by which a futures contract is terminated by a transaction that is equal and opposite from the one that initiated the position is called:
   - A. Open interest.
   - B. Offset.
   - C. Delivery.
   - D. Cash settlement.

4. Similar or identical futures contracts can be traded on:
   - A. Only one exchange in a given country.
   - B. Up to three exchanges in the same country.
   - C. Multiple exchanges regardless of location.

5. Which of the following items in a futures contract is standardized?
   - A. The total number of contracts available for purchase and sale
   - B. The size—the amount of the underlying item covered by the contract
   - C. The price of the underlying commodity
   - D. None of the above

6. Who determines the size, grades, delivery locations and delivery months of a futures contract?
   - A. The CFTC
   - B. The exchange on which the contract is traded
   - C. The USDA
   - D. National Futures Association

7. In contrast to futures, stocks or equities:
   - A. Have price and position limits.
   - B. Have expiration dates.
   - C. Have a short for every long.
   - D. Are not regulated by the CFTC.
   - E. All of the above.

8. The number of futures contracts bought or sold over a specified period of time is called:
   - A. Open interest.
   - B. Visible supply.
   - C. Volume.

9. Open interest is:
   - A. The number of outstanding long or short futures contracts.
   - B. The number of traders in a particular market.
   - C. The number of outstanding long and short futures contracts.
   - D. A term applicable to futures but not options markets.

10. If a new long buys from a new short, open interest:
    - A. Stays the same.
    - B. Decreases.
    - C. Increases.
    - D. The change is indeterminate.

11. Which of the following is essential to the operation of a successful futures contract based on a physical commodity?
    - A. Viable cash or actuals market in the same or comparable cash commodities as those underlying the futures market
    - B. Competitive market conditions in both production and distribution channels of the cash market
    - C. Access to inspection and grading facilities
    - D. Active trade participation
    - E. All of the above

12. A principal function of a futures exchange is to:

   A. Conduct cash business.

   B. Provide a trading market for foreign exchange.

   C. Make it possible for hedgers to transfer unwanted price risks.

13. The speculator uses the futures markets to:

   A. Earn trading profits.

   B. Lower raw material costs.

   C. Earn interest.

   D. Offset hedges.

14. The activity of speculators in futures markets:

   A. Increases trading volume.

   B. Provides needed liquidity.

   C. Enables the filling of orders with a minimum of price disturbance.

   D. All of the above.

15. Through arbitrage, it is possible to earn virtually risk-less profits.

   A. True

   B. False

16. Futures markets can be used to defray the cost of carrying commodity inventories.

   A. True

   B. False

Answers to Questions

1. A (True)

A futures contract is a legal agreement that specifies the future delivery of a commodity or financial instrument. However, most such contracts are offset by another futures contract or cash settled rather than being settled by delivery.

2. B

In futures markets, the term long implies buying or taking a position that profits when prices rise.

3. B

Offset is the term used to describe the liquidation of a long futures position by the sale of the same number of the same futures contracts or the termination of a short futures position by the purchase of the same number of the particular futures contract.

4. C

The same or similar futures contracts can be traded on more than one exchange in the United States or elsewhere, although normally one contract tends to dominate its competitors on other exchanges in terms of trading volume and liquidity. Generally, for similar contracts traded in time zones that differ by several hours, the futures contract trading when the primary cash market is open will be the dominant contract.

5. B

A prerequisite for futures and options markets is that the underlying commodity or financial instrument be capable of standardization in terms of its size, quality, delivery, packaging, etc. The price of a futures contract and the number of contracts traded are determined by the forces of supply and demand on the exchange.

6. B

Exchange rules set the standardized terms and conditions of all futures contracts.

7. D

Futures, but not stocks, have price and position limits, expiration dates, and a long for every short. U.S. stock markets are regulated by the Securities and Exchange Commission (SEC), while futures are regulated by the Commodity Futures Trading Commission (CFTC).

8. C

The number of futures contracts bought or sold (but not both combined) over a period of time is that period's volume.

9. A

Open interest is defined as the number of outstanding—*i.e.*, initiated but not yet closed—futures contract on either the long or the short side of the market (but not both combined).

10. C

When a new long buys from a new short, one or more (depending on the size of the trade) positions are created, and open interest increases by that number.

11. E

Successful futures markets require a degree of competitiveness in both the underlying cash and futures markets and assurance that both markets have integrity. In addition, successful futures markets require participation by hedgers as well as speculators. Responses a through d reflect these conditions.

12. C

Futures markets are foremost hedging markets. At present, a few futures exchanges also provide facilities for cash business (principally in grains), but this is not essential to a futures exchange. Foreign exchange is one of many dozens of types of financial instruments and physical commodities on which futures contracts are traded.

13. A

The principal motivation for speculators to trade futures is to obtain profits.

14. D

Speculative activity in futures markets enables a large number of transactions to be completed quickly and at small price concessions. This is the essence of a liquid market.

15. A (True)

Arbitrage, the simultaneous purchase and resale of the same underlying commodity, currency, or security in different markets, allows traders to earn virtually riskless profits when futures and cash prices move temporarily out of line with each other. Traders will buy in the (relatively) cheaper market and simultaneously sell in the (relatively) more expensive market, thereby generating profits with low or no risks. Arbitrage ensures that futures and cash prices stay in proper alignment as traders, taking into account their transaction costs, take advantage of any move away from fair market values until prices fall back into line.

16. A (True)

Often the futures price of a storable commodity reflects at least part of the cost of storage, insurance and interest to carry the commodity until the futures contract expires. In such cases, persons holding an inventory of the commodity can sell futures and thereby cover at least part of the cost of carrying the commodity over the lifetime of the futures contract.

Futures Industry Institutions and Professionals

2

Learning Objectives

Candidates, after completing this reading, should be able to:

- Describe the features of a modern futures exchange and identify typical contract terms and trading rules.
- Explain the organization and administration of an exchange and clearinghouse.
- Describe exchange membership, the different types of exchange members, and the exchange rules for member trading.
- Explain original and variation margin, daily settlement, the guaranty deposit, and the clearing process.

- Describe the steps that are taken when a clearinghouse member is unable to meet its financial obligations on its open contracts.
- Describe the mechanics of futures delivery and the roles of the clearinghouse, buyers, and sellers in this process.
- Explain the role of futures commission merchants, introducing brokers, account executives, commodity trading advisors, commodity pool operators, and customers.

Excerpt is Chapter 2 of Futures and Options, *The Institute for Financial Markets.*

DEVELOPMENT OF U.S. FUTURES EXCHANGES

The Board of Trade of the City of Chicago (more commonly referred to as the Chicago Board of Trade) was established in 1848 to provide a central marketplace where buyers and sellers could meet to exchange commodities. At first, customized forward contracts were exchanged. In 1865, the Chicago Board of Trade developed standardized agreements called futures contracts and published a set of rules to govern futures trading of the type widely used today.

In the following years, the model pioneered by the Chicago Board of Trade was adopted by nascent exchanges in other parts of the U.S. More recently, the U.S. futures contract model has served as the template for many exchanges around the world. The majority of these newer exchanges specialize in financial contracts and trade electronically, rather than by open outcry in the trading pits.

CBOT trading floor, circa 1900
Photo courtesy of the Chicago Board of Trade

THE MODERN FUTURES EXCHANGE

Despite the fact that there are many futures exchanges offering an array of contracts, many aspects of these exchanges are similar. Historically, most futures exchanges have been associations of members organized principally to provide the facilities needed for buying, selling, or otherwise marketing commodities under rules that protect the interests of all concerned.

This not-for-profit membership model was not always followed by new exchanges, particularly those that emerged in Europe in the second half of the 1990s. In addition, the situation in the U.S. began changing rapidly in 2000 with the demutualization of the Chicago Mercantile Exchange. Such demutualization usually is accompanied by a change from a non-profit to a for-profit status of the exchange.

Futures exchanges changing from membership organizations to for-profit corporations generally issue two or more different classes of stock. For example, each exchange membership might be entitled to a specified number of "Class A" shares that confer equity and voting powers in a holding company created by the exchange and one or more "Class B" shares that convey trading privileges on the exchange as well as certain core but limited voting rights. Normally, there also are provisions for the two classes of shares to be bought and sold separately and for the trading rights to be leased as well as used directly by the owners of the Class B shares.

The exchange itself, whether or not it is a membership organization, does not own any of the underlying commodities or instruments, nor does it trade or take positions in the futures or options contracts. Its role is to provide the physical or electronic facilities, operational mechanisms and rules needed to conduct competitive futures trading.

Because a futures exchange does not trade or take positions, the trading venue provided by the exchange is a "secondary market." That is, the members transact amongst themselves for their own accounts and those of their customers. In this respect, a futures exchange serves a role similar to that of a stock exchange. However, a futures exchange is also the author of the contracts that trade there. This means that the exchange writes all the terms and conditions of the standardized futures contract.

Generally, these contract terms and trading rules include:

- The delivery or contract months in which trading is permitted;

- Initial and maintenance margin levels for each commodity;

- For physical delivery contracts, the designation of delivery locations and grades (ranging from warehouses for grain to the coupons and maturities for

Treasury futures) and inspection procedures for all commodities tendered for delivery against futures contracts;

- For cash-settled contracts, the cash price series used for final settlement of the contract;
- Pricing conventions and minimum price fluctuations;
- Supervision of the day-to-day activity of those who participate in futures trading, either for customers or for themselves;
- Market surveillance programs to prevent market congestion or attempts at price manipulation;
- The distribution of price data on a real-time basis.

Exchange Organization and Administration

Futures exchanges historically have been associations of members formed to provide an orderly market for trading in futures and options on futures. In the U.S., exchange membership or the holding of trading permits is a privilege available only to individuals. An individual may be permitted, however, after making appropriate application to the exchange, to confer certain privileges of his or her membership on another person, corporation, cooperative organization, partnership or company by which he or she is employed or with which he or she is affiliated.

The organization of futures exchanges differs from one to another. In general, a board of directors or board of governors, elected by the membership, governs the exchange. The president is generally the full-time, paid, non-member executive responsible for day-to-day administrative oversight of the exchange and for carrying out the policies approved by the board of directors. Exchange policies are generally formulated after debate by various member committees before recommendation to the board of directors for approval. The board may either approve or reject committee recommendations. Changes in the bylaws and certain exchange rules may require the favorable vote of a majority of the exchange's members or holders of trading privileges.

The daily operations and administrative functions of an exchange are performed generally by the exchange staff. The staff works in areas such as legal and compliance, data processing, research, and facilities maintenance. Revenue to cover the operating expenses of an exchange are generated by transaction fees, assessments and dues paid by exchange members, as well as from fees charged for access to the exchange's real-time data. Most open-outcry exchanges obtain additional revenue from the rental of desk space and floor telephone booths.

Exchange Members

Only persons holding membership or other trading rights or privileges on an exchange may participate in exchange trading. The following discussion focuses on an open-outcry, rather than an electronic, trading environment.

An exchange member who trades in the pit or ring only for his or her own account is known as a local. This member makes trades and takes positions with his or her own capital and earns income based on trading skill and market analysis. While most are usually seen as short-term traders, locals employ as many different styles and methods of trading and analysis as any other type of trader. A scalper is an exchange member who buys and sells frequently, normally being ready to buy at a fraction below the last transaction price and sell at a fraction above, thus creating liquidity in the market. The term day trader applies to an exchange member who, despite frequent trading during the day, normally has a flat (zero) position at the end of the day. An exchange member who makes his or her living from commissions earned by executing buy and sell orders for others is referred to as a floor broker.

In general, an exchange member can complete a transaction only after making an open, competitive outcry of the bid or offer in hand. A floor broker is required to use due diligence in executing all customer orders. Any losses that result from errors made in handling customer orders become the broker's personal liability. With a few notable exceptions, non-competitive trades (bids or offers not made openly in the pit) are prohibited. Any member participating in a trade not allowed by exchange rules is subject to disciplinary action.

The practice of a member trading for himself or herself and also handling customer business is known as dual trading. Exchange rules vary regarding the circumstances under which dual trading is permitted, but all exchanges and other regulators give priority to a customer's order over an exchange member's or trader's own trades.

THE CLEARINGHOUSE OR CLEARING ASSOCIATION

Every futures exchange in the U.S. has an affiliation with a clearinghouse, sometimes known as a clearing association. The primary role of the clearinghouse is to provide the financial mechanisms to guarantee performance on the exchange's futures and options contracts. To accomplish this, the clearinghouse substitutes itself for each counterparty for the purpose of settling gains and losses, paying out funds to those with profits and collecting from those with losses. This is known as the principle of substitution. Additionally, the clearinghouse facilitates deliveries by matching the parties making and taking delivery.

Operating Structure

At most U.S. commodity exchanges, the two notable exceptions being the Chicago Mercantile Exchange and the New York Mercantile Exchange, the related clearinghouse is organized as a separate member corporation. At the two Mercantile exchanges, the clearinghouse is organized as a department within the exchange. While every member of the clearinghouse also must be a member of the related exchange, not all exchange members are members of the clearinghouse.

Applicants for clearinghouse membership are carefully screened by each clearinghouse board, with financial strength, reputation for integrity and administrative capabilities being prime considerations before approval is granted. Only those applicants who can meet the stringent financial and other requirements are approved.

The clearinghouse functions under the guidance of a board of directors or a committee of the exchange. It is the duty of the board or the exchange to set policy, pass on the admission or expulsion of members and elect clearinghouse officers or, on some exchanges, appoint members to an oversight committee.

As a protection for all clearing members, it is not unusual for the board of directors to establish a maximum limit on the number of contracts that individual clearing members can carry at any time, as well as requiring higher original margin (as discussed in the following text) per contract from clearing members whose positions exceed a stipulated size.

The clearinghouse obtains funds to support its operations from fees charged for clearing trades and for other services performed for its members, such as the handling of delivery notices. Some revenue also may be derived from interest on invested capital or from interest realized from the temporary investment of member guaranty-fund deposits, as discussed later in this chapter.

Original and Variation Margin

All clearinghouses require clearing member firms to deposit funds, known as original margin, with the clearinghouse to support open contracts submitted for clearance. The amount of margin required per contract is determined by the clearinghouse board. It is important to note that the Commodity Futures Trading Commission, the federal agency that regulates the U.S. futures and related options markets, requires that customer funds be segregated from member firms' proprietary funds. To maintain this segregation of funds, each clearinghouse member with customer accounts must establish two separate margin accounts at the clearinghouse: one for customer funds and one for its own funds.

Margin levels generally reflect the historical volatility of futures prices and are set to protect the clearinghouse against one day's (statistically) large price movement in a particular market. Different margin rates may apply to spot month positions, i.e., those in or near delivery, and to hedge or spread positions, as described in a later chapter.

Types of acceptable original margin vary by clearinghouse. Generally, clearing member margin deposits may be in the form of cash, letters of credit, government securities or registered securities. Non-dollar futures contracts—contracts priced in terms of a foreign currency, such as futures contracts on a foreign stock index—may have original and variation margin payments denominated in a foreign currency. Customer margin deposits with the clearinghouse member may include other negotiable instruments such as warehouse receipts.

The clearinghouse may collect margin either on a gross customer-position basis or a net customer-position basis. The Chicago Mercantile Exchange and the New York Mercantile Exchange require gross original margin from clearing members for each short and each long contract. Most other clearinghouses currently permit a clearing member firm to net customers' open long and short positions in a particular delivery month of a futures contract and to deposit with the clearinghouse only that margin needed to support the net position. For example, if a clearinghouse member's customers are long a total of 500 contracts of May wheat and short a total of 400 contracts of May wheat, a clearinghouse that collects customer margin on a net basis would charge margin on the net long position of 100 contracts.

Variation margin, the settlement of daily gains and losses between clearinghouse member firms, also is effected through the clearinghouse. At the end of each trading day the committee on quotations (or other exchange member committee) of each exchange determines the settlement price for each contract market, in effect, a closing value for that day's trading.

Settlement prices are determined for each delivery month and usually fall within the range of prices traded on the close, although the settlement price of a relatively inactive delivery month that does not trade on the close may be a nominal price fixed by the committee. A nominal price is not actually a trade price but one selected after considering the price relationship between the delivery month in question and the settlement prices for other delivery months of the same futures or options contract that did trade on the close. The settlement price usually represents an average between the closing bid and offer of an inactive trading month.

Each day all clearinghouse member firms either must pay to or receive from the clearinghouse the difference between the current settlement price and the trade price or, for an existing position, the previous day's settlement price. This difference is known as the variation margin. Variation margin is collected separately for customer positions and the clearing member's own positions and is paid to or from the clearinghouse before the opening of trading on the following business day. Payment is made by automatic debit or credit to the clearing member's customer or house (proprietary) margin account. In some cases, payment is made by certified check. In some markets, variation margin also is collected intraday based on the previous day's open positions, and clearinghouse members are required to deposit funds within one hour of the intraday margin call.

Guaranty Deposit

Members of a clearinghouse, in addition to providing the original and variation margin needed to support their own and customer positions, also must maintain a sizable guaranty deposit with the clearinghouse. This deposit, which may not be withdrawn as long as the firm remains a

The International Petroleum Exchange building in London
Photo courtesy of the International Petroleum Exchange

member of the clearinghouse, can range from a few thousand dollars to as much as several million dollars, depending upon the clearing organization and the member involved. Generally, the guaranty deposit may be in cash, securities or letters of credit. This reserve must be freely available to the clearinghouse at all times to be used, if necessary, to meet the financial obligations of any defaulting member.

Should an individual customer of a clearinghouse member become unable to fulfill either his financial or delivery obligation, the obligation must be assumed by the carrying clearinghouse member itself, using its own funds to make up any customer deficit. That is why brokers insist that margin calls be answered promptly and in full and why the commodity account agreement of each brokerage house gives the broker the right to liquidate any customer positions, without recourse, in the event margin calls are not met promptly.

In the event a clearinghouse member is unable to meet its financial obligations on its open contracts, as has happened on various occasions throughout history, the following procedure generally is followed:

- All open and fully margined customer positions on the failed member's books are transferred to a solvent clearinghouse member. Under-margined customer positions and the firm's proprietary positions are liquidated.

- If, as a result of this liquidation, the member's customer account with the clearinghouse is in deficit, any remaining margin the member had deposited at the clearinghouse is applied toward the deficit on customer positions.

- If the failed member's margin deposits on hand are not sufficient, his exchange membership may be sold and his contribution to the clearinghouse guaranty fund may be used.
- If the member's account is still in deficit, the surplus fund of the clearinghouse, if any, may then be drawn upon at the discretion of the clearinghouse board.
- If necessary, further recourse can be made to the contributions of other clearinghouse members to the guaranty fund.
- Finally, if necessary, a special assessment can be made against all remaining members of the clearinghouse; that is, the remaining members may be asked, by special pro-rata assessment, to make up any deficiency in the guaranty fund resulting from recourse to the preceding procedure.

The selection criteria of clearinghouse members, the guaranty-fund deposits and the ability of the clearinghouse to assess clearinghouse members to fulfill its obligations buttress the financial integrity of each futures contract. There have been no instances in which the failure of a clearinghouse member has resulted in the failure of a U.S. clearinghouse to meet its financial obligations.

Clearing Process

One of the primary activities of the clearinghouse is matching trade data submitted by clearinghouse members. Throughout each trading day, clearinghouse member firms provide to the clearinghouse the details of all trades executed on behalf of their customers or for the member's proprietary trading account. Before the clearinghouse can substitute itself as the opposite party to any trade, it must have a confirming record of the trade from both the buying and selling clearinghouse member.

In the modern clearinghouse, the member firm provides electronic data entry of trade details by computer-to-computer link. Strict deadlines are enforced for submission of trade data, because the clearinghouse must have all data records in hand to match buy and sell records for each completed transaction. Trade records that do not match, either because of a discrepancy in the details or because one side of the transaction is missing, are

Order booths at the International Petroleum Exchange building
Photo courtesy of the International Petroleum Exchange

returned to the submitting clearinghouse members for resolution. The two exchange members involved are required to resolve the discrepancy before or on the opening of trading the next morning. Such a contract is then cleared a day late, as of the preceding day.

When the accuracy of all reported transactions has been verified—and when original margin has been deposited for the position—the clearinghouse assumes the legal and financial obligations of the other party to all trades; that is, the clearinghouse becomes the buyer to everyone who has sold a contract and the seller to everyone who has bought a contract. This insertion, or substitution, of the clearinghouse as the counterparty to every trade enables a trader to liquidate his position without having to wait until the other party to his original contract also decides to liquidate. The individual trader thus relies on the clearinghouse to get him out of his market obligations when he has completed offsetting trades in an identical futures contract.

On the clearinghouse books the two trades—the one opening a position and the one closing it—offset each other, and no open contracts then remain. Using the principle of offset, futures traders are able to move freely in and out of the futures markets, without any residual obligation to the other party involved in either the original purchase (sale) or subsequent sale (purchase). The difference between the trader's purchase price and selling price represents his or her gross profit or loss, before the commission charge that must be paid to the broker.

DELIVERIES AND CASH SETTLEMENT

Futures contracts not offset by the end of trading are settled by delivery or by cash settlement. Actual delivery involves the transfer of ownership of a specific quantity of a physical commodity or financial instrument. While the clearinghouse can and does guarantee the financial fulfillment of each futures contract open on its books, it does not guarantee that the long who stands for delivery will actually receive the specified merchandise. This assurance is provided, as noted in the following text, through the clearinghouse member firm, which is required to fulfill the terms of a futures contract even though its customer may default on a particular delivery. Fortunately, there have been few instances when a member firm's customer has defaulted on either making or taking delivery.

Some futures and futures options contracts, such as those based on eurodollar interest rates and stock indexes, are satisfied by cash payments rather than delivery of a time deposit or basket of securities. As noted in Chapter 1, the exchange determines for all its markets whether there will be actual (physical) delivery or cash settlement. In the case of a cash-settled contract, the buyer and seller pay or receive, through the clearinghouse, the difference between their trade prices and the spot price of the underlying instrument or index at the maturity of the futures contract.

Where physical delivery is required, the substitution of the clearinghouse as the counterparty to every trade permits deliveries to be made directly by a short to an eligible long, even though the two parties may never have traded with each other. A seller with open short contracts during the delivery period must either deliver the commodity or other instrument called for by his position or close out the position by purchasing an equal number of futures contracts.

The clearinghouse performs the function of receiving delivery notices from sellers (shorts) and assigning the notices to buyers (longs). The clearinghouse also may act as a depository for warehouse receipts, arrange for inspection of physical commodities or, for foreign currencies and some financial instruments, receive delivery from sellers and make delivery to buyers.

Delivery can be made from any location or warehouse approved by the exchange and chosen by the seller. The option of selecting the day when delivery is to be made, if more than one day is permitted by the terms of the futures contract, rests with the seller as well. Buyers, on the other hand, only know that if they remain in the market during the delivery period they will receive an actual delivery on some day at some permitted delivery point. The long plays no part in selecting the particular day, the particular location or the particular form or grade of the commodity or financial instrument being delivered. This concept is known as seller's option, and its impact on pricing is discussed in a later chapter.

When the seller is ready to make delivery, he or she instructs the broker to submit a notice of intention to deliver to the clearinghouse within the time span permitted. For this service the broker carrying the account charges a fee. Delivery procedures and requirements differ among futures contracts and exchanges, depending on the nature of the deliverable good or instrument and prevailing cash market practices. For warehouse commodities traded on the Chicago Board of Trade, a notice of intent to deliver is submitted two business days prior to making an actual delivery. For other futures contracts, the notice of intent to deliver may be submitted from one day to several weeks before the intended delivery date. The notice of intent to deliver contains all of the essential facts regarding the delivery: the grade of the commodity, the weight to be delivered, the place where delivery will be made, the date of intended delivery and the delivery price.

When a delivery notice is received by the clearinghouse, the clearinghouse must immediately identify a buyer to receive the delivery. Three general methods of selection are commonly used. At the Chicago Board of Trade and the Chicago Mercantile Exchange, the clearinghouse usually assigns delivery to the clearinghouse member that has the oldest long position open on the clearinghouse books. The clearinghouse member, in turn, passes the notice to that customer on its books having the oldest open long position.

In other clearing organizations, the assignment of delivery notices to eligible clearing firms may be made on a net basis, *i.e.,* allocation of notices is made to member firms in proportion to the size of their net long position open on the clearinghouse books. Still other exchanges permit allocation of notices to clearing members on the basis of the size of their gross open long position: those clearing firms with the largest gross open long positions get the largest number of delivery notices. Under any of these systems, the clearing member receiving a delivery notice may allocate the notice to a long customer position using any of the methods mentioned earlier.

At this point the clearinghouse undertakes to bring the seller and buyer together. This is done either by exchanging the names of the deliverer and receiver with the two clearing firms involved, who then get the two parties to complete delivery and settlement directly, or by handling the actual exchange of delivery documents and payment via the clearinghouse.

If delivery is made through the clearinghouse, the clearing member whose customer is making delivery must provide the required documents, together with a bill for the amount due, to the clearinghouse. Upon receiving payment by certified check, the clearinghouse will release the documents to the receiver's carrying firm. This procedure must be completed within a time span specified in the delivery rules of each exchange. Finally, the clearinghouse will turn over the certified check it has received to the delivering customer's clearing firm, which passes the check along to its customer.

The last trading day of a futures contract is the last day on which open positions can be offset. Any positions remaining open beyond that date must be settled by actual delivery or cash settlement, per the exchange's procedures. The last notice day, or tender day as it is sometimes called, is the last day on which notices of intention to make delivery may be issued. For some futures contracts the last tender day and the last trading day are the same day, so that at the end of trading that day all shorts either have covered their positions with offsetting purchases or have issued delivery notices. By the same token, all of the open longs on that day either have liquidated their long positions by offset or have remained long to be in position to receive delivery. All that remains is for the actual exchange of delivery documents and certified checks to take place in the manner provided for by exchange rules. Figure 2-1 summarizes the general sequence of delivery procedures.

Speculators and Deliveries

A speculator who is long futures during the delivery period is liable for delivery just as a hedger would be. Should the speculator receive a delivery notice, he will own the commodity for at least one day (possibly longer

PHYSICAL DELIVERY I
(SIMULTANEOUS TRADING AND DELIVERY)

First Notice Day

- First day a short may issue a delivery notice; however, the short is not required to issue the notice on that day but may do so on subsequent days, according to the terms of the futures contract.
- Trading continues concurrent with deliveries. Shorts may issue notices, and longs are liable for delivery, anytime in the specified delivery period.

Last Notice Day

- Last day a short may issue a delivery notice.

Last Trading Day

- Last day on which the contract may be traded.

PHYSICAL DELIVERY II
(DELIVERY FOLLOWING THE END OF TRADING)

Last Trading Day

- Last day on which the contract may be traded. No further trading may take place in that contract. All remaining open positions are to be satisfied by delivery.

First Notice Day

- First day a short may issue a delivery notice; however, the short is not required to issue the notice on that day but may do so on subsequent days, according to the terms of the futures contract.

Last Notice Day

- Last day a short may issue a delivery notice.

CASH SETTLEMENT

Last Trading Day

- Last day on which the contract may be traded, with cash settlement of all positions remaining open after trading ceases.

Cash Settlement Day

- Day on which all remaining open positions are settled by cash debit or credit using a final cash-market value as of a specific date and time, as required by exchange rules.

FIGURE 2-1   General sequence of delivery.

if a weekend is involved) while beginning the process of delivering to someone else. The speculator will be responsible for all the associated expenses of delivery and ownership for at least that one day. He must pay his carrying broker the full value of the contract or arrange with his broker for financing and incur interest expenses. Once payment is made the merchandise becomes the property of the speculator. Of course, at this point there may be storage and insurance charges. If the commodity requires another inspection before it can be redelivered on the current or a later futures contract month, this cost must be borne by the speculator as well. If the commodity fails inspection, it will have to be unloaded in the cash market as distressed merchandise. For these reasons, the average speculator should have little interest in receiving delivery of commodities on a futures contract.

If a speculator wishes to maintain his long position in a futures market as first notice day approaches, he can do so without risk of delivery by selling his position in the spot month and simultaneously buying an equivalent number of contracts in a later delivery month. This operation is known as switching or rolling a futures position. While it will cost the speculator an extra commission and other transaction costs to do this, a rollover eliminates the hazards and costs that can accompany delivery.

FUTURES COMMISSION MERCHANTS AND INTRODUCING BROKERS

Futures Commission Merchants

A futures brokerage firm, known under the Commodity Exchange Act as a futures commission merchant (FCM), is the intermediary between public customers, including hedgers and institutional investors, and the exchanges. An FCM, known informally as a commission house or carrying firm, provides the facilities to execute customer orders on the exchange and maintains records of each customer's open positions, margin deposits, money balances and completed transactions. An FCM is the only entity outside the futures clearinghouse that can hold customer funds. In return for providing its array of services, an FCM collects commissions.

An FCM may be a full service or a discount firm. Some FCMs are part of national or regional brokerage companies that also offer securities and other financial services, while other FCMs offer only futures and/or futures options. In addition, some FCMs have as a parent or are related to a commercial bank, agribusiness company or other commercial enterprise.

Introducing Brokers

An introducing broker (IB) is an individual or firm that has established a relationship with one or more futures brokerage firms. Similar to an FCM, an IB is responsible for maintaining customer relationships and servicing customer accounts, and its sales force receives commissions. However, an IB cannot accept funds from its customers, and, as a result, all customers of an IB must open and maintain accounts with an FCM on a fully disclosed basis, *i.e.*, where each customer's account is identified and carried separately on the books of the FCM.

There are two types of introducing brokerage firms—independent and guaranteed. IBs that have sufficient capital to meet regulatory requirements may choose to introduce their clients through a number of different FCMs. Such IBs, which operate independently of any particular brokerage firm, are known as independent or non-guaranteed IBs. A guaranteed IB has a legal and regulatory relationship with the guarantor futures commission merchant through which the IB introduces its customers.

Futures commission merchants and introducing brokers must be registered under the Commodity Exchange Act, and their account executives, discussed in the following text, must be registered as Associated Persons (APs) of the FCM or IB.

Account Executives

Account executives or APs are the agents of the FCM or IB who deal directly with the firm's customers. Generally, an account executive is paid on the basis of the commissions his clients pay to the firm where he is employed. (Other futures industry firms and their agents that deal with the public are discussed later in this chapter.) It is the account executive who:

- Supplies the proper documents for new accounts and sees to it that they are signed;
- Explains disclosure requirements, trading rules and procedures to customers;
- Keeps customers informed of prices and market conditions as required;
- Enters orders received from customers for execution;
- Reports prices of executed trades and the status of pending orders;

Clerks on the floor signal bid and offer prices to phone clerks in contact with worldwide customers
Photo courtesy of the Chicago Mercantile Exchange

- Acts as a link between the customer and the firm's research department;
- Contacts the customer when margin calls arise.

In establishing and maintaining a customer account, it is usually the account executive who must obtain, and keep current, the required information about the customer. National Futures Association (NFA) rule 2-30, Customer Information and Risk Disclosure, calls for FCMs to know their customers by ascertaining at least the customer's:

- Name, address and occupation;
- Estimated annual income and net worth;
- Approximate age;
- Previous investment and futures trading experience.

The account executive obtains this information to assure himself and his firm of the customer's financial means and relevant investment experience and to ascertain whether futures trading provides a suitable vehicle for the customer.

Even though the account executive may be qualified to do so, most commission houses do not permit a commodity account executive to write a personal commodity advisory or market letter for distribution to existing customers or for use in soliciting new customers. The NFA's rule 2-29, Promotional Material and Communication with the Public, outlines strict rules covering the content

of such material and the supervisory responsibilities of the FCM or IB with respect to such communication. To maintain compliance many firms only permit the use of research reports or solicitation materials that have been prepared by the firm's research or marketing departments and approved for firm-wide use. (Pertinent NFA rules are discussed in detail in the IFM's *Guide to U.S. Futures Regulation*.)

COMMODITY TRADING ADVISORS AND COMMODITY POOL OPERATORS

Money managers in the futures and options industry fall into two broad categories: Commodity Trading Advisors (CTAs) and Commodity Pool Operators (CPOs), each regulated by both the Commodity Futures Trading Commission and the National Futures Association. CTAs trade individual accounts for single clients (whether individuals, corporations or institutions), while CPOs, as their name implies, pool the funds of many investors and trade for all individuals consolidated under one account. In addition, some money management firms, especially those that direct their services toward large corporate or institutional investors, have assumed the role of managers of managers. In this context such firms oversee the selection of traders and match CTAs with particular clients' investment objectives and risk tolerance or, alternately, these firms assemble groups of CTAs that satisfy the investment needs of a large client. In terms of regulatory requirements, such managers of managers may be registered as either CPOs or CTAs.

Commodity Trading Advisors (CTAs)

The Commodity Exchange Act generally defines a CTA as an individual or organization who, for compensation or profit, advises others on the value or advisability of trading futures or options on futures. A managed futures or options account is similar to other brokerage accounts, except that decisions about what and when to trade are delegated to a professional trading advisor who manages or has discretion over trading in the account. This discretionary authority is documented in a written power of attorney.

An investor who decides to open an account with a commodity trading advisor should make sure that the advisor is using a trading philosophy that will achieve the investor's goals. The potential investor also should determine

Trading on the New York Futures Exchange, a subsidiary of the New York Board of Trade
Photo courtesy of the New York Board of Trade

acceptable risk and profit levels and whether he or she wishes to place funds with an advisor who employs a fundamental or a technical approach to the market.

In addition to managing the accounts of single clients, CTAs also trade the funds raised and controlled by commodity pool operators, as discussed in the following text. It should be noted that CTAs that are not also FCMs may not accept funds from customers in the CTA's name. Instead, clients of such CTAs must place their funds at a futures commission merchant who carries the customers' accounts.

Trading advisors usually charge fees for their services, which generally include:

- An incentive or performance fee, which is a percentage of the trading profits in the client's managed account, most often as of the end of each calendar quarter. This fee is usually payable only on cumulative profits to the extent that such profits exceed a specified level.

- A management fee, which is levied whether the account makes or loses money and is usually a yearly

percentage of the assets the advisor is managing. This fee can be charged either monthly or quarterly.

- Brokerage commissions, in which some, but not all, CTAs participate. If a CTA shares commissions with its FCM, this fact must be disclosed to the CTA's clients.

Commodity Pool Operators (CPOs)

The central concept of a commodity pool is to combine or pool the funds of a number of investors to trade futures and options, rather than trading for clients one at a time. The Commodity Exchange Act defines a CPO as any person engaged in a business that is of the nature of an investment trust, syndicate or similar form of enterprise and who, in that respect, solicits, accepts or receives from others funds, securities or property for the purpose of trading in futures. In effect, commodity pools play a role similar to mutual funds in the securities industry.

Commodity pools, whose sponsors include major brokerage firms, have become popular investment vehicles largely because of several beneficial characteristics. For one, a client can participate in a commodity pool and receive professional management of his or her funds for a relatively small investment, normally $5,000. In contrast, an individually managed account may require ten or more times that amount. In addition, pools permit investors with a larger amount of capital to invest in several different pools that may be managed by different commodity trading advisors with different approaches and using different systems, thereby providing diversification.

Limited liability is another key benefit of a commodity pool. Commodity pools are normally limited partnerships, with the CPO acting as the general partner. Such an organizational form permits the pool to take advantage of flow-through taxation and limits the risk of pool participants. In effect, the investor's risk is no greater than the amount of capital he or she invests. In an individual commodities account, the investor can lose more money than initially placed in the account. Some pools also incorporate a dissolution clause. For example, if the initial value of a unit were $1,000 and there were a 50 percent dissolution clause, then when the value of a unit reached $500 the fund would stop trading, and the investor would receive about one half of his or her money back.

CUSTOMERS

Futures and options customers of an FCM may include:

- Individual speculative traders;

- Hedging firms or companies;

- Money managers, money management firms and institutional investors;

- Floor brokers who do not belong to the clearinghouse and who wish to avail themselves of the clearing facilities of the commission house;

- Other brokerage firms that are not members of the particular clearinghouse and/or exchange.

Futures transactions made through one commission house by another, depending upon the agreement between the two firms, may be carried on the books of the clearing firm either on a disclosed basis (under the actual names of the other firm's customers) or in an omnibus account (one bookkeeping and margin account that includes all the trades and positions of the other firm's customers, with the originating firm keeping the detailed accounting records required for the individual customers).

Customer Funds

As previously mentioned, special rules govern the handling by a commission house of customer margin funds deposited with the firm. For example, customer funds received by the firm to margin open positions in futures cannot, by law, be mingled with funds belonging to the commission house itself. Such customer margin funds, plus all profits realized and unrealized from futures positions, must be deposited in a bank account separate from the firm's own funds. The reason for this is that if the commission house should fail in business, residual margin funds and profits belonging to customers cannot be used to meet obligations of the firm to its general creditors; such funds are available only for the firm's futures customers. Customer margin funds, however, may be used by the commission house to meet the clearinghouse's margin requirements for the firm's customer business.

FOR YOUR CONSIDERATION

The advent of new types of electronic communication is having an impact on futures traders just as it is on stock traders, often allowing them to bypass contact with a live person at the FCM. This dramatically affects the traditional role of the account executive as the "customer's man." FCMs traditionally have relied on the account executive as the point of contact with clients in collecting margin funds and keeping customers' trading within their means, that is, assuring that the FCM does not have compliance or bad debt problems related to customer accounts. What new methods, technology or regulation might be required to accomplish these objectives without the account executive as intermediary?

APPENDIX

Type of Accounts

The types of customer accounts that a commission house may open include, but are not limited to, the following:

- *Individual customer account:* an account in which are recorded all of the money transactions and futures trading activity of an individual customer. Documentation required to support such an account usually includes a New Account Information form, a

Commodity Account Agreement form, a Risk Disclosure Statement and a Transfer of Funds Authorization. The last named form may not legally be required of a customer by the carrying firm, but most speculative customers will sign such a document when it is explained that, without it, each required transfer of the customer's funds from his futures account to any other type of account—for example, a securities account—will require specific authorization in writing.

- *Joint account (either as tenants in common or with rights of survivorship):* an account of two persons, who may or may not be related, who wish to trade in futures in a joint venture. In a joint account with right of survivorship, if one of the joint account owners dies, the entire interest in the account immediately vests in the survivor, and the deceased's estate has no further interest in the account. In a tenants-in-common account, without rights of survivorship, upon receiving written notice of the death of either of the joint owners, the carrying member firm is required to divide the account into equal parts, one under the name of the survivor and one under the name of the estate of the deceased. In addition to the documentation required of an individual customer, a joint account must be supported by a joint-account form, signed by both parties, on which the rights and obligations of each party to the account are set forth.

- *Partnership account:* the account of two or more individuals whose concerted operation in the business world is governed by a signed partnership agreement. Such an account may be for a closed partnership or for an open-end partnership, in which new partners may be added from time to time. To document such an account, all of the forms required of an Individual Customer Account must be furnished, plus a copy of the partnership agreement and a partnership form that outlines, among other things, who among the partners is legally authorized to commit the partnership by giving orders, withdrawing funds and conducting other business for the partnership.

- *Corporate account:* the account of a customer for whom a state has granted a charter to do business as a corporation. Many hedging customers are corporate accounts. When such an account is opened, the commission house asks to see a copy of the customer's corporate charter or board resolution to satisfy itself that the corporation is legally empowered to trade in

futures. If it is not, and the corporate customer later decides to back away from losing trades, there is not much the carrying commission firm can do but absorb any loss, because the customer could not legally trade in futures. If the corporate charter includes the required trading authority, then the corporate customer will be asked to fill out and sign, at a minimum, a New Account Information Card, a Risk Disclosure Statement, a Commodity Account Agreement and a Corporate Account form. The last, among other things, names the officers of the corporation to whom its board of directors has delegated the authority to place orders and enter into positions that will be legally binding on the corporation. The commission house also may suggest that the customer sign a Transfer of Funds Authorization.

- *Omnibus account:* an account of a commission house that clears, or carries, its trading (house omnibus) account or that of its customers (customers' omnibus) account through another commission house, known as the carrying firm. The customer of the carrying firm is the other commission house, whose customers may remain unknown to the carrying firm.

- *Power of attorney or discretionary account:* an account over which the owner or owners have delegated either discretionary power to trade, or full power of attorney (including authority to withdraw funds as well as to trade), to another. The person controlling the trading may be an employee of the FCM or a Commodity Trading Advisor (CTA), a futures money manager. (There are special rules regarding the approval of an FCM employee as power of attorney holder and covering the conduct of such accounts.) Documentation required for discretionary accounts includes the forms required for an Individual Customer Account plus a signed copy of the applicable power of attorney form. This latter form usually holds the commission house blameless for actions taken on the customer's behalf by the person to whom the power of attorney has been granted.

- *Fiduciary or trust account:* before opening a futures account for such an entity, the commission house will verify whether or not the fiduciary organization or trust is empowered by its indenture to trade in futures and related option contracts; not all are so empowered.

- *Investment company account:* provides for trading by a number of investors who pool their resources into one fund for the specific purpose of trading in futures. Power to trade is usually delegated to one or two participants in the fund or to an outsider. Special documentation to support such an account is required.

As noted earlier, most hedge accounts are under a corporate ownership structure. This is due to the nature of hedging as a "business" activity. However, a hedger may use any account ownership form that matches the structure of the hedger's business. As an example, many farmers are sole proprietors, and their futures hedging accounts are individual accounts. The FCM must make an effort to verify the general business activity and hedging needs of its hedge accounts. In any case, a hedger will be asked to complete additional documentation, such as a Hedge Account Agreement or Hedge Letter, and provide an approximation of the size of its hedging positions.

Study Questions

1. All futures exchanges in the U.S. are membership organizations.
   A. True
   B. False

2. Only persons who own or lease seats or trading rights on an exchange may execute futures contracts on the exchange's trading floor or via the exchange's electronic trading system.
   A. True
   B. False

3. The clearinghouse is the guarantor of the financial integrity of every futures contract open on its books.
   A. True
   B. False

4. Variation margin:
   A. Is collected each day by a futures clearinghouse from clearing members who have gains on their futures contracts.
   B. Is paid each day by a futures clearinghouse to clearing members who have gains on their futures contracts.
   C. Must be paid within three days of the loss.
   D. Both a and b.

5. Which of the following prices does a clearinghouse use in paying or collecting variation margins?
   A. Closing price
   B. Average of high and low prices

C. Settlement price
D. Opening price

6. Delivery against a futures position is initiated by:
   A. The buyer.
   B. The seller.
   C. The exchange.
   D. Either the buyer or the seller.

7. At maturity, all futures contracts are settled by delivery or by cash settlement.
   A. True
   B. False

8. An introducing broker (IB) in the futures industry:
   A. Must be guaranteed by a futures commission merchant.
   B. Services customer accounts.
   C. Cannot pay commissions to its sales force.
   D. Pays funds to and accepts funds from futures and options customers.

9. A commodity trading advisor (CTA):
   A. Is permitted to trade individually managed accounts.
   B. Is not permitted to trade for a commodity pool or fund.
   C. Is not permitted to charge an incentive fee.
   D. Does not have to be registered with the CFTC.

10. If an exchange member is "dual trading," under certain circumstances he or she can give priority to his/her own trades over customers' orders.
    A. True
    B. False

11. Clearinghouses use guaranty deposits to:
    A. Margin clearing members' positions.
    B. Meet the financial obligations of a defaulting member to other clearing members.
    C. Open accounts at other clearinghouses to diversify their holdings.
    D. Guarantee that customers' funds are not commingled with proprietary funds.

12. Why are some futures transactions cleared a day late, "as of" the preceding day?
    A. The contract market in which the transaction occurred was closed on the transaction day.

B. The transaction occurred after-hours.

C. Trade records did not match so the exchange members involved in the transaction had to resolve the discrepancy before or on the opening of trading the next morning.

D. The transaction occurred in a different time-zone and therefore could not meet clearing deadlines.

13. Because the clearinghouse substitutes itself as the counterparty to every trade, individual traders can liquidate their positions without having to wait for the other party to the original contract to liquidate.

    A. True

    B. False

14. NFA Rule 2-30 (Customer Information and Risk Disclosure) requires members and associates to obtain from customers who are individuals:

    A. The customer's true name, address, and principal occupation.

    B. The customer's current estimated annual income and net worth.

    C. The customer's approximate age.

    D. An indication of the customer's previous investment and futures trading experience.

    E. All of the above.

15. CFTC regulations provide that customer funds generally, but not always, must be segregated from the firm's proprietary funds.

    A. True

    B. False

16. Limited liability is a key benefit of a commodity pool.

    A. True

    B. False

17. First notice day is:

    A. The first day a long can take delivery.

    B. The first day a short can make delivery.

    C. The first day a long can issue a delivery notice.

    D. The first day a short can issue a delivery notice.

    E. None of the above

18. An omnibus account is the account of an individual customer that carries a variety of futures and options contracts.

    A. True

    B. False

Answers to Questions

1. **B** (False)

   For nearly 150 years all U.S. exchanges were membership organizations. However, in 1999 the Chicago Mercantile Exchange's board of directors approved the change of the exchange's structure from a membership to a shareholder form of organization. In 2002 there was an initial public offering (IPO) of the CME's common stock, which now trades on the New York Stock Exchange. Currently, several other U.S. exchanges are in the process of demutualizing and becoming shareholder corporations.

2. **A** (True)

   Only owners or lessees of seats or trading rights may trade on the floor of an exchange or execute trades over an exchange's screen-based trading system. Other traders must send their orders through a seat or trading rights owner or lessee.

3. **A** (True)

   Once a futures trade is cleared and therefore "on the books" of the clearinghouse, the clearinghouse interposes itself between the original buyer and seller and becomes the "buyer to every seller" and the "seller to every buyer." This, along with the futures margining system and other clearinghouse safeguards, permits the clearinghouse to guarantee the open contracts on its books.

4. **D**

   As a result of a futures clearinghouse's daily calculation of the gains and losses in all clearing members' accounts, variation margin is paid to members who have gains on their futures accounts and collected from members who have losses on their accounts.

5. **C**

   Futures contracts are marked to market each day based on that day's settlement price for each expiration month of a particular futures contract.

6. **B**

   The seller of a futures contract initiates delivery.

7. **A** (True)

   There are only two means to settle an open futures contract at maturity—by delivery or by cash settlement—as specified in the exchange rules for the particular contract.

8. B

Introducing brokers service customer accounts that they introduce to futures commission merchants, and for these activities introducing brokers are paid commissions. There are two types of introducing brokers—those that are guaranteed by one or more futures commission merchants and those that are independent.

9. A

Commodity trading advisors trade individually managed accounts and on behalf of commodity pools or funds. Commodity trading advisors are permitted to receive management and incentive fees and must be registered with the CFTC.

10. B (False)

Under all circumstances, dual traders, who trade for themselves and also handle customer business, are required by exchange and other regulatory rules to give priority to a customer's order over their own activities.

11. B

Guaranty deposits are used to meet the financial obligations of a defaulting clearing member to other members of the clearinghouse.

12. C

When trade records do not match in the clearing process, either because of a discrepancy in the details or because one side of the transaction is missing, the disputed trade is returned to the submitting clearinghouse members for resolution. The two exchange members involved in the transaction are required to resolve the discrepancy before or on the opening of trading the next morning. Such a contract is then cleared a day late, as of the preceding day.

13. A (True)

The clearinghouse inserts itself as the buyer to every seller and the seller to every buyer, thereby allowing traders to offset trades with any other trader rather than only with the trader with whom the trade originated.

14. E

NFA Rule 2-30 (Customer Information and Risk Disclosure) requires members to obtain from customers who are individuals at least the following information: (1) the customer's true name, address, and principal occupation or business; (2) the customer's current estimated annual income and net worth; (3) the customer's approximate age; and (4) an indication of the customer's previous investment and futures-trading experience.

15. B (False)

CFTC regulations require that all customer funds received by an FCM be segregated and accounted for separately from the firm's proprietary funds. The account in which customer funds are deposited must be clearly identified and acknowledged as a customer segregated funds account.

16. A (True)

Limited liability is a key benefit of a commodity pool.

17. D

First notice day is the first day a short can issue a delivery notice.

18. B (False)

An omnibus account is a futures commission merchant's customer or proprietary account that the FCM carries or clears through another FCM (called the carrying broker).

Hedging with Futures and Options

3

■ Learning Objectives

Candidates, after completing this reading, should be able to:

- Define the terms "long the basis" and "short the basis."
- Explain exchange for physical (EFP) transactions and their role in the energy and financial futures markets.

- Describe and calculate the payoffs on the various scenarios for hedging with options on futures.

Excerpt is Chapter 7 of Futures and Options, *The Institute for Financial Markets.*

As discussed in earlier chapters, futures contracts and many of the rules governing futures trading exist to meet the risk-management needs of commercial traders known as hedgers. In the context of futures and options markets, hedging may be defined as using such instruments to manage the price risks associated with the production, processing, ownership or other use of a commodity, financial instrument or other item or measure.

The hedger has a risk generated from a business or investment activity, whether it be raising livestock, manufacturing, merchandizing, exporting products or managing investment portfolios. Futures and options are used to reduce the price risk of the underlying commodity or other item. A hedger's futures and options positions are solely for the purpose of net risk management. By contrast, a speculator's futures and options positions represent net risk-taking in pursuit of profit.

Hedging and associated pricing concepts such as basis are among the most important and least understood aspects of futures. However, a general comprehension of these topics begins with the relatively simple task of identifying the hedger's risk and the futures or options position that will balance or diminish that risk.

BASIC CONCEPTS

Cash and Futures Price Correlation

In general, futures and options markets are used to manage price risk and not as a means for acquiring or disposing of the actual cash commodity or other underlying item, because futures and options normally are not the most efficient vehicles for the actual transfer of ownership. There are several reasons why even hedgers rarely take or make delivery against futures:

- The futures delivery grade may not be the same as that which the hedger needs or produces.
- The futures delivery location may be inconvenient or unsuitable for the hedger.
- The futures delivery date may not match the hedger's timing for delivery or receipt of the commodity.

However, because there is generally a very high correlation in price movement between the futures market and the cash market item specified in the futures contract, futures or related options hedges are extremely

effective in balancing cash market exposures, even absent any intention by the hedger to make or take delivery. In fact, hedging in futures and options is possible precisely because of the price correlation between cash and futures; the closer this correlation, the more perfect the hedge. Later sections of this chapter discuss the relationship between cash and futures prices, known as basis.

References to cash markets in this chapter are generic. However, it should be stated emphatically that for the purpose of evaluating hedges, it is critical for a hedger to use the specific cash markets in which he or she operates. In particular, a hedger must be aware of the cash markets for the grade of the commodity in the locations in which he does business, as well as the associated costs of the cash business such as transportation, storage, and financing.

Futures Position as a Temporary Substitute for a Later Cash Transaction

In examining a hedger's risk and the futures position that may be used to balance that risk, it can be helpful to conceive of the hedge as "a futures trade made today that is a substitute for a later cash market transaction." This concept provides a guide to the futures position the hedger must take to accomplish his or her risk management goals, even when the hedger has no intention of making or taking delivery against the futures.

Consider the example of a farmer who produces cotton and so is naturally long the cash crop. (We say naturally long whenever a normal course of business leaves one with a long position in the cash market. Other hedgers, for example those who lack a commodity they will need in the future, are referred to as naturally short.) Eventually, the farmer will sell his cotton in his local cash market. He might choose not to do this now for any number of reasons, including the fact that he may not yet have harvested (or even planted) the cotton. The farmer can sell futures now as a temporary substitute for his later sale in the cash market. This hedge means the farmer has locked in a selling price for his crop, regardless of what happens to prices after the hedge is established.

When harvest time arrives, the farmer is likely to make a local sale of his cotton and offset the futures position; the farmer sold futures with no intention of delivering, using the futures only as a price-setting mechanism. The farmer will offset the futures position when making an actual sale in his local cash market, because at that point he no longer needs the futures sale as the "temporary substitute."

The cotton processor is in the opposite position of the farmer; he will need raw material, i.e., cotton, in the months ahead. Therefore, he buys cotton futures now, as a temporary substitute for his later purchase in the cash market. Although this hedger, or any trader, is free to take delivery against a futures contract when it matures (if it is not a cash-settled contract), generally it will be more efficient for the hedger to purchase in the cash market at that time and simultaneously offset the futures position.

Equal and Opposite Positions in Cash and Futures

An alternative approach to examining a hedger's needs is to remember that a hedger takes "equal and opposite positions in cash and futures." This approach emphasizes the concept of using futures to take a risk that is a counterbalance to the hedger's cash market exposure.

(Note: Both the "futures as a substitute transaction" approach and the "equal and opposite transaction" approach are guides to the analysis of a hedger's risk and related risk-management activities. When undertaking such an analysis, either approach results in the same conclusion. However, as more complex scenarios evolve, one approach may be more useful than the other in analyzing a particular situation, despite the fact that the results will be identical.)

For example, if a portfolio manager responsible for a broadly based equities portfolio were concerned about upcoming economic reports and the possibility of their negative impact on the stock market, he might consider hedging the price risk of the portfolio. Clearly, this hedger is long cash; in this case, the cash commodity is shares of stock. To take an opposite position in futures would require a short position in futures, perhaps the S&P 500 futures, in a rough dollar equivalence to the dollar value of the portfolio (assuming the price of the cash portfolio is highly correlated with that of the S&P 500 index). Of course, the hedger never had any plan to sell or deliver any stock, but the cash and the futures positions now counterbalance each other in their sensitivity to changes in the stock market.

EXAMPLES OF HEDGING WITH FUTURES

The Selling Hedge

A hedger who takes a short position in futures is said to be placing a "short hedge" or a "selling hedge." Consider a businesswoman who is a dealer in a commodity traded on a futures market. She buys, sells, places orders to purchase and takes orders to supply the commodity to customers. Most important, however, is the fact that she owns inventories. In all of these activities, changing prices affect both her business and her profits. If she could find a way to have all of her transactions arranged so that every purchase was matched simultaneously with a sale, she would neutralize the possible adverse effects of changing market prices, essentially never having an inventory exposure.

Hedging in futures enables her to accomplish this kind of matching in the many instances when it is impossible to accomplish such matched buying and selling in the cash market. The way she would do this is to assume a futures or futures option hedge when she first acquires the inventory (that is, take a short position in futures or buy a put option when she goes long in the cash commodity) and then offset the futures or options position when the inventory is sold. Because trading is continuous in liquid futures and options markets, there is rarely a problem making a virtually simultaneous futures or options sale to match a commitment to buy in the cash market, or a simultaneous buy in futures or options to match a sale of the cash commodity.

For the moment, it is assumed that the long cash position precisely matches the futures contract's terms. Stated otherwise, the cash and futures price correlation is perfect. Although this correlation is rarely if ever perfect, the assumption serves to illustrate the basic concepts of hedging. In such a case, the hedger translates the amount of the cash position into the correct number of futures contracts and takes an equal and opposite position in futures. For example, if the dealer above has 4,000 ounces of gold, she would sell 40 gold futures on the New York Mercantile Exchange. (The contract size is 100 ounces of gold.) Figure 3-1 shows this dealer's hedge. In other words:

$$\text{\# of Futures to Hedge} = \frac{\text{Size (value) of Cash Position}}{\text{Size (value) of 1 Futures Contract}}$$

Cash (Actuals)	Futures
Long 4,000 ounces gold	Short 40 gold futures contracts

FIGURE 3-1 Futures hedge position for a dealer with 4,000 ounces of gold.

The short hedge protects the value of inventory against possible price declines. If the price of gold falls, the dealer would suffer a financial loss on the inventory. The short futures position, because its price moves with that of the commodity, will gain at approximately the same rate as losses accrue on the long cash side. The net value of the hedged position does not change at all. This is true also when the cash price rises: profits on the cash market side of the position will be balanced by corresponding losses in the futures market. Always keep in mind, however, that any variation in price correlation between the cash and futures positions will yield a result other than a perfect net between the cash and futures values. Nonetheless, significant risk protection can be achieved when the cash and futures prices are highly correlated and that correlation is stable over time.

Suppose that on October 20 a farmer brings 10,000 bushels of corn to a country elevator. The operator buys the grain for $2.50 per bushel. Concurrently, the elevator operator sells 2 contracts (10,000 bushels) of December corn futures at $2.52. By selling futures as a hedge, he protects his grain inventory against exposure to changing prices for several months ahead. Two weeks later, however, the elevator operator is able to sell the corn. In the interim, the cash market price of corn has declined to $2.35. The elevator operator now has a 15¢ per bushel loss on his inventory of 10,000 bushels, a total of $1,500. When the operator sells the corn, he closes out the short hedge in futures with an offsetting purchase. If the futures price also declined by 15¢ per bushel (*i.e.*, it was a perfect hedge in which the futures and cash prices were perfectly

correlated), the December futures are offset at $2.37. The gain realized on the futures position offsets the loss on the cash market transaction, as shown in Figure 3-2.

These examples did not include any costs for the futures transaction, such as commissions and the application of the hedger's working capital to margin requirements. Commissions tend to be very small when compared to the value of goods hedged; still, they should not be ignored as a cost of doing business. Cash flow issues related to margin requirements, particularly capital to meet any maintenance margin calls, can be very significant to a hedger. Such costs apply to buying as well as selling hedges.

The Buying Hedge

A hedger who takes a long position in futures is said to be placing a long hedge or a buying hedge. The buying or long hedge is used to protect against a possible price increase in the actual commodity when the underlying risk exposure is short the cash market, for example, if the potential hedger will need the commodity in the future and does not currently own it. Conceptually, the buying hedge is exactly the opposite of the selling hedge described above.

A copper fabricator, for example, wins a contract to supply copper wire and plumbing for a new office complex. The price he will receive for these products is fixed based on his winning bid. However, he does not yet own enough copper to manufacture the required product. Part of his strategy in bidding for the contract, of course, was to use current copper prices in his own cost estimates.

The hedger could wait to buy the copper, hoping the price would fall or, at the least, remain at about the same level he used in making his contract bid. If the copper price falls, a speculative profit would result. However, if the copper price rises, the fabricator would suffer a financial loss, and this loss could be substantial enough to put him out of business.

	Cash (Actuals)			Futures	
October 20	Buy 10,000 bushels	$2.50/bu.		Sell short 2 Dec. corn futures	$2.52/bu.
November 3	Sell 10,000 bushels	$2.35/bu.		Buy 2 Dec. corn futures to offset	$2.37/bu.
Gain (loss)		($ .15/bu.)			$ .15/bu.
Net result			$0.00		

FIGURE 3-2 Selling hedge: Loss on cash position offset by gain on futures position.

	Cash (Actuals)			Futures	
December 1	Sell 100,000 lbs.	$.8850/lb.		Buy 4 Mar. copper futures	$.8775/lb.
November 3	Buy 100,000 lbs.	$.8300/lb.		Sell 4 Mar. copper futures to offset	$.8225/lb.
Gain (loss)		$.0550/lb.			($.0550/lb.)
Net result			$0.00		

FIGURE 3-3 Buying hedge: Gain on cash position offset by loss on futures position.

Because the goal of this fabricator is to make merchandising and manufacturing profits, and not to risk the survival of his business on a single favorable price change, he chooses to hedge in the futures markets. By doing so, he is able to concentrate on running an efficient manufacturing and marketing operation. In terms of the substitute-transaction approach, the hedger buys futures today as a hedge against his need to buy cash copper in the future. When the fabricator subsequently buys his copper in the cash market, he will offset his long position in copper futures. Figure 3-3 illustrates a buying-hedge transaction.

BASIS: CASH/FUTURES PRICE RELATIONSHIPS

As previously mentioned, the relationship between cash and futures prices, termed the cash-futures basis, is a central concept in futures markets and the use of futures to hedge cash market risks. Traditionally, basis has been defined as:

Basis = Cash Price − Futures Price

With this definition, a positive basis (often described as cash over futures) indicates that the cash price exceeds the futures price; alternately, a negative basis (often described as cash under futures) reflects cash prices that are below the futures. However, caution is in order when classifying a particular cash-futures basis as positive or negative: it is necessary to assure that the same definition is used by all parties in the discussion.

In the preceding examples, the assumption was made that prices in both the cash and futures markets rise and fall by exactly the same amount; perfect correlation produces a perfect hedge. This is the same as saying that, from the time the hedge was established to the time it was lifted, the basis did not change. This rarely, if ever, happens. There is certainly a tendency for prices in cash and futures markets to move in the same direction, because the two markets share a value relationship. However, cash market prices may change more or less than futures prices over a given period of time.

Basis considerations are extremely important to hedging. In fact, it is often said that the hedger has traded outright price risk (having unhedged inventory or needs) for basis risk. This residual risk is why a hedger is said to reduce, but normally not eliminate, risk.

Many of the reasons for changes in the basis are closely related to the particular commodity or instrument being hedged. Market and economic events that have varying impacts on the supply of and demand for different grades or types of the commodity, or on different delivery locations, may have a strong impact on the basis. As emphasized earlier, each hedger must relate the cash market in which he or she operates to prices in the futures and options markets and remain abreast of developments that affect that relationship.

The hedger's location in comparison to the futures contract's specifications is one factor that will affect basis differently for different commodities. For example, price fluctuations of cash grain for export at the Gulf of Mexico may vary from price fluctuations for the futures contract, which specifies delivery in the upper midwest of the U.S. These differences might be caused by transportation issues related to railroads or barges or to the current status of foreign demand for U.S. grain. An exporter in New Orleans will hedge using the Chicago Board of Trade's futures, knowing that these and other factors will affect his basis: cash grain prices in New Orleans compared to Chicago grain futures.

Another source of basis risk is variation in the exact grade or type of the commodity to be hedged. This, too, will weigh differently on hedgers in different commodities. An example is a corporation wanting to hedge long-term interest rate risk due to an upcoming bond issuance. In this case, the corporation will be hedging corporate bonds with Treasury bond (or note) futures. This hedger must track closely the price relationship between corporate bonds of the quality the firm issues and Treasury futures.

Finally, the fact that the futures contract unit is not necessarily the same as the quantity to be hedged is another factor that prevents hedging from automatically giving complete price protection. For example, the CME's frozen pork belly futures contract specifies delivery of 40,000 pounds of frozen bellies. Hedging any quantity of pork bellies that is not a multiple of this amount causes some of the cash market exposure to be overhedged or underhedged.

INTERTEMPORAL PRICE RELATIONSHIPS

In addition to the circumstances mentioned above, there are basis and other price relationship issues that arise from the fact that futures and options markets price items for future, not current, delivery. These factors, too, weigh differently on different markets but are relevant in all futures and options markets.

A look at prices of the various futures months within a market reveals that these contracts do not usually trade at the same price but, rather, at premiums or discounts to each other. These premiums or discounts generally reflect the different maturity dates of the futures contract. For example, unleaded gasoline might sell at $.8120 per gallon in the cash market, while February futures are trading at $.8216 and March futures at $.8385. These price differences are the result of open market forces and vary from time to time with changing market conditions.

Normal, Carrying Charge or Contango Markets

A normal or carrying charge market, also known as contango, describes a market in which successive futures are at higher prices. That is, the greater the time until contract expiration or delivery, the higher the futures price. The difference, or spread, between the prices of the futures delivery months reflects supply and demand conditions as well as the influence of carrying costs. These latter generally include storage, insurance and financing. Clearly, the three parts of carrying costs apply differently, if at all, to different markets. Physical storage of metal, for instance, would generate all three of these expenses. Carrying debt instruments would generate only a net interest expense (net

because the debt instrument earns interest, while financing the purchase of the instrument requires payment of interest). Futures prices in a normal or carrying-charge market might look like those illustrated in Figure 3-4.

Inverted or Backwardation Markets

Sometimes the highest price is for the spot or nearby month, and each successive delivery month is priced lower than the preceding one. This is referred to as an inverted market, or one in backwardation, as illustrated in Figure 3-5. In futures markets for physical goods,

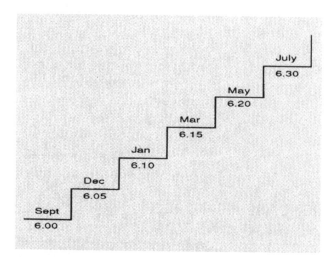

FIGURE 3-4 Prices of succeeding delivery months in a carrying-charge (contango) market.

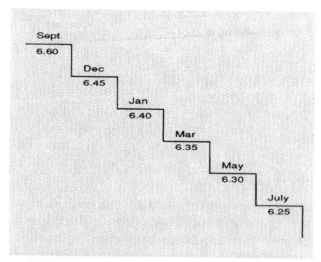

FIGURE 3-5 Prices of succeeding delivery months in an inverted (backwardation) market.

such as grain, oil or industrial metals, inverted markets sometimes occur when there is a current shortage of a commodity and those in need bid nearby supplies to a premium over the deferred contracts whose supply will not become available for some time. In futures markets for financial instruments, such as U.S. Treasury bonds or currencies, a backwardation or contango is caused by the relationship between interest earned on the cash instrument (which, for example, may be a long-term or foreign interest rate) and the interest expense of carrying the instrument (which, normally, is a short-term rate). As an example, U.S. Treasury bond futures trade in an inverted market when long-term interest rates exceed short-term rates.

Convergence

The prices of futures and the underlying cash commodity are closely related, because the futures price must converge to the cash price at expiration of the futures contract. For physical delivery contracts on the first delivery date, the price for that futures and the cash price for the identical grade of the commodity, in the same location, must be the same, because at delivery the futures contract is the same as the cash commodity. For cash-settled contracts, the expiring futures contract is settled against the specified cash price.

The fact that futures and cash prices always converge at delivery or cash settlement means that futures and cash prices should be closely related, given the carrying costs and supply and demand scenario that may exist at the time. If prices get too far out of line, for instance if the futures are too expensive relative to cash, then it should be possible to make a risk-free profit by selling the relatively overpriced futures and buying the relatively underpriced cash instrument. Since at expiration these prices must converge, the trader earns a profit at expiration by delivering the cash instrument against the short future. This is called an arbitrage trade, and because profits can be earned while taking little or no risk, futures prices rarely get out of line with cash prices for significant periods of time.

Further, the possibility of arbitrage means that prices in the futures markets are driven by the same economic factors as those affecting the underlying commodity or security. As a result, developments affecting cash commodity prices, or that can be expected to do so in the future, have a corresponding effect on the futures market.

An Illustration

These concepts are best understood with a simple example of a hedger in a tangible, storable commodity such as cocoa. On April 1, the hedger anticipates the need for cocoa on September 1. The hedger will research both the quoted price levels for cocoa from his normal suppliers and the futures prices relative to those cash quotes. (Cash and futures prices are quoted in dollars per ton.)

	Cash Cocoa	September Futures	Basis
April 1	810	872	62 under

These prices reflect a normal market, with a basis of "cash 62 under September futures." The hedger calculates the cost of carrying the cocoa for five months, perhaps arriving at a figure of $75 per ton. The hedger decides to buy cocoa now, at $810, and hedge by selling September futures at $872. On September 1, the cash and futures prices will converge, yielding proceeds of $62 per ton for this hedger.

These proceeds are not profit, however, because the hedger has incurred $75 in expenses for carrying the commodity for five months. (As discussed above, the basis should not be such that the hedger could receive more than the $75 in carrying costs. This would represent an arbitrage opportunity which, if it existed at all, would be relatively minute and fleeting.) The normal market, however, did enable him to earn a large portion of those carrying costs, while assuring inventory and price protection. The inevitability of convergence guarantees this result. In this illustration, the carrying charge price structure encourages hedgers to place the commodity in storage by creating a subsidy for the expense of carrying the commodity.

In the interim, there may be other price structures that appear, for example, a dramatic change in the market price structure from normal to inverted, as illustrated below.

	Cash Cocoa	September Futures	Basis
June 15	985	960	25 over

Although the hedger entered the position on April 1 willing to wait until September 1 to receive the $62 in proceeds (while maintaining his inventory), on June 15 he sees the opportunity to receive $87, and in a far shorter time period. These proceeds would yield a net profit beyond the cost of carrying the commodity for what has now been only 2½ months.

The earlier discussion of inverted markets indicated that they often result from tight supply situations. In order to realize this profit, the hedger would have to sell the inventory as well as offset the futures. Therefore, despite the unexpected and very favorable basis change, the hedger may decide to maintain his cash inventory and futures hedge so as to be certain of having inventory when he needs it.

Had the market been inverted on April 1, it is likely that the hedger would not have purchased the inventory at all. Instead of buying cash and selling futures (a favorable position for the short hedger in a normal market), the hedger might have chosen to buy September futures and let the futures market "carry his inventory." For example:

	Cash Cocoa	September Futures	Basis
April 1	1030	990	40 over

The inverted market would allow him to buy supplies for later delivery in the futures market at a price below the spot price and without the expense of carrying material. While the inverted market indicates an immediate need for supplies by many commercial users of cocoa, this hedger is rewarded for not being in desperate need of the commodity at the current time.

BASIS AND HEDGING

Price structures and basis in futures markets present hedgers with additional dimensions, beyond the price level, to consider. Great emphasis is placed on understanding and tracking the cash/futures basis, because the net result of a hedge will be the net price change between the cash and futures positions, that is, the change in the basis. (Recall the definition: Basis = Cash − Futures.)

So important is the basis that its changes are noted using terms similar to those used to describe outright prices. The basis is said to be strengthening when cash prices are stronger than futures prices: cash rises more (or falls less) than futures over the time the hedge is held. The basis is said to be weakening when cash prices are weaker than futures prices: cash falls more (or rises less) than futures over the time the hedge is held.

Long the Basis

A short hedge, or selling hedge, was described earlier as a short position in the futures market. Alternatively, in basis terms, we can say that a hedger who is long cash and short futures is "long the basis." As with any other long position, this hedger will profit from a strengthening in price: specifically a strengthening in the basis. This strengthening occurs when cash prices are stronger than futures prices: when cash rises more (or falls less) than futures over the time the hedge is held. As discussed in the previous illustration, in contango or carrying charge markets short hedgers may have an opportunity to subsidize their carrying costs. Figure 3-6 shows an example of a cash and carry hedge.

Short the Basis

A long hedge, or buying hedge, was described earlier as a long position in the futures market. Alternatively, in basis terms, we can say that a hedger who is short cash and long futures is "short the basis." As with any other short position, this hedger will profit from a weakening in price, specifically a weakening in the basis. This weakening occurs when cash prices are weaker than futures prices: cash falls more (or rises less) than futures over the time the hedge is held. As also illustrated earlier, in inverted or backwardation markets, long hedgers may be able to replace inventory at lower cost, if they are not in immediate need. Figure 3-7 shows an example of a hedger who is short the basis.

	Cash (Actuals)			Futures		Basis
January 15	Buy 100 tons cocoa	$750/ton		Sell 10 May cocoa futures	$790/ton	40 under
May 1	Sell	$738/ton		Buy to offset	$738/ton	0
Gain (loss)		($ 12/ton)			$ 52/ton	+ 40
Net result			$40/ton			

FIGURE 3-6 Hedger is long the basis/cash and carry hedge.

Cash (Actuals)				Futures		Basis
April 1	Sell 560,000 lbs. sugar	8.70¢/lb.		Buy 5 July sugar futures	8.30¢/lb.	40 over
June 1	Buy 560,000 lbs.	8.80¢/lb.		Sell 5 July sugar futures to offset	8.60¢/lb.	20 over
Gain (loss)		(.10¢/lb.)			.30¢/lb.	–20
Net result			.20/lb.			

FIGURE 3-7 Hedger is short the basis.

EXCHANGE FOR PHYSICALS (EFPs)

There are times when someone holding a futures position may want to make or take delivery on terms that are different from the futures' contract specifications. Similarly, there are occasions when cash merchants may want to transact a cash deal and set futures hedges simultaneously. These happen often enough that futures exchanges have set up a special procedure, called exchange of futures for physicals, or EFPs for short, to handle this situation. EFPs have been common historically in the grain markets and are now used extensively in other futures markets as well.

An EFP is a transaction in which one party buys the physical commodity and simultaneously sells futures to the other party while the latter sells the physical commodity and simultaneously buys the futures. The price of the futures position, the quantity of the futures and cash commodity to be exchanged, the price of the cash commodity and other terms are privately negotiated by the parties rather than being standardized in the futures contract or competitively determined in the trading pit.

EFPs are an exception to the general prohibition against prearranged trading in futures contracts. In other words, an EFP allows trading of futures positions without going through the trading pits. Generally, exchange rules require EFPs to be used only by people or firms who are trading the underlying cash commodity. Exchanges sometimes audit EFP traders to ensure that the procedure is properly used.

The energy markets make heavy use of EFPs. Cash crude oil, gasoline and heating oil transactions, for instance, are often made with reference to the relevant futures price. These prices are usually quoted in terms of a "differential," another name for the basis. For example, assume you wanted to buy 100,000 barrels of Alaskan Slope crude oil. Instead of getting a price of $18.00 (which might be the cash value of a barrel of this particular crude), you are quoted a price of "50 points over the April Merc," which means that there is a 50-cent difference between Alaskan Slope crude and the price of the April crude oil futures contract traded on the New York Mercantile Exchange (NYMEX). When the EFP is posted, one trader is long cash and short the futures, and the other trader is short cash and long the futures.

EFPs serve the same role in financial futures markets. Currency dealers, hedgers and arbitrageurs use EFPs to establish or offset hedges and to move easily between cash and futures. Equity trading desks use EFPs to hedge and/or transact baskets of stock efficiently.

CROSS-HEDGING

Cross-hedging involves using a futures market to hedge a cash position for which there is no actual or sufficiently liquid futures contract. The key to successful cross-hedging is finding a futures contract whose price movements closely correlate with the cash instrument to be hedged. Correlation involves a statistical relationship, and care must be taken to evaluate properly the relationship between the commodity underlying the futures contract and the cash commodity being hedged. Many complications can arise in such an evaluation because, among other things, price relationships can change over time.

The array of possible cross-hedges can be large. Some popular examples include using heating oil futures to hedge jet fuel exposure or using Treasury bond futures to hedge risks related to owning or issuing corporate bonds. Cross-hedging is necessitated in these cases by the lack of futures on either jet fuel or corporate bonds.

Another reason to cross-hedge is to substitute a liquid futures contract for a less liquid one, even though the more liquid contract might not represent the underlying cash exposure as precisely. An example is hedging in the S&P 500 stock index futures contract, even if there is another stock index product that more closely matches a particular equities portfolio. The liquidity afforded by the S&P 500 contract may be worth more than the higher price correlation of a less liquid contract.

Cross-hedges also are used when a hedger has exposure to a processed product, but futures exist only on the unprocessed commodity. For example, a bread maker may have exposure to changes in the price of flour, but no flour futures contract exists. As a result, she may choose to hedge with wheat futures, knowing that the price of flour includes factors other than the price of wheat (and thus recognizing the basis risk).

Cross-hedging, as with any hedge activity, requires monitoring of the cash-futures basis and basis changes; however, there is an additional dimension to the basis in these cases. Specifically, the relationship between the cash instrument or commodity being hedged and the cash item that underlies the futures contract also must be tracked. In this sense, it might be said that hedges based on delivery locations, timing, grades, etc., different from those of the futures contract also can be considered cross-hedges.

The subject of cross-hedging is an appropriate time to revisit the "equal and opposite positions in cash and futures" concept discussed earlier. Although the opposite portion of this axiom is always valid, the equal portion requires some elaboration. The example of a portfolio manager hedging a portfolio of stocks using the S&P 500 futures serves to illustrate this point. Perhaps the portfolio to be hedged is broadly-based and correlates closely enough with this index to make the hedge viable, although the portfolio is not a replica of the S&P 500 index. The manager will calculate the correlation of the portfolio with the underlying S&P 500 index, a measure called the "beta" of the portfolio. A beta of 1.05 means that, on average, the portfolio moves 105 percent of the movement of the underlying index. The portfolio manager does not hedge with futures equal to the dollar value of the portfolio but uses the beta to hedge the volatility of the portfolio. In this case, he sells futures with a dollar value of 105 percent of the dollar value of the portfolio.

This is an example in which equal was not a function of weights, measures or value but rather a function of volatility, or change in value. This arose from the cross-hedging nature of this hedge: a commodity (the portfolio) to be hedged that is related to, but not the same as, the commodity (S&P 500 index) underlying the futures contract.

HEDGING WITH OPTIONS ON FUTURES

This is an appropriate point at which to look more closely at using options on futures to hedge. The hedging concepts, as well as the option basics, that already have been covered remain applicable here. The hedger will take a position in options which is "equal and opposite" to the risk in the cash market. For example, a loss on the value of cash market inventory will be balanced by a gain in the options position.

Hedges can be established by buying or selling options. That is, buying puts and selling calls share a market-direction bias, and each can be used for hedging inventory and other long cash positions. Similarly, both buying calls and selling puts can be used for hedging short cash positions. However, there are major differences in the hedge protection achieved when buying options compared to selling options and when compared to futures. The illustrations that follow highlight some of these distinctions.

Due to the nature of options and the differing rights and obligations of calls and puts, the phrases "short hedge" and "long hedge" do not apply when hedging with options. Also in this context, the notion of basis and price correlation must be extended an additional level. In addition to the correlation between the cash commodity or instrument to be hedged and the futures contract underlying the option, the relationship between the futures contract and the options position also must be monitored.

Hedging Inventory with a Long Put Position

A hedger who owns inventory could establish a short position in futures. That is, the short hedge in futures will gain if prices (and the value of the cash inventory) fall. Just as the futures hedge mitigates risk, it also removes the possibility of gain, changes in the basis notwithstanding.

Instead of selling futures, a hedger who holds inventory could buy put options. As an example, consider a hedger who owns 500 ounces of gold and buys 5 December gold puts on May 1. The hedger's position represents an equal weight of gold. However, the options hedge will provide outcomes that differ markedly from futures.

On May 1

Cash	December Futures	December 285 Put
$276.00	$285.00	$11.00

If cash gold prices fall $25 per ounce by the expiration date of the options, the inventory will lose that amount in value. What gain might there be on the long puts? Assume that the futures also fall exactly $25, i.e., the basis has not changed. With the futures now at $260 at option expiration, the options have only intrinsic value remaining, i.e., $25 or the difference between the option's strike price and the futures price.

On expiration date of options

Cash	December Futures	December 285 Put
$251.00	$260.00	$25.00

After accounting for the cost of the option, the hedge yields only a $14 per ounce gain towards the $25 loss on the inventory. Therefore, this hedge did not provide as high a degree of protection as a futures hedge, even assuming an unchanged cash-futures basis. Of course, if gold had fallen more dramatically, say $70 per ounce, the hedger would be very pleased to have suffered a loss of only $11.

What if gold cash and futures prices strengthen by $30 during the period this hedge is in place? Examine the following prices for another possible outcome of the same option hedge discussed above.

On expiration date of options

Cash	December Futures	December 285 Put
$306.00	$315.00	$0

If this had been a short hedge in futures, the $30 gain on the value of the gold inventory would have been negated by a loss on the short futures position, assuming no change in the basis. The long put position, however, sustains only the loss of the premium, $11, while the hedger benefits from the $30 rise in the value of the gold held in inventory, for a net gain of $19.

Hedging Inventory with a Short Call Position

A short call position has the same market-direction bias as a long put position. The hedger could choose to sell 5 December 285 calls in lieu of buying 5 December 285 puts.

On May 1

Cash	December Futures	December 285 Call
$276.00	$285.00	$10.00

If cash gold prices fall $25 per ounce by the expiration date of the options, the inventory will lose that amount in value. What gain might there be on the short calls? Assume that the futures also fall exactly $25, i.e., the basis has not changed. With the futures now at $260 at option expiration, the options are out of the money, have no intrinsic value and are worthless.

On expiration date of options

Cash	December Futures	December 285 Call
$251.00	$260.00	$0

The premium received for selling the puts was $10; this is what the option hedge has contributed versus the $25 loss on the inventory. Therefore, this hedge did not provide as high a degree of protection as a futures hedge, even assuming an unchanged cash-futures basis. Additionally, if gold had fallen more dramatically, say by $70 per ounce, the short call hedge would still yield only the $10 in premium received. This is tantamount to not being hedged at all.

What if gold prices strengthened during the period this hedge was in place? Examine the following prices for another possible outcome of the same short call hedge:

On expiration date of options

Cash	December Futures	December 285 Call
$306.00	$315.00	$30.00

In this example, cash gold and futures both have rallied $30 since May 1. If this had been a short hedge in futures, the total gain on the value of the gold inventory would have been negated by a loss on the short futures position, assuming no change in the basis. The short call position, however, sustains a net loss of $20, while the hedger benefits from the $30 rise in the value of the gold held in inventory, for a net gain of $10. This gain is the price of the option premium the hedger received for writing the call. In this example, no matter how high the price of gold rises, the most the hedger will make from the favorable gold

(Most suited for hedging against and participating in larger cash price movements)

Risk Protection at Option Expiration	Favorable Price Opportunity
• Unlimited, less premium paid • Futures price must be beyond breakeven at expiration before protection is effective.	• Unlimited, less premium paid • Cash position must change more than premium paid before favorable cash price opportunity becomes profitable.

FIGURE 3-8 Purchasing options to hedge.

(Most suited for hedging against and participating in smaller cash price movements)

Risk Protection at Option Expiration	Favorable Price Opportunity
• Limited to premium received • Cash position must lose less than premium received for full protection.	• Limited to premium received • Futures price must be less than breakeven at expiration for any favorable price opportunity to generate profit.

FIGURE 3-9 Selling options to hedge.

price change is a net of $10 between the cash and options prices, i.e., the value of the premium received when the option was written.

For simplicity, inventory hedged by buying puts or selling calls has been used in the proceeding examples. An analysis of hedging short cash positions by purchasing calls or selling puts would be parallel.

These concepts are summarized in Figures 3-8 and 3-9, where it is assumed that there is perfect tracking between cash and futures prices and that all hedges are held until expiration of the options.

Hedging and the Option Delta

All of these illustrations have been based on the outcome of the hedge at the option expiration date. Under these circumstances, the option either had intrinsic value or was worthless. Of course, during the time the hedge is in place, the option premium will rise and fall with changes in the futures price, time to expiration and the price volatility of the underlying futures contract. Therefore, the outcome of an options hedge not held to expiration is more difficult to forecast.

In cases in which the options hedge will not be held to expiration, the option delta becomes a particularly useful tool.

On May 1

Cash	December Futures	December 285 Put	Delta
$276.00	$285.00	$11.00	−.50

These are the same sample prices on May 1 for the December 285 put as shown above. The delta for the December put has been added. In the options chapter, delta was defined as the expected change in the option premium for a given change in the futures price. Put options have a negative delta, because the premium correlates negatively (or moves inversely) with the futures price. As stated above, the hedger is long 500 ounces of gold and buys 5 December 285 puts.

If cash gold prices and gold futures were to drop $10, we might expect the put option to rise in value $5. Although the hedge may be equal by weight of the gold and the hedger can be confident in the ultimate risk protection at expiration, this would not be a very effective short-term hedge. Therefore, some hedgers prefer to hedge by making their cash and options positions equal by delta rather than by weight or volume. In this case, 10 puts would be required to balance the delta of the 500 ounces of gold. (Each futures contract for 100 ounces of gold has a delta of +1.) This entails paying the premium for two options and results in an "overhedge" if the plan is to hold the hedge until expiration. However, it is the appropriate course of action for the hedger attempting to neutralize shorter-term price changes.

FOR YOUR CONSIDERATION

In the past, stock index arbitrage was considered by some as a cause of, or aid in, the stock market decline in 1987. Theoretically, such arbitrage should be market neutral, keeping the equivalent instruments in alignment ahead of convergence. From what you know of how stocks and futures are traded, why do you think so many arbitrage opportunities existed at that time? Do you think that they were a negative factor in the market events of 1987? Why?

Study Questions

1. Futures and options positions that represent a substitute for transactions to be made at a later time in a physical marketing channel and that are economically appropriate for the reduction of risk are generally classified as:

   A. Market-exempted positions.

   B. Hedge positions.

   C. Non-customer positions.

   D. Spread positions.

2. A hedger's principal motivation for using futures markets is:

   A. To earn speculative profits.

   B. To transfer the risk of price changes.

   C. To find out the future price.

   D. To assure a profitable price.

3. A hedge may not give complete price protection for changes in the spot price if:

   A. The basis changes while the hedge is on.

   B. The quantity hedged differs from the size of the futures contract.

   C. The grade of the commodity hedged is different from the grade on which the futures contract is based.

   D. All of the above.

4. A selling or short hedge:

   A. Can be the same as a buying or long hedge.

   B. Protects the hedger against an unexpected price rise.

   C. Helps a dealer with unsold inventory to remain competitive.

   D. Is less prone to basis risk than a buying hedge.

5. A buying hedge is used to protect against a possible later price decrease in the actual commodity.

   A. True

   B. False

6. Hedging cash corporate bonds with T-bond or T-note futures is known as a (an):

   A. Cross-hedge.

   B. Straddle.

   C. Ratio hedge.

   D. Anticipatory hedge.

7. The cash-futures basis is:

   A. The difference between a commodity's cash and futures price.

   B. The unexpected change in the short-term interest rate.

   C. The underlying cash price of a commodity plus the carrying charge on the commodity.

   D. Relevant only for commodity futures.

8. If cash cotton is 63.75 cents per pound and the nearby futures contract is 63.50, the basis is:

   A. Plus .25¢.

   B. Minus .25¢.

   C. 63.50¢.

   D. Undetermined.

9. Which of the following is not a factor in determining the futures carrying costs; i.e., the difference between cash and futures prices?

   A. Interest

   B. Insurance

   C. Transaction costs

   D. Storage costs

10. An exporter who is "short the basis" (i.e., has made a fixed price sales commitment for a commodity not owned or purchased) would establish a short hedge.

    A. True

    B. False

11. It is April. A hog farmer plans to sell live hogs in October and decides to use options to hedge. (The contract size is 40,000 pounds.) What should he do?

    A. Buy a call.

    B. Buy a put.

    C. Sell a put.

    D. Buy a put straddle.

12. If a coffee grower wanted to hedge against lower coffee prices, he would:

    A. Buy coffee futures.

    B. Sell coffee futures.

    C. Buy a put option on coffee futures.

    D. Either b or c.

13. Which type of market would you anticipate seeing when there is a current shortage of grain?

    A. Inverted market

    B. Contango market

    C. Carrying-charge market

    D. Short market

14. A borrower who plans in May to issue 10 million dollars in 90-day commercial paper in September wishes to protect himself against higher interest rates in the future. He can do so by taking which of the following T-bill futures positions? (The T-bill futures contract has a face value of $1,000,000.)

    A. Buying 10 September 90-day T-bill contracts

    B. Selling 10 September 90-day T-bill contracts

    C. Buying 100 September 90-day T-bill contracts

    D. Selling 100 September 90-day T-bill contracts

15. It is June. A soybean farmer plans to harvest 50,000 bushels of beans in October. He decides to use put options to hedge. Cash beans are now $5.17 per bushel, and the November 520 soybean put has a premium of 28 cents/bu. The farmer buys 10 of the puts at 28 cents/bu. each. Four months later he sells his cash beans for $4.88 per bushel and his 10 puts at a premium of 43 cents/bu. Ignoring transaction costs, what was the effective price the farmer received for his beans, per bushel?

    A. $5.03

    B. $4.88

    C. $4.73

    D. $4.98

Answers to Questions

1. B

The CFTC hedge definition includes positions that normally represent a substitute for transactions to be made or positions to be taken at a later time in a physical marketing channel. Such positions also must be economically appropriate to the reduction of risks in the conduct and management of a commercial enterprise.

2. B

The essence of hedging is the reduction of risk, although there may be other benefits including price discovery and locking in a profitable price.

3. D

Whenever the specification of the cash commodity and the commodity underlying the futures contract differ, a hedge may not give complete price protection. This difference in the cash commodity and that underlying the futures position is most often reflected in the hedger's cash-futures basis.

4. C

A selling hedge protects an inventory against a decline in price.

5. B (False)

The purchase of a futures contract (long position) provides a hedge again price increases in the actual commodity.

6. A

A cross-hedge involves using a futures market whose underlying instrument is related to but different from the cash instrument at risk.

7. A

Basis is defined as the difference between the cash price and the futures price. It reflects a number of factors including the cost of carrying the underlying commodity or security; the yield, if any, generated by the underlying instrument; and differences in grade and location between the particular cash market item and the one specified in the futures contract. While hedging in the futures market can virtually eliminate the risk of a price level change, hedging cannot eliminate the risk of a change in the basis.

8. A

The cotton basis can be calculated as follows:

$$\text{Basis} = \text{Cash Price} - \text{Futures Price}$$
$$\text{Basis} = \$63.75¢ - 63.50¢ = +.25¢$$

N.B. A minus basis is referred to as "under"; a positive basis is referred to as "over."

9. C

The futures carrying costs are a function of interest, insurance and storage costs. Transaction costs are not included in the basis.

10. B (False)

An exporter who is "short the basis" would profit if the basis declines. Such a hedger would establish a long futures position, i.e., a long hedge.

11. B

To hedge the risk that hogs will be selling at a lower price in October, the hog farmer should buy a put option. A put guarantees that the farmer can earn at least the option's strike price, minus the premium he paid for the option, regardless of where futures prices have moved when the option expires.

12. D

To hedge against price declines of a long cash position, a hedger would sell futures or buy put options; both are positions on the short (or bearish) side of the market.

13. A

Inverted markets, also referred to as markets in backwardation, are markets where the highest price is for the spot or nearby month, and successive delivery months are priced lower than preceding ones. Inverted markets sometimes occur when there is a current shortage of grain, or other physical commodity, and those needing the commodity bid nearby supplies to a premium over deferred contracts. Certain financial futures markets are inverted when the cost of carrying the position (e.g., short-term interest rate) is less than the income generated by the cash position (e.g., the long-term interest rate).

14. B

If interest rates rise, the price of a fixed-income instrument declines. A short futures position protects against price declines in the cash market. Since the face value of the T-bill futures contract is $1,000,000, and the terms of both the cash instrument and futures contract are 90 days, the hedger would sell 10 T-bill contracts to hedge $10,000,000 face value of 90-day commercial paper.

15. A

The farmer received an effective price of $5.03 per bushel ($4.88 cash price plus $.43 premium received, minus $.28 premium paid = $5.03).

Introduction: Options, Futures, and Other Derivatives

4

Learning Objectives

Candidates, after completing this reading, should be able to:

- Differentiate between an open outcry system and electronic trading.
- Describe the over-the-counter market and how it differs from trading on an exchange, and its advantages and disadvantages.
- Differentiate between options, forwards, and futures contracts.
- Identify and calculate option and forward contract payoffs.

- Describe, contrast, and calculate the payoffs from hedging strategies involving forward contracts and options.
- Describe, contrast, and calculate the payoffs from speculative strategies involving futures and options.
- Calculate an arbitrage payoff and describe how arbitrage opportunities are temporary.
- Describe some of the risks that can arise from the use of derivatives.

Excerpt is Chapter 4 of Options, Futures, and Other Derivatives, *Eighth Edition, by John Hull.*

In the last 30 years, derivatives have become increasingly important in finance. Futures and options are now traded actively on many exchanges throughout the world. Many different types of forward contracts, swaps, options, and other derivatives are regularly traded by financial institutions, fund managers, and corporate treasurers in the over-the-counter market. Derivatives are added to bond issues, used in executive compensation plans, embedded in capital investment opportunities, and so on. We have now reached the stage where anyone who works in finance needs to understand how derivatives work, how they are used, and how they are priced.

Whether you love derivatives or hate them, you cannot ignore them! The derivatives market is huge—much bigger than the stock market when measured in terms of underlying assets. The value of the assets underlying outstanding derivatives transactions is several times the world gross domestic product. As we shall see in this chapter, derivatives can be used for hedging or speculation or arbitrage. They play a key role in transferring a wide range of risks in the economy from one entity to another.

A *derivative* can be defined as a financial instrument whose value depends on (or derives from) the values of other, more basic, underlying variables. Very often the variables underlying derivatives are the prices of traded assets. A stock option, for example, is a derivative whose value is dependent on the price of a stock. However, derivatives can be dependent on almost any variable, from the price of hogs to the amount of snow falling at a certain ski resort.

Since the first edition of this book was published in 1988 there have been many developments in derivatives markets. There is now active trading in credit derivatives, electricity derivatives, weather derivatives, and insurance derivatives. Many new types of interest rate, foreign exchange, and equity derivative products have been created. There have been many new ideas in risk management and risk measurement. Capital investment appraisal now often involves the evaluation of what are known as *real options*. The book has kept up with all these developments.

Derivatives markets have come under a great deal of criticism because of their role in the credit crisis that started in 2007. Derivative products were created from portfolios of risky mortgages in the United States using a procedure know as securitization. Many of the products that were created became worthless when house prices declined. Financial institutions, and investors throughout the world, lost a huge amount of money and the world was plunged into the worst recession it had experienced for many generations. As a result of the credit crisis, derivatives markets are now more heavily regulated than they used to be. For example, banks are required to keep more capital for the risks they are taking and to pay more attention to liquidity.

In this opening chapter, we take a first look at forward, futures, and options markets and provide an overview of how they are used by hedgers, speculators, and arbitrageurs. Later chapters will give more details and elaborate on many of the points made here.

EXCHANGE-TRADED MARKETS

A derivatives exchange is a market where individuals trade standardized contracts that have been defined by the exchange. Derivatives exchanges have existed for a long time. The Chicago Board of Trade (CBOT, www.cbot .com) was established in 1848 to bring farmers and merchants together. Initially its main task was to standardize the quantities and qualities of the grains that were traded. Within a few years the first futures-type contract was developed. It was known as a *to-arrive contract*. Speculators soon became interested in the contract and found trading the contract to be an attractive alternative to trading the grain itself. A rival futures exchange, the Chicago Mercantile Exchange (CME), was established in 1919. Now futures exchanges exist all over the world. CME and CBOT have merged to form the CME Group (www.cmegroup.com), which also includes the New York Mercantile Exchange.

The Chicago Board Options Exchange (CBOE, www.cboe .com) started trading call option contracts on 16 stocks in 1973. Options had traded prior to 1973, but the CBOE succeeded in creating an orderly market with well-defined contracts. Put option contracts started trading on the exchange in 1977. The CBOE now trades options on well over 1,000 stocks and many different stock indices. Like futures, options have proved to be very popular contracts. Many other exchanges throughout the world now trade options. The underlying assets include foreign currencies and futures contracts as well as stocks and stock indices.

Electronic Markets

Traditionally derivatives exchanges have used what is known as the *open outcry system*. This involves traders physically meeting on the floor of the exchange, shouting, and using a complicated set of hand signals to indicate the trades they would like to carry out. Exchanges are increasingly replacing the open outcry system by *electronic trading*. This involves traders entering their desired trades at a keyboard and a computer being used to match buyers and sellers. The open outcry system has its advocates, but, as time passes, it is becoming less and less used.

Electronic trading has led to a growth in algorithmic trading (also know as black-box trading, automated trading, high-frequency trading, or robo trading). This involves the use of computer programs to initiate trades, often without human intervention.

OVER-THE-COUNTER MARKETS

Not all trading is done on exchanges. The *over-the-counter market* is an important alternative to exchanges and, measured in terms of the total volume of trading, has become much larger than the exchange-traded market. It is a telephone- and computer-linked network of dealers. Trades are done over the phone and are usually between two financial institutions or between a financial institution and one of its clients (typically a corporate treasurer or fund manager). Financial institutions often act as market makers for the more commonly traded instruments. This means that they are always prepared to quote both a bid price (a price at which they are prepared to buy) and an offer price (a price at which they are prepared to sell).

Telephone conversations in the over-the-counter market are usually taped. If there is a dispute about what was agreed, the tapes are replayed to resolve the issue. Trades in the over-the-counter market are typically much larger than trades in the exchange-traded market. A key advantage of the over-the-counter market is that the terms of a contract do not have to be those specified by an exchange. Market participants are free to negotiate any mutually attractive deal. A disadvantage is that there is usually some credit risk in an over-the-counter trade (i.e., there is a small risk that the contract will not be honored). As we shall see in the next chapter, exchanges have organized themselves to eliminate virtually all credit risk.

Lehman Brothers was a very active trader of over-the-counter derivatives. As discussed in Box 4-1, its bankruptcy in 2008 provided a dramatic test for the market.

BOX 4-1 The Lehman Bankruptcy

On September 15, 2008, Lehman Brothers filed for Chapter 11 bankruptcy protection. This was the largest bankruptcy filing in US history and its ramifications were felt throughout derivatives markets. Almost until the end, it seemed as though there was a good chance that Lehman would survive. A number of companies (e.g., the Korean Development Bank, Barclays Bank in the UK, and Bank of America) expressed interest in buying it, but none of these was able to close a deal. Many people thought that Lehman was "too big to fail" and that the US government would have to bail it out if no purchaser could be found. This proved not to be the case.

How did this happen? It was a combination of high leverage, risky investments, and liquidity problems. Commercial banks that take deposits are subject to regulations on the amount of capital they must keep. Lehman was an investment bank and not subject to these regulations. By 2007, its leverage ratio had increased to 31:1, which means that a 3–4% decline in the value of its assets would wipe out its capital. Dick Fuld, Lehman's Chairman and Chief Executive Officer, encouraged an aggressive deal-making, risk-taking culture. He is reported to have told his executives: "Every day is a battle. You have to kill the enemy." The Chief Risk Officer at Lehman was competent, but did not have much influence and was even removed from the executive committee in 2007. The risks taken by Lehman included large positions in the instruments created from subprime mortgages. Lehman funded much of its operations with short-term debt. When there was a loss of confidence in the company, lenders refused to roll over this funding, forcing it into bankruptcy.

Lehman was very active in the over-the-counter derivatives markets. It had hundreds of thousands of transactions outstanding with about 8,000 different counterparties. Lehman's counterparties were often required to post collateral and this collateral had in many cases been used by Lehman for various purposes. It is easy to see that sorting out who owes what to whom in this type of situation is a nightmare!

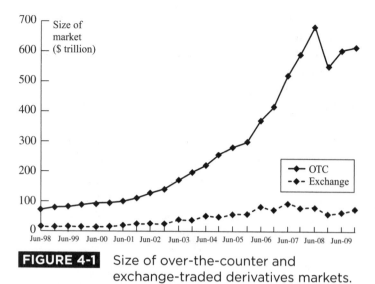

FIGURE 4-1 Size of over-the-counter and exchange-traded derivatives markets.

Market Size

Both the over-the-counter and the exchange-traded market for derivatives are huge. Although the statistics that are collected for the two markets are not exactly comparable, it is clear that the over-the-counter market is much larger than the exchange-traded market. The Bank for International Settlements (www.bis.org) started collecting statistics on the markets in 1998. Figure 4-1 compares (a) the estimated total principal amounts underlying transactions that were outstanding in the over-the-counter markets between June 1998 and December 2009 and (b) the estimated total value of the assets underlying exchange-traded contracts during the same period. Using these measures, we see that, by December 2009, the over-the-counter market had grown to $614.7 trillion and the exchange-traded market had grown to $73.1 trillion.

In interpreting these numbers, we should bear in mind that the principal underlying an over-the-counter transaction is not the same as its value. An example of an over-the-counter contract is an agreement to buy 100 million US dollars with British pounds at a predetermined exchange rate in 1 year. The total principal amount underlying this transaction is $100 million. However, the value of the contract might be only $1 million. The Bank for International Settlements estimates the gross market value of all over-the-counter contracts outstanding in December 2009 to be about $21.6 trillion.[1]

---

[1] A contract that is worth $1 million to one side and –$1 million to the other side would be counted as having a gross market value of $1 million.

FORWARD CONTRACTS

A relatively simple derivative is a *forward contract*. It is an agreement to buy or sell an asset at a certain future time for a certain price. It can be contrasted with a *spot contract*, which is an agreement to buy or sell an asset today. A forward contract is traded in the over-the-counter market—usually between two financial institutions or between a financial institution and one of its clients.

One of the parties to a forward contract assumes a *long position* and agrees to buy the underlying asset on a certain specified future date for a certain specified price. The other party assumes a *short position* and agrees to sell the asset on the same date for the same price.

Forward contracts on foreign exchange are very popular. Most large banks employ both spot and forward foreign-exchange traders. Spot traders are trading a foreign currency for almost immediate delivery. Forward traders are trading for delivery at a future time. Table 4-1 provides the quotes on the exchange rate between the British pound (GBP) and the US dollar (USD) that might be made by a large international bank on May 24, 2010. The quote is for the number of USD per GBP. The first row indicates that the bank is prepared to buy GBP (also known as sterling) in the spot market (i.e., for virtually immediate delivery) at the rate of $1.4407 per GBP and sell sterling in the spot market at $1.4411 per GBP. The second, third, and fourth rows indicate that the bank is prepared to buy sterling in 1, 3, and 6 months at $1.4408, $1.4410, and $1.4416 per GBP, respectively, and to sell sterling in 1, 3, and 6 months at $1.4413, $1.4415, and $1.4422 per GBP, respectively.

TABLE 4-1 Spot and Forward Quotes for the USD/ GBP Exchange Rate, May 24, 2010 (GBP = British pound; USD = US dollar; quote is number of USD per GBP)

	Bid	**Offer**
Spot	1.4407	1.4411
1-month forward	1.4408	1.4413
3-month forward	1.4410	1.4415
6-month forward	1.4416	1.4422

Forward contracts can be used to hedge foreign currency risk. Suppose that, on May 24, 2010, the treasurer of a US corporation knows that the corporation will pay £1 million in 6 months (i.e., on November 24, 2010) and wants to hedge against exchange rate moves. Using the quotes in Table 4-1, the treasurer can agree to buy £1 million 6 months forward at an exchange rate of 1.4422. The corporation then has a long forward contract on GBP. It has agreed that on November 24, 2010, it will buy £1 million from the bank for $1.4422 million. The bank has a short forward contract on GBP. It has agreed that on November 24, 2010, it will sell £1 million for $1.4422 million. Both sides have made a binding commitment.

Payoffs from Forward Contracts

Consider the position of the corporation in the trade we have just described. What are the possible outcomes? The forward contract obligates the corporation to buy £1 million for $1,442,200. If the spot exchange rate rose to, say, 1.5000, at the end of the 6 months, the forward contract would be worth $57,800 (= $1,500,000 − $1,442,200) to the corporation. It would enable 1 million pounds to be purchased at an exchange rate of 1.4422 rather than 1.5000. Similarly, if the spot exchange rate fell to 1.3500 at the end of the 6 months, the forward contract would have a negative value to the corporation of $92,200 because it would lead to the corporation paying $92,200 more than the market price for the sterling.

In general, the payoff from a long position in a forward contract on one unit of an asset is

$$S_T - K$$

where K is the delivery price and S_T is the spot price of the asset at maturity of the contract. This is because the holder of the contract is obligated to buy an asset worth S_T for K. Similarly, the payoff from a short position in a forward contract on one unit of an asset is

$$K - S_T$$

These payoffs can be positive or negative. They are illustrated in Figure 4-2. Because it costs nothing to enter into a forward contract, the payoff from the contract is also the trader's total gain or loss from the contract.

In the example just considered, $K = 1.4422$ and the corporation has a long contract. When $S_T = 1.5000$, the payoff is $0.0578 per £1; when $S_T = 1.3500$, it is −$0.0922 per £1.

Forward Prices and Spot Prices

We shall be discussing in some detail the relationship between spot and forward prices in Chapter 8. For a quick preview of why the two are related, consider a stock that pays no dividend and is worth $60. You can borrow or lend money for 1 year at 5%. What should the 1-year forward price of the stock be?

The answer is $60 grossed up at 5% for 1 year, or $63. If the forward price is more than this, say $67, you could borrow $60, buy one share of the stock, and sell it forward for $67. After paying of the loan, you would net a profit of $4 in 1 year. If the forward price is less than $63, say $58, an investor owning the stock as part of a portfolio would sell the stock for $60 and enter into a forward contract to buy it back for $58 in 1 year. The proceeds of investment would be invested at 5% to earn $3. The investor would end up $5 better off than if the stock were kept in the portfolio for the year.

FUTURES CONTRACTS

Like a forward contract, a futures contract is an agreement between two parties to buy or sell an asset at a

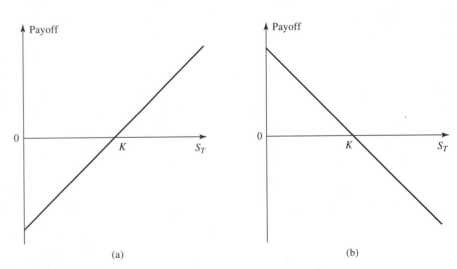

(a)

(b)

FIGURE 4-2 Payoffs from forward contracts: (a) long position, (b) short position. Delivery price = K; price of asset at contract maturity = S_T.

certain time in the future for a certain price. Unlike forward contracts, futures contracts are normally traded on an exchange. To make trading possible, the exchange specifies certain standardized features of the contract. As the two parties to the contract do not necessarily know each other, the exchange also provides a mechanism that gives the two parties a guarantee that the contract will be honored.

The largest exchanges on which futures contracts are traded are the Chicago Board of Trade (CBOT) and the Chicago Mercantile Exchange (CME). On these and other exchanges throughout the world, a very wide range of commodities and financial assets form the underlying assets in the various contracts. The commodities include pork bellies, live cattle, sugar, wool, lumber, copper, aluminum, gold, and tin. The financial assets include stock indices, currencies, and Treasury bonds. Futures prices are regularly reported in the financial press. Suppose that, on September 1, the December futures price of gold is quoted as $1,080. This is the price, exclusive of commissions, at which traders can agree to buy or sell gold for December delivery. It is determined on the floor of the exchange in the same way as other prices (i.e., by the laws of supply and demand). If more traders want to go long than to go short, the price goes up; if the reverse is true, then the price goes down.

Further details on issues such as margin requirements, daily settlement procedures, delivery procedures, bid–offer spreads, and the role of the exchange clearinghouse are given in Chapter 5.

OPTIONS

Options are traded both on exchanges and in the over-the-counter market. There are two types of option. A *call option* gives the holder the right to buy the underlying asset by a certain date for a certain price. A *put option* gives the holder the right to sell the underlying asset by a certain date for a certain price. The price in the contract is known as the *exercise price* or *strike price*; the date in the contract is known as the *expiration date* or *maturity*. *American options* can be exercised at any time up to the expiration date. *European options* can be exercised only on the expiration date itself.[2] Most of the

___
[2] Note that the terms *American* and *European* do not refer to the location of the option or the exchange. Some options trading on North American exchanges are European.

options that are traded on exchanges are American. In the exchange-traded equity option market, one contract is usually an agreement to buy or sell 100 shares. European options are generally easier to analyze than American options, and some of the properties of an American option are frequently deduced from those of its European counterpart.

It should be emphasized that an option gives the holder the right to do something. The holder does not have to exercise this right. This is what distinguishes options from forwards and futures, where the holder is obligated to buy or sell the underlying asset. Whereas it costs nothing to enter into a forward or futures contract, there is a cost to acquiring an option.

The largest exchange in the world for trading stock options is the Chicago Board Options Exchange (CBOE; www.cboe.com). Table 4-2 gives the bid and offer quotes for some of the call options trading on Google (ticker symbol: GOOG) on June 15, 2010. Table 4-3 does the same for put options trading on Google on that date. The quotes are taken from the CBOE website. The Google stock price at the time of the quotes was bid 497.07, offer 497.25. The bid–offer spread on an option is usually greater than that on the underlying stock and depends on the volume of trading. The option strike prices are $460, $480, $ 500, $520, $540, and $560. The maturities are July 2010, September 2010, and December 2010. The July options expire on July 17, 2010, the September options on September 18, 2010, and the December options on December 18, 2010.

The tables illustrate a number of properties of options. The price of a call option decreases as the strike price increases, while the price of a put option increases as the strike price increases. Both types of option tend to become more valuable as their time to maturity increases.

Suppose an investor instructs a broker to buy one December call option contract on Google with a strike price of $520. The broker will relay these instructions to a trader at the CBOE and the deal will be done. The (offer) price is $32.00, as indicated in Table 4-2. This is the price for an option to buy one share. In the United States, an option contract is a contract to buy or sell 100 shares. Therefore the investor must arrange for $3,200 to be remitted to the exchange through the broker. The exchange will then arrange for this amount to be passed on to the party on the other side of the transaction.

TABLE 4-2 Prices of call options on Google, June 15, 2010; stock price: bid $497.07; offer $497.25. (*Source:* CBOE)

Strike price ($)	July 2010		September 2010		December 2010	
	Bid	Offer	Bid	Offer	Bid	Offer
460	43.30	44.00	51.90	53.90	63.40	64.80
480	28.60	29.00	39.70	40.40	50.80	52.30
500	17.00	17.40	28.30	29.30	40.60	41.30
520	9.00	9.30	19.10	19.90	31.40	32.00
540	4.20	4.40	12.70	13.00	23.10	24.00
560	1.75	2.10	7.40	8.40	16.80	17.70

TABLE 4-3 Prices of put options on Google, June 15, 2010; stock price: bid $497.07; offer $497.25. (*Source:* CBOE)

Strike price ($)	July 2010		September 2010		December 2010	
	Bid	Offer	Bid	Offer	Bid	Offer
460	6.30	6.60	15.70	16.20	26.00	27.30
480	11.30	11.70	22.20	22.70	33.30	35.00
500	19.50	20.00	30.90	32.60	42.20	43.00
520	31.60	33.90	41.80	43.60	52.80	54.50
540	46.30	47.20	54.90	56.40	64.90	66.20
560	64.30	66.70	70.00	71.30	78.60	80.00

In our example, the investor has obtained at a cost of $3,200 the right to buy 100 Google shares for $520 each. If the price of Google does not rise above $520 before December 18, 2010, the option is not exercised and the investor loses $3,200.[3] But if the Google does well and the option is exercised when the bid price for the stock is $600, the investor is able to buy 100 shares at $520 and immediately sell them for $600 for a profit of $8,000, or $4,800 when the initial cost of the options is taken into account.[4]

An alternative trade for the investor would be the sale of one September put option contract with a strike price of $480. This would lead to an immediate cash inflow of 100 × 22.20 = $2,220. If the Google stock price stays above $480, the option is not exercised and the investor makes a profit of this amount. However, if stock price falls and the option is exercised when the stock price is $420, then there is a loss. The investor must buy 100 shares at $480 when they are only $420. This leads to a loss of $6,000, or $3,780 when the initial amount received for the option contract is taken into account.

The stock options trading on the CBOE are American. If we assume for simplicity that they are European, so that they can be exercised only at maturity, the investor's profit as a function of the final stock price for the two trades we have considered is shown in Figure 4-3.

---

[3] The calculations here ignore commissions paid by the investor.

[4] The calculations here ignore the effect of discounting. Theoretically, the $8,000 should be discounted from the time of exercise to June 15, 2010, when calculating the profit.

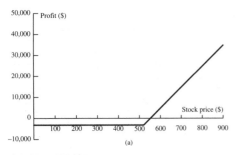
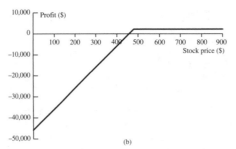

FIGURE 4-3 Net profit per share from (a) purchasing a contract consisting of 100 Google December call options with a strike price of $520 and (b) selling a contract consisting of 100 Google September put options with a strike price of $480.

Further details about the operation of options markets and how prices such as those in Tables 4-2 and 4-3 are determined by traders are given in later chapters. At this stage we note that there are four types of participants in options markets:

1. Buyers of calls
2. Sellers of calls
3. Buyers of puts
4. Sellers of puts

Buyers are referred to as having *long positions;* sellers are referred to as having *short positions.* Selling an option is also known as *writing the option.*

TYPES OF TRADERS

Derivatives markets have been outstandingly successful. The main reason is that they have attracted many different types of traders and have a great deal of liquidity. When an investor wants to take one side of a contract, there is usually no problem in finding someone that is prepared to take the other side.

Three broad categories of traders can be identified: hedgers, speculators, and arbitrageurs. Hedgers use derivatives to reduce the risk that they face from potential future movements in a market variable. Speculators use them to bet on the future direction of a market variable. Arbitrageurs take offsetting positions in two or more instruments to lock in a profit. In the next few sections, we will consider the activities of each type of trader in more detail.

HEDGERS

In this section we illustrate how hedgers can reduce their risks with forward contracts and options.

Hedging Using Forward Contracts

Suppose that it is May 24, 2010, and ImportCo, a company based in the United States, knows that it will have to pay £10 million on August 24, 2010, for goods it has purchased from a British supplier. The USD–GBP exchange rate quotes made by a financial institution are shown in Table 4-1. ImportCo could hedge its foreign exchange risk by buying pounds (GBP) from the financial institution in the 3-month forward market at 1.4415. This would have the effect of fixing the price to be paid to the British exporter at $14,415,000.

Consider next another US company, which we will refer to as ExportCo, that is exporting goods to the United Kingdom and, on May 24, 2010, knows that it will receive £30 million 3 months later. ExportCo can hedge its foreign exchange risk by selling £30 million in the 3-month forward market at an exchange rate of 1.4410. This would have the effect of locking in the US dollars to be realized for the sterling at $43,230,000.

Note that a company might do better if it chooses not to hedge than if it chooses to hedge. Alternatively, it might do worse. Consider ImportCo. If the exchange rate is 1.3000 on August 24 and the company has not hedged, the £10 million that it has to pay will cost $13,000,000, which is less than $14,415,000. On the other hand, if the exchange rate is 1.5000, the £10 million will cost $15,000,000—and the company will wish that it had hedged! The position of ExportCo if it does not hedge is the reverse. If the exchange rate in August proves to be less than 1.4410, the company will wish that it had hedged; if the rate is greater than 1.4410, it will be pleased that it has not done so.

This example illustrates a key aspect of hedging. The purpose of hedging is to reduce risk. There is no guarantee that the outcome with hedging will be better than the outcome without hedging

Hedging Using Options

Options can also be used for hedging. Consider an investor who in May of a particular year owns 1,000 Microsoft shares. The share price is $28 per share. The investor is concerned about a possible share price decline in the next 2 months and wants protection. The investor could buy ten July put option contracts on Microsoft on the Chicago Board Options Exchange with a strike price of $27.50. This would give the investor the right to sell a total of 1,000 shares for a price of $27.50. If the quoted option price is $1, then each option contract would cost 100 × $1 = $100 and the total cost of the hedging strategy would be 10 × $100 = $1,000.

The strategy costs $1,000 but guarantees that the shares can be sold for at least $27.50 per share during the life of the option. If the market price of Microsoft falls below $27.50, the options will be exercised, so that $27,500 is realized for the entire holding. When the cost of the options is taken into account, the amount realized is $26,500. If the market price stays above $27.50, the options are not exercised and expire worthless. However, in this case the value of the holding is always above $27,500 (or above $26,500 when the cost of the options is taken into account). Figure 4-4 shows the net value of the portfolio (after taking the cost of the options into account) as a function of Microsoft's stock price in 2 months. The dotted line shows the value of the portfolio assuming no hedging.

A Comparison

There is a fundamental difference between the use of forward contracts and options for hedging. Forward contracts are designed to neutralize risk by fixing the price that the hedger will pay or receive for the underlying asset. Option contracts, by contrast, provide insurance. They offer a way for investors to protect themselves against adverse price movements in the future while still allowing them to benefit from favorable price movements. Unlike forwards, options involve the payment of an up-front fee.

SPECULATORS

We now move on to consider how futures and options markets can be used by speculators. Whereas hedgers want to avoid exposure to adverse movements in the

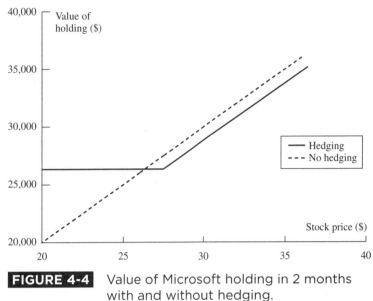

FIGURE 4-4 Value of Microsoft holding in 2 months with and without hedging.

price of an asset, speculators wish to take a position in the market. Either they are betting that the price of the asset will go up or they are betting that it will go down.

Speculation Using Futures

Consider a US speculator who in February thinks that the British pound will strengthen relative to the US dollar over the next 2 months and is prepared to back that hunch to the tune of £250,000. One thing the speculator can do is purchase £250,000 in the spot market in the hope that the sterling can be sold later at a higher price. (The sterling once purchased would be kept in an interest-bearing account.) Another possibility is to take a long position in four CME April futures contracts on sterling. (Each futures contract is for the purchase of £62,500.) Table 4-4 summarizes the two alternatives on the assumption that the current exchange rate is 1.4470 dollars per pound and the April futures price is 1.4410 dollars per pound. If the exchange rate turns out to be 1.5000 dollars per pound in April, the futures contract alternative enables the speculator to realize a profit of (1.5000 − 1.4410) × 250,000 = $14,750. The spot market alternative leads to 250,000 units of an asset being purchased for $1.4470 in February and sold for $1.5000 in April, so that a profit of (1.5000 − 1.4470) × 250,000 = $13,250 is made. If the exchange rate falls to 1.4000 dollars per pound, the futures

TABLE 4-4 Speculation Using Spot and Futures Contracts. One futures contract is on £62,500. Initial margin on four futures contracts = $20,000.

	Possible Trades	
	Buy £250,000 **Spot price = 1.4470**	**Buy 4 futures contracts** **Futures price = 1.4410**
Investment	$361,750	$20,000
Profit if April spot = 1.5000	$13,250	$14,750
Profit if April spot = 1.4000	−$11,750	−$10,250

contract gives rise to a (1.4410 − 1.4000) × 250,000 = $10,250 loss, whereas the spot market alternative gives rise to a loss of (1.4470 − 1.4000) × 250,000 = $11,750. The spot market alternative appears to give rise to slightly worse outcomes for both scenarios. But this is because the calculations do not reflect the interest that is earned or paid.

What then is the difference between the two alternatives? The first alternative of buying sterling requires an up-front investment of $361,750 (= 250,000 × 1.4470). In contrast, the second alternative requires only a small amount of cash to be deposited by the speculator in what is termed a "margin account." The operation of margin accounts is explained in Chapter 5. In Table 4-4, the initial margin requirement is assumed to be $5,000 per contract, or $20,000 in total, but in practice it might be even less than this. The futures market allows the speculator to obtain leverage. With a relatively small initial outlay, the investor is able to take a large speculative position.

Speculation Using Options

Options can also be used for speculation. Suppose that it is October and a speculator considers that a stock is likely to increase in value over the next 2 months. The stock price is currently $20, and a 2-month call option with a $22.50 strike price is currently selling for $1. Table 4-5 illustrates two possible alternatives, assuming that the speculator is willing to invest $2,000. One alternative is to purchase 100 shares; the other involves the purchase of 2,000 call options (i.e., 20 call option contracts). Suppose that the speculator's hunch is correct and the price of the stock rises to $27 by December. The first alternative of buying the stock yields a profit of

$$100 \times (\$27 - \$20) = \$700$$

TABLE 4-5 Comparison of Profits (losses) from Two Alternative Strategies for Using $2,000 to Speculate on a Stock Worth $20 in October

	December Stock Price	
Investor's Strategy	**$15**	**$27**
Buy 100 shares	−$500	$700
Buy 2,000 call options	−$2,000	$7,000

However, the second alternative is far more profitable. A call option on the stock with a strike price of $22.50 gives a payoff of $4.50, because it enables something worth $27 to be bought for $22.50. The total payoff from the 2,000 options that are purchased under the second alternative is

$$2,000 \times \$4.50 = \$9,000$$

Subtracting the original cost of the options yields a net profit of

$$\$9,000 - \$2,000 = \$7,000$$

The options strategy is, therefore, 10 times more profitable than directly buying the stock.

Options also give rise to a greater potential loss. Suppose the stock price falls to $15 by December. The first alternative of buying stock yields a loss of

$$100 \times (\$20 - \$15) = \$500$$

Because the call options expire without being exercised, the options strategy would lead to a loss of $2,000—the original amount paid for the options. Figure 4-5 shows the profit or loss from the two strategies as a function of the stock price in 2 months.

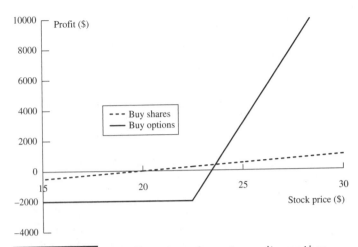

FIGURE 4-5 Profit or loss from two alternative strategies for speculating on a stock currently worth $20.

Options like futures provide a form of leverage. For a given investment, the use of options magnifies the financial consequences. Good outcomes become very good, while bad outcomes result in the whole initial investment being lost.

A Comparison

Futures and options are similar instruments for speculators in that they both provide a way in which a type of leverage can be obtained. However, there is an important difference between the two. When a speculator uses futures, the potential loss as well as the potential gain is very large. When options are used, no matter how bad things get, the speculator's loss is limited to the amount paid for the options.

ARBITRAGEURS

Arbitrageurs are a third important group of participants in futures, forward, and options markets. Arbitrage involves locking in a riskless profit by simultaneously entering into transactions in two or more markets. In later chapters we will see how arbitrage is sometimes possible when the futures price of an asset gets out of line with its spot price. We will also examine how arbitrage can be used in options markets. This section illustrates the concept of arbitrage with a very simple example.

Let us consider a stock that is traded on both the New York Stock Exchange (www.nyse.com) and the London Stock Exchange (www.stockex.co.uk). Suppose that the stock price is $140 in New York and £100 in London at a time when the exchange rate is $1.4300 per pound. An arbitrageur could simultaneously buy 100 shares of the stock in New York and sell them in London to obtain a risk-free profit of

$$100 \times [(\$1.43 \times 100) - \$140]$$

or $300 in the absence of transactions costs. Transactions costs would probably eliminate the profit for a small investor. However, a large investment bank faces very low transactions costs in both the stock market and the foreign exchange market. It would find the arbitrage opportunity very attractive and would try to take as much advantage of it as possible.

Arbitrage opportunities such as the one just described cannot last for long. As arbitrageurs buy the stock in New York, the forces of supply and demand will cause the dollar price to rise. Similarly, as they sell the stock in London, the sterling price will be driven down. Very quickly the two prices will become equivalent at the current exchange rate. Indeed, the existence of profit-hungry arbitrageurs makes it unlikely that a major disparity between the sterling price and the dollar price could ever exist in the first place. Generalizing from this example, we can say that the very existence of arbitrageurs means that in practice only very small arbitrage opportunities are observed in the prices that are quoted in most financial markets. In this book most of the arguments concerning futures prices, forward prices, and the values of option contracts will be based on the assumption that no arbitrage opportunities exist.

DANGERS

Derivatives are very versatile instruments. As we have seen, they can be used for hedging, for speculation, and for arbitrage. It is this very versatility that can cause problems. Sometimes traders who have a mandate to hedge risks or follow an arbitrage strategy become (consciously or unconsciously) speculators. The results can be disastrous. One example of this is provided by the activities of Jérôme Kerviel at Société Général (see Box 4-2).

To avoid the sort of problems Société Général encountered, it is very important for both financial and nonfinancial corporations to set up controls to ensure that derivatives are being used for their intended purpose. Risk limits should be set and the activities of traders should be monitored daily to ensure that these risk limits are adhered to.

Unfortunately, even when traders follow the risk limits that have been specified, big mistakes can happen. Some of the activities of traders in the dervatives market during the period leading up to the start of the credit crisis in July 2007 proved to be much riskier than they were thought to be by the financial institutions they worked for. House prices in the United States had been rising fast. Most people thought that the increases would continue—or, at worst, that house prices would simply level off. Very few were prepared for the steep decline that actually happened. Furthermore, very few were prepared for the high correlation between mortgage default rates in different parts of the country. Some risk managers did express reservations about the exposures of the companies for which they worked to the US real estate market. But, when times are good (or appear to be good), there is an unfortunate tendency to ignore risk managers and this is what happened at many financial institutions during the 2006–2007 period. The key lesson from the credit crisis is that financial institutions should always be dispassionately asking "What can go wrong?", and they should follow that up with the question "If it does go wrong, how much will we lose?"

SUMMARY

One of the exciting developments in finance over the last 30 years has been the growth of derivatives markets. In many situations, both hedgers and speculators find it more attractive to trade a derivative on an asset than to trade the asset itself. Some derivatives are traded on exchanges; others are traded by financial institutions, fund managers, and corporations in the over-the-counter market, or added to new issues of debt and equity securities. Much of this book is concerned with the valuation of derivatives. The aim is to present a unifying framework within which all derivatives—not just options or futures—can be valued.

In this chapter we have taken a first look at forward, futures, and options contracts. A forward or futures contract involves an obligation to buy or sell an asset at a certain time in the future for a certain price. There are two types of options: calls and puts. A call option gives the holder the right to buy an asset by a certain date for a certain price. A put option gives the holder the right to sell an asset by a certain date for a certain price. Forwards, futures, and options trade on a wide range of different underlying assets.

Derivatives have been very successful innovations in capital markets. Three main types of traders can be identified: hedgers, speculators, and arbitrageurs. Hedgers are in the position where they face risk associated with the price of an asset. They use derivatives to reduce or eliminate this risk. Speculators wish to bet on future movements in the price of an asset. They use derivatives to get extra leverage. Arbitrageurs are in business to take advantage of a discrepancy between prices in two different markets. If, for example, they see the futures price of an asset getting out of line with the cash price, they will take offsetting positions in the two markets to lock in a profit.

Further Reading

Chancellor, E. *Devil Take the Hindmost—A History of Financial Speculation.* New York: Farra Straus Giroux, 2000.

Merton, R. C. "Finance Theory and Future Trends: The Shift to Integration," *Risk,* 12, 7 (July 1999): 48–51.

Miller, M. H. "Financial Innovation: Achievements and Prospects," *Journal of Applied Corporate Finance,* 4 (Winter 1992): 4–11.

Zingales, L., "Causes and Effects of the Lehman Bankruptcy," Testimony before Committee on Oversight and Government Reform, United States House of Representatives, October 6, 2008.

Mechanics of Futures Markets

5

■ Learning Objectives

Candidates, after completing this reading, should be able to:

- Define and describe the key features of a futures contract, including the asset, the contract price and size, delivery, and limits.
- Explain the convergence of futures and spot prices.
- Describe the rationale for margin requirements and explain how they work.
- Describe the role of a clearinghouse in futures and over-the-counter market transactions.
- Describe the role of collateralization in the over-the-counter market and compare it to the margining system.

- Identify and describe the differences between a normal and inverted futures market.
- Describe the mechanics of the delivery process and contrast it with cash settlement.
- Describe and explain the impact of different trading order types.
- Compare and contrast forward and futures contracts.

Excerpt is Chapter 2 of Options, Futures, and Other Derivatives, *Eighth Edition, by John Hull.*

In Chapter 4 we explained that both futures and forward contracts are agreements to buy or sell an asset at a future time for a certain price. Futures contracts are traded on an organized exchange, and the contract terms are standardized by that exchange. By contrast, forward contracts are private agreements between two financial institutions or between a financial institution and one of its clients.

This chapter covers the details of how futures markets work. We examine issues such as the specification of contracts, the operation of margin accounts, the organization of exchanges, the regulation of markets, the way in which quotes are made, and the treatment of futures transactions for accounting and tax purposes. We compare futures contracts with forward contracts and explain the difference between the payoffs realized from them.

BACKGROUND

As we saw in Chapter 4, futures contracts are now traded actively all over the world. The Chicago Board of Trade, the Chicago Mercantile Exchange, and the New York Mercantile Exchange have merged to form the CME Group (www.cmegroup.com). Other large exchanges include NYSE Euronext (www.euronext.com), Eurex (www.eurexchange.com), BM&F BOVESPA (wwwbmfbovespa.com.br), and the Tokyo International Financial Futures Exchange (www.tfx.co.jp).

We examine how a futures contract comes into existence by considering the corn futures contract traded on the Chicago Board of Trade (CBOT). On March 5 a trader in New York might call a broker with instructions to buy 5,000 bushels of corn for delivery in July of the same year. The broker would immediately issue instructions to a trader to buy (i.e., take a long position in) one July corn contract. (Each corn contract on CBOT is for the delivery of exactly 5,000 bushels.) At about the same time, another trader in Kansas might instruct a broker to sell 5,000 bushels of corn for July delivery. This broker would then issue instructions to sell (i.e., take a short position in) one corn contract. A price would be determined and the deal would be done. Under the traditional open outcry system, floor traders representing each party would physically meet to determine the price. With electronic trading, a computer would match the traders.

<table>
<tr><td>BOX 5-1</td><td>The Unanticipated Delivery of a Futures Contract</td></tr>
</table>

This story (which may well be apocryphal) was told to the author of this book by a senior executive of a financial institution. It concerns a new employee of the financial institution who had not previously worked in the financial sector. One of the clients of the financial institution regularly entered into a long futures contract on live cattle for hedging purposes and issued instructions to close out the position on the last day of trading. (Live cattle futures contracts trade on the Chicago Mercantile Exchange and each contract is on 40,000 pounds of cattle.) The new employee was given responsibility for handling the account.

When the time came to close out a contract the employee noted that the client was long one contract and instructed a trader at the exchange to buy (not sell) one contract. The result of this mistake was that the financial institution ended up with a long position in two live cattle futures contracts. By the time the mistake was spotted trading in the contract had ceased.

The financial institution (not the client) was responsible for the mistake. As a result, it started to look into the details of the delivery arrangements for live cattle futures contracts—something it had never done before. Under the terms of the contract, cattle could be delivered by the party with the short position to a number of different locations in the United States during the delivery month. Because it was long, the financial institution could do nothing but wait for a party with a short position to issue *a notice of intention to deliver* to the exchange and for the exchange to assign that notice to the financial institution.

It eventually received a notice from the exchange and found that it would receive live cattle at a location 2,000 miles away the following Tuesday. The new employee was sent to the location to handle things. It turned out that the location had a cattle auction every Tuesday. The party with the short position that was making delivery bought cattle at the auction and then immediately delivered them. Unfortunately the cattle could not be resold until the next cattle auction the following Tuesday. The employee was therefore faced with the problem of making arrangements for the cattle to be housed and fed for a week. This was a great start to a first job in the financial sector!

The trader in New York who agreed to buy has a *long futures position* in one contract; the trader in Kansas who agreed to sell has a *short futures position* in one contract. The price agreed to is the current *futures price* for July corn, say 300 cents per bushel. This price, like any other price, is determined by the laws of supply and demand. If, at a particular time, more traders wish to sell rather than buy July corn, the price will go down. New buyers then enter the market so that a balance between buyers and sellers is maintained. If more traders wish to buy rather than sell July corn, the price goes up. New sellers then enter the market and a balance between buyers and sellers is maintained.

Closing Out Positions

The vast majority of futures contracts do not lead to delivery. The reason is that most traders choose to close out their positions prior to the delivery period specified in the contract. Closing out a position means entering into the opposite trade to the original one. For example, the New York investor who bought a July corn futures contract on March 5 can close out the position by selling (i.e., shorting) one July corn futures contract on, say, April 20. The Kansas investor who sold (i.e., shorted) a July contract on March 5 can close out the position by buying one July contract on, say, May 25. In each case, the investor's total gain or loss is determined by the change in the futures price between March 5 and the day when the contract is closed out.

Delivery is so unusual that traders sometimes forget how the delivery process works (see Box 5-1). Nevertheless we will spend part of this chapter reviewing the delivery arrangements in futures contracts. This is because it is the possibility of final delivery that ties the futures price to the spot price.[1]

SPECIFICATION OF A FUTURES CONTRACT

When developing a new contract, the exchange must specify in some detail the exact nature of the agreement between the two parties. In particular, it must specify the asset, the contract size (exactly how much of the asset will be delivered under one contract), where delivery will be made, and when delivery will be made.

Sometimes alternatives are specified for the grade of the asset that will be delivered or for the delivery locations. As a general rule, it is the party with the short position (the party that has agreed to sell the asset) that chooses

what will happen when alternatives are specified by the exchange. When the party with the short position is ready to deliver, it files a *notice of intention to deliver* with the exchange. This notice indicates selections it has made with respect to the grade of asset that will be delivered and the delivery location.

The Asset

When the asset is a commodity, there may be quite a variation in the quality of what is available in the marketplace. When the asset is specified, it is therefore important that the exchange stipulate the grade or grades of the commodity that are acceptable. The New York Board of Trade (NYBOT) has specified the asset in its frozen concentrated orange juice futures contract as orange solids from Florida and/or Brazil that are US Grade A with Brix value of not less than 62.5 degrees.

For some commodities a range of grades can be delivered, but the price received depends on the grade chosen. For example, in the Chicago Board of Trade corn futures contract, the standard grade is "No. 2 Yellow," but substitutions are allowed with the price being adjusted in a way established by the exchange. No. 1 Yellow is deliverable for 1.5 cents per bushel more than No. 2 Yellow. No. 3 Yellow is deliverable for 1.5 cents per bushel less than No. 2 Yellow.

The financial assets in futures contracts are generally well defined and unambiguous. For example, there is no need to specify the grade of a Japanese yen. However, there are some interesting features of the Treasury bond and Treasury note futures contracts traded on the Chicago Board of Trade. The underlying asset in the Treasury bond contract is any long-term US Treasury bond that has a maturity of greater than 15 years and is not callable within 15 years. In the Treasury note futures contract, the underlying asset is any long-term Treasury note with a maturity of no less than 6.5 years and no more than 10 years from the date of delivery. In both cases, the exchange has a formula for adjusting the price received according to the coupon and maturity date of the bond delivered. This is discussed in Chapter 9.

The Contract Size

The contract size specifies the amount of the asset that has to be delivered under one contract. This is an

---

[1] As mentioned in Chapter 4, the spot price is the price for almost immediate delivery.

important decision for the exchange. If the contract size is too large, many investors who wish to hedge relatively small exposures or who wish to take relatively small speculative positions will be unable to use the exchange. On the other hand, if the contract size is too small, trading may be expensive as there is a cost associated with each contract traded.

The correct size for a contract clearly depends on the likely user. Whereas the value of what is delivered under a futures contract on an agricultural product might be $10,000 to $20,000, it is much higher for some financial futures. For example, under the Treasury bond futures contract traded on the Chicago Board of Trade, instruments with a face value of $100,000 are delivered.

In some cases exchanges have introduced "mini" contracts to attract smaller investors. For example, the CME's Mini Nasdaq 100 contract is on 20 times the Nasdaq 100 index, whereas the regular contract is on 100 times the index. (We will cover futures on indices more fully in Chapter 6.)

Delivery Arrangements

The place where delivery will be made must be specified by the exchange. This is particularly important for commodities that involve significant transportation costs. In the case of the NYBOT frozen concentrate orange juice contract, delivery is to exchange-licensed warehouses in Florida, New Jersey, or Delaware.

When alternative delivery locations are specified, the price received by the party with the short position is sometimes adjusted according to the location chosen by that party. The price tends to be higher for delivery locations that are relatively far from the main sources of the commodity.

Delivery Months

A futures contract is referred to by its delivery month. The exchange must specify the precise period during the month when delivery can be made. For many futures contracts, the delivery period is the whole month.

The delivery months vary from contract to contract and are chosen by the exchange to meet the needs of market participants. For example, corn futures traded on the Chicago Board of Trade have delivery months of March, May,

July, September, and December. At any given time, contracts trade for the closest delivery month and a number of subsequent delivery months. The exchange specifies when trading in a particular month's contract will begin. The exchange also specifies the last day on which trading can take place for a given contract. Trading generally ceases a few days before the last day on which delivery can be made.

Price Quotes

The exchange defines how prices will be quoted. For example, crude oil futures prices are quoted in dollars and cents. Treasury bond and Treasury note futures prices are quoted in dollars and thirty-seconds of a dollar.

Price Limits and Position Limits

For most contracts, daily price movement limits are specified by the exchange. If in a day the price moves down from the previous day's close by an amount equal to the daily price limit, the contract is said to be *limit down*. If it moves up by the limit, it is said to be *limit up*. A *limit move* is a move in either direction equal to the daily price limit. Normally, trading ceases for the day once the contract is limit up or limit down. However, in some instances the exchange has the authority to step in and change the limits.

The purpose of daily price limits is to prevent large price movements from occurring because of speculative excesses. However, limits can become an artificial barrier to trading when the price of the underlying commodity is advancing or declining rapidly. Whether price limits are, on balance, good for futures markets is controversial.

Position limits are the maximum number of contracts that a speculator may hold. The purpose of these limits is to prevent speculators from exercising undue influence on the market.

CONVERGENCE OF FUTURES PRICE TO SPOT PRICE

As the delivery period for a futures contract is approached, the futures price converges to the spot price of the underlying asset. When the delivery period is reached, the futures price equals—or is very close to—the spot price.

To see why this is so, we first suppose that the futures price is above the spot price during the delivery period. Traders then have a clear arbitrage opportunity:

1. Sell (i.e., short) a futures contract
2. Buy the asset
3. Make delivery

These steps are certain to lead to a profit equal to the amount by which the futures price exceeds the spot price. As traders exploit this arbitrage opportunity, the futures price will fall. Suppose next that the futures price is below the spot price during the delivery period. Companies interested in acquiring the asset will find it attractive to enter into a long futures contract and then wait for delivery to be made. As they do so, the futures price will tend to rise.

The result is that the futures price is very close to the spot price during the delivery period. Figure 5-1 illustrates the convergence of the futures price to the spot price. In Figure 5-1(a) the futures price is above the spot price prior to the delivery period. In Figure 5-1(b) the futures price is below the spot price prior to the delivery period. The circumstances under which these two patterns are observed are discussed in Chapter 8.

THE OPERATION OF MARGINS

If two investors get in touch with each other directly and agree to trade an asset in the future for a certain price, there are obvious risks. One of the investors may regret the deal and try to back out. Alternatively, the investor simply may not have the financial resources to honor the agreement. One of the key roles of the exchange is to organize trading so that contract defaults are avoided. This is where margins come in.

Daily Settlement

To illustrate how margins work, we consider an investor who contacts his or her broker to buy two December gold futures contracts on the COMEX division of the New York Mercantile Exchange (NYMEX), which is part of the CME Group. We suppose that the current futures price is $1,250 per ounce. Because the contract size is 100 ounces, the investor has contracted to buy a total of 200 ounces at this price. The broker will require the investor to deposit funds in a *margin account*. The amount that must be deposited at the time the contract is entered into is known as the *initial margin*. We suppose this is $6,000 per contract, or $12,000 in total. At the end of each trading day, the margin account is adjusted to reflect the investor's gain or loss. This practice is referred to as *daily settlement* or *marking to market*.

Suppose, for example, that by the end of the first day the futures price has dropped by $9 from $1,250 to $1,241. The investor has a loss of $1,800 (= 200 x $9), because the 200 ounces of December gold, which the investor contracted to buy at $1,250, can now be sold for only $1,241. The balance in the margin account would therefore be reduced by $1,800 to $10,200. Similarly, if the price of December gold rose to $1,259 by the end of the first day, the balance in the margin account would be increased by $1,800 to $13,800. A trade is first settled at the close of the day on which it takes place. It is then settled at the close of trading on each subsequent day.

Note that daily settlement is not merely an arrangement between broker and client. When there is a decrease in the futures price so that the margin account of an investor with a long position is reduced by $1,800,

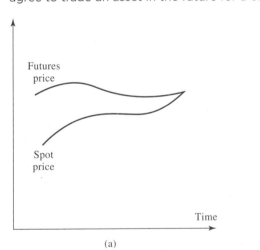

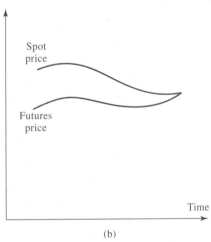

(a)

(b)

FIGURE 5-1 Relationship between futures price and spot price as the delivery period is approached: (a) Futures price above spot price; (b) futures price below spot price.

the investor's broker has to pay the exchange $1,800 and the exchange passes the money on to the broker of an investor with a short position. Similarly, when there is an increase in the futures price, brokers for parties with short positions pay money to the exchange and brokers for parties with long positions receive money from the exchange. Later we will examine in more detail the mechanism by which this happens.

The investor is entitled to withdraw any balance in the margin account in excess of the initial margin. To ensure that the balance in the margin account never becomes negative a *maintenance margin*, which is somewhat lower than the initial margin, is set. If the balance in the margin

account falls below the maintenance margin, the investor receives a margin call and is expected to top up the margin account to the initial margin level the next day. The extra funds deposited are known as a *variation margin*. If the investor does not provide the variation margin, the broker closes out the position. In the case of the investor considered earlier, closing out the position would involve neutralizing the existing contract by selling 200 ounces of gold for delivery in December.

Table 5-1 illustrates the operation of the margin account for one possible sequence of futures prices in the case of the investor considered earlier. The maintenance margin is assumed to be $4,500 per contract, or $9,000 in total.

TABLE 5-1 Operation of Margins for a Long Position in Two Gold Futures Contracts. The initial margin is $6,000 per contract, or $12,000 in total; the maintenance margin is $4,500 per contract, or $9,000 in total. The contract is entered into on Day 1 at $1,250 and closed out on Day 16 at $1226.90.

Day	Trade Price ($)	Settlement Price ($)	Daily Gain ($)	Cumulative Gain ($)	Margin Account Balance ($)	Margin Call ($)
1	1,250.00				12,000	
1		1,241.00	–1,800	–1,800	10,200	
2		1,238.30	–540	–2,340	9,660	
3		1,244.60	1,260	–1,080	10,920	
4		1,241.30	–660	–1,740	10,260	
5		1,240.10	–240	–1,980	10,020	
6		1,236.20	–780	–2,760	9,240	
7		1,229.90	–1,260	–4,020	7,980	4,020
8		1,230.80	180	–3,840	12,180	
9		1,225.40	–1,080	–4,920	11,100	
10		1,228.10	540	–4,380	11,640	
11		1,211.00	–3,420	–7,800	8,220	3,780
12		1,211.00	0	–7,800	12,000	
13		1,214.30	660	–7,140	12,660	
14		1,216.10	360	–6,780	13,020	
15		1,223.00	1,380	–5,400	14,400	
16	1,226.90		780	–4,620	15,180	

On Day 7, the balance in the margin account falls $1,020 below the maintenance margin level. This drop triggers a margin call from the broker for an additional $4,020 to bring the account balance up to the initial margin level of $12,000. It is assumed that the investor provides this margin by the close of trading on Day 8. On Day 11, the balance in the margin account again falls below the maintenance margin level, and a margin call for $3,780 is sent out. The investor provides this margin by the close of trading on Day 12. On Day 16, the investor decides to close out the position by selling two contracts. The futures price on that day is $1,226.90, and the investor has a cumulative loss of $4,620. Note that the investor has excess margin on Days 8, 13, 14, and 15. It is assumed that the excess is not withdrawn.

Further Details

Most brokers pay investors interest on the balance in a margin account. The balance in the account does not, therefore, represent a true cost, provided that the interest rate is competitive with what could be earned elsewhere. To satisfy the initial margin requirements (but not subsequent margin calls), an investor can sometimes deposit securities with the broker. Treasury bills are usually accepted in lieu of cash at about 90% of their face value. Shares are also sometimes accepted in lieu of cash—but at about 50% of their market value.

Whereas a forward contract is settled at the end of its life, a futures contract is, as we have seen, settled daily. At the end of each day, the investor's gain (loss) is added to (subtracted from) the margin account, bringing the value of the contract back to zero. A futures contract is in effect closed out and rewritten at a new price each day.

Minimum levels for initial and maintenance margins are set by the exchange. Individual brokers may require greater margins from their clients than those specified by the exchange. However, they cannot require lower margins than those specified by the exchange. Margin levels are determined by the variability of the price of the underlying asset. The higher this variability, the higher the margin levels. The maintenance margin is usually about 75% of the initial margin.

Margin requirements may depend on the objectives of the trader. A bona fide hedger, such as a company that produces the commodity on which the futures contract is written, is often subject to lower margin requirements than a speculator. The reason is that there is deemed to be less risk of default. Day trades and spread transactions often give rise to lower margin requirements than do hedge transactions. In a *day trade* the trader announces to the broker an intent to close out the position in the same day. In a *spread transaction* the trader simultaneously buys (i.e., takes a long position in) a contract on an asset for one maturity month and sells (i.e., takes a short position in) a contract on the same asset for another maturity month.

Note that margin requirements are the same on short futures positions as they are on long futures positions. It is just as easy to take a short futures position as it is to take a long one. The spot market does not have this symmetry. Taking a long position in the spot market involves buying the asset for immediate delivery and presents no problems. Taking a short position involves selling an asset that you do not own. This is a more complex transaction that may or may not be possible in a particular market. It is discussed further in Chapter 8.

The Clearing House and Clearing Margins

A *clearing house* acts as an intermediary in futures transactions. It guarantees the performance of the parties to each transaction. The clearing house has a number of members, who must post funds with the exchange. Brokers who are not members themselves must channel their business through a member. The main task of the clearing house is to keep track of all the transactions that take place during a day, so that it can calculate the net position of each of its members.

Just as an investor is required to maintain a margin account with a broker, the broker is required to maintain a margin account with a clearing house member and the clearinghouse member is required to maintain a margin account with the clearing house. The latter is known as a *clearing margin*. The margin accounts for clearing house members are adjusted for gains and losses at the end of each trading day in the same way as are the margin accounts of investors. However, in the case of the clearing house member, there is an original margin, but no maintenance margin. Every day the account balance for each contract must be maintained at an amount equal to the original margin times the number of contracts outstanding. Thus, depending on transactions during the day and price movements, the clearing house member may have to add funds to its margin account at the end of the day. Alternatively, it may find it can remove funds from the account at this time. Brokers who are not clearing house members must maintain a margin account with a clearing house member.

In determining clearing margins, the exchange clearing house calculates the number of contracts outstanding on either a gross or a net basis. When the gross basis is used, the number of contracts equals the sum of the long and short positions. When the net basis is used, these are off-set against each other. Suppose a clearing house member has two clients: one with a long position in 20 contracts, the other with a short position in 15 contracts. Gross margining would calculate the clearing margin on the basis of 35 contracts; net margining would calculate the clearing margin on the basis of 5 contracts. Most exchanges currently use net margining.

Credit Risk

The whole purpose of the margining system is to ensure that funds are available to pay traders when they make a profit. Overall the system has been very successful. Traders entering into contracts at major exchanges have always had their contracts honored. Futures markets were tested on October 19, 1987, when the S&P 500 index declined by over 20% and traders with long positions in S&P 500 futures found they had negative margin balances. Traders who did not meet margin calls were closed out but still owed their brokers money. Some did not pay and as a result some brokers went bankrupt because, without their clients' money, they were unable to meet margin calls on contracts they entered into on behalf of their clients. However, the exchanges had sufficient funds to ensure that everyone who had a short futures position on the S&P 500 got paid off.

OTC MARKETS

Credit risk has traditionally been a feature of the over-the-counter markets. There is always a chance that the party on the other side of an over-the-counter trade will default. It is interesting that, in an attempt to reduce credit risk, the over-the-counter market has adopted, or has been compelled to adopt, some of the procedures used by exchanges.

Collateralization

Collateralization has been used in OTC markets for some time and is similar to the practice of posting margin in futures markets.

Consider two companies A and B, that have entered into an OTC derivatives transaction such as a forward. A collateralization agreement applying to the transaction might involve the transaction being valued each day. If, from one day to the next, the value of the transaction to company A increases by a positive amount X (so that the value to company B decreases by X), company B is required to pay X to company A. Similarly, if the value to company B increases by a positive amount X (so that the value to company A decreases by X), company A is required to pay X to company B. The contract is not settled daily, as in the case of futures. The payments are a security deposit designed to ensure that obligations will be honored. Interest is paid on the full amount of the funds that have been deposited by one party with the other.

Collateralization significantly reduces the credit risk in OTC contracts. As described in Box 5-2, it was used by the hedge fund Long-Term Capital Management (LTCM) in the 1990s. As a result LTCM's counterparties were prepared to accept LTCM's credit risk.

The Use of Clearing Houses in OTC Markets

Since the 2007–2009 crisis, governments in the US and elsewhere have passed legislation requiring clearing houses to be used for some OTC transactions.

The way in which clearing houses work in the OTC market is as follows. An OTC transaction is negotiated between two parties, A and B, in the usual way. It is then presented to a clearing house (sometimes called a central clearing party). Assuming the clearing house accepts the transaction, it becomes the counterparty to both A and B. (This is similar to the way the clearing house for a futures exchange becomes the counterparty to the two sides of a futures trade.) The clearing house takes on the credit risk of both A and B. It manages this risk by requiring an initial margin and daily variation margins from them.

The OTC market has traditionally been a series of bilateral agreements between market participants as illustrated

Long-Term Capital Management (LTCM), a hedge fund formed in the mid-1990s, always collateralized its transactions. The hedge fund's investment strategy was known as convergence arbitrage. A very simple example of what it might do is the following. It would find two bonds, X and Y, issued by the same company that promised the same payoffs, with X being less liquid (i.e., less actively traded) than Y. The market always places a value on liquidity. As a result the price of X would be less than the price of Y. LTCM would buy X, short Y, and wait, expecting the prices of the two bonds to converge at some future time.

When interest rates increased, the company expected both bonds to move down in price by about the same amount, so that the collateral it paid on bond X would be about the same as the collateral it received on bond Y. Similarly, when interest rates decreased, LTCM expected both bonds to move up in price by about the same amount, so that the collateral it received on bond X would be about the same as the collateral it

paid on bond Y. It therefore expected that there would be no significant outflow of funds as a result of its collateralization agreements.

In August 1998, Russia defaulted on its debt and this led to what is termed a "flight to quality" in capital markets. One result was that investors valued liquid instruments more highly than usual and the spreads between the prices of the liquid and illiquid instruments in LTCM's portfolio increased dramatically. The prices of the bonds LTCM had bought went down and the prices of those it had shorted increased. It was required to post collateral on both. The company was highly leveraged and unable to make the payments required under the collateralization agreements. The result was that positions had to be closed out and LTCM lost about $4 billion. If the company had been less highly leveraged it would probably have been able to survive the flight to quality and could have waited for the prices of the liquid and illiquid bonds to move closer to each other.

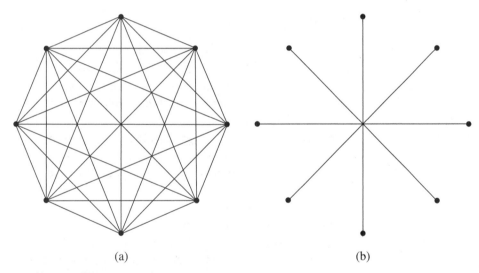

(a)   (b)

FIGURE 5-2   (a) The traditional way in which OTC markets have operated: a series of bilateral agreements between market participants; (b) how OTC markets would operate with a single central clearing house.

In practice, because not all OTC transactions are routed through clearing houses, the market has elements of both Figure 5-2a and 5-2b.

A number of arguments have been cited for the use of clearing houses in OTC markets. Collateral will automatically have to be posted; credit risk in the financial system will (hopefully) be reduced;[2] and the trades taking place in the OTC market will become more transparent. A major concern of governments since the credit crisis of 2007 is *systemic risk*. This is the risk that a failure by a large financial institution will lead to failures by other large financial institutions and a collapse of the financial system. The way this can happen is described in Box 5-3.

in Figure 5-2a. If all OTC contract were cleared in the way that has just been described, the OTC market would move to the situation where each participant deals with one or more clearing houses, as illustrated in Figure 5-2b.

---

[2] The impact of clearing houses on credit risk depends on the number of clearing houses and the proportion of all OTC trades that are cleared through them. See D. Duffie and H. Zhu (2010), "Does a Central Clearing Counterparty Reduce Counterparty Risk?" Working Paper, Stanford University.

One of the motivations for the legislation requiring that clearing houses be used for OTC transactions is what might be termed the "AIG fiasco." During the period leading up to the credit crisis, the insurance company AIG provided protection to other financial institutions against a huge volume of credit risks that were related to subprime mortgages. Since AIG had a AAA credit rating at the time the transactions were negotiated, it was not required to post collateral by its counterparties. The transactions resulted in big losses for AIG and led to an $85 billion bailout of the company by the US government. Whether the clearing house legislation by itself will prevent companies taking risks as large as those of AIG in the future is doubtful. This is because the legislation applies only to "standardized" OTC transactions and AIG's transactions were nonstandard. However, mandatory collateralization for nonstandard OTC contracts will go a long way toward preventing another AIG occurring in the future.

MARKET QUOTES

Futures quotes are available from exchanges and from several online sources (see, for example, futures .tradingcharts.com/marketquotes). Table 5-2 shows quotes provided by exchanges for a number of different commodities on May 26, 2010. Quotes for index, currency,

and interest rate futures are given in Chapter 6, 8, and 9, respectively.

The asset underlying the futures contract, the contract size, and how the price is quoted are all shown at the top of each section in Table 5-2. The first asset is gold, traded on COMEX (a division of the New York Mercantile Exchange, which is not part of the CME Group). The contract size is 100 ounces, and the price is quoted in dollars per ounce. The maturity month of the contract is shown in the first column.

Prices

The first three numbers in each row show the opening price, the highest price achieved in trading during the day, and the lowest price achieved in trading during the day. The opening price is representative of the prices at which contracts were trading immediately after the start of trading. For June 2010 gold, the opening price on May 26, 2010, was $1,203.80. During the day, the price traded between $1,201.00 and $1,216.90.

Settlement Price

The fourth number is the *settlement price*. This is the price used for calculating daily gains and losses and margin requirements. It is usually calculated as the price at which the contract traded immediately before the end of a day's trading session (1:30 p.m. for gold). The fifth number is the change in the settlement price from the previous day. For the June 2010 gold futures contract, the settlement price on May 26, 2010, was $1,213.40, up $15.40 from the previous trading day. In this case, an investor with a long position in one contract would find his or her margin account balance increased by $1,540 (= 100 × $15.40) on May 26, 2010. Similarly, an investor with a short position in one contract would find that the margin balance decreased by $1,540 on this date.

The numbers in the fifth column show that, by chance, settlement prices for all the contracts considered increased between May 25 and May 26, 2010.

Trading Volume and Open Interest

The final two columns in Table 5-2 show the trading volume for the day and the open interest at the end of the previous day. The trading volume is the number of

TABLE 5-2 Futures Quotes for a Selection of CME Group Contracts on Commodities on May 26, 2010

	Open	High	Low	Settlement	Change	Volume	Open Interest
Gold 100 oz, $ per oz							
June 2010	1203.80	1216.90	1201.00	1213.40	15.40	194,461	156,156
July 2010	1205.00	1217.50	1202.00	1214.20	15.50	838	714
Aug. 2010	1205.00	1218.70	1202.70	1215.30	15.50	130,676	240,074
Oct. 2010	1208.30	1220.20	1205.30	1217.50	15.60	2,445	21,792
Dec. 2010	1208.80	1222.90	1207.50	1219.90	15.60	7,885	61,497
June 2011	1215.90	1228.00	1215.20	1227.80	15.80	408	13,461
Crude oil 1,000 barrels, $ per barrel							
July 2010	70.06	71.70	69.21	71.51	2.76	6,315	388,902
Aug. 2010	71.25	72.77	70.42	72.54	2.44	3,746	115,305
Dec. 2010	74.00	75.34	73.17	75.23	2.19	5,055	196,033
Dec. 2011	77.01	78.59	76.51	78.53	2.00	4,175	100,674
Dec. 2012	78.50	80.21	78.50	80.18	1.86	1,258	7,0126
Corn 5,000 bushels, cents per bushel							
July 2010	369.50	372.00	368.75	371.50	7.25	122,528	491,587
Sept. 2010	379.50	381.00	379.00	381.00	7.75	24,186	175,798
Dec. 2010	389.00	390.75	380.25	390.75	8.00	47,428	373,026
Mar. 2011	400.00	403.25	400.00	403.25	7.75	4,581	55,836
May 2011	410.50	411.50	410.50	411.50	7.25	830	8,995
July 2011	417.50	419.50	417.50	419.50	7.50	3,491	31,939
Dec. 2011	416.25	418.00	415.75	418.00	7.25	4,760	59,061
Soybeans 5,000 bushels, cents per bushel							
July 2010	934.25	939.75	933.00	938.00	7.50	41,816	220,712
Aug. 2010	922.00	931.50	922.00	929.50	8.50	4,881	15,674
Sept. 2010	914.50	918.75	912.50	916.50	7.00	1,935	12,983
Nov. 2010	906.00	912.50	905.00	910.00	7.00	18,908	157,826
Jan. 2011	917.75	921.50	914.75	919.75	7.00	2,621	12,391
Mar. 2011	926.00	930.00	925.00	928.50	8.00	1,406	5,857
May 2011	933.50	935.50	931.00	933.50	7.50	942	5,626
Wheat 5,000 bushels, cents per bushel							
July 2010	462.75	742.00	459.00	461.75	1.25	45,283	246,683
Sept. 2010	480.00	489.00	476.50	479.00	1.00	13,941	90,257
Dec. 2010	510.75	519.50	507.25	510.00	1.25	9,756	70,618
Mar. 2011	541.50	548.50	536.75	539.00	0.75	2,748	27,879
May 2011	557.00	563.50	552.75	555.50	1.25	923	8,199
July 2011	574.25	583.00	571.00	573.75	0.75	4,938	34,300
Live Cattle 40,000 lb, cents per lb							
June 2010	90.800	90.850	90.450	90.800	0.775	12,410	51,817
Aug. 2010	89.700	90.050	89.525	89.925	0.850	19,341	144,587
Oct. 2010	91.100	91.150	90.750	91.100	0.750	7,718	78,300
Dec. 2010	92.100	92.250	91.875	92.175	0.800	3,347	41,102
Feb. 2011	93.200	93.550	93.200	93.550	0.800	792	18,428

contracts traded. The open interest is the number of contracts outstanding, that is, the number of long positions or, equivalently, the number of short positions.

Trading volume can be greater than both the beginning-of-day and end-of-day open interest. (This was the case for June 2010 gold on May 26, 2010.) This indicates that many traders who entered into positions during the day closed them out before the end of the day. (Traders who do this are referred to as *day traders*.)

Patterns of Futures Prices

Futures prices can show a number of different patterns. The futures price of gold generally increases with the maturity of the contract. Table 5-2 shows that this was the case on May 26, 2010. The settlement price on that day increased from $1213.40 to $1227.80 as the contract maturity month increased from June 2010 to June 2011. Markets where the futures price is an increasing function of the time to maturity are known as *normal markets*. Markets where the futures price decreases with the maturity of the futures contract are known as *inverted markets*.[3]

Table 5-2 shows that there was a normal market for crude oil on May 26, 2010. This is not always the case. For example, on October 15, 2007, oil futures prices were inverted. The November 2007, December 2007, January 2008, February 2008, March 2008, and April 2008 settlement prices were 86.13, 85.13, 84.25, 83.41, 82.69, and 82.05, respectively. Sometimes futures prices, perhaps because of seasonality, show a mixture of normal and inverted markets. For example, on May 26, 2010, the futures price of soybeans first decreased and then increased as the maturity of the contract increased.

DELIVERY

As mentioned earlier in this chapter, very few of the futures contracts that are entered into lead to delivery of the underlying asset. Most are closed out early.

---

[3] The term *contango* is sometimes used to describe situations where the futures price is an increasing function of the maturity of the contract and the term *backwardation* is sometimes used to describe the situation where the futures price is a decreasing function of the maturity of the contract. Strictly speaking, as will be explained in Chapter 8, these terms refer to whether the price of the underlying asset is expected to increase or decrease over time.

Nevertheless, it is the possibility of eventual delivery that determines the futures price. An understanding of delivery procedures is therefore important.

The period during which delivery can be made is defined by the exchange and varies from contract to contract. The decision on when to deliver is made by the party with the short position, whom we shall refer to as investor A. When investor A decides to deliver, investor A's broker issues a notice of intention to deliver to the exchange clearinghouse. This notice states how many contracts will be delivered and, in the case of commodities, also specifies where delivery will be made and what grade will be delivered. The exchange then chooses a party with a long position to accept delivery.

Suppose that the party on the other side of investor A's futures contract when it was entered into was investor B. It is important to realize that there is no reason to expect that it will be investor B who takes delivery. Investor B may well have closed out his or her position by trading with investor C, investor C may have closed out his or her position by trading with investor D, and so on. The usual rule chosen by the exchange is to pass the notice of intention to deliver on to the party with the oldest outstanding long position. Parties with long positions must accept delivery notices. However, if the notices are transferable, long investors have a short period of time, usually half an hour, to find another party with a long position that is prepared to accept the notice from them.

In the case of a commodity, taking delivery usually means accepting a warehouse receipt in return for immediate payment. The party taking delivery is then responsible for all warehousing costs. In the case of livestock futures, there may be costs associated with feeding and looking after the animals (see Box 5-1). In the case of financial futures, delivery is usually made by wire transfer. For all contracts, the price paid is usually the most recent settlement price. If specified by the exchange, this price is adjusted for grade, location of delivery, and so on. The whole delivery procedure from the issuance of the notice of intention to deliver to the delivery itself generally takes about two to three days.

There are three critical days for a contract. These are the first notice day, the last notice day, and the last trading day. The *first notice day* is the first day on which a notice of intention to make delivery can be submitted to the exchange. The *last notice day* is the last such day. The *last trading day* is generally a few days before the last notice day. To avoid the risk of having to take delivery, an investor with a long position should close out his or her contracts prior to the first notice day.

Cash Settlement

Some financial futures, such as those on stock indices discussed in Chapter 6, are settled in cash because it is inconvenient or impossible to deliver the underlying asset. In the case of the futures contract on the S&P 500, for example, delivering the underlying asset would involve delivering a portfolio of 500 stocks. When a contract is settled in cash, all outstanding contracts are declared closed on a predetermined day. The final settlement price is set equal to the spot price of the underlying asset at either the opening or close of trading on that day. For example, in the S&P 500 futures contract traded by the CME Group, the predetermined day is the third Friday of the delivery month and final settlement is at the opening price.

TYPES OF TRADERS AND TYPES OF ORDERS

There are two main types of traders executing trades: *futures commission merchants* (FCMs) and *locals*. FCMs are following the instructions of their clients and charge a commission for doing so; locals are trading on their own account.

Individuals taking positions, whether locals or the clients of FCMs, can be categorized as hedgers, speculators, or arbitrageurs, as discussed in Chapter 4. Speculators can be classified as scalpers, day traders, or position traders. *Scalpers* are watching for very short-term trends and attempt to profit from small changes in the contract price. They usually hold their positions for only a few minutes. *Day traders* hold their positions for less than one trading day. They are unwilling to take the risk that adverse news will occur overnight. *Position traders* hold their positions for much longer periods of time. They hope to make significant profits from major movements in the markets.

Orders

The simplest type of order placed with a broker is a *market order*. It is a request that a trade be carried out

immediately at the best price available in the market. However, there are many other types of orders. We will consider those that are more commonly used.

A *limit order* specifies a particular price. The order can be executed only at this price or at one more favorable to the investor. Thus, if the limit price is $30 for an investor wanting to buy, the order will be executed only at a price of $30 or less. There is, of course, no guarantee that the order will be executed at all, because the limit price may never be reached.

A *stop order* or *stop-loss order* also specifies a particular price. The order is executed at the best available price once a bid or offer is made at that particular price or a less-favorable price. Suppose a stop order to sell at $30 is issued when the market price is $35. It becomes an order to sell when and if the price falls to $30. In effect, a stop order becomes a market order as soon as the specified price has been hit. The purpose of a stop order is usually to close out a position if unfavorable price movements take place. It limits the loss that can be incurred.

A *stop-limit order* is a combination of a stop order and a limit order. The order becomes a limit order as soon as a bid or offer is made at a price equal to or less favorable than the stop price. Two prices must be specified in a stop-limit order: the stop price and the limit price. Suppose that at the time the market price is $35, a stop-limit order to buy is issued with a stop price of $40 and a limit price of $41. As soon as there is a bid or offer at $40, the stop-limit becomes a limit order at $41. If the stop price and the limit price are the same, the order is sometimes called a *stop-and-limit order*.

A *market-if-touched* (MIT) *order* is executed at the best available price after a trade occurs at a specified price or at a price more favorable than the specified price. In effect, an MIT becomes a market order once the specified price has been hit. An MIT is also known as a *board order*. Consider an investor who has a long position in a futures contract and is issuing instructions that would lead to closing out the contract. A stop order is designed to place a limit on the loss that can occur in the event of unfavorable price movements. By contrast, a market-if-touched order is designed to ensure that profits are taken if sufficiently favorable price movements occur.

A *discretionary order* or *market-not-held order* is traded as a market order except that execution may be delayed at the broker's discretion in an attempt to get a better price.

Some orders specify time conditions. Unless otherwise stated, an order is a day order and expires at the end of the trading day. A *time-of-day order* specifies a particular period of time during the day when the order can be executed. An *open order* or a *good-till-canceled order* is in effect until executed or until the end of trading in the particular contract. A *fill-or-kill order*, as its name implies, must be executed immediately on receipt or not at all.

REGULATION

Futures markets in the United States are currently regulated federally by the Commodity Futures Trading Commission (CFTC; www.cftc.gov), which was established in 1974. This body is responsible for licensing futures exchanges and approving contracts. All new contracts and changes to existing contracts must be approved by the CFTC. To be approved, the contract must have some useful economic purpose. Usually this means that it must serve the needs of hedgers as well as speculators.

The CFTC looks after the public interest. It is responsible for ensuring that prices are communicated to the public and that futures traders report their outstanding positions if they are above certain levels. The CFTC also licenses all individuals who offer their services to the public in futures trading. The backgrounds of these individuals are investigated, and there are minimum capital requirements. The CFTC deals with complaints brought by the public and ensures that disciplinary action is taken against individuals when appropriate. It has the authority to force exchanges to take disciplinary action against members who are in violation of exchange rules.

With the formation of the National Futures Association (NFA; www.nfa.futures. org) in 1982, some responsibilities of the CFTC were shifted to the futures industry itself. The NFA is an organization of individuals who participate in the futures industry. Its objective is to prevent fraud and to ensure that the market operates in the best interests of the general public. It is authorized to monitor trading and take disciplinary action when appropriate. The agency has set up an efficient system for arbitrating disputes between individuals and its members.

From time to time, other bodies, such as the Securities and Exchange Commission (SEC; www.sec.gov), the Federal Reserve Board (www.federalreserve.gov), and the US Treasury Department (www.treas.gov), have claimed jurisdictional rights over some aspects of futures trading. These bodies are concerned with the effects of futures trading on the spot markets for securities such as stocks, Treasury bills, and Treasury bonds. The SEC currently has an effective veto over the approval of new stock or bond index futures contracts. However, the basic responsibility for all futures and options on futures rests with the CFTC.

Trading Irregularities

Most of the time futures markets operate efficiently and in the public interest. However, from time to time, trading irregularities do come to light. One type of trading irregularity occurs when an investor group tries to "corner the market".[4] The investor group takes a huge long futures position and also tries to exercise some control over the supply of the underlying commodity. As the maturity of the futures contracts is approached, the investor group does not close out its position, so that the number of outstanding futures contracts may exceed the amount of the commodity available for delivery. The holders of short positions realize that they will find it difficult to deliver and become desperate to close out their positions. The result is a large rise in both futures and spot prices. Regulators usually deal with this type of abuse of the market by increasing margin requirements or imposing stricter position limits or prohibiting trades that increase a speculator's open position or requiring market participants to close out their positions.

Other types of trading irregularity can involve the traders on the floor of the exchange. These received some publicity early in 1989, when it was announced that the FBI had carried out a two-year investigation, using undercover agents, of trading on the Chicago Board of Trade and the Chicago Mercantile Exchange. The investigation was initiated because of complaints filed by a large agricultural concern.

---

[4] Possibly the best known example of this was the attempt by the Hunt brothers to corner the silver market in 1979–80. Between the middle of 1979 and the beginning of 1980, their activities led to a price rise from $9 per ounce to $50 per ounce.

The alleged offenses included overcharging customers, not paying customers the full proceeds of sales, and traders using their knowledge of customer orders to trade first for themselves (an offence known as *front running*).

ACCOUNTING AND TAX

The full details of the accounting and tax treatment of futures contracts are beyond the scope of this book. A trader who wants detailed information on this should consult experts. In this section we provide some general background information.

Accounting

Accounting standards require changes in the market value of a futures contract to be recognized when they occur unless the contract qualifies as a hedge. If the contract does qualify as a hedge, gains or losses are generally recognized for accounting purposes in the same period in which the gains or losses from the item being hedged are recognized. The latter treatment is referred to as *hedge accounting*.

Consider a company with a December year end. In September 2011 it buys a March 2012 corn futures contract and closes out the position at the end of February 2012. Suppose that the futures prices are 250 cents per bushel when the contract is entered into, 270 cents per bushel at the end of 2011, and 280 cents per bushel when the contract is closed out. The contract is for the delivery of 5,000 bushels. If the contract does not qualify as a hedge, the gains for accounting purposes are

$$5,000 \times (2.70 - 2.50) = \$1,000$$

in 2011 and

$$5,000 \times (2.80 - 2.70) = \$500$$

in 2012. If the company is hedging the purchase of 5,000 bushels of corn in February 2012 so that the contract qualifies for hedge accounting, the entire gain of $1,500 is realized in 2012 for accounting purposes.

The treatment of hedging gains and losses is sensible. If the company is hedging the purchase of 5,000 bushels of corn in February 2012, the effect of the futures contract is to ensure that the price paid is close to 250 cents per bushel. The accounting treatment reflects that this price is paid in 2012.

In June 1998, the Financial Accounting Standards Board issued FASB Statement No. 133 (FAS 133), Accounting for Derivative Instruments and Hedging Activities. FAS 133 applies to all types of derivatives (including futures, forwards, swaps, and options). It requires all derivatives to be included on the balance sheet at fair market value.[5] It increases disclosure requirements. It also gives companies far less latitude than previously in using hedge accounting. For hedge accounting to be used, the hedging instrument must be highly effective in offsetting exposures and an assessment of this effectiveness is required every three months. A similar standard IAS 39 has been issued by the International Accounting Standards Board.

Tax

Under the US tax rules, two key issues are the nature of a taxable gain or loss and the timing of the recognition of the gain or loss. Gains or losses are either classified as capital gains or losses or alternatively as part of ordinary income.

For a corporate taxpayer, capital gains are taxed at the same rate as ordinary income, and the ability to deduct losses is restricted. Capital losses are deductible only to the extent of capital gains. A corporation may carry back a capital loss for three years and carry it forward for up to five years. For a noncorporate taxpayer, short-term capital gains are taxed at the same rate as ordinary income, but long-term capital gains are subject to a maximum capital gains tax rate of 15%. (Long-term capital gains are gains from the sale of a capital asset held for longer than one year; short-term capital gains are the gains from the sale of a capital asset held one year or less.) For a noncorporate taxpayer, capital losses are deductible to the extent of capital gains plus ordinary income up to $3,000 and can be carried forward indefinitely.

Generally, positions in futures contracts are treated as if they are closed out on the last day of the tax year. For the noncorporate taxpayer, this gives rise to capital gains and losses that are treated as if they were 60% long term and 40% short term without regard to the holding period. This is referred to as the "60/40" rule. A noncorporate taxpayer may elect to carry back for three years any net losses from the 60/40 rule to offset any gains recognized under the rule in the previous three years.

---

[5] Previously the attraction of derivatives in some situations was that they were "off-balance-sheet" items.

Hedging transactions are exempt from this rule. The definition of a hedge transaction for tax purposes is different from that for accounting purposes. The tax regulations define a hedging transaction as a transaction entered into in the normal course of business primarily for one of the following reasons:

1. To reduce the risk of price changes or currency fluctuations with respect to property that is held or to be held by the taxpayer for the purposes of producing ordinary income

2. To reduce the risk of price or interest rate changes or currency fluctuations with respect to borrowings made by the taxpayer

A hedging transaction must be clearly identified as such in the company's records. Gains or losses from hedging transactions are treated as ordinary income. The timing of the recognition of gains or losses from hedging transactions generally matches the timing of the recognition of income or expense associated with the transaction being hedged.

FORWARD VS. FUTURES CONTRACTS

The main differences between forward and futures contracts are summarized in Table 5-3. Both contracts are agreements to buy or sell an asset for a certain price at a certain future time. A forward contract is traded in the over-the-counter market and there is no standard contract size or standard delivery arrangements. A single delivery date is usually specified and the contract is usually held to the end of its life and then settled. A futures contract is a standardized contract traded on an exchange. A range of delivery dates is usually specified. It is settled daily and usually closed out prior to maturity.

Profits from Forward and Futures Contracts

Suppose that the sterling exchange rate for a 90-day forward contract is 1.5000 and that this rate is also the futures price for a contract that will be delivered in exactly 90 days. What is the difference between the gains and losses under the two contracts?

Under the forward contract, the whole gain or loss is realized at the end of the life of the contract. Under the futures contract, the gain or loss is realized day by day because of the daily settlement procedures. Suppose that investor A is long £1 million in a 90-day forward contract and investor B is long £1 million in 90-day futures contracts. (Because each futures contract is for the purchase or sale of £62,500, investor B must purchase a total of 16 contracts.) Assume that the spot exchange rate in 90 days proves to be 1.7000 dollars per pound. Investor A makes a gain of $200,000 on the 90th day. Investor B makes the same gain—but spread out over the 90-day period. On some days investor B may realize a loss, whereas on other days he or she makes a gain. However, in total, when losses are netted against gains, there is a gain of $200,000 over the 90-day period.

Foreign Exchange Quotes

Both forward and futures contracts trade actively on foreign currencies. However, there is sometimes a difference in the way exchange rates are quoted in the two markets. For example, futures prices where one currency is the US dollar are always quoted as the number of US dollars per unit of the foreign currency or as the number of US cents per unit of the foreign currency. Forward prices are always quoted in the same way as spot prices. This means that, for the British pound, the euro, the Australian dollar, and the New Zealand dollar, the forward quotes show the number of US dollars per unit of the foreign currency and are directly comparable with futures quotes. For other major currencies, forward quotes show the number of

| **TABLE 5-3** | Comparison of Forward and Futures Contracts |

Forward	Futures
Private contract between two parties	Traded on an exchange
Not standardized	Standardized contract
Usually one specified delivery date	Range of delivery dates
Settled at end of contract	Settled daily
Delivery or final cash settlement usually takes place	Contract is usually closed out prior to maturity
Some credit risk	Virtually no credit risk

units of the foreign currency per US dollar (USD). Consider the Canadian dollar (CAD). A futures price quote of 0.9500 USD per CAD corresponds to a forward price quote of 1.0526 CAD per USD (1.0526 = 1/0.9500).

SUMMARY

A very high proportion of the futures contracts that are traded do not lead to the delivery of the underlying asset. Traders usually enter into offsetting contracts to close out their positions before the delivery period is reached. However, it is the possibility of final delivery that drives the determination of the futures price. For each futures contract, there is a range of days during which delivery can be made and a well-defined delivery procedure. Some contracts, such as those on stock indices, are settled in cash rather than by delivery of the underlying asset.

The specification of contracts is an important activity for a futures exchange. The two sides to any contract must know what can be delivered, where delivery can take place, and when delivery can take place. They also need to know details on the trading hours, how prices will be quoted, maximum daily price movements, and so on. New contracts must be approved by the Commodity Futures Trading Commission before trading starts.

Margins are an important aspect of futures markets. An investor keeps a margin account with his or her broker. The account is adjusted daily to reflect gains or losses, and from time to time the broker may require the account to be topped up if adverse price movements have taken place. The broker either must be a clearinghouse member or must maintain a margin account with a clearinghouse member. Each clearinghouse member maintains a margin account with the exchange clearinghouse. The balance in the account is adjusted daily to reflect gains and losses on the business for which the clearinghouse member is responsible.

Information on futures prices is collected in a systematic way at exchanges and relayed within a matter of seconds to investors throughout the world. Many daily newspapers such as the *Wall Street Journal* carry a summary of the previous day's trading.

Forward contracts differ from futures contracts in a number of ways. Forward contracts are private arrangements between two parties, whereas futures contracts are traded on exchanges. There is generally a single delivery date in a forward contract, whereas futures contracts frequently involve a range of such dates. Because they are not traded on exchanges, forward contracts do not need to be standardized. A forward contract is not usually settled until the end of its life, and most contracts do in fact lead to delivery of the underlying asset or a cash settlement at this time.

In the next few chapters we shall examine in more detail the ways in which forward and futures contracts can be used for hedging. We shall also look at how forward and futures prices are determined.

Further Reading

Duffie, D., and H. Zhu. "Does a Central Clearing Counterparty Reduce Counterparty Risk?" Working Paper, Stanford University, 2010.

Gastineau, G. L., D. J. Smith, and R. Todd. *Risk Management, Derivatives, and Financial Analysis under SFAS No. 133.* The Research Foundation of AIMR and Blackwell Series in Finance, 2001.

Hull, J., "OTC Derivatives and Central Clearing: Can All Transactions Be Cleared," *Financial Stability Review*, 14 (July 2010): 71–80.

Jones, F. J., and R. J. Teweles. In: *The Futures Game*, edited by B. Warwick, 3rd ed. New York: McGraw-Hill, 1998.

Jorion, P. "Risk Management Lessons from Long-Term Capital Management," *European Financial Management*, 6, 3 (September 2000): 277–300.

Kawaller, I. G., and P. D. Koch. "Meeting the Highly Effective Expectation Criterion for Hedge Accounting," *Journal of Derivatives*, 7, 4 (Summer 2000): 79–87.

Lowenstein, R. *When Genius Failed: The Rise and Fall of Long-Term Capital Management*. New York: Random House, 2000.

Hedging Strategies Using Futures

6

Learning Objectives

Candidates, after completing this reading, should be able to:

- Define and differentiate between short and long hedges and identify their appropriate uses.
- Describe the arguments for and against hedging and the potential impact of hedging on firm profitability.
- Define the basis and explain the various sources of basis risk, and explain how basis risks arise when hedging with futures.
- Define cross hedging, and compute and interpret the minimum variance hedge ratio and hedge effectiveness.

- Compute the optimal number of futures contracts needed to hedge an exposure, and explain and calculate the "tailing the hedge" adjustment.
- Explain how to use stock index futures contracts to change a stock portfolio's beta.
- Explain the term "rolling the hedge forward" and describe some of the risks that arise from this strategy.

Excerpt is Chapter 3 of Options, Futures, and Other Derivatives, *Eighth Edition, by John Hull.*

Many of the participants in futures markets are hedgers. Their aim is to use futures markets to reduce a particular risk that they face. This risk might relate to fluctuations in the price of oil, a foreign exchange rate, the level of the stock market, or some other variable. A *perfect hedge* is one that completely eliminates the risk. Perfect hedges are rare. For the most part, therefore, a study of hedging using futures contracts is a study of the ways in which hedges can be constructed so that they perform as close to perfect as possible.

In this chapter we consider a number of general issues associated with the way hedges are set up. When is a short futures position appropriate? When is a long futures position appropriate? Which futures contract should be used? What is the optimal size of the futures position for reducing risk? At this stage, we restrict our attention to what might be termed *hedge-and-forget* strategies. We assume that no attempt is made to adjust the hedge once it has been put in place. The hedger simply takes a futures position at the beginning of the life of the hedge and closes out the position at the end of the life of the hedge.

The chapter initially treats futures contracts as forward contracts (that as, it ignores daily settlement). Later it explains an adjustment known as "tailing" that takes account of the difference between futures and forwards.

BASIC PRINCIPLES

When an individual or company chooses to use futures markets to hedge a risk, the objective is usually to take a position that neutralizes the risk as far as possible. Consider a company that knows it will gain $10,000 for each 1 cent increase in the price of a commodity over the next 3 months and lose $10,000 for each 1 cent decrease in the price during the same period. To hedge, the company's treasurer should take a short futures position that is designed to offset this risk. The futures position should lead to a loss of $10,000 for each 1 cent increase in price of the commodity over the 3 months and a gain of $10,000 for each 1 cent decrease in the price during this period. If the price of the commodity goes down, the gain on the futures position offsets the loss on the rest of the company's business. If the price of the commodity goes

up, the loss on the futures position is offset by the gain on the rest of the company's business.

Short Hedges

A *short hedge* is a hedge, such as the one just described, that involves a short position in futures contracts. A short hedge is appropriate when the hedger already owns an asset and expects to sell it at some time in the future. For example, a short hedge could be used by a farmer who owns some hogs and knows that they will be ready for sale at the local market in two months. A short hedge can also be used when an asset is not owned right now but will be owned at some time in the future. Consider, for example, a US exporter who knows that he or she will receive euros in 3 months. The exporter will realize a gain if the euro increases in value relative to the US dollar and will sustain a loss if the euro decreases in value relative to the US dollar. A short futures position leads to a loss if the euro increases in value and a gain if it decreases in value. It has the effect of offsetting the exporter's risk.

To provide a more detailed illustration of the operation of a short hedge in a specific situation, we assume that it is May 15 today and that an oil producer has just negotiated a contract to sell 1 million barrels of crude oil. It has been agreed that the price that will apply in the contract is the market price on August 15. The oil producer is therefore in the position where it will gain $10,000 for each 1 cent increase in the price of oil over the next 3 months and lose $10,000 for each 1 cent decrease in the price during this period. Suppose that on May 15 the spot price is $80 per barrel and the crude oil futures price for August delivery is $79 per barrel. Because each futures contract is for the delivery of 1,000 barrels, the company can hedge its exposure by shorting (i.e., selling) 1,000 futures contracts. If the oil producer closes out its position on August 15, the effect of the strategy should be to lock in a price close of $79 per barrel.

To illustrate what might happen, suppose that the spot price on August 15 proves to be $75 per barrel. The company realizes $75 million for the oil under its sales contract. Because August is the delivery month for the futures contract, the futures price on August 15 should be very close to the spot price of $75 on that date. The company therefore gains approximately

$$\$79 - \$75 = \$4$$

per barrel, or $4 million in total from the short futures position. The total amount realized from both the futures position and the sales contract is therefore approximately $79 per barrel, or $79 million in total.

For an alternative outcome, suppose that the price of oil on August 15 proves to be $85 per barrel. The company realizes $85 per barrel for the oil and loses approximately

$$\$85 - \$79 = \$6$$

per barrel on the short futures position. Again, the total amount realized is approximately $79 million. It is easy to see that in all cases the company ends up with approximately $79 million.

Long Hedges

Hedges that involve taking a long position in a futures contract are known as *long hedges*. A long hedge is appropriate when a company knows it will have to purchase a certain asset in the future and wants to lock in a price now.

Suppose that it is now January 15. A copper fabricator knows it will require 100,000 pounds of copper on May 15 to meet a certain contract. The spot price of copper is 340 cents per pound, and the futures price for May delivery is 320 cents per pound. The fabricator can hedge its position by taking a long position in four futures contracts offered by the COMEX division of the CME Group and closing its position on May 15. Each contract is for the delivery of 25,000 pounds of copper. The strategy has the effect of locking in the price of the required copper at close to 320 cents per pound.

Suppose that the spot price of copper on May 15 proves to be 325 cents per pound. Because May is the delivery month for the futures contract, this should be very close to the futures price. The fabricator therefore gains approximately

$$100,000 \times (\$3.25 - \$3.20) = \$5,000$$

on the futures contracts. It pays $100,000 \times \$3.25 = $325,000 for the copper, making the net cost approximately $325,000 - $5,000 = $320,000. For an alternative outcome, suppose that the spot price is 305 cents per pound on May 15. The fabricator then loses approximately

$$100,000 \times (\$3.20 - \$3.05) = \$15,000$$

on the futures contract and pays $100,000 \times \$3.05 = $305,000 for the copper. Again, the net cost is approximately $320,000, or 320 cents per pound.

Note that, in this case, it is clearly better for the company to use futures contracts than to buy the copper on January 15 in the spot market. If it does the latter, it will pay 340 cents per pound instead of 320 cents per pound and will incur both interest costs and storage costs. For a company using copper on a regular basis, this disadvantage would be offset by the convenience of having the copper on hand.[1] However, for a company that knows it will not require the copper until May 15, the futures contract alternative is likely to be preferred.

The examples we have looked at assume that the futures position is closed out in the delivery month. The hedge has the same basic effect if delivery is allowed to happen. However, making or taking delivery can be costly and inconvenient. For this reason, delivery is not usually made even when the hedger keeps the futures contract until the delivery month. As will be discussed later, hedgers with long positions usually avoid any possibility of having to take delivery by closing out their positions before the delivery period.

We have also assumed in the two examples that there is no daily settlement. In practice, daily settlement does have a small effect on the performance of a hedge. As explained in Chapter 5, it means that the payoff from the futures contract is realized day by day throughout the life of the hedge rather than all at the end.

ARGUMENTS FOR AND AGAINST HEDGING

The arguments in favor of hedging are so obvious that they hardly need to be stated. Most companies are in the business of manufacturing, or retailing or wholesaling, or providing a service. They have no particular skills or expertise in predicting variables such as interest rates,

---

[1] See Chapter 9 for a discussion of convenience yields.

exchange rates, and commodity prices. It makes sense for them to hedge the risks associated with these variables as they become aware of them. The companies can then focus on their main activities—for which presumably they do have particular skills and expertise. By hedging, they avoid unpleasant surprises such as sharp rises in the price of a commodity that is being purchased.

In practice, many risks are left unhedged. In the rest of this section we will explore some of the reasons for this.

Hedging and Shareholders

One argument sometimes put forward is that the shareholders can, if they wish, do the hedging themselves. They do not need the company to do it for them. This argument is, however, open to question. It assumes that shareholders have as much information as the company's management about the risks faced by a company. In most instances, this is not the case. The argument also ignores commissions and other transactions costs. These are less expensive per dollar of hedging for large transactions than for small transactions. Hedging is therefore likely to be less expensive when carried out by the company than when it is carried out by individual shareholders. Indeed, the size of futures contracts makes hedging by individual shareholders impossible in many situations.

One thing that shareholders can do far more easily than a corporation is diversify risk. A shareholder with a well-diversified portfolio may be immune to many of the risks faced by a corporation. For example, in addition to holding shares in a company that uses copper, a well-diversified shareholder may hold shares in a copper producer, so that there is very little overall exposure to the price of copper. If companies are acting in the best interests of well-diversified shareholders, it can be argued that hedging is unnecessary in many situations. However, the extent to which managers are in practice influenced by this type of argument is open to question.

Hedging and Competitors

If hedging is not the norm in a certain industry, it may not make sense for one particular company to choose to be different from all others. Competitive pressures within the industry may be such that the prices of the goods and services produced by the industry fluctuate to reflect raw material costs, interest rates, exchange rates, and so on. A company that does not hedge can expect its profit margins to be roughly constant. However, a company that does hedge can expect its profit margins to fluctuate!

To illustrate this point, consider two manufacturers of gold jewelry, SafeandSure Company and TakeaChance Company. We assume that most companies in the industry do not hedge against movements in the price of gold and that TakeaChance Company is no exception. However, SafeandSure Company has decided to be different from its competitors and to use futures contracts to hedge its purchase of gold over the next 18 months. If the price of gold goes up, economic pressures will tend to lead to a corresponding increase in the wholesale price of jewelry, so that TakeaChance Company's gross profit margin is unaffected. By contrast, SafeandSure Company's profit margin will increase after the effects of the hedge have been taken into account. If the price of gold goes down, economic pressures will tend to lead to a corresponding decrease in the wholesale price of jewelry. Again, TakeaChance Company's profit margin is unaffected. However, SafeandSure Company's profit margin goes down. In extreme conditions, SafeandSure Company's profit margin could become negative as a result of the "hedging" carried out! The situation is summarized in Table 6-1.

This example emphasizes the importance of looking at the big picture when hedging. All the implications of price changes on a company's profitability should be taken into account in the design of a hedging strategy to protect against the price changes.

TABLE 6-1 Danger in Hedging When Competitors Do Not Hedge

Change in gold price	Effect on price of gold jewelry	Effect on profits of TakeaChance Co.	Effect on profits of SafeandSure Co.
Increase	Increase	None	Increase
Decrease	Decrease	None	Decrease

Hedging Can Lead to a Worse Outcome

It is important to realize that a hedge using futures contracts can result in a decrease or an increase in a company's profits relative to the position it would be in with no hedging. In the example involving the oil producer considered earlier, if the price of oil goes down, the company loses money on its sale of 1 million barrels of oil, and the futures position leads to an offsetting gain. The treasurer can be congratulated for having had the foresight to put the hedge in place. Clearly, the company is better off than it would be with no hedging. Other executives in the organization, it is hoped, will appreciate the contribution made by the treasurer. If the price of oil goes up, the company gains from its sale of the oil, and the futures position leads to an offsetting loss. The company is in a worse position than it would be with no hedging. Although the hedging decision was perfectly logical, the treasurer may in practice have a difficult time justifying it. Suppose that the price of oil at the end of the hedge is $89, so that the company loses $10 per barrel on the futures contract. We can imagine a conversation such as the following between the treasurer and the president:

> **President:** This is terrible. We've lost $10 million in the futures market in the space of three months. How could it happen? I want a full explanation.
>
> **Treasurer:** The purpose of the futures contracts was to hedge our exposure to the price of oil, not to make a profit. Don't forget we made $10 million from the favorable effect of the oil price increases on our business.
>
> **President:** What's that got to do with it? That's like saying that we do not need to worry when our sales are down in California because they are up in New York.
>
> **Treasurer:** If the price of oil had gone down . . .
>
> **President:** I don't care what would have happened if the price of oil had gone down. The fact is that it went up. I really do not know what you were doing playing the futures markets like this. Our shareholders will expect us to have done particularly well this quarter. I'm going to have to explain to them that your actions reduced profits by $10 million. I'm afraid this is going to mean no bonus for you this year.
>
> **Treasurer:** That's unfair. I was only . . .

> **President:** Unfair! You are lucky not to be fired. You lost $10 million.
>
> **Treasurer:** It all depends on how you look at it . . .

It is easy to see why many treasurers are reluctant to hedge! Hedging reduces risk for the company. However, it may increase risk for the treasurer if others do not fully understand what is being done. The only real solution to this problem involves ensuring that all senior executives within the organization fully understand the nature of hedging before a hedging program is put in place. Ideally, hedging strategies are set by a company's board of directors and are clearly communicated to both the company's management and the shareholders. (See Box 6-1 for a discussion of hedging by gold mining companies.)

BOX 6-1   Hedging by Gold Mining Companies

It is natural for a gold mining company to consider hedging against changes in the price of gold. Typically it takes several years to extract all the gold from a mine. Once a gold mining company decides to go ahead with production at a particular mine, it has a big exposure to the price of gold. Indeed a mine that looks profitable at the outset could become unprofitable if the price of gold plunges.

Gold mining companies are careful to explain their hedging strategies to potential shareholders. Some gold mining companies do not hedge. They tend to attract shareholders who buy gold stocks because they want to benefit when the price of gold increases and are prepared to accept the risk of a loss from a decrease in the price of gold. Other companies choose to hedge. They estimated the number of ounces of gold they will produce each month for the next few years and enter into short futures or forward contracts to lock in the price for all or part of this.

Suppose you are Goldman Sachs and are approached by a gold mining company that wants to sell you a large amount of gold in 1 year at a fixed price. How do you set the price and then hedge your risk? The answer is that you can hedge by borrowing the gold from a central bank, selling it immediately in the spot market, and investing the proceeds at the risk-free rate. At the end of the year, you buy the gold from the gold mining company and use it to repay the central bank. The fixed forward price you set for the gold reflects the risk-free rate you can earn and the lease rate you pay the central bank for borrowing the gold.

BASIS RISK

The hedges in the examples considered so far have been almost too good to be true. The hedger was able to identify the precise date in the future when an asset would be bought or sold. The hedger was then able to use futures contracts to remove almost all the risk arising from the price of the asset on that date. In practice, hedging is often not quite as straightforward as this. Some of the reasons are as follows:

1. The asset whose price is to be hedged may not be exactly the same as the asset underlying the futures contract.

2. The hedger may be uncertain as to the exact date when the asset will be bought or sold.

3. The hedge may require the futures contract to be closed out before its delivery month.

These problems give rise to what is termed *basis risk*. This concept will now be explained.

The Basis

The *basis* in a hedging situation is as follows:[2]

> Basis = Spot price of asset to be hedged
> **− Futures price of contract used**

If the asset to be hedged and the asset underlying the futures contract are the same, the basis should be zero at the expiration of the futures contract. Prior to expiration, the basis may be positive or negative. From Table 5-2, we see that, on May 26, 2010, the basis was negative for gold and positive for short maturity contracts on soybeans.

As time passes, the spot price and the futures price for a particular month do not necessarily change by the same amount. As a result, the basis changes. An increase in the basis is referred to as a *strengthening of the basis*; a decrease in the basis is referred to as a *weakening of the basis*. Figure 6-1 illustrates how a basis might change over time in a situation where the basis is positive prior to expiration of the futures contract.

---

[2] This is the usual definition. However, the alternative definition Basis = Futures price − Spot price is sometimes used, particularly when the futures contract is on a financial asset.

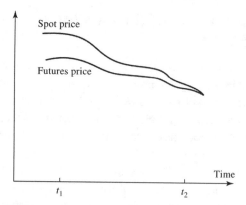

FIGURE 6-1   Variation of basis over time.

To examine the nature of basis risk, we will use the following notation:

> S_1: Spot price at time t_1
> S_2: Spot price at time t_2
> F_1: Futures price at time t_1
> F_2: Futures price at time t_2
> b_1: Basis at time t_1
> b_2: Basis at time t_2.

We will assume that a hedge is put in place at time t_1 and closed at time t_2. As an example, we will consider the case where the spot and futures prices at the time the hedge is initiated are \$2.50 and \$2.20, respectively, and that at the time the hedge is closed out they are \$2.00 and \$1.90, respectively. This means that $S_1 = 2.50$, $F_1 = 2.20$, $S_2 = 2.00$, and $F_2 = 1.90$.

From the definition of the basis, we have

$$b_1 = S_1 - F_1 \quad \text{and} \quad b_2 = S_2 - F_2$$

so that, in our example, $b_1 = 0.30$ and $b_2 = 0.10$.

Consider first the situation of a hedger who knows that the asset will be sold at time t_2 and takes a short futures position at time t_1. The price realized for the asset is S_2 and the profit on the futures position is $F_1 - F_2$. The effective price that is obtained for the asset with hedging is therefore

$$S_2 + F_1 - F_2 = F_1 + b_2$$

In our example, this is \$2.30. The value of F_1 is known at time t_1. If b_2 were also known at this time, a perfect hedge

---

would result. The hedge risk is the uncertainty associated with b_2 and is known as *basis risk*. Consider next a situation where a company knows it will buy the asset at time t_2 and initiates a long hedge at time t_1. The price paid for the asset is S_2 and the loss on the hedge is $F_1 - F_2$. The effective price that is paid with hedging is therefore

$$S_2 + F_1 - F_2 = F_1 + b_2$$

This is the same expression as before and is $2.30 in the example. The value of F_1 is known at time t_1, and the term b_2 represents basis risk.

Note that basis risk can lead to an improvement or a worsening of a hedger's position. Consider a short hedge. If the basis strengthens (i.e., increases) unexpectedly, the hedger's position improves; if the basis weakens (i.e., decreases) unexpectedly, the hedger's position worsens. For a long hedge, the reverse holds. If the basis strengthens unexpectedly, the hedger's position worsens; if the basis weakens unexpectedly, the hedger's position improves.

The asset that gives rise to the hedger's exposure is sometimes different from the asset underlying the futures contract that is used for hedging. This is known as cross hedging and is discussed in the next section. It leads to an increase in basis risk. Define S_2^* as the price of the asset underlying the futures contract at time t_2. As before, S_2 is the price of the asset being hedged at time t_2. By hedging, a company ensures that the price that will be paid (or received) for the asset is

$$S_2 + F_1 - F_2$$

This can be written as

$$F_1 + (S_2^* - F_2) + (S_2 - S_2^*)$$

The terms $S_2^* - F_2$ and $S_2 - S_2^*$ represent the two components of the basis. The $S_2^* - F_2$ term is the basis that would exist if the asset being hedged were the same as the asset underlying the futures contract. The $S_2 - S_2^*$ term is the basis arising from the difference between the two assets.

Choice of Contract

One key factor affecting basis risk is the choice of the futures contract to be used for hedging. This choice has two components:

1. The choice of the asset underlying the futures contract
2. The choice of the delivery month.

If the asset being hedged exactly matches an asset underlying a futures contract, the first choice is generally fairly easy. In other circumstances, it is necessary to carry out a careful analysis to determine which of the available futures contracts has futures prices that are most closely correlated with the price of the asset being hedged.

The choice of the delivery month is likely to be influenced by several factors. In the examples given earlier in this chapter, we assumed that, when the expiration of the hedge corresponds to a delivery month, the contract with that delivery month is chosen. In fact, a contract with a later delivery month is usually chosen in these circumstances. The reason is that futures prices are in some instances quite erratic during the delivery month. Moreover, a long hedger runs the risk of having to take delivery of the physical asset if the contract is held during the delivery month. Taking delivery can be expensive and inconvenient. (Long hedgers normally prefer to close out the futures contract and buy the asset from their usual suppliers.)

In general, basis risk increases as the time difference between the hedge expiration and the delivery month increases. A good rule of thumb is therefore to choose a delivery month that is as close as possible to, but later than, the expiration of the hedge. Suppose delivery months are March, June, September, and December for a futures contract on a particular asset. For hedge expirations in December, January, and February, the March contract will be chosen; for hedge expirations in March, April, and May, the June contract will be chosen; and so on. This rule of thumb assumes that there is sufficient liquidity in all contracts to meet the hedger's requirements. In practice, liquidity tends to be greatest in short-maturity futures contracts. Therefore, in some situations, the hedger may be inclined to use short-maturity contracts and roll them forward. This strategy is discussed later in the chapter.

Example 6.1

It is March 1. A US company expects to receive 50 million Japanese yen at the end of July. Yen futures contracts on the CME Group have delivery months of March, June, September, and December. One contract is for the delivery of 12.5 million yen. The company therefore shorts four September yen futures contracts on March 1. When the yen are received at the end of July, the company closes out its position. We suppose that the futures price on March 1 in cents per yen is 0.7800 and that the spot and futures prices when the contract is closed out are 0.7200 and 0.7250, respectively.

The gain on the futures contract is 0.7800 − 0.7250 = 0.0550 cents per yen. The basis is 0.7200 − 0.7250 = − 0.0050 cents per yen when the contract is closed out. The effective price obtained in cents per yen is the final spot price plus the gain on the futures:

$$0.7200 + 0.0550 = 0.7750$$

This can also be written as the initial futures price plus the final basis:

$$0.7800 + (-0.0050) = 0.7750$$

The total amount received by the company for the 50 million yen is 50 × 0.00775 million dollars, or $387,500.

Example 6.2

It is June 8 and a company knows that it will need to purchase 20,000 barrels of crude oil at some time in October or November. Oil futures contracts are currently traded for delivery every month on the NYMEX division of the CME Group and the contract size is 1,000 barrels. The company therefore decides to use the December contract for hedging and takes a long position in 20 December contracts. The futures price on June 8 is $68.00 per barrel. The company finds that it is ready to purchase the crude oil on November 10. It therefore closes out its futures contract on that date. The spot price and futures on November 10 are $70.00 per barrel and $69.10 per barrel.

The gain on the futures contract is 69.10 − 68.00 = $1.10 per barrel. The basis when the contract is closed out is 70.00 − 69.10 = $0.90 per barrel. The effective price paid (in dollars per barrel) is the final spot price less the gain on the futures, or

$$70.00 - 1.10 = 68.90$$

This can also be calculated as the initial futures price plus the final basis,

$$68.00 + 0.90 = 68.90$$

The total price paid is 68.90 × 20,000 = $1,378,000.

CROSS HEDGING

In Examples 6.1 and 6.2, the asset underlying the futures contract was the same as the asset whose price is being hedged. *Cross hedging* occurs when the two assets are different. Consider, for example, an airline that is concerned about the future price of jet fuel. Because jet fuel futures are not actively traded, it might choose to use heating oil futures contracts to hedge its exposure.

The *hedge ratio* is the ratio of the size of the position taken in futures contracts to the size of the exposure. When the asset underlying the futures contract is the same as the asset being hedged, it is natural to use a hedge ratio of 1.0. This is the hedge ratio we have used in the examples considered so far. For instance, in Example 6.2, the hedger's exposure was on 20,000 barrels of oil, and futures contracts were entered into for the delivery of exactly this amount of oil.

When cross hedging is used, setting the hedge ratio equal to 1.0 is not always optimal. The hedger should choose a value for the hedge ratio that minimizes the variance of the value of the hedged position. We now consider how the hedger can do this.

Calculating the Minimum Variance Hedge Ratio

The minimum variance hedge ratio depends on the relationship between changes in the spot price and changes in the futures price. Define:

ΔS: Change in spot price, S, during a period of time equal to the life of the hedge

ΔF: Change in futures price, F, during a period of time equal to the life of the hedge.

We will denote the minimum variance hedge ratio by h^*. It can be shown that h^* is the slope of the best-fit line from a linear regression of ΔS against ΔF (see Figure 6-2). This result is intuitively reasonable. We would expect h^* to be the ratio of the average change in S for a particular change in F.

The formula for h^* is:

$$h^* = \rho \frac{\sigma_S}{\sigma_F} \qquad \text{(6.1)}$$

where σ_S is the standard deviation of ΔS, σ_F is the standard deviation of ΔF, and ρ is the coefficient of correlation between the two.

Equation (6.1) shows that the optimal hedge ratio is the product of the coefficient of correlation between ΔS and ΔF and the ratio of the standard deviation of ΔS to the standard deviation of ΔF. Figure 6-3 shows how the

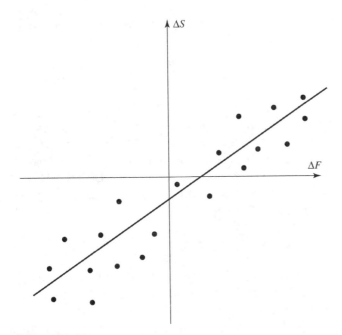

FIGURE 6-2 Regression of change in spot price against change in futures price.

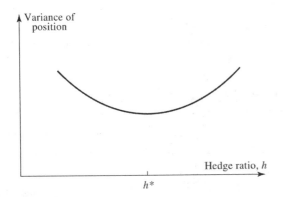

FIGURE 6-3 Dependence of variance of hedger's position on hedge ratio.

variance of the value of the hedger's position depends on the hedge ratio chosen.

If $\rho = 1$ and $\sigma_F = \sigma_S$, the hedge ratio, h^*, is 1.0. This result is to be expected, because in this case the futures price mirrors the spot price perfectly. If $\rho = 1$ and $\sigma_F = 2\sigma_S$, the hedge ratio h^* is 0.5. This result is also as expected, because in this case the futures price always changes by twice as much as the spot price. The *hedge effectiveness* can be defined as the proportion of the variance that is eliminated by hedging. This is the R^2 from the regression of ΔS against ΔF and equals ρ^2.

The parameters ρ, σ_F, and σ_S in Equation (6.1) are usually estimated from historical data on ΔS and ΔF. (The implicit assumption is that the future will in some sense be like the past.) A number of equal nonoverlapping time intervals are chosen, and the values of ΔS and ΔF for each of the intervals are observed. Ideally, the length of each time interval is the same as the length of the time interval for which the hedge is in effect. In practice, this sometimes severely limits the number of observations that are available, and a shorter time interval is used.

Optimal Number of Contracts

To calculate the number of contracts that should be used in hedging, define:

Q_A: Size of position being hedged (units)

Q_F: Size of one futures contract (units)

N^*: Optimal number of futures contracts for hedging

The futures contracts should be on h^*Q_A units of the asset. The number of futures contracts required is therefore given by

$$N^* = \frac{h^* Q_A}{Q_F} \qquad (6.2)$$

Example 6.3 will show how the results in this section can be used by an airline hedging the purchase of jet fuel.[3]

Example 6.3

An airline expects to purchase 2 million gallons of jet fuel in 1 month and decides to use heating oil futures for hedging. We suppose that Table 6-2 gives, for 15 successive months, data on the change, ΔS, in the jet fuel price per gallon and the corresponding change, ΔF, in the futures price for the contract on heating oil that would be used for hedging price changes during the month. In this case, the usual formulas for calculating standard deviations and correlations give $\sigma_F = 0.0313$, $\sigma_S = 0.263$, and $\rho = 0.928$.

From Equation (6.1), the minimum variance hedge ratio, h^*, is therefore

$$0.928 \times \frac{0.0263}{0.0313} = 0.7777$$

---

[3] Heating oil futures are more actively traded than jet fuel futures contracts. For an account of how Delta Airlines used heating oil futures to hedge its future purchases of jet fuel, see A. Ness, "Delta Wins on Fuel," *Risk*, June 2001: 8.

TABLE 6-2 Data to Calculate Minimum Variance Hedge Ratio When Heating Oil Futures Contract Is Used to Hedge Purchase of Jet Fuel

Month i	Change in heating oil futures price per gallon ($= \Delta F$)	Change in jet fuel price per gallon ($= \Delta S$)
1	0.021	0.029
2	0.035	0.020
3	−0.046	−0.044
4	0.001	0.008
5	0.044	0.026
6	−0.029	−0.019
7	−0.026	−0.010
8	−0.029	−0.007
9	0.048	0.043
10	−0.006	0.011
11	−0.036	−0.036
12	−0.011	−0.018
13	0.019	0.009
14	−0.027	−0.032
15	0.029	0.023

Each heating oil contract traded on NYMEX is on 42,000 gallons of heating oil. From Equation (6.2), the optimal number of contracts is

$$\frac{0.7777 \times 2,000,000}{42,000} = 37.03$$

or, rounding to the nearest whole number, 37.

Tailing the Hedge

When futures are used for hedging, a small adjustment, known as *tailing the hedge*, can be made to allow for the impact of daily settlement. In practice this means that Equation (6.2) becomes[4]

$$N^* = \frac{h * V_A}{V_F} \qquad \textbf{(6.3)}$$

where V_A is the dollar value of the position being hedged and V_F is the dollar value of one futures contract (the futures price times Q_F). Suppose that in Example 6.3 the spot price and the futures price are 1.94 and 1.99 dollars per gallon, respectively. Then $V_A = 2,000,000 \times 1.94 = 3,880,000$ while $V_F = 42,000 \times 1.99 = 83,580$, so that the optimal number of contracts is

$$\frac{0.7777 \times 3,880,000}{83,580} = 36.10$$

If we round this to the nearest whole number, the optimal number of contracts is now 36 rather than 37. The effect of tailing the hedge is to multiply the hedge ratio in Equation (6.2) by the ratio of the spot price to the futures price. Theoretically, the futures position used for hedging should then be adjusted as the spot price and futures price change, but in practice this usually makes very little difference.

If forward contracts rather than futures contracts are used, there is no daily settlement and Equation (6.2) should be used.

STOCK INDEX FUTURES

We now move on to consider stock index futures and how they are used to hedge or manage exposures to equity prices.

A *stock index* tracks changes in the value of a hypothetical portfolio of stocks. The weight of a stock in the portfolio at a particular time equals the proportion of the hypothetical portfolio invested in the stock at that time. The percentage increase in the stock index over a small interval of time is set equal to the percentage increase in the value of the hypothetical portfolio. Dividends are usually not included in the calculation so that the index tracks the capital gain/loss from investing in the portfolio.[5]

---

[4] See Problem 23 in Chapter 8 for an explanation of Equation (6.3).

[5] An exception to this is a *total return index.* This is calculated by assuming that dividends on the hypothetical portfolio are reinvested in the portfolio.

If the hypothetical portfolio of stocks remains fixed, the weights assigned to individual stocks in the portfolio do not remain fixed. When the price of one particular stock in the portfolio rises more sharply than others, more weight is automatically given to that stock. Sometimes indices are constructed from a hypothetical portfolio consisting of one of each of a number of stocks. The weights assigned to the stocks are then proportional to their market prices, with adjustments being made when there are stock splits. Other indices are constructed so that weights are proportional to market capitalization (stock price × number of shares outstanding). The underlying portfolio is then automatically adjusted to reflect stock splits, stock dividends, and new equity issues.

TABLE 6-3 Index Futures Quotes as Reported by Exchanges on May 26, 2010

	Open	High	Low	Settlement	Change	Volume	Open interest
Dow Jones Industrial Average, $10 times index (CME Group)							
June 2010	10080	10160	9921	9921	−104	533	12,353
Sept. 2010	10080	10085	9864	9864	−104	2	225
S&P 500, $250 times index (CME Group)							
June 2010	1080.0	1089.5	1060.5	1061.2	−11.8	43,076	296,397
Sept. 2010	1084.0	1085.5	1057.5	1057.0	−11.9	6,850	26,966
Dec. 2010	1074.0	1081.9	1052.9	1053.1	−11.8	7	4,326
Nasdaq-100, $100 times index (CME Group)							
June 2010	1827.0	1850.0	1788.0	1791.5	−24.0	2,350	20,674
Russell 1000, $100 times index (ICE)							
June 2010	595.4	601.0	586.4	585.7	−5.8	−1,214	19,275
US Dollar Index, $1000 times index (ICE)							
June 2010	86.725	87.480	86.625	87.244	0.356	37,321	35,401
Sept. 2010	87.270	87.800	87.050	87.584	0.356	74	2,533

Stock Indices

Table 6-3 shows futures prices for contracts on a number of different stock indices on May 26, 2010.

The *Dow Jones Industrial Average* is based on a portfolio consisting of 30 blue-chip stocks in the United States. The weights given to the stocks are proportional to their prices. The CME Group trades two futures contracts on the index. The one shown is on $10 times the index. The other (the Mini DJ Industrial Average) is on $5 times the index.

The *Standard & Poor's 500* (S&P 500) *Index* is based on a portfolio of 500 different stocks: 400 industrials, 40 utilities, 20 transportation companies, and 40 financial institutions. The weights of the stocks in the portfolio at any given time are proportional to their market capitalizations. The stocks are those of large publicly held companies that trade on NYSE Euronext or Nasdaq OMX. The CME Group trades two futures contracts on the S&P 500. The one shown is on $250 times the index; the other (the Mini S&P 500 contract) is on $50 times the index.

The *Nasdaq-100* is based on 100 stocks using the National Association of Securities Dealers Automatic Quotations Service. The CME Group trades two futures contracts. The one shown is on $100 times the index; the other (the Mini Nasdaq-100 contract) is on $20 times the index.

The *Russell 1000 Index* is an index of the prices of the 1,000 largest capitalization stocks in the United States. The *US Dollar Index* is a trade-weighted index of the values of six foreign currencies (the euro, yen, pound, Canadian dollar, Swedish krona, and Swiss franc).

As mentioned in Chapter 5, futures contracts on stock indices are settled in cash, not by delivery of the underlying asset. All contracts are marked to market to either the opening price or the closing price of the index on the last trading day, and the positions are then deemed to be closed. For example, contracts on the S&P 500 are closed out at the opening price of the S&P 500 index on the third Friday of the delivery month.

Hedging an Equity Portfolio

Stock index futures can be used to hedge a well-diversified equity portfolio. Define:

V_A: Current value of the portfolio

V_F: Current value of one futures contract (the futures price times the contract size).

If the portfolio mirrors the index, the optimal hedge ratio, h^*, equals 1.0 and Equation (6.3) shows that the number of futures contracts that should be shorted is

$$N^* = \frac{V_A}{V_F} \qquad \text{(6.4)}$$

Suppose, for example, that a portfolio worth $5,050,000 mirrors the S&P 500. The index futures price is 1,010 and each futures contract is on $250 times the index. In this case $V_A = 5,050,000$ and $V_F = 1,010 \times 250 = 252,500$, so that 20 contracts should be shorted to hedge the portfolio.

When the portfolio does not exactly mirror the index, we can use the capital asset pricing model. The parameter beta (β) from the capital asset pricing model is the slope of the best-fit line obtained when excess return on the portfolio over the risk-free rate is regressed against the excess return of the index over the risk-free rate. When β =1.0, the return on the portfolio tends to mirror the return on the index; when β = 2.0, the excess return on the portfolio tends to be twice as great as the excess return on the index; when β = 0.5, it tends to be half as great; and so on.

A portfolio with a β of 2.0 is twice as sensitive to movements in the index as a portfolio with a beta 1.0. It is therefore necessary to use twice as many contracts to hedge the portfolio. Similarly, a portfolio with a beta of 0.5 is half as sensitive to market movements as a portfolio with a beta of 1.0 and we should use half as many contracts to hedge it. In general,

$$N^* = \beta \frac{V_A}{V_F} \qquad \text{(6.5)}$$

This formula assumes that the maturity of the futures contract is close to the maturity of the hedge.

Comparing Equation (6.5) with Equation (6.3), we see that they imply $h^* = \beta$. This is not surprising. The hedge ratio h^* is the slope of the best-fit line when changes in the portfolio are regressed against changes in the futures price of the index. Beta (β) is the slope of the best-fit line when the return from the portfolio is regressed against the return for the index.

We illustrate that this formula gives good results by extending our earlier example. Suppose that a futures contract with 4 months to maturity is used to hedge the value of a portfolio over the next 3 months in the following situation:

> Value of S&P 500 index = 1,000
>
> S&P 500 futures price = 1,010
>
> Value of portfolio = $5,050,00
>
> Risk-free interest rate = 4% per annum
>
> Dividend yield on index = 1% per annum
>
> Beta of portfolio = 1.5.

One futures contract is for delivery of $250 times the index. As before $V_F = 250 \times 1,010 = 252,500$. From Equation (6.5), the number of futures contracts that should be shorted to hedge the portfolio is

$$1.5 \times \frac{5,050,000}{252,500} = 30$$

Suppose the index turns out to be 900 in 3 months and futures price is 902. The gain from the short futures position is then

$$30 \times (1010 - 902) \times 250 = \$810,000$$

The loss on the index is 10%. The index pays a dividend of 1% per annum, or 0.25% per 3 months. When dividends are taken into account, an investor in the index would therefore earn −9.75% over the 3-month period. Because the portfolio has a β of 1.5, the capital asset pricing model gives

> Expected return on portfolio − Risk-free interest rate
> = 1.5 × (Return on index − Risk-free interest rate)

The risk-free interest rate is approximately 1% per 3 months. It follows that the expected return (%) on the portfolio during the 3 months when the 3-month return on the index is −9.75% is

$$1.0 + [1.5 \times (-9.75 -1.0)] = -15.25$$

The expected value of the portfolio (inclusive of dividends) at the end of the 3 months is therefore

$$\$5,050,000 \times (1 - 015125) = \$4,286,187$$

It follows that the expected value of the hedger's position, including the gain on the hedge, is

$$\$4,286,187 + \$810,000 = \$5,096,187$$

Table 6-4 summarizes these calculations together with similar calculations for other values of the index at maturity. It can be seen that the total expected value of the

TABLE 6-4 Performance of Stock Index Hedge

Value of index in three months:	900	950	1,000	1,050	1,100
Futures price of index today:	1,010	1,010	1,010	1,010	1,010
Futures price of index in three months:	902	952	1,003	1,053	1,103
Gain on futures position ($):	810,000	435,000	52,500	−322,500	−697,500
Return on market:	−9.750%	−4.750%	0.250%	5.250%	10.250%
Expected return on portfolio:	−15.125%	−7.625%	−0.125%	7.375%	14.875%
Expected portfolio value in three months including dividends ($):	4,286,187	4,664,937	5,043,687	5,422,437	5,801,187
Total value of position in three months ($):	5,096,187	5,099,937	5,096,187	5,099,937	5,103,687

hedger's position in 3 months is almost independent of the value of the index.

The only thing we have not covered in this example is the relationship between futures prices and spot prices. We will see in Chapter 8 that the 1,010 assumed for the futures price today is roughly what we would expect given the interest rate and dividend we are assuming. The same is true of the futures prices in 3 months shown in Table 6-4.[6]

Reasons for Hedging an Equity Portfolio

Table 6-4 shows that the hedging procedure results in a value for the hedger's position at the end of the 3-month period being about 1% higher than at the beginning of the 3-month period. There is no surprise here. The risk-free rate is 4% per annum, or 1% per 3 months. The hedge results in the investor's position growing at the risk-free rate.

It is natural to ask why the hedger should go to the trouble of using futures contracts. To earn the risk-free

interest rate, the hedger can simply sell the portfolio and invest the proceeds in risk-free instruments such as Treasury bills.

One answer to this question is that hedging can be justified if the hedger feels that the stocks in the portfolio have been chosen well. In these circumstances, the hedger might be very uncertain about the performance of the market as a whole, but confident that the stocks in the portfolio will outperform the market (after appropriate adjustments have been made for the beta of the portfolio). A hedge using index futures removes the risk arising from market moves and leaves the hedger exposed only to the performance of the portfolio relative to the market. This will be discussed further shortly. Another reason for hedging may be that the hedger is planning to hold a portfolio for a long period of time and requires short-term protection in an uncertain market situation. The alternative strategy of selling the portfolio and buying it back later might involve unacceptably high transaction costs.

---

[6] The calculations in Table 6-4 assume that the dividend yield on the index is predictable, the risk-free interest rate remains constant, and the return on the index over the 3-month period is perfectly correlated with the return on the portfolio. In practice, these assumptions do not hold perfectly, and the hedge works rather less well than is indicated by Table 6-4.

Changing the Beta of a Portfolio

In the example in Table 6-4, the beta of the hedger's portfolio is reduced to zero so that the hedger's expected return is almost independent of the performance of the index. Sometimes futures contracts are used to change the beta of a portfolio to some value other than zero. Continuing with our earlier example:

S&P 500 index = 1,000

S&P 500 futures price = 1,010

Value of portfolio = $5,050,000

Beta of portfolio = 1.5

As before, $V_F = 250 \times 1,010 = 252,500$ and a complete hedge requires

$$1.5 \times \frac{5,050,000}{252,500} = 30$$

contracts to be shorted. To reduce the beta of the portfolio from 1.5 to 0.75, the number of contracts shorted should be 15 rather than 30; to increase the beta of portfolio to 2.0, a long position in 10 contracts should be taken; and so on. In general, to change the beta of the portfolio from β to β^*, where $\beta > \beta^*$, a short position in

$$(\beta - \beta^*)\frac{V_A}{V_F}$$

contracts is required. When $\beta < \beta^*$, a long position in

$$(\beta^* - \beta)\frac{V_A}{V_F}$$

contracts is required.

Locking in the Benefits of Stock Picking

Suppose you consider yourself to be good at picking stocks that will outperform the market. You own a single stock or a small portfolio of stocks. You do not know how well the market will perform over the next few months, but you are confident that your portfolio will do better than the market. What should you do?

You should short $\beta V_A / V_F$ index futures contracts, where β is the beta of your portfolio, V_A is the total value of the portfolio, and V_F is the current value of one index futures contract. If your portfolio performs better than a well-diversified portfolio with the same beta, you will then make money.

Consider an investor who in April holds 20,000 IBM shares, each worth $100. The investor feels that the market will be very volatile over the next three months but that IBM has a good chance of outperforming the market. The investor decides to use the August futures contract on the S&P 500 to hedge the market's return during the three-month period. The β of IBM is estimated at 1.1. Suppose that the current futures price for the August contract on the S&P 500 is 900. Each contract is for delivery of $250 times the index. In this case, $V_A = 20,000 \times 100 = 2,000,000$ and $V_F = 900 \times 250 = 225,000$. The number of contracts that should be shorted is therefore

$$1.1 \times \frac{2,000,000}{225,000} = 9.78$$

Rounding to the nearest integer, the investor shorts 10 contracts, closing out the position in July. Suppose IBM falls to $90 and the futures price of the S&P 500 falls to 750. The investor loses $20,000 \times (\$100 - \$90) = \$200,000$ on IBM, while gaining $10 \times 250 \times (900 - 750) = \$375,500$ on the futures contracts.

The overall gain to the investor in this case is $175,000 because IBM did not go down by as much as a well-diversified portfolio with a β of 1.1. If the market had gone up and IBM went up by more than a portfolio with a β of 1.1 (as expected by the investor), then a profit would be made in this case as well.

STACK AND ROLL

Sometimes the expiration date of the hedge is later than the delivery dates of all the futures contracts that can be used. The hedger must then roll the hedge forward by closing out one futures contract and taking the same position in a futures contract with a later delivery date. Hedges can be rolled forward many times. The procedure is known as *stack and roll*. Consider a company that wishes to use a short hedge to reduce the risk associated with the price to be received for an asset at time T. If there are futures contracts 1, 2, 3, . . . , n (not all necessarily in existence at the present time) with progressively later delivery dates, the company can use the following strategy:

Time t_1: Short futures contract 1

Time t_2: Close out futures contract 1
           Short futures contract 2

Time t_3: Close out futures contract 2
           Short futures contract 3

⋮

Time t_n: Close out futures contract $n - 1$
           Short futures contract n

Time T: Close our futures contract n.

Suppose that in April 2011 a company realizes that it will have 100,000 barrels of oil to sell in June 2012 and decides to hedge its risk with a hedge ratio of 1.0. (In this example, we do not make the "tailing" adjustment described earlier). The current spot price is $69. Although futures contracts are traded with maturities stretching several years into the future, we suppose that only the first six delivery months have sufficient liquidity to meet the company's needs. The company therefore shorts 100 October 2011 contracts. In September 2011, it rolls the hedge forward into the March 2012 contract. In February 2012, it rolls the hedge forward again into the July 2010 contract.

One possible outcome is shown in Table 6-5. The October 2011 contract is shorted at $68.20 per barrel and closed out at $67.40 per barrel for a profit of $0.80 per barrel; the March 2012 contract is shorted at $67.00 per barrel and closed out at $66.50 per barrel for a profit of $0.50 per barrel. The July 2012 contract is shorted at $66.30 per barrel and closed out at $65.90 per barrel for a profit of $0.40 per barrel. The final spot price is $66.

The dollar gain per barrel of oil from the short futures contracts is

$$(68.20 - 67.40) + (67.00 - 66.50) + (66.30 - 65.90) = 1.70$$

The oil price declined from $69 to $66. Receiving only $1.70 per barrel compensation for a price decline of $3.00 may appear unsatisfactory. However, we cannot expect total compensation for a price decline when futures prices are below spot prices. The best we can hope for is to lock in the futures price that would apply to a June 2012 contract if it were actively traded.

In practice, a company usually has an exposure every month to the underlying asset and uses a 1-month futures contract for hedging because it is the most liquid. Initially it enters into ("stacks") sufficient contracts to cover its exposure to the end of its hedging horizon. One month later, it closes out all the contracts and "rolls" them into new 1-month contracts to cover its new exposure, and so on.

As described in Box 6-2, a German company, Metallgesellschaft, followed this strategy in the early 1990s to hedge contracts it had entered into to supply commodities at a fixed price. It ran into difficulties because the prices of the commodities declined so that there were immediate cash outflows on the futures and, at that time, only the expectation of eventual gains on the contracts. This mismatch between the timing of the cash flows on the hedge and the timing of the cash flows from the position being hedged led to liquidity problems that could not be handled. The moral of the story is that potential liquidity problems should always be considered when a hedging strategy is being planned.

TABLE 6-5 Data for the Example on Rolling Oil Hedge Forward

Date	Apr. 2011	Sept. 2011	Feb. 2012	June 2012
Oct. 2011 futures price	68.20	67.40		
Mar. 2012 futures price		67.00	66.50	
July 2012 futures price			66.30	65.90
Spot price	69.00			66.00

BOX 6-2 Metallgesellschaft: Hedging Gone Awry

Sometimes rolling hedges forward can lead to cash flow pressures. The problem was illustrated dramatically by the activities of a German company, Metallgesellschaft (MG), in the early 1990s.

MG sold a huge volume of 5- to 10-year heating oil and gasoline fixed-price supply contracts to its customers at 6 to 8 cents above market prices. It hedged its exposure with long positions in short-dated futures contracts that were rolled forward. As it turned out, the price of oil fell and there were margin calls on the futures positions. Considerable short-term cash flow pressures were placed on MG. The members of MG who devised the hedging strategy argued that these short-term cash outflows were offset by positive cash flows that would ultimately be realized on the long-term fixed-price contracts. However, the company's senior management and its bankers became concerned about the huge cash drain. As a result, the company closed out all the hedge positions and agreed with its customers that the fixed-price contracts would be abandoned. The outcome was a loss to MG of $1.33 billion.

SUMMARY

This chapter has discussed various ways in which a company can take a position in futures contracts to offset an exposure to the price of an asset. If the exposure is such that the company gains when the price of the asset increases and loses when the price of the asset decreases, a short hedge is appropriate. If the exposure is the other way round (i.e., the company gains when the price of the asset decreases and loses when the price of the asset increases), a long hedge is appropriate.

Hedging is a way of reducing risk. As such, it should be welcomed by most executives. In reality, there are a number of theoretical and practical reasons why companies do not hedge. On a theoretical level, we can argue that shareholders, by holding well-diversified portfolios, can eliminate many of the risks faced by a company.

They do not require the company to hedge these risks. On a practical level, a company may find that it is increasing rather than decreasing risk by hedging if none of its competitors does so. Also, a treasurer may fear criticism from other executives if the company makes a gain from movements in the price of the underlying asset and a loss on the hedge.

An important concept in hedging is basis risk. The basis is the difference between the spot price of an asset and its futures price. Basis risk arises from uncertainty as to what the basis will be at maturity of the hedge.

The hedge ratio is the ratio of the size of the position taken in futures contracts to the size of the exposure. It is not always optimal to use a hedge ratio of 1.0. If the hedger wishes to minimize the variance of a position, a hedge ratio different from 1.0 may be appropriate. The optimal hedge ratio is the slope of the best-fit line obtained when changes in the spot price are regressed against changes in the future price.

Stock index futures can be used to hedge the systematic risk in an equity portfolio. The number of futures contracts required is the beta of the portfolio multiplied by the ratio of the value of the portfolio to the value of one futures contract. Stock index futures can also be used to change the beta of a portfolio without changing the stocks that make up the portfolio.

When there is no liquid futures contract that matures later than the expiration of the hedge, a strategy known as stack and roll may be appropriate. This involves entering into a sequence of futures contracts. When the first futures contract is near expiration, it is closed out and the hedger enters into a second contract with a later delivery month. When the second contract is close to expiration, it is closed out and the hedger enters into a third contract with a later delivery month; and so on. The result of all this is the creation of a long-dated futures contract by trading a series of short-dated contracts.

Further Reading

Allayannis, G., and J. Wetson. "The Use of Foreign Currency Derivatives and Firm Market Value," *Review of Financial Studies*, 14, 1 (Spring 2001): 243–76.

Bodnar, G. M., G. S. Hayt, and R. C. Marston. "1998 Wharton Survey of Financial Risk Management by U.S. Non-Financial Firms," *Financial Management*, 2, 4 (1998): 70–91.

Brown G. W. "Managing Foreign Exchange Risk with Derivatives." *Journal of Financial Economics*, 60 (2001): 401–48.

Culp, C. and M. H. Miller. "Metallgesellschaft and the Economics of Synthetic Storage," *Journal of Applied Corporate Finance*, 7, 4 (Winter 1995): 62–76.

Campbell, J. Y., K. Serfaty-de Mederios, and L. M. Viceira. "Global Currency Hedging," *Journal of Finance*, 65, 1 (February 2010): 87–121.

Cotter, J., and J. Hanly. "Hedging: Scaling and the Investor Horizon," *Journal of Risk*, 12, 2 (Winter 2009/2010): 49–77.

Ederington, L. H. "The Hedging Performance of the New Futures Market," *Journal of Finance*, 34 (March 1979): 157–70.

Edwards, F. R. and M. S. Canter. "The Collapse of Metallgesellschaft: Unhedgeable Risks, Poor Hedging Strategy, or Just Bad Luck?" *Journal of Applied Corporate Finance*, 8, 1 (Spring 1995): 86–105.

Geczy, C., B. A. Minton, and C. Schrand. "Why Firms Use Currency Derivatives," *Journal of Finance*, 52, 4 (1997): 1323–54.

Graham, J. R. and C. W. Smith, Jr. "Tax Incentives to Hedge," *Journal of Finance*, 54, 6 (1999): 2241–62.

Haushalter, G. D. "Financing Policy, Basis Risk, and Corporate Hedging: Evidence from Oil and Gas Producers," *Journal of Finance*, 55, 1 (2000): 107–52.

Mello, A. S. and J. E. Parsons. "Hedging and Liquidity," *Review of Financial Studies*, 13 (Spring 2000): 127–53.

Neuberger, A. J. "Hedging Long-Term Exposures with Multiple Short-Term Futures Contracts," *Review of Financial Studies*, 12 (1999): 429–59.

Petersen, M. A. and S. R. Thiagarajan, "Risk Management and Hedging: With and Without Derivatives," *Financial Management*, 29, 4 (Winter 2000): 5–30.

Rendleman, R. "A Reconciliation of Potentially Conflicting Approaches to Hedging with Futures," *Advances in Futures and Options*, 6 (1993): 81–92.

Stulz, R. M. "Optimal Hedging Policies," *Journal of Financial and Quantitative Analysis*, 19 (June 1984): 127–40.

Tufano, P. "Who Manages Risk? An Empirical Examination of Risk Management Practices in the Gold Mining Industry," *Journal of Finance*, 51, 4 (1996): 1097–1138.

Tufano, P. "The Determinants of Stock Price Exposure: Financial Engineering and the Gold Mining Industry," *Journal of Finance*, 53, 3 (1998): 1015–52.

Interest Rates

7

Learning Objectives

Candidates, after completing this reading, should be able to:

- Describe Treasury rates, LIBOR, and repo rates, and explain what is meant by the "risk-free" rate.
- Calculate the value of an investment using different compounding frequencies.
- Convert interest rates based on different compounding frequencies.
- Calculate the theoretical price of a bond using spot rates.
- Calculate forward interest rates from a set of spot rates.

- Calculate the value of the cash flows from a forward rate agreement (FRA).
- Calculate the duration, modified duration, and dollar duration of a bond.
- Describe the limitations of duration and explain how convexity addresses some of them.
- Calculate the change in a bond's price given its duration, its convexity, and a change in interest rates.
- Describe the major theories of the term structure of interest rates.

Excerpt is Chapter 4 of Options, Futures, and Other Derivatives, *Eighth Edition, by John Hull.*

Interest rates are a factor in the valuation of virtually all derivatives and will feature prominently in much of the material that will be presented in the rest of this book. This chapter deals with some fundamental issues concerned with the way interest rates are measured and analyzed. It explains the compounding frequency used to define an interest rate and the meaning of continuously compounded interest rates, which are used extensively in the analysis of derivatives. It covers zero rates, par yields, and yield curves, discusses bond pricing, and outlines a "bootstrap" procedure commonly used by a derivatives trading desk to calculate zero-coupon Treasury interest rates. It also covers forward rates and forward rate agreements and reviews different theories of the term structure of interest rates. Finally, it explains the use of duration and convexity measures to determine the sensitivity of bond prices to interest rate changes.

Chapter 9 will cover interest rate futures and show how the duration measure can be used when interest rate exposures are hedged. For ease of exposition, day count conventions will be ignored throughout this chapter. The nature of these conventions and their impact on calculations will be discussed in Chapters 9 and 10.

TYPES OF RATES

An interest rate in a particular situation defines the amount of money a borrower promises to pay the lender. For any given currency, many different types of interest rates are regularly quoted. These include mortgage rates, deposit rates, prime borrowing rates, and so on. The interest rate applicable in a situation depends on the credit risk. This is the risk that there will be a default by the borrower of funds, so that the interest and principal are not paid to the lender as promised. The higher the credit risk, the higher the interest rate that is promised by the borrower.

Treasury Rates

Treasury rates are the rates an investor earns on Treasury bills and Treasury bonds. These are the instruments used by a government to borrow in its own currency. Japanese Treasury rates are the rates at which the Japanese government borrows in yen; US Treasury rates are the rates

at which the US government borrows in US dollars; and so on. It is usually assumed that there is no chance that a government will default on an obligation denominated in its own currency. Treasury rates are therefore totally risk-free rates in the sense that an investor who buys a Treasury bill or Treasury bond is certain that interest and principal payments will be made as promised.

LIBOR

LIBOR is short for *London Interbank Offered Rate*. It is a reference interest rate, produced once a day by the British Bankers' Association, and is designed to reflect the rate of interest at which banks are prepared to make large wholesale deposits with other banks. LIBOR is quoted in all major currencies for maturities up to 12 months: 1-month LIBOR is the rate at which 1-month deposits are offered, 3-month LIBOR is the rate at which 3-month deposits are offered, and so on.

A deposit with a bank can be regarded as a loan to that bank. A bank must therefore satisfy certain creditworthiness criteria in order to be able to receive deposits from another bank at LIBOR. Typically it must have a AA credit rating.[1]

A rate closely related to LIBOR is LIBID. This is the *London Interbank Bid Rate* and is the rate at which banks will accept deposits from other banks. At any specified time, there is a small spread between LIBID and LIBOR rates (with LIBOR higher than LIBID). The rates themselves are determined by active trading between banks and adjust so that the supply of funds in the interbank market equals the demand for funds in that market. For example, if more banks want to borrow US dollars for 3 months than lend US dollars for 3 months, the 3-month US LIBID and LIBOR rates will increase. Similarly, if more banks want to lend 3-month funds than borrow these funds, the 3-month LIBID and LIBOR rates will decrease. This interbank market is known as the *Eurocurrency market*. It is outside the control of any one government.

Repo Rates

Sometimes trading activities are funded with a *repurchase agreement*, or *repo*. This is a contract where an investment

---

[1] The best credit rating given to a company by rating agencies S&P and Fitch is AAA. The second best is AA. The corresponding ratings from Moody's are Aaa and Aa, respectively.

dealer who owns securities agrees to sell them to another company now and buy them back later at a slightly higher price. The other company is providing a loan to the investment dealer. The difference between the price at which the securities are sold and the price at which they are repurchased is the interest it earns. The interest rate is referred to as the *repo rate.* If structured carefully, the loan involves very little credit risk. If the borrower does not honor the agreement, the lending company simply keeps the securities. If the lending company does not keep to its side of the agreement, the original owner of the securities keeps the cash. The most common type of repo is an *overnight repo,* in which the agreement is renegotiated each day. However, longer-term arrangements, known as *term repos,* are sometimes used.

The Risk-Free Rate

The "risk-free rate" is used extensively in the evaluation of derivatives. It might be thought that derivatives traders would use the interest rates implied by Treasury bills and bonds as risk-free rates. In fact, they do not do this. As indicated in Box 7-1, there are a number of tax and regulatory issues that cause Treasury rates to be artificially low.

Financial institutions have traditionally used LIBOR rates as risk-free rates. For a AA-rated financial institution LIBOR is the short-term opportunity cost of capital. The financial institution can borrow short-term funds at the LIBOR quotes of other financial institutions and can lend funds to other financial institutions at its own LIBOR quotes. LIBOR rates are not totally free of credit risk. For example, when funds are lent at 3-month LIBOR to a AA-rated financial institution, there is a small chance that it will default during the 3 months. However, they are close to risk-free in normal market conditions. LIBOR rates have maturities up to 1 year. As we will explain later, traders have traditionally used Eurodollar futures and interest rate swaps to extend the risk-free LIBOR yield curve beyond 1 year.

The credit crisis that started in 2007 caused many derivatives dealers to critically review their practices. This is because banks became very reluctant to lend to each other during the crisis and LIBOR rates soared. Many dealers have now switched to using the overnight indexed swap (OIS) rate as a proxy for the risk-free rate. It is closer to risk-free than LIBOR.

MEASURING INTEREST RATES

A statement by a bank that the interest rate on one-year deposits is 10% per annum sounds straightforward and unambiguous. In fact, its precise meaning depends on the way the interest rate is measured.

If the interest rate is measured with annual compounding, the bank's statement that the interest rate is 10% means that $100 grows to

$$\$100 \times 1.1 = \$110$$

at the end of 1 year. When the interest rate is measured with semiannual compounding, it means that 5% is earned every 6 months, with the interest being reinvested. In this case $100 grows to

$$\$100 \times 1.05 \times 1.05 = \$110.25$$

at the end of 1 year. When the interest rate is measured with quarterly compounding, the bank's statement means

TABLE 7-1 Effect of the Compounding Frequency on the Value of $100 at the End of 1 Year When the Interest Rate Is 10% per Annum

Compounding Frequency	Value of $100 at End of Year ($)
Annually ($m = 1$)	110.00
Semiannually ($m = 2$)	110.25
Quarterly ($m = 4$)	110.38
Monthly ($m = 12$)	110.47
Weekly ($m = 52$)	110.51
Daily ($m = 365$)	110.52

that 2.5% is earned every 3 months, with the interest being reinvested. The $100 then grows to

$$\$100 \times 1.025^4 = \$110.38$$

at the end of 1 year. Table 7-1 shows the effect of increasing the compounding frequency further.

The compounding frequency defines the units in which an interest rate is measured. A rate expressed with one compounding frequency can be converted into an equivalent rate with a different compounding frequency. For example, from Table 7-1 we see that 10.25% with annual compounding is equivalent to 10% with semiannual compounding. We can think of the difference between one compounding frequency and another to be analogous to the difference between kilometers and miles. They are two different units of measurement.

To generalize our results, suppose that an amount A is invested for n years at an interest rate of R per annum. If the rate is compounded once per annum, the terminal value of the investment is

$$A(1 + R)^n$$

If the rate is compounded m times per annum, the terminal value of the investment is

$$A\left(1 + \frac{R}{m}\right)^{mn} \qquad \textbf{(7.1)}$$

When $m = 1$, the rate is sometimes referred to as the *equivalent annual interest rate.*

Continuous Compounding

The limit as the compounding frequency, m, tends to infinity is known as *continuous compounding.*[2] With continuous compounding, it can be shown that an amount A invested for n years at rate R grows to

$$Ae^{Rn} \qquad \textbf{(7.2)}$$

where $e = 2.71828$. The exponential function, e^x, is built into most calculators, so the computation of the expression in Equation (7.2) presents no problems. In the example in Table 7-1, $A = 100$, $n = 1$, and $R = 0.1$, so that the value to which A grows with continuous compounding is

$$100e^{0.1} = \$110.52$$

This is (to two decimal places) the same as the value with daily compounding. For most practical purposes, continuous compounding can be thought of as being equivalent to daily compounding. Compounding a sum of money at a continuously compounded rate R for n years involves multiplying it by e^{Rn}. Discounting it at a continuously compounded rate R for n years involves multiplying by e^{-Rn}.

In this book, interest rates will be measured with continuous compounding except where stated otherwise. Readers used to working with interest rates that are measured with annual, semiannual, or some other compounding frequency may find this a little strange at first. However, continuously compounded interest rates are used to such a great extent in pricing derivatives that it makes sense to get used to working with them now.

Suppose that R_c is a rate of interest with continuous compounding and R_m is the equivalent rate with compounding m times per annum. From the results in Equations (7.1) and (7.2), we have

$$Ae^{R_c n} = A\left(1 + \frac{R_m}{m}\right)^{mn}$$

or

$$e^{R_c} = \left(1 + \frac{R_m}{m}\right)^{m}$$

This means that

$$R_c = m \ln\left(1 + \frac{R_m}{m}\right) \qquad \textbf{(7.3)}$$

---

[2] Actuaries sometimes refer to a continuously compounded rate as the *force of interest.*

and

$$R_m = m(e^{R_c/m} - 1) \qquad \textbf{(7.4)}$$

These equations can be used to convert a rate with a compounding frequency of m times per annum to a continuously compounded rate and vice versa. The natural logarithm function $\ln x$, which is built into most calculators, is the *inverse* of the exponential function, so that, if $y = \ln x$, then $x = e^y$.

Example 7.1

Consider an interest rate that is quoted as 10% per annum with semiannual compounding. From Equation (7.3) with $m = 2$ and $R_m = 0.1$, the equivalent rate with continuous compounding is

$$2 \ln\left(1 + \frac{0.1}{2}\right) = 0.09758$$

or 9.758% per annum.

Example 7.2

Suppose that a lender quotes the interest rate on loans as 8% per annum with continuous compounding, and that interest is actually paid quarterly. From Equation (7.4) with $m = 4$ and $R_c = 0.08$, the equivalent rate with quarterly compounding is

$$4 \times (e^{0.08/4} - 1) = 0.0808$$

or 8.08% per annum. This means that on a $1,000 loan, interest payments of $20.20 would be required each quarter.

ZERO RATES

The n-year zero-coupon interest rate is the rate of interest earned on an investment that starts today and lasts for n years. All the interest and principal is realized at the end of n years. There are no intermediate payments. The n-year zero-coupon interest rate is sometimes also referred to as the n-year *spot rate,* the n-year *zero rate,* or just the n-year *zero.* Suppose a 5-year zero rate with continuous compounding is quoted as 5% per annum. This means that $100, if invested for 5 years, grows to

$$100 \times e^{0.05 \times 5} = 128.40$$

Most of the interest rates we observe directly in the market are not pure zero rates. Consider a 5-year government bond

that provides a 6% coupon. The price of this bond does not by itself determine the 5-year Treasury zero rate because some of the return on the bond is realized in the form of coupons prior to the end of year 5. Later in this chapter we will discuss how we can determine Treasury zero rates from the market prices of coupon-bearing bonds.

BOND PRICING

Most bonds pay coupons to the holder periodically. The bond's principal (which is also known as its par value or face value) is paid at the end of its life. The theoretical price of a bond can be calculated as the present value of all the cash flows that will be received by the owner of the bond. Sometimes bond traders use the same discount rate for all the cash flows underlying a bond, but a more accurate approach is to use a different zero rate for each cash flow.

To illustrate this, consider the situation where Treasury zero rates, measured with continuous compounding, are as in Table 7-2. (We explain later how these can be calculated.) Suppose that a 2-year Treasury bond with a principal of $100 provides coupons at the rate of 6% per annum semiannually. To calculate the present value of the first coupon of $3, we discount it at 5.0% for 6 months; to calculate the present value of the second coupon of $3, we discount it at 5.8% for 1 year; and so on. Therefore the theoretical price of the bond is

$$3e^{-0.05 \times 0.5} + 3e^{-0.058 \times 1.0} + 3e^{-0.064 \times 1.5} + 103e^{-0.068 \times 2.0} = 98.39$$

or $98.39.

Bond Yield

A bond's yield is the single discount rate that, when applied to all cash flows, gives a bond price equal to its

TABLE 7-2 Treasury Zero Rates

Maturity (Years)	Zero Rate (%) (Continuously Compounded)
0.5	5.0
1.0	5.8
1.5	6.4
2.0	6.8

market price. Suppose that the theoretical price of the bond we have been considering, $98.39, is also its market value (i.e., the market's price of the bond is in exact agreement with the data in Table 7-2). If y is the yield on the bond, expressed with continuous compounding, it must be true that

$$3e^{-y \times 0.5} + 3e^{-y \times 1.0} + 3e^{-y \times 1.5} + 103e^{-y \times 2.0} = 98.39$$

This equation can be solved using an iterative ("trial and error") procedure to give $y = 6.76\%$.[3]

Par Yield

The *par yield* for a certain bond maturity is the coupon rate that causes the bond price to equal its par value. (The par value is the same as the principal value.) Usually the bond is assumed to provide semiannual coupons. Suppose that the coupon on a 2-year bond in our example is c per annum (or $\frac{1}{2}c$ per 6 months). Using the zero rates in Table 7-2, the value of the bond is equal to its par value of 100 when

$$\frac{c}{2}e^{-0.05 \times 0.5} + \frac{c}{2}e^{-0.058 \times 1.0} + \frac{c}{2}e^{-0.064 \times 1.5} + \left(100 + \frac{c}{2}\right)e^{-0.068 \times 2.0} = 100$$

This equation can be solved in a straightforward way to give $c = 6.87$. The 2-year par yield is therefore 6.87% per annum. This has semiannual compounding because payments are assumed to be made every 6 months. With continuous compounding, the rate is 6.75% per annum.

More generally, if d is the present value of $1 received at the maturity of the bond, A is the value of an annuity that pays one dollar on each coupon payment date, and m is the number of coupon payments per year, then the par yield c must satisfy

$$100 = A\frac{c}{m} + 100d$$

so that

$$c = \frac{(100 - 100d)m}{A}$$

In our example, $m = 2$, $d = e^{-0.068 \times 2} = 0.87284$, and

$$A = e^{-0.05 \times 0.5} + e^{-0.058 \times 1.0} + e^{-0.064 \times 1.5} + e^{-0.068 \times 2.0} = 3.70027$$

The formula confirms that the par yield is 6.87% per annum.

DETERMINING TREASURY ZERO RATES

One way of determining Treasury zero rates such as those in Table 7-2 is to observe the yields on "strips." These are zero-coupon bonds that are synthetically created by traders when they sell coupons on a Treasury bond separately from the principal.

Another way to determine Treasury zero rates is from Treasury bills and coupon-bearing bonds. The most popular approach is known as the *bootstrap method*. To illustrate the nature of the method, consider the data in Table 7-3 on the prices of five bonds. Because the first three bonds pay no coupons, the zero rates corresponding to the maturities of these bonds can easily be calculated. The 3-month bond has the effect of turning an investment of 97.5 into 100 in 3 months. The continuously compounded 3-month rate R is therefore given by solving

$$100 = 97.5e^{R \times 0.25}$$

It is 10.127% per annum. The 6-month continuously compounded rate is similarly given by solving

$$100 = 94.9e^{R \times 0.5}$$

TABLE 7-3 Data for Bootstrap Method

Bond Principal ($)	Time to Maturity (Years)	Annual Coupon* ($)	Bond Price ($)
100	0.25	0	97.5
100	0.50	0	94.9
100	1.00	0	90.0
100	1.50	8	96.0
100	2.00	12	101.6

*Half the stated coupon is assumed to be paid every 6 months.

---

[3] One way of solving nonlinear equations of the form $f(y) = 0$, such as this one, is to use the Newton–Raphson method. We start with an estimate y_0 of the solution and produce successively better estimates $y_1, y_2, y_3, \ldots$ using the formula $y_{i+1} = y_i - f(y_i)/f'(y_i)$, where $f'(y)$ denotes the derivative of f with respect to y.

It is 10.469% per annum. Similarly, the 1-year rate with continuous compounding is given by solving

$$100 = 90e^{R \times 1.0}$$

It is 10.536% per annum.

The fourth bond lasts 1.5 years. The payments are as follows:

6 months: $4

1 year: $4

1.5 years: $104

From our earlier calculations, we know that the discount rate for the payment at the end of 6 months is 10.469% and that the discount rate for the payment at the end of 1 year is 10.536%. We also know that the bond's price, $96, must equal the present value of all the payments received by the bondholder. Suppose the 1.5-year zero rate is denoted by R. It follows that

$$4e^{-0.10469 \times 0.5} + 4e^{-0.10536 \times 1.0} + 104e^{-R \times 1.5} = 96$$

This reduces to

$$e^{-1.5R} = 0.85196$$

or

$$R = -\frac{\ln(0.85196)}{1.5} = 0.10681$$

The 1.5-year zero rate is therefore 10.681%. This is the only zero rate that is consistent with the 6-month rate, 1-year rate, and the data in Table 7-3.

The 2-year zero rate can be calculated similarly from the 6-month, 1-year, and 1.5-year zero rates, and the information on the last bond in Table 7-3. If R is the 2-year zero rate, then

$$6e^{-0.10469 \times 0.5} + 6e^{-0.10536 \times 1.0} + 6e^{-0.10681 \times 1.5} + 106e^{-R \times 2.0} = 101.6$$

This gives $R = 0.10808$, or 10.808%.

The rates we have calculated are summarized in Table 7-4. A chart showing the zero rate as a function of maturity is known as the *zero curve*. A common assumption is that the zero curve is linear between the points determined using the bootstrap method. (This means that the 1.25-year zero rate is $0.5 \times 10.536 + 0.5 \times 10.681 = 10.6085\%$ in our example.) It is also usually assumed that the zero curve is horizontal prior to the first point and horizontal

beyond the last point. Figure 7-1 shows the zero curve for our data using these assumptions. By using longer maturity bonds, the zero curve would be more accurately determined beyond 2 years.

In practice, we do not usually have bonds with maturities equal to exactly 1.5 years, 2 years, 2.5 years, and so on. The approach often used by analysts is to interpolate between the bond price data before it is used to calculate the zero curve. For example, if they know that a 2.3-year bond with a coupon of 6% sells for 98 and a 2.7-year bond with a coupon of 6.5% sells for 99, it might be assumed that a 2.5-year bond with a coupon of 6.25% would sell for 98.5.

FORWARD RATES

Forward interest rates are the rates of interest implied by current zero rates for periods of time in the future. To illustrate how they are calculated, we suppose that LIBOR zero

TABLE 7-4 Continuously Compounded Zero Rates Determined from Data in Table 7-3

Maturity (Years)	Zero Rate (%) (Continuously Compounded)
0.25	10.127
0.50	10.469
1.00	10.536
1.50	10.681
2.00	10.808

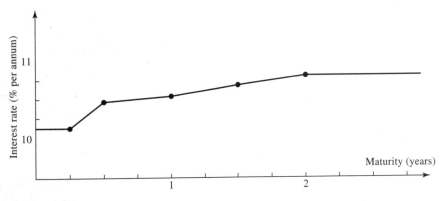

FIGURE 7-1 Zero rates given by the bootstrap method.

TABLE 7-5   Calculation of Forward LIBOR Rates

Year (n)	Zero Rate for an n-Year Investment (% per Annum)	Forward Rate for nth Year (% per Annum)
1	3.0	
2	4.0	5.0
3	4.6	5.8
4	5.0	6.2
5	5.3	6.5

rates are as shown in the second column of Table 7-5. (As we shall see in Chapter 10, LIBOR zero rates are calculated in a similar way to the Treasury zero rates calculated in the previous section.) The rates are assumed to be continuously compounded. Thus, the 3% per annum rate for 1 year means that, in return for an investment of $100 today, an amount $100e^{0.03 \times 1} = \$103.05$ is received in 1 year; the 4% per annum rate for 2 years means that, in return for an investment of $100 today, an amount $100e^{0.04 \times 2} = \$108.33$ is received in 2 years; and so on.

The forward interest rate in Table 7-5 for year 2 is 5% per annum. This is the rate of interest that is implied by the zero rates for the period of time between the end of the first year and the end of the second year. It can be calculated from the 1-year zero interest rate of 3% per annum and the 2-year zero interest rate of 4% per annum. It is the rate of interest for year 2 that, when combined with 3% per annum for year 1, gives 4% overall for the 2 years. To show that the correct answer is 5% per annum, suppose that $100 is invested. A rate of 3% for the first year and 5% for the second year gives

$$100e^{0.03 \times 1}e^{0.05 \times 1} = \$108.33$$

at the end of the second year. A rate of 4% per annum for 2 years gives

$$100e^{0.04 \times 2}$$

which is also $108.33. This example illustrates the general result that when interest rates are continuously compounded and rates in successive time periods are combined, the overall equivalent rate is simply the average rate during the whole period. In our example, 3% for the first year and 5% for the second year average to 4% over

the 2 years. The result is only approximately true when the rates are not continuously compounded.

The forward rate for year 3 is the rate of interest that is implied by a 4% per annum 2-year zero rate and a 4.6% per annum 3-year zero rate. It is 5.8% per annum. The reason is that an investment for 2 years at 4% per annum combined with an investment for one year at 5.8% per annum gives an overall average return for the three years of 4.6% per annum. The other forward rates can be calculated similarly and are shown in the third column of the table. In general, if R_1 and R_2 are the zero rates for maturities T_1 and T_2, respectively, and R_F is the forward interest rate for the period of time between T_1 and T_2, then

$$R_F = \frac{R_2 T_2 - R_1 T_1}{T_2 - T_1} \quad (7.5)$$

To illustrate this formula, consider the calculation of the year-4 forward rate from the data in Table 7-5: $T_1 = 3$, $T_2 = 4$, $R_1 = 0.046$, and $R_2 = 0.05$, and the formula gives $R_F = 0.062$.

Equation (7.5) can be written as

$$R_F = R_2 + (R_2 - R_1)\frac{T_1}{T_2 - T_1} \quad (7.6)$$

This shows that if the zero curve is upward sloping between T_1 and T_2, so that $R_2 > R_1$, then $R_F > R_2$ (i.e., the forward rate for a period of time ending at T_2 is greater than the T_2 zero rate). Similarly, if the zero curve is downward sloping with $R_2 < R_1$, then $R_F < R_2$ (i.e., the forward rate is less than the T_2 zero rate). Taking limits as T_2 approaches T_1 in Equation (7.6) and letting the common value of the two be T, we obtain

$$R_F = R + T\frac{\partial R}{\partial T}$$

where R is the zero rate for a maturity of T. The value of R_F obtained in this way is known as the *instantaneous forward rate* for a maturity of T. This is the forward rate that is applicable to a very short future time period that begins at time T. Define $P(0, T)$ as the price of a zero-coupon bond maturing at time T. Because $P(0, T) = e^{-RT}$, the equation for the instantaneous forward rate can also be written as

$$R_F = -\frac{\partial}{\partial T}\ln P(0, T)$$

By borrowing and lending at LIBOR, a large financial institution can lock in LIBOR forward rates. Suppose LIBOR zero rates are as in Table 7-5. It can borrow $100 at 3% for 1 year and invest the money at 4% for 2 years, the result is a cash outflow of $100e^{0.03 \times 1} = \$103.05$ at the end of year 1 and an inflow of $100e^{0.04 \times 2} = \$108.33$ at the end of year 2. Since $108.33 = 103.05e^{0.05}$, a return equal to the forward rate (5%) is earned on $103.05 during the second year. Alternatively, it can borrow $100 for four years at 5% and invest it for three years at 4.6%. The result is a cash inflow of $100e^{0.046 \times 3} = \$114.80$ at the end of the third year and a cash outflow of $100e^{0.05 \times 4} = \$122.14$ at the end of the fourth year. Since $122.14 = 114.80e^{0.062}$, money is being borrowed for the fourth year at the forward rate of 6.2%.

If a large investor thinks that rates in the future will be different from today's forward rates there are many trading strategies that the investor will find attractive (see Box 7-2). One of these involves entering into a contract known as a *forward rate agreement*. We will now discuss how this contract works and how it is valued.

FORWARD RATE AGREEMENTS

A forward rate agreement (FRA) is an over-the-counter agreement designed to ensure that a certain interest rate will apply to either borrowing or lending a certain principal during a specified future period of time. The assumption underlying the contract is that the borrowing or lending would normally be done at LIBOR.

Consider a forward rate agreement where company X is agreeing to lend money to company Y for the period of time between T_1 and T_2. Define:

R_K: The rate of interest agreed to in the FRA

R_F: The forward LIBOR interest rate for the period between times T_1 and T_2, calculated today[4]

R_M: The actual LIBOR interest rate observed in the market at time T_1 for the period between times T_1 and T_2

L: The principal underlying the contract

We will depart from our usual assumption of continuous compounding and assume that the rates R_K, R_F, and R_M are all measured with a compounding frequency reflecting

---

[4] LIBOR forward rates are calculated as described earlier from the LIBOR/swap zero curve. The latter is determined in the way described in Chapter 10.

the length of the period to which they apply. This means that if $T_2 - T_1 = 0.5$, they are expressed with semiannual compounding; if $T_2 - T_1 = 0.25$, they are expressed with quarterly compounding; and so on. (This assumption corresponds to the usual market practice for FRAs.)

Normally company X would earn R_M from the LIBOR loan. The FRA means that it will earn R_K. The extra interest rate (which may be negative) that it earns as a result of entering into the FRA is $R_K - R_M$. The interest rate is set at time T_1 and paid at time T_2. The extra interest rate therefore leads to a cash flow to company X at time T_2 of

$$L(R_K - R_M)(T_2 - T_1) \tag{7.7}$$

Similarly there is a cash flow to company Y at time T_2 of

$$L(R_M - R_K)(T_2 - T_1) \qquad (7.8)$$

From Equations (7.7) and (7.8), we see that there is another interpretation of the FRA. It is an agreement where company X will receive interest on the principal between T_1 and T_2 at the fixed rate of R_K and pay interest at the realized LIBOR rate of R_M. Company Y will pay interest on the principal between T_1 and T_2 at the fixed rate of R_K and receive interest at R_M.

Usually FRAs are settled at time T_1 rather than T_2. The payoff must then be discounted from time T_2 to T_1. For company X, the payoff at time T_1 is

$$\frac{L(R_K - R_M)(T_2 - T_1)}{1 + R_M(T_2 - T_1)}$$

and, for company Y, the payoff at time T_1 is

$$\frac{L(R_M - R_K)(T_2 - T_1)}{1 + R_M(T_2 - T_1)}$$

Example 7.3

Suppose that a company enters into an FRA that is designed to ensure it will receive a fixed rate of 4% on a principal of $100 million for a 3-month period starting in 3 years. The FRA is an exchange where LIBOR is paid and 4% is received for the 3-month period. If 3-month LIBOR proves to be 4.5% for the 3-month period the cash flow to the lender will be

$$100,000,000 \times (0.04 - 0.045) \times 0.25 = -\$125,000$$

at the 3.25-year point. This is equivalent to a cash flow of

$$-\frac{125,000}{1 + 0.045 \times 0.25} = -\$123,609$$

at the 3-year point. The cash flow to the party on the opposite side of the transaction will be +$125,000 at the 3.25-year point or +$123,609 at the 3-year point. (All interest rates quoted in this example are expressed with quarterly compounding.)

Valuation

To value an FRA we first note that it is always worth zero when $R_K = R_F$.[5] This is because, as noted earlier, a large financial institution can at no cost lock in the forward rate for a future time period. For example, it can ensure that it earns the forward rate for the time period between years 2 and 3 by borrowing a certain amount of money for 2 years and investing it for 3 years. Similarly, it can ensure that it pays the forward rate for the time period between years 2 and 3 by borrowing for a certain amount of money for 3 years and investing it for 2 years.

Compare two FRAs. The first promises that the LIBOR forward rate R_F will be received on a principal of L between times T_1 and T_2; the second promises that R_K will be received on the same principal between the same two dates. The two contracts are the same except for the interest payments received at time T_2. The excess of the value of the second contract over the first is, therefore, the present value of the difference between these interest payments, or

$$L(R_K - R_F)(T_2 - T_1)e^{-R_2 T_2}$$

where R_2 is the continuously compounded riskless zero rate for a maturity T_2.[6] Because the value of the first FRA, where R_F is received, is zero, the value of the second FRA, where R_K is received, is

$$V_{FRA} = L(R_K - R_F)(T_2 - T_1)e^{-R_2 T_2} \qquad (7.9)$$

Similarly, the value of an FRA where R_K is paid is

$$V_{FRA} = L(R_F - R_K)(T_2 - T_1)e^{-R_2 T_2} \qquad (7.10)$$

By comparing Equations (7.7) and (7.9), or Equations (7.8) and (7.10), we see that an FRA can be valued if we:

1. Calculate the payoff on the assumption that forward rates are realized (that is, on the assumption that $R_M = R_F$).
2. Discount this payoff at the risk-free rate.

We will use this result when we value swaps (which are portfolios of FRAs) in Chapter 10.

Example 7.4

Suppose that LIBOR zero and forward rates are as in Table 7-5. Consider an FRA where we will receive a rate of 6%, measured with annual compounding, and pay LIBOR on a principal of $100 million between the end of year 1

---

[5] It is usually the case that R_K is set equal to R_F when the FRA is first initiated.

[6] Note that R_K, R_M, and R_F are expressed with a compounding frequency corresponding to $T_2 - T_1$, whereas R_2 is expressed with continuous compounding.

and the end of year 2. In this case, the forward rate is 5% with continuous compounding or 5.127% with annual compounding. From equation (7.9), it follows that the value of the FRA is

$$100{,}000{,}000 \times (0.06 - 0.05127)e^{-0.04 \times 2} = \$805{,}800$$

DURATION

The *duration* of a bond, as its name implies, is a measure of how long on average the holder of the bond has to wait before receiving cash payments. A zero-coupon bond that lasts n years has a duration of n years. However, a coupon-bearing bond lasting n years has a duration of less than n years, because the holder receives some of the cash payments prior to year n.

Suppose that a bond provides the holder with cash flows c_i at time t_i ($1 \leqslant i \leqslant n$). The bond price B and bond yield y (continuously compounded) are related by

$$B = \sum_{i=1}^{n} c_i e^{-yt_i} \qquad (7.11)$$

The duration of the bond, D, is defined as

$$D = \frac{\sum_{i=1}^{n} t_i c_i e^{-yt_i}}{B} \qquad (7.12)$$

This can be written

$$D = \sum_{i=1}^{n} t_i \left[\frac{c_i e^{-yt_i}}{B} \right]$$

The term in square brackets is the ratio of the present value of the cash flow at time t_i to the bond price. The bond price is the present value of all payments. The duration is therefore a weighted average of the times when payments are made, with the weight applied to time t_i being equal to the proportion of the bond's total present value provided by the cash flow at time t_i. The sum of the weights is 1.0. Note that for the purposes of the definition of duration all discounting is done at the bond yield rate of interest, y. (We do not use a different zero rate for each cash flow in the way described in the section "Bond Pricing.")

When a small change Δy in the yield is considered, it is approximately true that

$$\Delta B = \frac{dB}{dy} \Delta y \qquad (7.13)$$

From Equation (7.11), this becomes

$$\Delta B = -\Delta y \sum_{i=1}^{n} c_i t_i e^{-yt_i} \qquad (7.14)$$

(Note that there is a negative relationship between B and y. When bond yields increase, bond prices decrease. When bond yields decrease, bond prices increase.) From Equations (7.12) and (7.14), the key duration relationship is obtained:

$$\Delta B = -BD\Delta y \qquad (7.15)$$

This can be written

$$\frac{\Delta B}{B} = -D\Delta y \qquad (7.16)$$

Equation (7.16) is an approximate relationship between percentage changes in a bond price and changes in its yield. It is easy to use and is the reason why duration, which was first suggested by Macaulay in 1938, has become such a popular measure.

Consider a 3-year 10% coupon bond with a face value of $100. Suppose that the yield on the bond is 12% per annum with continuous compounding. This means that $y = 0.12$. Coupon payments of \$5 are made every 6 months. Table 7-6 shows the calculations necessary to determine the bond's duration. The present values of the bond's cash flows, using the yield as the discount rate, are shown in column 3 (e.g., the present value of the first cash flow is $5e^{-0.12 \times 0.5} = 4.709$). The sum of the numbers in column 3 gives the bond's price as 94.213. The weights are calculated by dividing the numbers in column 3 by 94.213. The sum of the numbers in column 5 gives the duration as 2.653 years.

Small changes in interest rates are often measured in *basis points*. As mentioned earlier, a basis point is 0.01% per annum. The following example investigates the accuracy of the duration relationship in Equation (7.15).

Example 7.5

For the bond in Table 7-6, the bond price, B, is 94.213 and the duration, D, is 2.653, so that Equation (7.15) gives

$$\Delta B = -94.213 \times 2.653 \times \Delta y$$

or

$$\Delta B = -249.95 \times \Delta y$$

When the yield on the bond increases by 10 basis points (= 0.1%), $\Delta y = +0.001$. The duration relationship predicts that $\Delta B = -249.95 \times 0.001 = -0.250$, so that the bond price goes down to $94.213 - 0.250 = 93.963$. How accurate is this? Valuing the bond in terms of its yield in the usual way, we find that, when the bond yield increases by 10 basis points to 12.1%, the bond price is

$$5e^{-0.121 \times 0.5} + 5e^{-0.121 \times 1.0} + 5e^{-0.121 \times 1.5} + 5e^{-0.121 \times 2.0}$$

$$+ 5e^{-0.121 \times 2.5} + 105e^{-0.121 \times 3.0} = 93.963$$

which is (to three decimal places) the same as that predicted by the duration relationship.

Modified Duration

The preceding analysis is based on the assumption that y is expressed with continuous compounding. If y is expressed with annual compounding, it can be shown that the approximate relationship in Equation (7.15) becomes

$$\Delta B = -\frac{BD\Delta y}{1 + y}$$

More generally, if y is expressed with a compounding frequency of m times per year, then

$$\Delta B = -\frac{BD\Delta y}{1 + y/m}$$

A variable D^*, defined by

$$D^* = \frac{D}{1 + y/m}$$

is sometimes referred to as the bond's *modified duration*. It allows the duration relationship to be simplified to

$$\Delta B = -BD^*\Delta y \qquad \textbf{(7.17)}$$

when y is expressed with a compounding frequency of m times per year. The following example investigates the accuracy of the modified duration relationship.

Example 7.6

The bond in Table 7-6 has a price of 94.213 and a duration of 2.653. The yield, expressed with semiannual compounding is 12.3673%. The modified duration, D^*, is given by

$$D^* = \frac{2.653}{1 + 0.123673/2} = 2.499$$

From Equation (7.17),

$$\Delta B = -94.213 \times 2.4985 \times \Delta y$$

or

$$\Delta B = -235.39 \times \Delta y$$

When the yield (semiannually compounded) increases by 10 basis points (= 0.1 %), we have $\Delta y = +0.001$. The duration relationship predicts that we expect ΔB to be $-235.39 \times 0.001 = -0.235$, so that the bond price goes down to $94.213 - 0.235 = 93.978$. How accurate is this? An exact calculation similar to that in the previous example shows that, when the bond yield (semiannually compounded) increases by 10 basis points to 12.4673%, the bond price becomes 93.978. This shows that the modified duration calculation gives good accuracy for small yield changes.

Another term that is sometimes used is *dollar duration*. This is the product of modified duration and bond price, so that $\Delta B = -D^{**}\Delta y$, where D^{**} is dollar duration.

Bond Portfolios

The duration, D, of a bond portfolio can be defined as a weighted average of the durations of the individual bonds in the portfolio, with the weights being proportional to the bond prices. Equations (7.15) to (7.17) then apply, with B being defined as the value of the bond portfolio. They estimate the change in the value of the bond portfolio for a small change Δy in the yields of all the bonds.

It is important to realize that, when duration is used for bond portfolios, there is an implicit assumption that the

TABLE 7-6 Calculation of Duration

Time (Years)	Cash Flow ($)	Present Value	Weight	Time × Weight
0.5	5	4.709	0.050	0.025
1.0	5	4.435	0.047	0.047
1.5	5	4.176	0.044	0.066
2.0	5	3.933	0.042	0.083
2.5	5	3.704	0.039	0.098
3.0	105	73.256	0.778	2.333
Total:	130	94.213	1.000	2.653

yields of all bonds will change by approximately the same amount. When the bonds have widely differing maturities, this happens only when there is a parallel shift in the zero-coupon yield curve. We should therefore interpret Equations (7.15) to (7.17) as providing estimates of the impact on the price of a bond portfolio of a small parallel shift, Δy, in the zero curve.

By choosing a portfolio so that the duration of assets equals the duration of liabilities (i.e., the net duration is zero), a financial institution eliminates its exposure to small parallel shifts in the yield curve. But it is still exposed to shifts that are either large or nonparallel.

CONVEXITY

The duration relationship applies only to small changes in yields. This is illustrated in Figure 7-2, which shows the relationship between the percentage change in value and change in yield for two bond portfolios having the same duration. The gradients of the two curves are the same at the origin. This means that both bond portfolios change in value by the same percentage for small yield changes and is consistent with Equation (7.16). For large yield changes, the portfolios behave differently. Portfolio X has more curvature in its relationship with yields than portfolio Y.

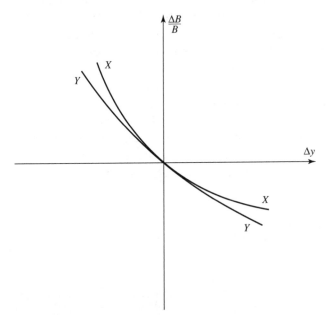

FIGURE 7-2   Two bond portfolios with the same duration.

A factor known as *convexity* measures this curvature and can be used to improve the relationship in Equation (7.16).

A measure of convexity is

$$C = \frac{1}{B}\frac{d^2B}{dy^2} = \frac{\sum_{i=1}^{n} c_i t_i^2 e^{-yt_i}}{B}$$

From Taylor series expansions, we obtain a more accurate expression than Equation (7.13), given by

$$\Delta B = \frac{dB}{dy}\Delta y + \frac{1}{2}\frac{d^2B}{dy^2}\Delta y^2$$

This leads to

$$\frac{\Delta B}{B} = -D\Delta y + \frac{1}{2}C(\Delta y)^2$$

For a portfolio with a particular duration, the convexity of a bond portfolio tends to be greatest when the portfolio provides payments evenly over a long period of time. It is least when the payments are concentrated around one particular point in time. By choosing a portfolio of assets and liabilities with a net duration of zero and a net convexity of zero, a financial institution can make itself immune to relatively large parallel shifts in the zero curve. However, it is still exposed to nonparallel shifts.

THEORIES OF THE TERM STRUCTURE OF INTEREST RATES

It is natural to ask what determines the shape of the zero curve. Why is it sometimes downward sloping, sometimes upward sloping, and sometimes partly upward sloping and partly downward sloping? A number of different theories have been proposed. The simplest is *expectations theory*, which conjectures that long-term interest rates should reflect expected future short-term interest rates. More precisely, it argues that a forward interest rate corresponding to a certain future period is equal to the expected future zero interest rate for that period. Another idea, *market segmentation theory*, conjectures that there need be no relationship between short-, medium-, and long-term interest rates. Under the theory, a major investor such as a large pension fund invests in bonds of a certain maturity and does not readily switch from one maturity to another. The short-term interest rate is determined by supply and demand in the short-term bond market; the medium-term interest rate is determined by supply and demand in the medium-term bond market; and so on.

The theory that is most appealing is *liquidity preference theory.* The basic assumption underlying the theory is that investors prefer to preserve their liquidity and invest funds for short periods of time. Borrowers, on the other hand, usually prefer to borrow at fixed rates for long periods of time. This leads to a situation in which forward rates are greater than expected future zero rates. The theory is also consistent with the empirical result that yield curves tend to be upward sloping more often than they are downward sloping.

The Management of Net Interest Income

To understand liquidity preference theory, it is useful to consider the interest rate risk faced by banks when they take deposits and make loans. The *net interest income* of the bank is the excess of the interest received over the interest paid and needs to be carefully managed.

Consider a simple situation where a bank offers consumers a one-year and a five-year deposit rate as well as a one-year and five-year mortgage rate. The rates are shown in Table 7-7. We make the simplifying assumption that the expected one-year interest rate for future time periods to equal the one-year rates prevailing in the market today. Loosely speaking this means that the market considers interest rate increases to be just as likely as interest rate decreases. As a result, the rates in Table 7-7 are "fair" in that they reflect the market's expectations (i.e., they correspond to expectations theory). Investing money for one year and reinvesting for four further one-year periods gives the same expected overall return as a single five-year investment. Similarly, borrowing money for one year and refinancing each year for the next four years leads to the same expected financing costs as a single five-year loan.

Suppose you have money to deposit and agree with the prevailing view that interest rate increases are just as likely

as interest rate decreases. Would you choose to deposit your money for one year at 3% per annum or for five years at 3% per annum? The chances are that you would choose one year because this gives you more financial flexibility. It ties up your funds for a shorter period of time.

Now suppose that you want a mortgage. Again you agree with the prevailing view that interest rate increases are just as likely as interest rate decreases. Would you choose a one-year mortgage at 6% or a five-year mortgage at 6%? The chances are that you would choose a five-year mortgage because it fixes your borrowing rate for the next five years and subjects you to less refinancing risk.

When the bank posts the rates shown in Table 7-7, it is likely to find that the majority of its customers opt for one-year deposits and five-year mortgages. This creates an asset/liability mismatch for the bank and subjects it to risks. There is no problem if interest rates fall. The bank will find itself financing the five-year 6% loans with deposits that cost less than 3% in the future and net interest income will increase. However, if rates rise, the deposits that are financing these 6% loans will cost more than 3% in the future and net interest income will decline. A 3% rise in interest rates would reduce the net interest income to zero.

It is the job of the asset/liability management group to ensure that the maturities of the assets on which interest is earned and the maturities of the liabilities on which interest is paid are matched. One way it can do this is by increasing the five-year rate on both deposits and mortgages. For example, it could move to the situation in Table 7-8 where the five-year deposit rate is 4% and the five-year mortgage rate 7%. This would make five-year deposits relatively more attractive and one-year mortgages relatively more attractive. Some customers who chose one-year deposits when the rates were as in Table 7-7 will switch to five-year deposits in the Table 7-8

TABLE 7-7 Example of Rates Offered by a Bank to Its Customers

Maturity (Years)	Deposit Rate	Mortgage Rate
1	3%	6%
5	3%	6%

TABLE 7-8 Five-Year Rates Are Increased in an Attempt to Match Maturities of Assets and Liabilities

Maturity (Years)	Deposit Rate	Mortgage Rate
1	3%	6%
5	4%	7%

situation. Some customers who chose five-year mortgages when the rates were as in Table 7-7 will choose one-year mortgages. This may lead to the maturities of assets and liabilities being matched. If there is still an imbalance with depositors tending to choose a one-year maturity and borrowers a five-year maturity, five-year deposit and mortgage rates could be increased even further. Eventually the imbalance will disappear.

The net result of all banks behaving in the way we have just described is liquidity preference theory. Long-term rates tend to be higher than those that would be predicted by expected future short-term rates. The yield curve is upward sloping most of the time. It is downward sloping only when the market expects a steep decline in short-term rates.

Many banks now have sophisticated systems for monitoring the decisions being made by customers so that, when they detect small differences between the maturities of the assets and liabilities being chosen by customers they can fine tune the rates they offer. Sometimes derivatives such as interest rate swaps (which will be discussed in Chapter 10) are also used to manage their exposure. The result of all this is that net interest income is usually very stable. This has not always been the case. In the United States, the failure of Savings and Loan companies in the 1980s and the failure of Continental Illinois in 1984 were to a large extent a result of the fact that they did not match the maturities of assets and liabilities. Both failures proved to be very expensive for US taxpayers.

Liquidity

In addition to creating problems in the way that has been described, a portfolio where maturities are mismatched can lead to liquidity problems. Consider a financial institution that funds 5-year fixed rate loans with wholesale deposits that last only 3 months. It might recognize its exposure to rising interest rates and hedge its interest rate risk.

(One way of doing this is by using interest rate swaps, as mentioned earlier.) However, it still has a liquidity risk. Wholesale depositors may, for some reason, lose confidence in the financial institution and refuse to continue to provide the financial institution with short-term funding. The financial institution, even if it has adequate equity capital, will then experience a severe liquidity problem that could lead to its downfall. As described in Box 7-3, these types of liquidity problems were the root cause of

---

> **BOX 7-3** Liquidity and the 2007–2009 Financial Crisis
>
> During the credit crisis that started in July 2007 there was a "flight to quality," where financial institutions and investors looked for safe investments and were less inclined than before to take credit risks. Financial institutions that relied on short-term funding experienced liquidity problems. One example is Northern Rock in the United Kingdom, which chose to finance much of its mortgage portfolio with wholesale deposits, some lasting only 3 months. Starting in September 2007, the depositors became nervous and refused to roll over the funding they were providing to Northern Rock, i.e., at the end of a 3-month period they would refuse to deposit their funds for a further 3-month period. As a result, Northern Rock was unable to finance its assets. It was taken over by the UK government in early 2008. In the US, financial institutions such as Bear Stearns and Lehman Brothers experienced similar liquidity problems because they had chosen to fund part of their operations with short-term funds.

some of the failures of financial institutions during the crisis that started in 2007.

SUMMARY

Two important interest rates for derivative traders are Treasury rates and LIBOR rates. Treasury rates are the rates paid by a government on borrowings in its own currency. LIBOR rates are short-term lending rates offered by banks in the interbank market. Derivatives traders have traditionally assumed that the LIBOR rate is the short-term risk-free rate at which funds can be borrowed or lent.

The compounding frequency used for an interest rate defines the units in which it is measured. The difference between an annually compounded rate and a quarterly compounded rate is analogous to the difference between a distance measured in miles and a distance measured in kilometers. Traders frequently use continuous compounding when analyzing the value of options and more complex derivatives.

Many different types of interest rates are quoted in financial markets and calculated by analysts. The n-year zero or spot rate is the rate applicable to an investment lasting for n years when all of the return is realized at the end. The par yield on a bond of a certain maturity is the coupon rate that causes the bond to sell for its par value. Forward rates are the rates applicable to future periods of time implied by today's zero rates.

The method most commonly used to calculate zero rates is known as the bootstrap method. It involves starting with short-term instruments and moving progressively to longer-term instruments, making sure that the zero rates calculated at each stage are consistent with the prices of the instruments. It is used daily by trading desks to calculate a Treasury zero-rate curve.

A forward rate agreement (FRA) is an over-the-counter agreement that the LIBOR rate will be exchanged for a specified interest rate during a specified future period of time. An FRA can be valued by assuming that forward LIBOR rates are realized and discounting the resulting payoff.

An important concept in interest rate markets is *duration*. Duration measures the sensitivity of the value of a bond portfolio to a small parallel shift in the zero-coupon yield curve. Specifically,

$$\Delta B = -BD\Delta y$$

where B is the value of the bond portfolio, D is the duration of the portfolio, Δy is the size of a small parallel shift in the zero curve, and ΔB is the resultant effect on the value of the bond portfolio.

Liquidity preference theory can be used to explain the interest rate term structures that are observed in practice.

The theory argues that most entities like to borrow long and lend short. To match the maturities of borrowers and lenders, it is necessary for financial institutions to raise long-term rates so that forward interest rates are higher than expected future spot interest rates.

Further Reading

Allen, S. L., and A. D. Kleinstein. *Valuing Fixed-Income Investments and Derivative Securities: Cash Flow Analysis and Calculations.* New York: New York Institute of Finance, 1991.

Fabozzi, F. J. *Duration, Convexity, and Other Bond Risk Measures.* Frank J. Fabozzi Assoc., 1999.

Fabozzi, F. J. *Fixed-Income Mathematics: Analytical and Statistical Techniques,* 4th ed. New York: McGraw-Hill, 2006.

Grinblatt, M., and F. A. Longstaff. "Financial Innovation and the Role of Derivatives Securities: An Empirical Analysis of the Treasury Strips Program," *Journal of Finance,* 55, 3 (2000): 1415–36.

Jorion, P. *Big Bets Gone Bad: Derivatives and Bankruptcy in Orange County.* New York: Academic Press, 1995.

Stigum, M., and F. L. Robinson. *Money Markets and Bond Calculations.* Chicago: Irwin, 1996.

Determination of Forward and Future Prices

■ Learning Objectives

Candidates, after completing this reading, should be able to:

- Differentiate between investment and consumption assets.
- Define short-selling and calculate the net profit of a short sale of a dividend-paying stock.
- Describe the differences between forward and futures contracts and explain the relationship between forward and spot prices.
- Calculate the forward price given the underlying asset's spot price, and describe an arbitrage argument between spot and forward prices.
- Explain the relationship between forward and futures prices.
- Calculate a forward foreign exchange rate using the interest rate parity relationship.
- Define income, storage costs, and convenience yield.

- Calculate the futures price on commodities incorporating income/storage costs and/or convenience yields.
- Define and calculate, using the cost-of-carry model, forward prices where the underlying asset either does or does not have interim cash flows.
- Describe the various delivery options available in the futures markets and how they can influence futures prices.
- Explain the relationship between current futures prices and expected future spot prices, including the impact of systematic and nonsystematic risk.
- Define and interpret contango and backwardation, and explain how they relate to the cost-of-carry model.

Excerpt is Chapter 5 of Options, Futures, and Other Derivatives, *Eighth Edition, by John Hull.*

In this chapter we examine how forward prices and futures prices are related to the spot price of the underlying asset. Forward contracts are easier to analyze than futures contracts because there is no daily settlement—only a single payment at maturity. We therefore start this chapter by considering the relationship between the forward price and the spot price. Luckily it can be shown that the forward price and futures price of an asset are usually very close when the maturities of the two contracts are the same. This is convenient because it means that results obtained for forwards are usually also true for futures.

In the first part of the chapter we derive some important general results on the relationship between forward (or futures) prices and spot prices. We then use the results to examine the relationship between futures prices and spot prices for contracts on stock indices, foreign exchange, and commodities. We will consider interest rate futures contracts in the next chapter.

INVESTMENT ASSETS VS. CONSUMPTION ASSETS

When considering forward and futures contracts, it is important to distinguish between investment assets and consumption assets. An *investment asset* is an asset that is held for investment purposes by significant numbers of investors. Stocks and bonds are clearly investment assets. Gold and silver are also examples of investment assets. Note that investment assets do not have to be held exclusively for investment. (Silver, for example, has a number of industrial uses.) However, they do have to satisfy the requirement that they are held by significant numbers of investors solely for investment. A *consumption asset* is an asset that is held primarily for consumption. It is not usually held for investment. Examples of consumption assets are commodities such as copper, oil, and pork bellies.

As we shall see later in this chapter, we can use arbitrage arguments to determine the forward and futures prices of an investment asset from its spot price and other observable market variables. We cannot do this for consumption assets.

SHORT SELLING

Some of the arbitrage strategies presented in this chapter involve *short selling*. This trade, usually simply referred to as "shorting", involves selling an asset that is not owned. It is something that is possible for some—but not all—investment assets. We will illustrate how it works by considering a short sale of shares of a stock.

Suppose an investor instructs a broker to short 500 IBM shares. The broker will carry out the instructions by borrowing the shares from another client and selling them in the market in the usual way. The investor can maintain the short position for as long as desired, provided there are always shares for the broker to borrow. At some stage, however, the investor will close out the position by purchasing 500 IBM shares. These are then replaced in the account of the client from which the shares were borrowed. The investor takes a profit if the stock price has declined and a loss if it has risen. If at any time while the contract is open the broker is not able to borrow shares, the investor is forced to close out the position, even if not ready to do so. Sometimes a fee is charged for lending shares or other securities to the party doing the shorting.

An investor with a short position must pay to the broker any income, such as dividends or interest, that would normally be received on the securities that have been shorted. The broker will transfer this income to the account of the client from whom the securities have been borrowed. Consider the position of an investor who shorts 500 shares in April when the price per share is $120 and closes out the position by buying them back in July when the price per share is $100. Suppose that a dividend of $1 per share is paid in May. The investor receives $500 \times \$120 = \$60,000$ in April when the short position is initiated. The dividend leads to a payment by the investor of $500 \times \$1 = \$500$ in May. The investor also pays $500 \times \$100 = \$50,000$ for shares when the position is closed out in July. The net gain, therefore, is

$$\$60,000 - \$500 - \$50,000 = \$9,500$$

assuming there is no fee for borrowing the shares. Table 8-1 illustrates this example and shows that the cash flows from the short sale are the mirror image of the cash

TABLE 8-1	Cash Flows from Short Sale and Purchase of Shares

Purchase of Shares	
April: Purchase 500 shares for $120	−$60,000
May: Receive dividend	+$500
July: Sell 500 shares for $100 per share	+$50,000
Net profit =	−$9,500

Short Sale of Shares	
April: Borrow 500 shares and sell them for $120	+$60,000
May: Pay dividend	−$500
July: Buy 500 shares for $100 per share Replace borrowed shares to close short position	−$50,000
Net profit =	+$9,500

flows from purchasing the shares in April and selling them in July. (Again, this assumes no borrowing fee.)

The investor is required to maintain a *margin account* with the broker. The margin account consists of cash or marketable securities deposited by the investor with the broker to guarantee that the investor will not walk away from the short position if the share price increases. It is similar to the margin account discussed in Chapter 5 for futures contracts. An initial margin is required and if there are adverse movements (i.e., increases) in the price of the asset that is being shorted, additional margin may be required. If the additional margin is not provided, the short position is closed out. The margin account does not represent a cost to the investor. This is because interest is usually paid on the balance in margin accounts and, if the interest rate offered is unacceptable, marketable securities such as Treasury bills can be used to meet margin requirements. The proceeds of the sale of the asset belong to the investor and normally form part of the initial margin.

From time to time regulations are changed on short selling. In 1938, the uptick rule was introduced. This allowed shares to be shorted only on an "uptick"—that is, when the most recent movement in the share price was an increase. The SEC abolished the uptick rule in July 2007, but introduced an "alternative uptick" rule in February 2010. Under this rule, when the price of a stock has decreased by more than 10% in one day, there are restrictions on short selling for that day and the next. These restrictions are that the stock can be shorted only at a price that is higher than the best current bid price. Occasionally there are temporary bans on short selling. This happened in a number of countries in 2008 because it was considered that short selling contributed to the high market volatility that was being experienced.

ASSUMPTIONS AND NOTATION

In this chapter we will assume that the following are all true for some market participants:

1. The market participants are subject to no transaction costs when they trade.

2. The market participants are subject to the same tax rate on all net trading profits.

3. The market participants can borrow money at the same risk-free rate of interest as they can lend money.

4. The market participants take advantage of arbitrage opportunities as they occur.

Note that we do not require these assumptions to be true for all market participants. All that we require is that they be true—or at least approximately true—for a few key market participants such as large derivatives dealers. It is the trading activities of these key market participants and their eagerness to take advantage of arbitrage opportunities as they occur that determine the relationship between forward and spot prices.

The following notation will be used throughout this chapter:

T: Time until delivery date in a forward or futures contract (in years)

S_0: Price of the asset underlying the forward or futures contract today

F_0: Forward or futures price today

r: Zero-coupon risk-free rate of interest per annum, expressed with continuous compounding, for an investment maturing at the delivery date (i.e., in T years)

The risk-free rate r is the rate at which money is borrowed or lent when there is no credit risk, so that the money is certain to be repaid. As discussed in Chapter 7, participants in derivatives markets have traditionally assumed that LIBOR rates rather than Treasury rates are the relevant risk-free rates.

FORWARD PRICE FOR AN INVESTMENT ASSET

The easiest forward contract to value is one written on an investment asset that provides the holder with no income. Non-dividend-paying stocks and zero-coupon bonds are examples of such investment assets.

Consider a long forward contract to purchase a non-dividend-paying stock in 3 months.[1] Assume the current stock price is $40 and the 3-month risk-free interest rate is 5% per annum.

Suppose first that the forward price is relatively high at $43. An arbitrageur can borrow $40 at the risk-free interest rate of 5% per annum, buy one share, and short a forward contract to sell one share in 3 months. At the end of the 3 months, the arbitrageur delivers the share and receives $43. The sum of money required to pay off the loan is

$$40e^{0.05 \times 3/12} = \$40.50$$

By following this strategy, the arbitrageur locks in a profit of $43.00 − $40.50 = $2.50 at the end of the 3-month period.

Suppose next that the forward price is relatively low at $39. An arbitrageur can short one share, invest the proceeds of the short sale at 5% per annum for 3 months, and take a long position in a 3-month forward contract. The proceeds of the short sale grow to $40e^{0.05 \times 3/12}$, or $40.50 in 3 months. At the end of the 3 months, the arbitrageur pays $39, takes delivery of the share under the terms of the forward contract, and uses it to close out the short position. A net gain of

$$\$40.50 - \$39.00 = \$1.50$$

is therefore made at the end of the 3 months. The two trading strategies we have considered are summarized in Table 8-2.

---

[1] Forward contracts on individual stocks do not often arise in practice. However, they form useful examples for developing our ideas. Futures on individual stocks started trading in the United States in November 2002.

TABLE 8-2 Arbitrage Opportunities When Forward Price Is Out of Line with Spot Price for Asset Providing No Income (asset price = $40; interest rate = 5%; maturity of forward contract = 3 months)

Forward Price = $43	Forward Price = $39
Action now: Borrow $40 at 5% for 3 months Buy one unit of asset Enter into forward contract to sell asset in 3 months for $43	*Action now:* Short 1 unit of asset to realize $40 Invest $40 at 5% for 3 months Enter into a forward contract to buy asset in 3 months for $39
Action in 3 months: Sell asset for $43 Use $40.50 to repay loan with interest	*Action in 3 months:* Buy asset for $39 Close short position Receive $40.50 from investment
Profit realized = $2.50	Profit realized = $1.50

Under what circumstances do arbitrage opportunities such as those in Table 8-2 not exist? The first arbitrage works when the forward price is greater than $40.50. The second arbitrage works when the forward price is less than $40.50. We deduce that for there to be no arbitrage the forward price must be exactly $40.50.

A Generalization

To generalize this example, we consider a forward contract on an investment asset with price S_0 that provides no income. Using our notation, T is the time to maturity, r is the risk-free rate, and F_0 is the forward price. The relationship between F_0 and S_0 is

$$F_0 = S_0 e^{rT} \tag{8.1}$$

If $F_0 > S_0 e^{rT}$, arbitrageurs can buy the asset and short forward contracts on the asset. If $F_0 < S_0 e^{rT}$, they can short the asset and enter into long forward contracts on it.[2] In

---

[2] For another way of seeing that Equation (8.1) is correct, consider the following strategy: buy one unit of the asset and enter into a short forward contract to sell it for F_0 at time T. This costs S_0 and is certain to lead to a cash inflow of F_0 at time T. Therefore S_0 must equal the present value of F_0; that is, $S_0 = F_0 e^{-rT}$, or equivalently $F_0 = S_0 e^{rT}$.

Kidder Peabody's Embarrassing Mistake

Investment banks have developed a way of creating a zero-coupon bond, called a *strip,* from a coupon-bearing Treasury bond by selling each of the cash flows underlying the coupon-bearing bond as a separate security. Joseph Jett, a trader working for Kidder Peabody, had a relatively simple trading strategy. He would buy strips and sell them in the forward market. As Equation (8.1) shows, the forward price of a security providing no income is always higher than the spot price. Suppose, for example, that the 3-month interest rate is 4% per annum and the spot price of a strip is $70. The 3-month forward price of the strip is $70e^{0.04 \times 3/12} = \$70.70$.

Kidder Peabody's computer system reported a profit on each of Jett's trades equal to the excess of the forward price over the spot price ($0.70 in our example). In fact this profit was nothing more than the cost of financing the purchase of the strip. But, by rolling his contracts forward, Jett was able to prevent this cost from accruing to him.

The result was that the system reported a profit of $100 million on Jett's trading (and Jett received a big bonus) when in fact there was a loss in the region of $350 million. This shows that even large financial institutions can get relatively simple things wrong!

our example, $S_0 = 40$, $r = 0.05$, and $T = 0.25$, so that Equation (8.1) gives

$$F_0 = 40e^{0.05 \times 0.25} = \$40.50$$

which is in agreement with our earlier calculations.

A long forward contract and a spot purchase both lead to the asset being owned at time T. The forward price is higher than the spot price because of the cost of financing the spot purchase of the asset during the life of the forward contract. This point was overlooked by Kidder Peabody in 1994, much to its cost (see Box 8-1).

Example 8.1

Consider a 4-month forward contract to buy a zero-coupon bond that will mature 1 year from today. (This means that the bond will have 8 months to go when the forward contract matures.) The current price of the bond is $930. We assume that the 4-month risk-free rate of interest (continuously compounded) is 6% per annum.

Because zero-coupon bonds provide no income, we can use Equation (8.1) with $T = 4/12$, $r = 0.06$, and $S_0 = 930$. The forward price, F_0, is given by

$$F_0 = 930e^{0.06 \times 4/12} = \$948.79$$

This would be the delivery price in a contract negotiated today.

What If Short Sales Are Not Possible?

Short sales are not possible for all investment assets and sometimes a fee is charged for borrowing assets. As it happens, this does not matter. To derive Equation (8.1), we do not need to be able to short the asset. All that we require is that there be a significant number of people who hold the asset purely for investment (and by definition this is always true of an investment asset). If the forward price is too low, they will find it attractive to sell the asset and take a long position in a forward contract.

Suppose that the underlying asset has no storage costs or income. If $F_0 > S_0e^{rT}$, an investor can adopt the following strategy:

1. Borrow S_0 dollars at an interest rate r for T years.
2. Buy 1 unit of the asset.
3. Short a forward contract on 1 unit of the asset.

At time T, the asset is sold for F_0. An amount S_0e^{rT} is required to repay the loan at this time and the investor makes a profit of $F_0 - S_0e^{rT}$.

Suppose next that $F_0 < S_0e^{rT}$. In this case, an investor who owns the asset can:

1. Sell the asset for S_0
2. Invest the proceeds at interest rate r for time T.
3. Take a long position in a forward contract on 1 unit of the asset.

At time T, the cash invested has grown to S_0e^{rT}. The asset is repurchased for F_0 and the investor makes a profit of $S_0e^{rT} - F_0$ relative to the position the investor would have been in if the asset had been kept.

As in the non-dividend-paying stock example considered earlier, we can expect the forward price to adjust so that neither of the two arbitrage opportunities we have considered exists. This means that the relationship in Equation (8.1) must hold.

KNOWN INCOME

In this section we consider a forward contract on an investment asset that will provide a perfectly predictable cash income to the holder. Examples are stocks paying known dividends and coupon-bearing bonds. We adopt the same approach as in the previous section. We first look at a numerical example and then review the formal arguments.

Consider a long forward contract to purchase a coupon-bearing bond whose current price is $900. We will suppose that the forward contract matures in 9 months. We will also suppose that a coupon payment of $40 is expected after 4 months. We assume that the 4-month and 9-month risk-free interest rates (continuously compounded) are, respectively, 3% and 4% per annum.

Suppose first that the forward price is relatively high at $910. An arbitrageur can borrow $900 to buy the bond and short a forward contract. The coupon payment has a present value of $40e^{-0.03 \times 4/12} = \$39.60$. Of the $900, $39.60 is therefore borrowed at 3% per annum for 4 months so that it can be repaid with the coupon payment. The remaining $860.40 is borrowed at 4% per annum for 9 months. The amount owing at the end of the 9-month period is $860.40e^{0.04 \times 0.75} = \$886.60$. A sum of $910 is received for the bond under the terms of the forward contract. The arbitrageur therefore makes a net profit of

$$910.00 - 886.60 = \$23.40$$

Suppose next that the forward price is relatively low at $870. An investor can short the bond and enter into a long forward contract. Of the $900 realized from shorting the bond, $39.60 is invested for 4 months at 3% per annum so that it grows into an amount sufficient to pay the coupon on the bond. The remaining $860.40 is invested for 9 months at 4% per annum and grows to $886.60. Under the terms of the forward contract, $870 is paid to buy the bond and the short position is closed out. The investor therefore gains

$$886.60 - 870 = \$16.60$$

The two strategies we have considered are summarized in Table 8-3.[3] The first strategy in Table 8-3 produces a profit

---

TABLE 8-3 Arbitrage Opportunities When 9-Month Forward Price Is Out of Line with Spot Price for Asset Providing Known Cash Income (asset price = $900; income of $40 occurs at 4 months; 4-month and 9-month rates are, respectively, 3% and 4% per annum)

Forward Price = $910	Forward Price = $870
Action now: Borrow $900: $39.60 for 4 months and $860.40 for 9 months. Buy 1 unit of asset. Enter into forward contract to sell asset in 9 months for $910	*Action now:* Short 1 unit of asset to realize $900. Invest $39.60 for 4 months and $860.40 for 9 months. Enter into a forward contract to buy asset in 9 months for $870
Action in 4 months: Receive $40 of income on asset. Use $40 to repay first loan with interest	*Action in 4 months:* Receive $40 from 4-month investment. Pay income of $40 on asset
Action in 9 months: Sell asset for $910. Use $886.60 to repay second loan with interest	*Action in 9 months:* Receive $886.60 from 9-month investment. Buy asset for $870. Close out short position
Profit realized = $23.40	Profit realized = $16.60

when the forward price is greater than $886.60, whereas the second strategy produces a profit when the forward price is less than $886.60. It follows that if there are no arbitrage opportunities then the forward price must be $886.60.

A Generalization

We can generalize from this example to argue that, when an investment asset will provide income with a present value of I during the life of a forward contract, we have

$$F_0 = (S_0 - I)e^{rT} \qquad \textbf{(8.2)}$$

In our example, $S_0 = 900.00$, $I = 40e^{-0.03 \times 4/12} = 39.60$, $r = 0.04$, and $T = 0.75$, so that

$$F_0 = (900.00 - 39.60)e^{0.04 \times 0.75} = \$886.60$$

This is in agreement with our earlier calculation. Equation (8.2) applies to any investment asset that provides a known cash income.

If $F_0 > (S_0 - I)e^{rT}$, an arbitrageur can lock in a profit by buying the asset and shorting a forward contract on the asset; if $F_0 < (S_0 - I)e^{rT}$, an arbitrageur can lock in a profit by shorting the asset and taking a long position in a forward contract. If short sales are not possible, investors who own the asset will find it profitable to sell the asset and enter into long forward contracts.[4]

Example 8.2

Consider a 10-month forward contract on a stock when the stock price is $50. We assume that the risk-free rate of interest (continuously compounded) is 8% per annum for all maturities. We also assume that dividends of $0.75 per share are expected after 3 months, 6 months, and 9 months. The present value of the dividends, I, is

$$I = 0.75e^{-0.08 \times 3/12} + 0.75e^{-0.08 \times 6/12} + 0.75e^{-0.08 \times 9/12} = 2.162$$

The variable T is 10 months, so that the forward price, F_0, from Equation (8.2), is given by

$$F_0 = (50 - 2.162)e^{0.08 \times 10/12} = \$51.14$$

If the forward price were less than this, an arbitrageur would short the stock and buy forward contracts. If the forward price were greater than this, an arbitrageur would short forward contracts and buy the stock in the spot market.

KNOWN YIELD

We now consider the situation where the asset underlying a forward contract provides a known yield rather than a known cash income. This means that the income is known when expressed as a percentage of the asset's price at the time the income is paid. Suppose that an asset is expected to provide a yield of 5% per annum. This could mean that income is paid once a year and is equal to 5% of the asset price at the time it is paid, in which case the yield would be 5% with annual compounding. Alternatively, it could mean that income is paid twice a year and

is equal to 2.5% of the asset price at the time it is paid, in which case the yield would be 5% per annum with semi-annual compounding. In Chapter 7 we explained that we will normally measure interest rates with continuous compounding. Similarly, we will normally measure yields with continuous compounding. Formulas for translating a yield measured with one compounding frequency to a yield measured with another compounding frequency are the same as those given for interest rates in Chapter 7.

Define q as the average yield per annum on an asset during the life of a forward contract with continuous compounding. It can be shown (see Exercise 20) that

$$F_0 = S_0 e^{(r - q)T} \tag{8.3}$$

Example 8.3

Consider a 6-month forward contract on an asset that is expected to provide income equal to 2% of the asset price once during a 6-month period. The risk-free rate of interest (with continuous compounding) is 10% per annum. The asset price is $25. In this case, $S_0 = 25$, $r = 0.10$, and $T = 0.5$. The yield is 4% per annum with semiannual compounding. From Equation (7.3), this is 3.96% per annum with continuous compounding. It follows that $q = 0.0396$, so that from Equation (8.3) the forward price, F_0, is given by

$$F_0 = 25e^{(0.10 - 0.0396) \times 0.5} = \$25.77$$

VALUING FORWARD CONTRACTS

The value of a forward contract at the time it is first entered into is zero. At a later stage, it may prove to have a positive or negative value. It is important for banks and other financial institutions to value the contract each day. (This is referred to as marking to market the contract.) Using the notation introduced earlier, we suppose K is the delivery price for a contract that was negotiated some time ago, the delivery date is T years from today, and r is the T-year risk-free interest rate. The variable F_0 is the forward price that would be applicable if we negotiated the contract today. In addition, we define f to be the value of forward contract today.

It is important to be clear about the meaning of the variables F_0, K, and f. At the beginning of the life of the forward contract, the delivery price, K, is set equal to the forward price and the value of the contract, f, is 0. As time passes, K stays the same (because it is part of the

---

[4] For another way of seeing that Equation (8.2) is correct, consider the following strategy: buy one unit of the asset and enter into a short forward contract to sell it for F_0 at time T. This costs S_0 and is certain to lead to a cash inflow of F_0 at time T and an income with a present value of I. The initial outflow is S_0. The present value of the inflows is $I + F_0 e^{-rT}$. Hence, $S_0 = I + F_0 e^{-rT}$, or equivalently $F_0 = (S_0 - I)e^{rT}$.

definition of the contract), but the forward price changes and the value of the contract becomes either positive or negative.

A general result, applicable to all long forward contracts (both those on investment assets and those on consumption assets), is

$$f = (F_0 - K)e^{-rT} \qquad \text{(8.4)}$$

To see why Equation (8.4) is correct, we use an argument analogous to the one we used for forward rate agreements in Chapter 7. We compare a long forward contract that has a delivery price of F_0 with an otherwise identical long forward contract that has a delivery price of K. The difference between the two is only in the amount that will be paid for the underlying asset at time T. Under the first contract, this amount is F_0; under the second contract, it is K. A cash outflow difference of $F_0 - K$ at time T translates to a difference of $(F_0 - K)e^{-rT}$ today. The contract with a delivery price F_0 is therefore less valuable than the contract with delivery price K by an amount $(F_0 - K)e^{-rT}$. The value of the contract that has a delivery price of F_0 is by definition zero. It follows that the value of the contract with a delivery price of K is $(F_0 - K)e^{-rT}$. This proves Equation (8.4). Similarly, the value of a short forward contract with delivery price K is

$$(K - F_0)e^{-rT}$$

Example 8.4

A long forward contract on a non-dividend-paying stock was entered into some time ago. It currently has 6 months to maturity. The risk-free rate of interest (with continuous compounding) is 10% per annum, the stock price is $25, and the delivery price is $24. In this case, $S_0 = 25$, $r = 0.10$, $T = 0.5$, and $K = 24$. From Equation (8.1), the 6-month forward price, F_0, is given by

$$F_0 = 25e^{0.1 \times 0.5} = \$26.28$$

From Equation (8.4), the value of the forward contract is

$$f = (26.28 - 24)e^{-0.1 \times 0.5} = \$2.17$$

Equation (8.4) shows that we can value a long forward contract on an asset by making the assumption that the price of the asset at the maturity of the forward contract equals the forward price F_0. To see this, note that when we make that assumption, a long forward contract provides a payoff at time T of $F_0 - K$. This has a present value of $(F_0 - K)e^{-rT}$, which is the value of f in Equation (8.4).

Similarly, we can value a short forward contract on the asset by assuming that the current forward price of the asset is realized. These results are analogous to the result in Chapter 7 that we can value a forward rate agreement on the assumption that forward rates are realized.

Using Equation (8.4) in conjunction with Equation (8.1) gives the following expression for the value of a forward contract on an investment asset that provides no income

$$f = S_0 - Ke^{-rT} \qquad \text{(8.5)}$$

Similarly, using Equation (8.4) in conjunction with Equation (8.2) gives the following expression for the value of a long forward contract on an investment asset that provides a known income with present value I:

$$f = S_0 - I - Ke^{-rT} \qquad \text{(8.6)}$$

Finally, using Equation (8.4) in conjunction with Equation (8.3) gives the following expression for the value of a long forward contract on an investment asset that provides a known yield at rate q:

$$f = S_0 e^{-qT} - Ke^{-rT} \qquad \text{(8.7)}$$

When a futures price changes, the gain or loss on a futures contract is calculated as the change in the futures price multiplied by the size of the position. This gain is realized almost immediately because of the way futures contracts are settled daily. Equation (8.4) shows that, when a forward price changes, the gain or loss is the present value of the change in the forward price multiplied by the size of the position. The difference between the gain/loss on forward and futures contracts can cause confusion on a foreign exchange trading desk (see Box 8-2).

ARE FORWARD PRICES AND FUTURES PRICES EQUAL?

Technical Note 24 at www.rotman.utoronto.ca/~hull/TechnicalNotes provides an arbitrage argument to show that, when the short-term risk-free interest rate is constant, the forward price for a contract with a certain delivery date is in theory the same as the futures price for a contract with that delivery date. The argument in the appendix can be extended to cover situations where the interest rate is a known function of time.

When interest rates vary unpredictably (as they do in the real world), forward and futures prices are in theory no

A foreign exchange trader working for a bank enters into a long forward contract to buy 1 million pounds sterling at an exchange rate of 1.5000 in 3 months. At the same time, another trader on the next desk takes a long position in 16 contracts for 3-month futures on sterling. The futures price is 1.5000 and each contract is on 62,500 pounds. The positions taken by the forward and futures traders are therefore the same. Within minutes of the positions being taken the forward and the futures prices both increase to 1.5040. The bank's systems show that the futures trader has made a profit of $4,000, while the forward trader has made a profit of only $3,900. The forward trader immediately calls the bank's systems department to complain. Does the forward trader have a valid complaint?

The answer is no! The daily settlement of futures contracts ensures that the futures trader realizes an almost immediate profit corresponding to the increase in the futures price. If the forward trader closed out the position by entering into a short contract at 1.5040, the forward trader would have contracted to buy 1 million pounds at 1.5000 in 3 months and sell 1 million pounds at 1.5040 in 3 months. This would lead to a $4,000 profit—but in 3 months, not today. The forward trader's profit is the present value of $4,000. This is consistent with Equation (8.4).

The forward trader can gain some consolation from the fact that gains and losses are treated symmetrically. If the forward/futures prices dropped to 1.4960 instead of rising to 1.5040, then the futures trader would take a loss of $4,000 while the forward trader would take a loss of only $3,900.

contract. Hence, when S is strongly positively correlated with interest rates, futures prices will tend to be slightly higher than forward prices. When S is strongly negatively correlated with interest rates, a similar argument shows that forward prices will tend to be slightly higher than futures prices.

The theoretical differences between forward and futures prices for contracts that last only a few months are in most circumstances sufficiently small to be ignored. In practice, there are a number of factors not reflected in theoretical models that may cause forward and futures prices to be different. These include taxes, transactions costs, and the treatment of margins. The risk that the counterparty will default may be less in the case of a futures contract because of the role of the exchange clearinghouse. Also, in some instances, futures contracts are more liquid and easier to trade than forward contracts. Despite all these points, for most purposes it is reasonable to assume that forward and futures prices are the same. This is the assumption we will usually make in this book. We will use the symbol F_0 to represent both the futures price and the forward price of an asset today.

One exception to the rule that futures and forward contracts can be assumed to be the same concerns Eurodollar futures. This will be discussed in Chapter 9.

FUTURES PRICES OF STOCK INDICES

We introduced futures on stock indices in Chapter 6 and showed how a stock index futures contract is a useful tool in managing equity portfolios. Table 6-3 shows futures prices for a number of different indices. We are now in a position to consider how index futures prices are determined.

A stock index can usually be regarded as the price of an investment asset that pays dividends.[5] The investment asset is the portfolio of stocks underlying the index, and the dividends paid by the investment asset are the dividends that would be received by the holder of this portfolio. It is usually assumed that the dividends provide a known yield rather than a known cash income. If q is the

longer the same. We can get a sense of the nature of the relationship by considering the situation where the price of the underlying asset, S, is strongly positively correlated with interest rates. When S increases, an investor who holds a long futures position makes an immediate gain because of the daily settlement procedure. The positive correlation indicates that it is likely that interest rates have also increased. The gain will therefore tend to be invested at a higher than average rate of interest. Similarly, when S decreases, the investor will incur an immediate loss. This loss will tend to be financed at a lower than average rate of interest. An investor holding a forward contract rather than a futures contract is not affected in this way by interest rate movements. It follows that a long futures contract will be slightly more attractive than a similar long forward

---

[5] Occasionally this is not the case: see Box 8-3.

BOX 8-3 The CME Nikkei 225 Futures Contract

The arguments in this chapter on how index futures prices are determined require that the index be the value of an investment asset. This means that it must be the value of a portfolio of assets that can be traded. The asset underlying the Chicago Mercantile Exchange's futures contract on the Nikkei 225 Index does not qualify, and the reason why is quite subtle. Suppose S is the value of the Nikkei 225 Index. This is the value of a portfolio of 225 Japanese stocks measured in yen. The variable underlying the CME futures contract on the Nikkei 225 has a *dollar value* of $5S$. In other words, the futures contract takes a variable that is measured in yen and treats it as though it is dollars.

We cannot invest in a portfolio whose value will always be $5S$ dollars. The best we can do is to invest in one that is always worth $5S$ yen or in one that is always worth $5QS$ dollars, where Q is the dollar value of 1 yen. The variable $5S$ dollars is not, therefore, the price of an investment asset and Equation (8.8) does not apply.

CME's Nikkei 225 futures contract is an example of a *quanto*. A quanto is a derivative where the underlying asset is measured in one currency and the payoff is in another currency.

dividend yield rate, Equation (8.3) gives the futures price, F_0, as

$$F_0 = S_0 e^{(r-q)T} \qquad \textbf{(8.8)}$$

This shows that the futures price increases at rate $r - q$ with the maturity of the futures contract. In Table 6-3, the December futures settlement price of the S&P 500 is about 0.76% less than the June settlement price. This indicates that, on May 26, 2010, the short-term risk-free rate r was less than the dividend yield q by about 1.52% per year.

Example 8.5

Consider a 3-month futures contract on an index. Suppose that the stocks underlying the index provide a dividend yield of 1% per annum, that the current value of the index is 1,300, and that the continuously compounded risk-free interest rate is 5% per annum. In this case, $r = 0.05$, $S_0 = 1,300$, $T = 0.25$, and $q = 0.01$. Hence, the futures price, F_0, is given by

$$F_0 = 1,300 e^{(0.05 - 0.01) \times 0.25} = \$1,313.07$$

In practice, the dividend yield on the portfolio underlying an index varies week by week throughout the year. For example, a large proportion of the dividends on the NYSE stocks are paid in the first week of February, May, August, and November each year. The chosen value of q should represent the average annualized dividend yield during the life of the contract. The dividends used for estimating q should be those for which the ex-dividend date is during the life of the futures contract.

Index Arbitrage

If $F_0 > S_0 e^{(r-q)T}$, profits can be made by buying the stocks underlying the index at the spot price (i.e., for immediate delivery) and shorting futures contracts. If $F_0 < S_0 e^{(r-q)T}$, profits can be made by doing the reverse—that is, shorting or selling the stocks underlying the index and taking a long position in futures contracts. These strategies are known as *index arbitrage*. When $F_0 < S_0 e^{(r-q)T}$, index arbitrage is often done by a pension fund that owns an indexed portfolio of stocks. When $F_0 > S_0 e^{(r-q)T}$, it might be done by a corporation holding short-term money market investments. For indices involving many stocks, index arbitrage is sometimes accomplished by trading a relatively small representative sample of stocks whose movements closely mirror those of the index. Usually index arbitrage is implemented through *program trading*. This involves using a computer system to generate the trades.

Most of the time the activities of arbitrageurs ensure that Equation (8.8) holds, but occasionally arbitrage is impossible and the futures price does get out of line with the spot price (see Box 8-4).

FORWARD AND FUTURES CONTRACTS ON CURRENCIES

We now move on to consider forward and futures foreign currency contracts from the perspective of a US investor. The underlying asset is one unit of the foreign currency. We will therefore define the variable S_0 as the current spot price in US dollars of one unit of the foreign currency and F_0 as the forward or futures price in US dollars of one unit of the foreign currency. This is consistent with the way we have defined S_0 and F_0 for other assets underlying forward and futures contracts. However, as mentioned earlier, it does not necessarily correspond to the way spot and

To do index arbitrage, a trader must be able to trade both the index futures contract and the portfolio of stocks underlying the index very quickly at the prices quoted in the market. In normal market conditions this is possible using program trading, and the relationship in Equation (8.8) holds well. Examples of days when the market was anything but normal are October 19 and 20 of 1987. On what is termed "Black Monday," October 19, 1987, the market fell by more than 20%, and the 604 million shares traded on the New York Stock Exchange easily exceeded all previous records. The exchange's systems were overloaded, and orders placed to buy or sell shares on that day could be delayed by up to two hours before being executed.

For most of October 19, 1987, futures prices were at a significant discount to the underlying index. For example, at the close of trading the S&P 500 Index was at 225.06 (down 57.88 on the day), whereas the futures price for December delivery on the S&P 500 was 201.50 (down 80.75 on the day). This was largely because the delays in processing orders made index arbitrage impossible. On the next day, Tuesday, October 20, 1987, the New York Stock Exchange placed temporary restrictions on the way in which program trading could be done. This also made index arbitrage very difficult and the breakdown of the traditional linkage between stock indices and stock index futures continued. At one point the futures price for the December contract was 18% less than the S&P 500 Index. However, after a few days the market returned to normal, and the activities of arbitrageurs ensured that Equation (8.8) governed the relationship between futures and spot prices of indices.

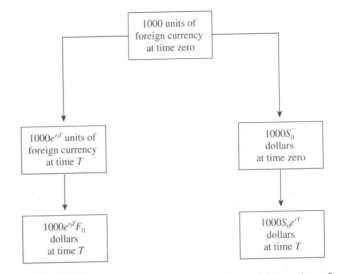

FIGURE 8-1   Two ways of converting 1,000 units of a foreign currency to dollars at time T. Here, S_0 is spot exchange rate, F_0 is forward exchange rate, and r and r_f are the dollar and foreign risk-free rates.

The relationship between F_0 and S_0 is

$$F_0 = S_0 e^{(r - r_f)T} \tag{8.9}$$

This is the well-known interest rate parity relationship from international finance. The reason it is true is illustrated in Figure 8-1. Suppose that an individual starts with 1,000 units of the foreign currency. There are two ways it can be converted to dollars at time T. One is by investing it for T years at r_f and entering into a forward contract to sell the proceeds for dollars at time T. This generates $1,000 e^{r_f T} F_0$ dollars. The other is by exchanging the foreign currency for dollars in the spot market and investing the proceeds for T years at rate r. This generates $1,000 S_0 e^{rT}$ dollars. In the absence of arbitrage opportunities, the two strategies must give the same result. Hence,

$$1,000 e^{r_f T} F_0 = 1,000 S_0 e^{rT}$$

so that

$$F_0 = S_0 e^{(r - r_f)T}$$

Example 8.6

Suppose that the 2-year interest rates in Australia and the United States are 5% and 7%, respectively, and the spot exchange rate between the Australian dollar (AUD) and the US dollar (USD) is 0.6200 USD per AUD.

forward exchange rates are quoted. For major exchange rates other than the British pound, euro, Australian dollar, and New Zealand dollar, a spot or forward exchange rate is normally quoted as the number of units of the currency that are equivalent to one US dollar.

A foreign currency has the property that the holder of the currency can earn interest at the risk-free interest rate prevailing in the foreign country. For example, the holder can invest the currency in a foreign-denominated bond. We define r_f as the value of the foreign risk-free interest rate when money is invested for time T. The variable r is the US dollar risk-free rate when money is invested for this period of time.

From Equation (8.9), the 2-year forward exchange rate should be

$$0.62e^{(0.07 - 0.05) \times 2} = 0.6453$$

Suppose first that the 2-year forward exchange rate is less than this, say 0.6300. An arbitrageur can:

1. Borrow 1,000 AUD at 5% per annum for 2 years, convert to 620 USD and invest the USD at 7% (both rates are continuously compounded).

2. Enter into a forward contract to buy 1,105.17 AUD for $1,105.17 \times 0.63 = 696.26$ USD.

The 620 USD that are invested at 7% grow to $620e^{0.07 \times 2} = 713.17$ USD in 2 years. Of this, 696.26 USD are used to purchase 1,105.17 AUD under the terms of the forward contract. This is exactly enough to repay principal and interest on the 1,000 AUD that are borrowed ($1,000e^{0.05 \times 2} = 1,105.17$). The strategy therefore gives rise to a riskless profit of $713.17 - 696.26 = 16.91$ USD. (If this does not sound very exciting, consider following a similar strategy where you borrow 100 million AUD!)

Suppose next that the 2-year forward rate is 0.6600 (greater than the 0.6453 value given by Equation (8.9)). An arbitrageur can:

1. Borrow 1,000 USD at 7% per annum for 2 years, convert to $1,000/0.6200 = 1,612.90$ AUD, and invest the AUD at 5%.

2. Enter into a forward contract to sell 1,782.53 AUD for $1,782.53 \times 0.66 = 1,176.47$ USD.

The 1,612.90 AUD that are invested at 5% grow to $1,612.90e^{0.05 \times 2} = 1,782.53$ AUD in 2 years. The forward contract has the effect of converting this to 1,176.47 USD. The amount needed to pay off the USD borrowings is $1,000e^{0.07 \times 2} = 1,150.27$ USD. The strategy therefore gives rise to a riskless profit of $1,176.47 - 1,150.27 = 26.20$ USD.

Table 8-4 shows currency futures quotes on May 26, 2010. The quotes are US dollars per unit of the foreign currency. (In the case of the Japanese yen, the quote is US dollars per 100 yen; for the Mexican peso, it is US dollars per 10 pesos.) This is the usual quotation convention for futures contracts. Equation (8.9) applies with r equal to the US risk-free rate and r_f equal to the foreign risk-free rate.

On May 26, 2010, short-term interest rates on the Japanese yen, British pound, Swiss franc, and euro were lower than the short-term interest rate on the US dollar.

This corresponds to the $r > r_f$ situation and explains why futures prices for these currencies increase with maturity in Table 8-4. For the Australian dollar, Canadian dollar, and Mexican peso, short-term interest rates were higher than in the United States. This corresponds to the $r_f > r$ situation and explains why the futures prices of these currencies decrease with maturity.

Example 8.7

In Table 8-4, the September settlement price for the Australian dollar is about 1% lower than the June settlement price. This indicates that the futures prices are decreasing at about 4% per year with maturity. From Equation (8.9) this is an estimate of the amount by which short-term Australian LIBOR interest rates exceeded short-term US LIBOR interest rates on May 26, 2010.

A Foreign Currency as an Asset Providing a Known Yield

Equation (8.9) is identical to Equation (8.3) with q replaced by r_f. This is not a coincidence. A foreign currency can be regarded as an investment asset paying a known yield. The yield is the risk-free rate of interest in the foreign currency.

To understand this, we note that the value of interest paid in a foreign currency depends on the value of the foreign currency. Suppose that the interest rate on British pounds is 5% per annum. To a US investor the British pound provides an income equal to 5% of the value of the British pound per annum. In other words it is an asset that provides a yield of 5% per annum.

FUTURES ON COMMODITIES

We now move on to consider futures contracts on commodities. First we look at the futures prices of commodities that are investment assets such as gold and silver.[6] We then go on to examine the futures prices of consumption assets.

---

[6] Recall that, for an asset to be an investment asset, it need not be held solely for investment purposes. What is required is that some individuals hold it for investment purposes and that these individuals be prepared to sell their holdings and go long forward contracts, if the latter look more attractive. This explains why silver, although it has significant industrial uses, is an investment asset.

TABLE 8-4 Currency Futures Quotes as Reported by Exchanges on May 26, 2010

	Open	High	Low	Settlement	Change	Volume	Open interest
Australian dollar, $100,000, USD per AUD (CME Group)							
June 2010	0.8266	0.8373	0.8171	0.8236	0.0062	146,968	101,448
Sept. 2010	0.8165	0.8285	0.8090	0.8152	0.0059	860	4,650
British pound, £62,500, USD per GBP (CME Group)							
June 2010	1.4429	1.4446	1.4330	1.4411	0.0046	105,256	140,369
Sept. 2010	1.4432	1.4450	1.4339	1.4416	0.0044	1,448	10,811
Canadian Dollar, $100,000, USD per CAD (CME Group)							
June 2010	0.9384	0.9452	0.9305	0.9393	0.0097	126,564	111,697
Sept. 2010	0.9378	0.9449	.0.9309	0.9392	0.0094	2,264	8,647
Euro, 125,000 euros, USD per EUR (CME Group)							
June 2010	1.2371	1.2380	1.2170	1.2201	-0.0117	400,948	267,552
Sept. 2010	1.2388	1.2388	1.2186	1.2216	-0.0118	4,702	13,939
Japanese Yen, 12,500,000 yen, USD per 100 yen (CME Group)							
June 2010	1.1073	1.1136	1.1031	1.1108	0.0009	172,240	135,113
Sept. 2010	1.1100	1.1156	1.1053	1.1129	0.0005	2,098	5,506
Mexican Peso, MXN500,000, USD per 20MXN (CME Group)							
June 2010	0.76800	0.77175	0.76000	0.76375	0.00225	37,776	84,207
Sept. 2010	0.76375	0.76375	0.75275	0.75625	0.00225	107	727
Swiss Franc, CHF125,000, USD per CHF (CME Group)							
June 2010	0.8661	0.8688	0.8613	0.8629	-0.0012	68,960	46,212
Sept. 2010	0.8693	0.8713	0.8644	0.8657	-0.0017	1,817	1,938

Income and Storage Costs

As explained in Box 6-1, the hedging strategies of gold producers leads to a requirement on the part of investment banks to borrow gold. Gold owners such as central banks charge interest in the form of what is known as the *gold lease rate* when they lend gold. The same is true of silver. Gold and silver can therefore provide income to the holder. Like other commodities they also have storage costs.

Equation (8.1) shows that, in the absence of storage costs and income, the forward price of a commodity that is an investment asset is given by

$$F_0 = S_0 e^{rT} \qquad \textbf{(8.10)}$$

Storage costs can be treated as negative income. If U is the present value of all the storage costs, net of income, during the life of a forward contract, it follows from Equation (8.2) that

$$F_0 = (S_0 + U)e^{rT} \qquad \textbf{(8.11)}$$

Example 8.8

Consider a 1-year futures contract on an investment asset that provides no income. It costs $2 per unit to store the asset, with the payment being made at the end of the year. Assume that the spot price is $450 per unit and the risk-free rate is 7% per annum for all maturities. This corresponds to $r = 0.07$, $S_0 = 450$, $T = 1$, and

$$U = 2e^{-0.07 \times 1} = 1.865$$

From Equation (8.11), the theoretical futures price, F_0, is given by

$$F_0 = (450 + 1.865)e^{0.07 \times 1} = \$484.63$$

If the actual futures price is greater than 484.63, an arbitrageur can buy the asset and short 1-year futures contracts to lock in a profit. If the actual futures price is less than 484.63, an investor who already owns the asset can improve the return by selling the asset and buying futures contracts.

If the storage costs (net of income) incurred at any time are proportional to the price of the commodity, they can be treated as negative yield. In this case, from Equation (8.3),

$$F_0 = S_0 e^{(r+u)T} \qquad \text{(8.12)}$$

where u denotes the storage costs per annum as a proportion of the spot price net of any yield earned on the asset.

Consumption Commodities

Commodities that are consumption assets rather than investment assets usually provide no income, but can be subject to significant storage costs. We now review the arbitrage strategies used to determine futures prices from spot prices carefully.[7]

Suppose that, instead of Equation (8.11), we have

$$F_0 > (S_0 + U)e^{rT} \qquad \text{(8.13)}$$

To take advantage of this opportunity, an arbitrageur can implement the following strategy:

1. Borrow an amount $S_0 + U$ at the risk-free rate and use it to purchase one unit of the commodity and to pay storage costs.

2. Short a futures contract on one unit of the commodity.

---

[7] For some commodities the spot price depends on the delivery location. We assume that the delivery location for spot and futures are the same.

If we regard the futures contract as a forward contract, so that there is no daily settlement, this strategy leads to a profit of $F_0 - (S_0 + U)e^{rT}$ at time T. There is no problem in implementing the strategy for any commodity. However, as arbitrageurs do so, there will be a tendency for S_0 to increase and F_0 to decrease until Equation (8.13) is no longer true. We conclude that Equation (8.13) cannot hold for any significant length of time.

Suppose next that

$$F_0 < (S_0 + U)e^{rT} \qquad \text{(8.14)}$$

When the commodity is an investment asset, we can argue that many investors hold the commodity solely for investment. When they observe the inequality in Equation (8.14), they will find it profitable to do the following:

1. Sell the commodity, save the storage costs, and invest the proceeds at the risk-free interest rate.

2. Take a long position in a futures contract.

The result is a riskless profit at maturity of $(S_0 + U)e^{rT} - F_0$ relative to the position the investors would have been in if they had held the commodity. It follows that Equation (8.14) cannot hold for long. Because neither Equation (8.13) nor (8.14) can hold for long, we must have $F_0 = (S_0 + U)e^{rT}$.

This argument cannot be used for a commodity that is a consumption asset rather than an investment asset. Individuals and companies who own a consumption commodity usually plan to use it in some way. They are reluctant to sell the commodity in the spot market and buy forward or futures contracts, because forward and futures contracts cannot be used in a manufacturing process or consumed in some other way. There is therefore nothing to stop Equation (8.14) from holding, and all we can assert for a consumption commodity is

$$F_0 \leq (S_0 + U)e^{rT} \qquad \text{(8.15)}$$

If storage costs are expressed as a proportion u of the spot price, the equivalent result is

$$F_0 \leq S_0 e^{(r + u)T} \qquad \text{(8.16)}$$

Convenience Yields

We do not necessarily have equality in Equations (8.15) and (8.16) because users of a consumption commodity may feel that ownership of the physical commodity provides benefits that are not obtained by holders of futures contracts. For example, an oil refiner is unlikely to regard a futures contract on crude oil in the same way as crude oil held in inventory. The crude oil in inventory can be an input to the refining process, whereas a futures contract cannot be used for this purpose. In general, ownership of the physical asset enables a manufacturer to keep a production process running and perhaps profit from temporary local shortages. A futures contract does not do the same. The benefits from holding the physical asset are sometimes referred to as the *convenience yield* provided by the commodity. If the dollar amount of storage costs is known and has a present value U, then the convenience yield y is defined such that

$$F_0 e^{yT} = (S_0 + U)e^{rT}$$

If the storage costs per unit are a constant proportion, u, of the spot price, then y is defined so that

$$F_0 e^{yT} = S_0 e^{(r + u)T}$$

or

$$F_0 = S_0 e^{(r + u - y)T} \qquad \textbf{(8.17)}$$

The convenience yield simply measures the extent to which the left-hand side is less than the right-hand side in Equation (8.15) or (8.16). For investment assets the convenience yield must be zero; otherwise, there are arbitrage opportunities. Table 5-2 in Chapter 5 shows that, on May 26, 2010, the futures price of soybeans decreased as the maturity of the contract increased from July 2010 to November 2010. This pattern suggests that the convenience yield, y, is greater than $r + u$.

The convenience yield reflects the market's expectations concerning the future availability of the commodity. The greater the possibility that shortages will occur, the higher the convenience yield. If users of the commodity have high inventories, there is very little chance of shortages in the near future and the convenience yield tends to be low. If inventories are low, shortages are more likely and the convenience yield is usually higher.

THE COST OF CARRY

The relationship between futures prices and spot prices can be summarized in terms of the *cost of carry*. This measures the storage cost plus the interest that is paid to finance the asset less the income earned on the asset. For a non-dividend-paying stock, the cost of carry is r, because there are no storage costs and no income is earned; for a stock index, it is $r - q$, because income is earned at rate q on the asset. For a currency, it is $r - r_f$; for a commodity that provides income at rate q and requires storage costs at rate u, it is $r - q + u$; and so on.

Define the cost of carry as c. For an investment asset, the futures price is

$$F_0 = S_0 e^{cT} \qquad \textbf{(8.18)}$$

For a consumption asset, it is

$$F_0 = S_0 e^{(c - y)T} \qquad \textbf{(8.19)}$$

where y is the convenience yield.

DELIVERY OPTIONS

Whereas a forward contract normally specifies that delivery is to take place on a particular day, a futures contract often allows the party with the short position to choose to deliver at any time during a certain period. (Typically the party has to give a few days' notice of its intention to deliver.) The choice introduces a complication into the determination of futures prices. Should the maturity of the futures contract be assumed to be the beginning, middle, or end of the delivery period? Even though most futures contracts are closed out prior to maturity, it is important to know when delivery would have taken place in order to calculate the theoretical futures price.

If the futures price is an increasing function of the time to maturity, it can be seen from Equation (8.19) that $c > y$, so that the benefits from holding the asset (including convenience yield and net of storage costs) are less than the risk-free rate. It is usually optimal in such a case for the party with the short position to deliver as early as possible, because the interest earned on the cash received outweighs the benefits of holding the asset. As a rule, futures prices in these circumstances should be calculated on the basis that delivery will take place at the beginning of the delivery period. If futures prices are decreasing as time to maturity increases ($c < y$), the reverse is true. It is then usually optimal for the party with the short position to deliver as late as possible, and futures prices should, as a rule, be calculated on this assumption.

FUTURES PRICES AND EXPECTED FUTURE SPOT PRICES

We refer to the market's average opinion about what the spot price of an asset will be at a certain future time as the *expected spot price* of the asset at that time. Suppose that it is now June and the September futures price of corn is 350 cents. It is interesting to ask what the expected spot price of corn in September is. Is it less than 350 cents, greater than 350 cents, or exactly equal to 350 cents? As illustrated in Figure 5-1, the futures price converges to the spot price at maturity. If the expected spot price is less than 350 cents, the market must be expecting the September futures price to decline, so that traders with short positions gain and traders with long positions lose. If the expected spot price is greater than 350 cents, the reverse must be true. The market must be expecting the September futures price to increase, so that traders with long positions gain while those with short positions lose.

Keynes and Hicks

Economists John Maynard Keynes and John Hicks argued that, if hedgers tend to hold short positions and speculators tend to hold long positions, the futures price of an asset will be below the expected spot price.[8] This is because speculators require compensation for the risks they are bearing. They will trade only if they can expect to make money on average. Hedgers will lose money on average, but they are likely to be prepared to accept this because the futures contract reduces their risks. If hedgers tend to hold long positions while speculators hold short positions, Keynes and Hicks argued that the futures price will be above the expected spot price for a similar reason.

Risk and Return

The modern approach to explaining the relationship between futures prices and expected spot prices is based on the relationship between risk and expected return in the economy. In general, the higher the risk of an investment, the higher the expected return demanded by an investor. The capital asset pricing model, which is

___
[8] See: J. M. Keynes, *A Treatise on Money*. London: Macmillan, 1930; and J. R. Hicks, *Value and Capital*. Oxford: Clarendon Press, 1939.

explained in the appendix to Chapter 6, shows that there are two types of risk in the economy: systematic and non-systematic. Nonsystematic risk should not be important to an investor. It can be almost completely eliminated by holding a well-diversified portfolio. An investor should not therefore require a higher expected return for bearing non-systematic risk. Systematic risk, in contrast, cannot be diversified away. It arises from a correlation between returns from the investment and returns from the whole stock market. An investor generally requires a higher expected return than the risk-free interest rate for bearing positive amounts of systematic risk. Also, an investor is prepared to accept a lower expected return than the risk-free interest rate when the systematic risk in an investment is negative.

The Risk in a Futures Position

Let us consider a speculator who takes a long position in a futures contract that lasts for T years in the hope that the spot price of the asset will be above the futures price at the end of the life of the futures contract. We ignore daily settlement and assume that the futures contract can be treated as a forward contract. We suppose that the speculator puts the present value of the futures price into a risk-free investment while simultaneously taking a long futures position. The proceeds of the risk-free investment are used to buy the asset on the delivery date. The asset is then immediately sold for its market price. The cash flows to the speculator are as follows:

Today: $-F_0 e^{-rT}$

End of futures contract: $+S_T$

where F_0 is the futures price today, S_T is the price of the asset at time T at the end of the futures contract, and r is the risk-free return on funds invested for time T.

How do we value this investment? The discount rate we should use for the expected cash flow at time T equals an investor's required return on the investment. Suppose that k is an investor's required return for this investment. The present value of this investment is

$$-F_0 e^{-rT} + E(S_T)e^{-kT}$$

where E denotes expected value. We can assume that all investments in securities markets are priced so that they have zero net present value. This means that

$$-F_0 e^{-rT} + E(S_T)e^{-kT} = 0$$

or

$$F_0 = E(S_T)e^{(r-k)T} \qquad (8.20)$$

As we have just discussed, the returns investors require on an investment depend on its systematic risk. The investment we have been considering is in essence an investment in the asset underlying the futures contract. If the returns from this asset are uncorrelated with the stock market, the correct discount rate to use is the risk-free rate r, so we should set $k = r$. Equation (8.20) then gives

$$F_0 = E(S_T)$$

This shows that the futures price is an unbiased estimate of the expected future spot price when the return from the underlying asset is uncorrelated with the stock market.

If the return from the asset is positively correlated with the stock market, $k > r$ and Equation (8.20) leads to $F_0 < E(S_T)$. This shows that, when the asset underlying the futures contract has positive systematic risk, we should expect the futures price to understate the expected future spot price. An example of an asset that has positive systematic risk is a stock index. The expected return of investors on the stocks underlying an index is generally more than the risk-free rate, r. The dividends provide a return of q. The expected increase in the index must therefore be more than $r - q$. Equation (8.8) is therefore consistent with the prediction that the futures price understates the expected future stock price for a stock index.

If the return from the asset is negatively correlated with the stock market, $k < r$ and Equation (8.20) gives $F_0 > E(S_T)$. This shows that, when the asset underlying the futures contract has negative systematic risk, we should expect the futures price to overstate the expected future spot price.

These results are summarized in Table 8-5.

Normal Backwardation and Contango

When the futures price is below the expected future spot price, the situation is known as *normal backwardation*; and when the futures price is above the expected future spot price, the situation is known as *contango*. However, it should be noted that sometimes these terms are used to refer to whether the futures price is below or above the current spot price, rather than the expected future spot price.

TABLE 8-5 Relationship between Futures Price and Expected Future Spot Price

Underlying Asset	Relationship of Expected Return k from Asset to Risk-Free Rate r	Relationship of Futures Price F to Expected Future Spot Price $E(S_T)$
No systematic risk	$k = r$	$F_0 = E(S_T)$
Positive systematic risk	$k > r$	$F_0 < E(S_T)$
Negative systematic risk	$k < r$	$F_0 > E(S_T)$

SUMMARY

For most purposes, the futures price of a contract with a certain delivery date can be considered to be the same as the forward price for a contract with the same delivery date. It can be shown that in theory the two should be exactly the same when interest rates are perfectly predictable.

For the purposes of understanding futures (or forward) prices, it is convenient to divide futures contracts into two categories: those in which the underlying asset is held for investment by a significant number of investors and those in which the underlying asset is held primarily for consumption purposes.

In the case of investment assets, we have considered three different situations:

1. The asset provides no income.
2. The asset provides a known dollar income.
3. The asset provides a known yield.

The results are summarized in Table 8-6. They enable futures prices to be obtained for contracts on stock indices, currencies, gold, and silver. Storage costs can be treated as negative income.

In the case of consumption assets, it is not possible to obtain the futures price as a function of the spot price and other observable variables. Here the parameter known as the asset's convenience yield becomes important. It measures the extent to which users of the commodity feel that

TABLE 8-6 Summary of Results for a Contract with Time to Maturity T on an Investment Asset with Price S_0 when the Risk-Free Interest Rate for a T-Year Period Is r.

Asset	Forward/ Futures Price	Value of Long Forward Contract with Delivery Price K
Provides no income:	S_0e^{rT}	$S_0 - Ke^{-rT}$
Provides known income with present value I:	$(S_0 - I)e^{rT}$	$S_0 - I - Ke^{-rT}$
Provides known yield q:	$S_0e^{(r-q)T}$	$S_0e^{-qT} - Ke^{-rT}$

ownership of the physical asset provides benefits that are not obtained by the holders of the futures contract. These benefits may include the ability to profit from temporary local shortages or the ability to keep a production process running. We can obtain an upper bound for the futures price of consumption assets using arbitrage arguments, but we cannot nail down an equality relationship between futures and spot prices.

The concept of cost of carry is sometimes useful. The cost of carry is the storage cost of the underlying asset plus the cost of financing it minus the income received from it. In the case of investment assets, the futures price is greater than the spot price by an amount reflecting the cost of carry. In the case of consumption assets, the futures price is greater than the spot price by an amount reflecting the cost of carry net of the convenience yield.

If we assume the capital asset pricing model is true, the relationship between the futures price and the expected future spot price depends on whether the return on the asset is positively or negatively correlated with the return on the stock market. Positive correlation will tend to lead to a futures price lower than the expected future spot price, whereas negative correlation will tend to lead to a futures price higher than the expected future spot price. Only when the correlation is zero will the theoretical futures price be equal to the expected future spot price.

Further Reading

Cox, J. C, J. E. Ingersoll, and S. A. Ross. "The Relation between Forward Prices and Futures Prices," *Journal of Financial Economics*, 9 (December 1981): 321–46.

Ghon, R. S. and R. P. Chang. "Intra-day Arbitrage in Foreign Exchange and Eurocurrency Markets," *Journal of Finance*, 47, 1 (1992): 363–380.

Jarrow, R. A., and G. S. Oldfield. "Forward Contracts and Futures Contracts," *Journal of Financial Economics*, 9 (December 1981): 373–82.

Kane, E. J. "Market Incompleteness and Divergences between Forward and Futures Interest Rates," *Journal of Finance*, 35 (May 1980): 221–34.

Pindyck, R. S. "Inventories and the Short-Run Dynamics of Commodity Prices," *Rand Journal of Economics*, 25, 1 (1994): 141–159.

Richard, S., and S. Sundaresan. "A Continuous-Time Model of Forward and Futures Prices in a Multigood Economy," *Journal of Financial Economics*, 9 (December 1981): 347–72.

Routledge, B. R., D. J. Seppi, and C. S. Spatt. "Equilibrium Forward Curves for Commodities," *Journal of Finance*, 55, 3 (2000) 1297-1338.

Interest Rate Futures

9

■ Learning Objectives

Candidates, after completing this reading, should be able to:

- Identify the most commonly used day count conventions, describe the markets that each one is typically used in, and apply each to an interest calculation.
- Calculate the conversion of a discount rate to a price for a US Treasury bill.
- Differentiate between the clean and dirty price for a US Treasury bond; calculate the accrued interest and dirty price on a US Treasury bond.
- Explain and calculate a US Treasury bond futures contract conversion factor.
- Calculate the cost of delivering a bond into a Treasury bond futures contract.
- Describe the impact of the level and shape of the yield curve on the cheapest-to-deliver Treasury bond decision.

- Calculate the theoretical futures price for a Treasury bond futures contract.
- Calculate the final contract price on a Eurodollar futures contract.
- Describe and compute the Eurodollar futures contract convexity adjustment.
- Explain how Eurodollar futures can be used to extend the LIBOR zero curve.
- Calculate the duration-based hedge ratio and describe a duration-based hedging strategy using interest rate futures.
- Explain the limitations of using a duration-based hedging strategy.

Excerpt is Chapter 6 of Options, Futures, and Other Derivatives, *Eighth Edition, by John Hull.*

So far we have covered futures contracts on commodities, stock indices, and foreign currencies. We have seen how they work, how they are used for hedging, and how futures prices are determined. We now move on to consider interest rate futures.

This chapter explains the popular Treasury bond and Eurodollar futures contracts that trade in the United States. Many of the other interest rate futures contracts throughout the world have been modeled on these contracts. The chapter also shows how interest rate futures contracts, when used in conjunction with the duration measure introduced in Chapter 7, can be used to hedge a company's exposure to interest rate movements.

DAY COUNT AND QUOTATION CONVENTIONS

As a preliminary to the material in this chapter, we consider the day count and quotation conventions that apply to bonds and other instruments dependent on the interest rate.

Day Counts

The day count defines the way in which interest accrues over time. Generally, we know the interest earned over some reference period (e.g., the time between coupon payments on a bond), and we are interested in calculating the interest earned over some other period.

The day count convention is usually expressed as X/Y. When we are calculating the interest earned between two dates, X defines the way in which the number of days between the two dates is calculated, and Y defines the way in which the total number of days in the reference period is measured. The interest earned between the two dates is

$$\frac{\text{Number of days between dates}}{\text{Number of days in reference period}} \times \frac{\text{Interest earned in}}{\text{reference period}}$$

Three day count conventions that are commonly used in the United States are:

1. Actual/actual (in period)
2. 30/360
3. Actual/360

The actual/actual (in period) day count is used for Treasury bonds in the United States. This means that the

interest earned between two dates is based on the ratio of the actual days elapsed to the actual number of days in the period between coupon payments. Assume that the bond principal is $100, coupon payment dates are March 1 and September 1, and the coupon rate is 8% per annum. (This means that $4 of interest is paid on each of March 1 and September 1.) Suppose that we wish to calculate the interest earned between March 1 and July 3. The reference period is from March 1 to September 1. There are 184 (actual) days in the reference period, and interest of $4 is earned during the period. There are 124 (actual) days between March 1 and July 3. The interest earned between March 1 and July 3 is therefore

$$\frac{124}{184} \times 4 = 2.6957$$

The 30/360 day count is used for corporate and municipal bonds in the United States. This means that we assume 30 days per month and 360 days per year when carrying out calculations. With the 30/360 day count, the total number of days between March 1 and September 1 is 180. The total number of days between March 1 and July 3 is $(4 \times 30) + 2 = 122$. In a corporate bond with the same terms as the Treasury bond just considered, the interest earned between March 1 and July 3 would therefore be

$$\frac{122}{180} \times 4 = 2.7111$$

As shown in Box 9-1, sometimes the 30/360 day count convention has surprising consequences.

The actual/360 day count is used for money market instruments in the United States. This indicates that the reference period is 360 days. The interest earned during part of a year is calculated by dividing the actual number of elapsed days by 360 and multiplying by the rate. The interest earned in 90 days is therefore exactly one-fourth of the quoted rate, and the interest earned in a whole year of 365 days is 365/360 times the quoted rate.

Conventions vary from country to country and from instrument to instrument. For example, money market instruments are quoted on an actual/365 basis in Australia, Canada, and New Zealand. LIBOR is quoted on an actual/360 for all currencies except sterling, for which it is quoted on an actual/365 basis. Euro-denominated and sterling bonds are usually quoted on an actual/actual basis.

Price Quotations of US Treasury Bills

The prices of money market instruments are sometimes quoted using a *discount rate*. This is the interest earned as a percentage of the final face value rather than as a percentage of the initial price paid for the instrument. An example is Treasury bills in the United States. If the price of a 91-day Treasury bill is quoted as 8, this means that the rate of interest earned is 8% of the face value per 360 days. Suppose that the face value is $100. Interest of $2.0222 (= $100 × 0.08 × 91/360) is earned over the 91-day life. This corresponds to a true rate of interest of 2.0222/(100 − 2.0222) = 2.064% for the 91-day period. In general, the relationship between the cash price and quoted price of a Treasury bill in the United States is

$$P = \frac{360}{n}(100 - Y)$$

where P is the quoted price, Y is the cash price, and n is the remaining life of the Treasury bill measured in calendar days.

Price Quotations of US Treasury Bonds

Treasury bond prices in the United States are quoted in dollars and thirty-seconds of a dollar. The quoted price is for a bond with a face value of $100. Thus, a quote of 90-05 indicates that the quoted price for a bond with a face value of $100,000 is $90,156.25.

The quoted price, which traders refer to as the *clean price*, is not the same as the cash price paid by the purchaser of the bond, which is referred to by traders as the *dirty price*. In general,

Cash price = Quoted price + Accrued interest since last coupon date

To illustrate this formula, suppose that it is March 5, 2010, and the bond under consideration is an 11% coupon bond maturing on July 10, 2018, with a quoted price of 95-16 or $95.50. Because coupons are paid semiannually on government bonds (and the final coupon is at maturity), the most recent coupon date is January 10, 2010, and the next coupon date is July 10, 2010. The number of days between January 10, 2010, and March 5, 2010, is 54, whereas the number of days between January 10, 2010, and July 10, 2010, is 181. On a bond with $100 face value, the coupon payment is $5.50 on January 10 and July 10. The accrued interest on March 5, 2010, is the share of the July 10 coupon accruing to the bondholder on March 5, 2010. Because actual/actual in period is used for Treasury bonds in the United States, this is

$$\frac{54}{181} \times \$5.50 = \$1.64$$

The cash price per $100 face value for the bond is therefore

$$\$95.50 + \$1.64 = \$97.14$$

Thus, the cash price of a $100,000 bond is $97,140.

TREASURY BOND FUTURES

Table 9-1 shows interest rate futures quotes on May 26, 2010. One of the most popular long-term interest rate futures contracts is the Treasury bond futures contract traded by the CME Group. In this contract, any government bond that has more than 15 years to maturity on the first day of the delivery month and is not callable within 15 years from that day can be delivered. As will be explained later in this section, the exchange has developed a procedure for adjusting the price received by the party with the short position according to the particular bond it chooses to deliver.

The 10-year, 5-year, and 2-year Treasury note futures contract in the United States are also very popular. In the 10-year Treasury note futures contract, any government bond (or note) with a maturity between 6½ and 10 years can be delivered. In the 5-year Treasury note futures contract, the bond delivered must have a remaining life

	Open	High	Low	Settlement	Change	Volume	Open interest
Treasury Bonds $100,000 (CME Group)							
June 2010	125-000	125-090	123-280	124-150	−25.0	691,927	462,946
Sept. 2010	124-170	124-290	123-130	124-010	−28.0	240,475	294,151
Treasury Notes 10 Year $100,000 (CME Group)							
June 2010	121-180	121-230	120-245	121-050	−16.5	2,139,365	1,085,236
Sept. 2010	120-230	120-295	119-300	120-105	−18.0	657,677	754,551
Treasury Notes 5 Year $100,000 (CME Group)							
June 2010	117-260	117-287	117-082	117-157	−12.0	1,008,580	710,630
Sept. 2010	116-312	117-035	116-140	116-217	−12.5	360,038	353,682
Treasury Notes 2 Year $100,000 (CME Group)							
June 2010	109-102	109-110	109-050	109-080	−2.5	595,833	642,470
Sept. 2010	109-002	109-010	108-272	108-302	−2.7	282,058	343,447
30-day Fed Funds Rate $5,000,000 (CME Group)							
May 2010	99.7950	99.7975	99.7925	99.7925	0.0000	2,440	63,402
Nov. 2010	99.7150	99.7250	99.7000	99.7150	0.0000	8,440	83,036
Eurodollar $1,000,000 (CME Group)							
June 2010	99.3400	99.3400	99.3050	99.3100	0.0425	370,183	1,110,424
Sept. 2010	99.1150	99.1150	99.0500	99.0500	0.0250	693,097	1,107,562
Dec. 2010	98.9700	98.9700	98.8950	98.8950	−0.0050	500,388	1,065,630
Dec. 2011	98.2200	98.2250	98.1750	98.2050	−0.0450	222,979	530,952
Dec. 2012	97.2950	97.3350	97.2750	97.3350	−0.0650	61,428	141,428
Dec. 2015	95.5100	95.5800	95.5100	95.5800	−0.0400	1,403	10,380

between 4.167 and 5.25 years; in the 2-year contract, the remaining life must be between 1.75 and 5.25 years.

The remaining discussion in this section focuses on the Treasury bond futures. The Treasury note futures traded in the United States and many other futures contracts in the rest of the world are designed in a similar way to the Treasury bond futures, so that many of the points we will make are applicable to these contracts as well.

Quotes

Treasury bond and Treasury note futures contracts are quoted in dollars and thirty-seconds of a dollar per $100 face value. This is similar to the way bonds and notes are quoted in the spot market. In Table 9-1, the settlement price of the June 2010 Treasury bond futures contract is specified as 124-150. This means $124\frac{15.0}{32}$, or 124.46875. The

settlement price of the September 2010 10-year Treasury note futures contract is quoted as 120-105. This means $120\frac{10.5}{32}$, or 120.328125. The settlement price of the June 2010 5-year Treasury bond price is quoted as 117-157. This means $117\frac{15.75}{32}$, or 117.492188. Finally, the settlement price of the September 2010 2-year Treasury note futures contract is quoted as 108-302. This means $108\frac{30.25}{32}$, or 108.945313.

Conversion Factors

As mentioned, the Treasury bond futures contract allows the party with the short position to choose to deliver any bond that has a maturity of more than 15 years and is not callable within 15 years. When a particular bond is delivered, a parameter known as its *conversion factor* defines the price received for the bond by the party with the short position. The applicable quoted price is the product of the conversion factor and the most recent settlement price for the futures contract. Taking accrued interest into account (see previous section), the cash received for each $100 face value of the bond delivered is

(Most recent settlement price × Conversion factor) + Accrued interest

Each contract is for the delivery of $100,000 face value of bonds. Suppose that the most recent settlement price is 90-00, the conversion factor for the bond delivered is 1.3800, and the accrued interest on this bond at the time of delivery is $3 per $100 face value. The cash received by the party with the short position (and paid by the party with the long position) is then

$$(1.3800 \times 90.00) + 3.00 = \$127.20$$

per $100 face value. A party with the short position in one contract would deliver bonds with a face value of $100,000 and receive $127,200.

The conversion factor for a bond is set equal to the quoted price the bond would have per dollar of principal on the first day of the delivery month on the assumption that the interest rate for all maturities equals 6% per annum (with semiannual compounding). The bond maturity and the times to the coupon payment dates are rounded down to the nearest 3 months for the purposes of the calculation. The practice enables the exchange to produce comprehensive tables. If, after rounding, the bond lasts for an exact number of 6-month periods, the first coupon is assumed to be paid in 6 months. If, after rounding, the bond does not last for an exact number of 6-month periods (i.e., there are an extra 3 months), the first coupon is assumed to be paid after 3 months and accrued interest is subtracted.

As a first example of these rules, consider a 10% coupon bond with 20 years and 2 months to maturity. For the purposes of calculating the conversion factor, the bond is assumed to have exactly 20 years to maturity. The first coupon payment is assumed to be made after 6 months. Coupon payments are then assumed to be made at 6-month intervals until the end of the 20 years when the principal payment is made. Assume that the face value is $100. When the discount rate is 6% per annum with semiannual compounding (or 3% per 6 months), the value of the bond is

$$\sum_{i=1}^{40} \frac{5}{1.03^i} + \frac{100}{1.03^{40}} = \$146.23$$

Dividing by the face value gives a conversion factor of 1.4623.

As a second example of the rules, consider an 8% coupon bond with 18 years and 4 months to maturity. For the purposes of calculating the conversion factor, the bond is assumed to have exactly 18 years and 3 months to maturity. Discounting all the payments back to a point in time 3 months from today at 6% per annum (compounded semi-annually) gives a value of

$$4 + \sum_{i=1}^{36} \frac{4}{1.03^i} + \frac{100}{1.03^{36}} = \$125.83$$

The interest rate for a 3-month period is $\sqrt{1.03} - 1$, or 1.4889%. Hence, discounting back to the present gives the bond's value as 125.83/1.014889 = $123.99. Subtracting the accrued interest of 2.0, this becomes $121.99. The conversion factor is therefore 1.2199.

Cheapest-to-Deliver Bond

At any given time during the delivery month, there are many bonds that can be delivered in the Treasury bond futures contract. These vary widely as far as coupon and maturity are concerned. The party with the short position can choose which of the available bonds is "cheapest" to deliver. Because the party with the short position receives

(Most recent settlement price × Conversion factor) + Accrued interest

the cost of purchasing a bond is

Quoted bond price + Accrued interest

the cheapest-to-deliver bond is the one for which

Quoted bond price − (Most recent settlement price × Conversion factor)

is least. Once the party with the short position has decided to deliver, it can determine the cheapest-to-deliver bond by examining each of the deliverable bonds in turn.

Example 9.1

The party with the short position has decided to deliver and is trying to choose between the three bonds in the table below. Assume the most recent settlement price is 93-08, or 93.25.

Bond	Quoted Bond Price ($)	Conversion Factor
1	99.50	1.0382
2	143.50	1.5188
3	119.75	1.2615

The cost of delivering each of the bonds is as follows:

Bond 1: $99.50 - (93.25 \times 1.0382) = \$2.69$

Bond 2: $143.50 - (93.25 \times 1.5188) = \$1.87$

Bond 3: $119.75 - (93.25 \times 1.2615) = \$2.12$

The cheapest-to-deliver bond is Bond 2.

A number of factors determine the cheapest-to-deliver bond. When bond yields are in excess of 6%, the conversion factor system tends to favor the delivery of low-coupon long-maturity bonds. When yields are less than 6%, the system tends to favor the delivery of high-coupon short-maturity bonds. Also, when the yield curve is upward-sloping, there is a tendency for bonds with a long time to maturity to be favored, whereas when it is downward-sloping, there is a tendency for bonds with a short time to maturity to be delivered.

In addition to the cheapest-to-deliver bond option, the party with a short position has an option known as the wild card play. This is described in Box 9-2.

BOX 9-2   The Wild Card Play

Trading in the CME Group's Treasury bond futures contract ceases at 2:00 p.m. Chicago time. However, Treasury bonds themselves continue trading in the spot market until 4:00 p.m. Furthermore, a trader with a short futures position has until 8:00 p.m. to issue to the clearinghouse a notice of intention to deliver. If the notice is issued, the invoice price is calculated on the basis of the settlement price that day. This is the price at which trading was conducted just before the closing bell at 2:00 p.m.

This practice gives rise to an option known as the *wild card play*. If bond prices decline after 2:00 p.m. on the first day of the delivery month, the party with the short position can issue a notice of intention to deliver at, say, 3:45 p.m. and proceed to buy bonds in the spot market for delivery at the 2:00 p.m. futures price. If the bond price does not decline, the party with the short position keeps the position open and waits until the next day when the same strategy can be used.

As with the other options open to the party with the short position, the wild card play is not free. Its value is reflected in the futures price, which is lower than it would be without the option.

Determining the Futures Price

An exact theoretical futures price for the Treasury bond contract is difficult to determine because the short party's options concerned with the timing of delivery and choice of the bond that is delivered cannot easily be valued. However, if we assume that both the cheapest-to-deliver bond and the delivery date are known, the Treasury bond futures contract is a futures contract on a traded security (the bond) that provides the holder with known income.[1] Equation (8.2) then shows that the futures price, F_0, is related to the spot price, S_0, by

$$F_0 = (S_0 - I)e^{rT} \qquad \textbf{(9.1)}$$

where I is the present value of the coupons during the life of the futures contract, T is the time until the futures contract matures, and r is the risk-free interest rate applicable to a time period of length T.

Example 9.2

Suppose that, in a Treasury bond futures contract, it is known that the cheapest-to-deliver bond will be a 12% coupon bond with a conversion factor of 1.6000. Suppose also that it is known that delivery will take place in 270 days. Coupons are payable semiannually on the bond. As illustrated in Figure 9-1, the last coupon date was 60 days ago, the next coupon date is in 122 days, and the coupon date thereafter is in 305 days. The term structure is flat, and the rate of interest (with continuous compounding) is 10% per annum. Assume that the current quoted bond price is $115. The cash price of the bond is obtained by adding to this quoted price the proportion of the next coupon payment that accrues to the holder. The cash price is therefore

$$115 + \frac{60}{60 + 122} \times 6 = 116.978$$

A coupon of $6 will be received after 122 days ($= 0.3342$ years). The present value of this is

$$6e^{-0.1 \times 0.3342} = 5.803$$

---

[1] In practice, for the purposes of determining the cheapest-to-deliver in this calculation, analysts usually assume that zero rates at the maturity of the futures contract will equal today's forward rates.

FIGURE 9-1   Time chart for Example 9.2.

The futures contract lasts for 270 days (= 0.7397 years). The cash futures price, if the contract were written on the 12% bond, would therefore be

$$(116.978 - 5.803)e^{0.1 \times 0.7397} = 119.711$$

At delivery, there are 148 days of accrued interest. The quoted futures price, if the contract were written on the 12% bond, is calculated by subtracting the accrued interest

$$119.711 - 6 \times \frac{148}{148 + 35} = 114.859$$

From the definition of the conversion factor, 1.6000 standard bonds are considered equivalent to each 12% bond. The quoted futures price should therefore be

$$\frac{114.859}{1.6000} = 71.79$$

EURODOLLAR FUTURES

The most popular interest rate futures contract in the United States is the three-month Eurodollar futures contract traded by the CME Group. A Eurodollar is a dollar deposited in a U.S. or foreign bank outside the United States. The Eurodollar interest rate is the rate of interest earned on Eurodollars deposited by one bank with another bank. It is essentially the same as the London Interbank Offered Rate (LIBOR) introduced in Chapter 7.

A three-month Eurodollar futures contract is a futures contract on the interest that will be paid (by someone who borrows at the Eurodollar interest rate) on $1 million for a future three-month period. It allows a trader to speculate on a future three-month interest rate or to hedge an exposure to a future three-month interest rate. Eurodollar futures contracts have maturities in March, June, September, and December for up to 10 years into the future. This means that in 2010 a trader can use Eurodollar futures to take a position on what interest rates will be as far into the future as 2020. Short-maturity contracts trade for months other than March, June, September, and December.

To understand how Eurodollar futures contracts work, consider the June 2010 contract in Table 9-1. The quoted settlement price on May 26, 2010, is 99.3100. The contract ends on the third Wednesday of the delivery month. In the case of this contract, the third Wednesday of the delivery month is June 16, 2010. The contract is settled daily in the usual way until that date. On June 16, 2010, the settlement price is set equal to $100 - R$, where R is the actual three-month Eurodollar interest rate on that day, expressed with quarterly compounding and an actual/360 day count convention. Thus, if the three-month Eurodollar interest rate on June 16, 2010, turned out to be 0.75% (actual/360 with quarterly compounding), the final settlement price would be 99.2500. Once a final settlement has taken place, all contracts are declared closed.

The contract is designed so that a one-basis-point (= 0.01) move in the futures quote corresponds to a gain or loss of $25 per contract. When a Eurodollar futures quote increases by one basis point, a trader who is long one contract gains $25 and a trader who is short one contract loses $25. Similarly, when the quote decreases by one basis point a trader who is long one contract loses $25 and a trader who is short one contract gains $25. Suppose, for example, a settlement price changes from 99.3100 to 99.2700. Traders with long positions lose $4 \times 25 = $100 per contract; traders with short positions gain $100 per contract. A one-basis-point change in the futures quote corresponds to a 0.01% change in the futures interest rate. This in turn leads to a

$$1,000,000 \times 0.0001 \times 0.25 = 25$$

or $25 change in the interest that will be earned on $1 million in three months. The $25 per basis point rule is therefore consistent with the point made earlier that the contract locks in an interest rate on $1 million for three months.

The futures quote is 100 minus the futures interest rate, an investor who is long gains when interest rates fall and one who is short gains when interest rates rise. Table 9–2 shows a possible set of outcomes for the June 2010 contract in Table 9–1.

TABLE 9-2 Possible Sequence of Prices for June 2010 Eurodollar Futures Contract

Date	Futures Price	Change	Gain per Contract ($)
May 26, 2010	99.3100		
May 27, 2010	99.2700	−0.0400	−100
May 28, 2010	99.3200	+0.0500	+125
⋮	⋮	⋮	⋮
June 16, 2010	99.5300	+0.0600	+150
Total		+0.2200	+550

The contract price is defined as

$$10,000 \times [100 - 0.25 \times (100 - Q)] \qquad (9.2)$$

where Q is the quote. Thus, the settlement price of 99.3100 for the June 2010 contract in Table 9-1 corresponds to a contract price of

$$10,000 \times [100 - 0.25 \times (100 - 93.3100)] = \$998,275$$

In Table 9-2, the final contract price is

$$10,000 \times [100 - 0.25 \times (100 - 99.5300)] = \$998,825$$

and the difference between the initial and final contract price is $550. This is consistent with the gain calculated in Table 9-2 using the "$25 per one-basis-point move" rule.

Example 9.3

An investor wants to lock in the interest rate for a three-month period beginning September 19, 2012, on a principal of $100 million. The September 2012 Eurodollar futures quote is 96.50, indicating that the investor can lock in an interest rate of 100 − 96.5 or 3.5% per annum. The investor hedges by buying 100 contracts. Suppose that on September 19, 2012, the three-month Eurodollar rate turns out to be 2.6%. The final settlement in the contract is then at a price of 97.40. The investor gains

$$100 \times 25 \times (9,740 - 9,650) = 225,000$$

or $225,000 on the Eurodollar futures contracts. The interest earned on the three-month investment is

$$100,000,000 \times 0.25 \times 0.026 = 650,000$$

or $650,000. The gain on the Eurodollar futures brings this up to $875,000, which is what the interest would be at 3.5% ($100,000,000 \times 0.25 \times 0.035 = 875,000$).

It appears that the futures trade has the effect of exactly locking an interest rate of 3.5% in all circumstances. In fact, the hedge is less than perfect because (a) futures contracts are settled daily (not all at the end) and (b) the final settlement in the futures contract happens on September 19, 2012, whereas the interest payment on the investment is three months later. One way of adjusting for the second point is to reduce the size of the hedge to reflect the difference between funds received on September 19, 2012, and funds received three months later. In this case, we would assume an interest rate of 3.5% for the three-month period and multiply the number of contracts by $1/(1 + 0.035 \times 0.25) = 0.9913$. This would lead to 99 rather than 100 contracts being purchased.

Example 9.3 shows how Eurodollar futures contracts can be used by an investor who wants to hedge the interest that will be earned during a future three-month period starting on September 19, 2012. Note that the timing of the cash flows from the hedge does not line up exactly with the timing of the interest cash flows. This is because the futures contract is settled daily. Also, the final settlement is on September 19, 2012, whereas interest payments on the investment are received three months after September 19, 2012. As indicated in the example, a small adjustment can be made to the hedge position in an attempt to allow for this second point.

Table 9-1 shows that the first year of the interest rate term structure in the U.S. was upward sloping on May 26, 2010. The futures rate for a three-month period beginning June 16, 2010, was 0.69%; for a three-month period beginning September 15, 2010, it was 0.95%; for a three-month period beginning December 15, 2010, it was 1.105%; and for a three-month period beginning December 16, 2015, it was 4.42%.

Other contracts similar to the CME Group's Eurodollar futures contracts trade on interest rates in other countries. The CME Group trades Euroyen contracts. The London International Financial Futures and Options Exchange (part of Euronext) trades three-month Euribor contracts (i.e., contracts on the three-month LIBOR rate for the euro) and three-month Euroswiss futures.

Forward vs. Futures Interest Rates

The Eurodollar futures contract is similar to a forward rate agreement (FRA: see Chapter 7) in that it locks in an interest rate for a future period. For short maturities (up to a year or so), the Eurodollar futures interest rate can be assumed to be the same as the corresponding forward interest rate. For longer-dated contracts, differences between the contracts become important. Compare a Eurodollar futures contract on an interest rate for the period between times T_1 and T_2 with an FRA for the same period. The Eurodollar futures contract is settled daily. The final settlement is at time T_1 and reflects the realized interest rate for the period between times T_1 and T_2. By contrast the FRA is not settled daily and the final settlement reflecting the realized interest rate between times T_1 and T_2 is made at time T_2.[2]

There are therefore two differences between a Eurodollar futures contract and an FRA. These are:

1. The difference between a Eurodollar futures contract and a similar contract where there is no daily settlement. The latter is a forward contract where a payoff equal to the difference between the forward interest rate and the realized interest rate is paid at time T_1.

2. The difference between a forward contract where there is settlement at time T_1 and a forward contract where there is settlement at time T_2.

These two components to the difference between the contracts cause some confusion in practice. Both decrease the forward rate relative to the futures rate, but for long-dated contracts the reduction caused by the second difference is much smaller than that caused by the first. The reason why the first difference (daily settlement) decreases the forward rate follows from the arguments in Chapter 8. Suppose you have a contract where the payoff is $R_M - R_F$ at time T_1, where R_F is a predetermined rate for the period between T_1 and T_2, and R_M is the realized rate for this period, and you have the option to switch to daily settlement. In this case daily settlement tends to lead to cash inflows when rates are high and cash outflows when rates are low. You would therefore find switching to daily settlement to be attractive because you tend to have more money in your margin account when rates are high. As a result the market would therefore set R_F higher for the daily settlement alternative (reducing your cumulative

expected payoff). To put this the other way around, switching from daily settlement to settlement at time T_1 reduces R_F.

To understand the reason why the second difference reduces the forward rate, suppose that the payoff of $R_M - R_F$ is at time T_2 instead of T_1 (as it is for a regular FRA). If R_M is high, the payoff is positive. Because rates are high, the cost to you of having the payoff that you receive at time T_2 rather than time T_1 is relatively high. If R_M is low, the payoff is negative. Because rates are low, the benefit to you of having the payoff you make at time T_2 rather than time T_1 is relatively low. Overall you would rather have the payoff at time T_1. If it is at time T_2 rather than T_1, you must be compensated by a reduction in R_F.[3]

Convexity Adjustment

Analysts make what is known as a *convexity adjustment* to account for the total difference between the two rates. One popular adjustment is[4]

$$\text{Forward rate} = \text{Futures rate} - \tfrac{1}{2}\sigma^2 T_1 T_2 \qquad \text{(9.3)}$$

where, as above, T_1 is the time to maturity of the futures contract and T_2 is the time to the maturity of the rate underlying the futures contract. The variable σ is the standard deviation of the change in the short-term interest rate in 1 year. Both rates are expressed with continuous compounding.[5]

Example 9.4

Consider the situation where $\sigma = 0.012$ and we wish to calculate the forward rate when the 8-year Eurodollar futures price quote is 94. In this case $T_1 = 8$, $T_2 = 8.25$, and the convexity adjustment is

$$\tfrac{1}{2} \times 0.012^2 \times 8 \times 8.25 = 0.00475$$

or 0.475% (47.5 basis points). The futures rate is 6% per annum on an actual/360 basis with quarterly compounding. This corresponds to 1.5% per 90 days or an annual

---

[2] As mentioned in Chapter 7, settlement may occur at time T_1, but it is then equal to the present value of what the forward contract payoff would be at time T_2.

[3] Quantifying the effect of this type of timing difference on the value of a derivative is discussed later.

[4] See Technical Note 1 at www.rotman.utoronto.ca/~hull/TechnicalNotes for a proof of this.

[5] This formula is based on the Ho–Lee interest rate model. See T.S.Y. Ho and S.-B. Lee, "Term structure movements and pricing interest rate contingent claims," *Journal of Finance,* 41 (December 1986), 1011–29.

rate of $(365/90) \ln 1.015 = 6.038\%$ with continuous compounding and an actual/365 day count. The estimate of the forward rate given by Equation (9.3), therefore, is $6.038 - 0.475 = 5.563\%$ per annum with continuous compounding. The table below shows how the size of the adjustment increases with the time to maturity.

Maturity of Futures (Years)	Convexity Adjustments (Basis Points)
2	3.2
4	12.2
6	27.0
8	47.5
10	73.8

We can see from this table that the size of the adjustment is roughly proportional to the square of the time to maturity of the futures contract. For example, when the maturity doubles from 2 to 4 years, the size of the convexity approximately quadruples.

Using Eurodollar Futures to Extend the LIBOR Zero Curve

The LIBOR zero curve out to 1 year is determined by the 1-month, 3-month, 6-month, and 12-month LIBOR rates. Once the convexity adjustment just described has been made, Eurodollar futures are often used to extend the zero curve. Suppose that the ith Eurodollar futures contract matures at time T_i ($i = 1, 2, \ldots$). It is usually assumed that the forward interest rate calculated from the ith futures contract applies to the period T_i to T_{i+1}. (In practice this is close to true.) This enables a bootstrap procedure to be used to determine zero rates. Suppose that F_i is the forward rate calculated from the ith Eurodollar futures contract and R_i is the zero rate for a maturity T_i. From Equation (7.5),

$$F_i = \frac{R_{i+1}T_{i+1} - R_i T_i}{T_{i+1} - T_i}$$

so that

$$R_{i+1} = \frac{F_i(T_{i+1} - T_i) + R_i T_i}{T_{i+1}} \qquad (9.4)$$

Other Euro rates such as Euroswiss, Euroyen, and Euribor are used in a similar way.

Example 9.5

The 400-day LIBOR zero rate has been calculated as 4.80% with continuous compounding and, from Eurodollar futures quotes, it has been calculated that (a) the forward rate for a 90-day period beginning in 400 days is 5.30% with continuous compounding, (b) the forward rate for a 90-day period beginning in 491 days is 5.50% with continuous compounding, and (c) the forward rate for a 90-day period beginning in 589 days is 5.60% with continuous compounding. We can use Equation (9.4) to obtain the 491-day rate as

$$\frac{0.053 \times 91 + 0.048 \times 400}{491} = 0.04893$$

or 4.893%. Similarly we can use the second forward rate to obtain the 589-day rate as

$$\frac{0.055 \times 98 + 0.04893 \times 491}{589} = 0.04994$$

or 4.994%. The next forward rate of 5.60% would be used to determine the zero curve out to the maturity of the next Eurodollar futures contract. (Note that, even though the rate underlying the Eurodollar futures contract is a 90-day rate, it is assumed to apply to the 91 or 98 days elapsing between Eurodollar contract maturities.)

DURATION-BASED HEDGING STRATEGIES USING FUTURES

We discussed duration in Chapter 7. Consider the situation where a position in an asset that is interest rate dependent, such as a bond portfolio or a money market security, is being hedged using an interest rate futures contract. Define:

F_c: Contract price for the interest rate futures contract

D_F: Duration of the asset underlying the futures contract at the maturity of the futures contract

P: Forward value of the portfolio being hedged at the maturity of the hedge (in practice, this is usually assumed to be the same as the value of the portfolio today)

D_P: Duration of the portfolio at the maturity of the hedge

If we assume that the change in the yield, Δy, is the same for all maturities, which means that only parallel shifts in the yield curve can occur, it is approximately true that

$$\Delta P = -PD_P \Delta y$$

It is also approximately true that

$$\Delta V_F = -V_F D_F \Delta y$$

The number of contracts required to hedge against an uncertain Δy, therefore, is

$$N^* = \frac{P D_P}{V_F D_F} \qquad \textbf{(9.5)}$$

This is the *duration-based hedge ratio*. It is sometimes also called the *price sensitivity hedge ratio*.[6] Using it has the effect of making the duration of the entire position zero.

When the hedging instrument is a Treasury bond futures contract, the hedger must base D_F on an assumption that one particular bond will be delivered. This means that the hedger must estimate which of the available bonds is likely to be cheapest to deliver at the time the hedge is put in place. If, subsequently, the interest rate environment changes so that it looks as though a different bond will be cheapest to deliver, then the hedge has to be adjusted and as a result its performance may be worse than anticipated.

When hedges are constructed using interest rate futures, it is important to bear in mind that interest rates and futures prices move in opposite directions. When interest rates go up, an interest rate futures price goes down. When interest rates go down, the reverse happens, and the interest rate futures price goes up. Thus, a company in a position to lose money if interest rates drop should hedge by taking a long futures position. Similarly, a company in a position to lose money if interest rates rise should hedge by taking a short futures position.

The hedger tries to choose the futures contract so that the duration of the underlying asset is as close as possible to the duration of the asset being hedged. Eurodollar futures tend to be used for exposures to short-term interest rates, whereas Treasury bond and Treasury note futures contracts are used for exposures to longer-term rates.

Example 9.6

It is August 2 and a fund manager with $10 million invested in government bonds is concerned that interest rates are expected to be highly volatile over the next 3 months. The fund manager decides to use the December T-bond futures contract to hedge the value of the portfolio. The current futures price is 93-02, or 93.0625. Because each contract is for the delivery of $100,000 face value of bonds, the futures contract price is $93,062.50.

Suppose that the duration of the bond portfolio in 3 months will be 6.80 years. The cheapest-to-deliver bond in the T-bond contract is expected to be a 20-year 12% per annum coupon bond. The yield on this bond is currently 8.80% per annum, and the duration will be 9.20 years at maturity of the futures contract.

The fund manager requires a short position in T-bond futures to hedge the bond portfolio. If interest rates go up, a gain will be made on the short futures position, but a loss will be made on the bond portfolio. If interest rates decrease, a loss will be made on the short position, but there will be a gain on the bond portfolio. The number of bond futures contracts that should be shorted can be calculated from Equation (9.5) as

$$\frac{10,000,000}{93,062.50} \times \frac{6.80}{9.20} = 79.42$$

To the nearest whole number, the portfolio manager should short 79 contracts.

HEDGING PORTFOLIOS OF ASSETS AND LIABILITIES

Financial institutions sometimes attempt to hedge themselves against interest rate risk by ensuring that the average duration of their assets equals the average duration of their liabilities. (The liabilities can be regarded as short positions in bonds.) This strategy is known as *duration matching* or *portfolio immunization*. When implemented, it ensures that a small parallel shift in interest rates will have little effect on the value of the portfolio of assets and liabilities. The gain (loss) on the assets should offset the loss (gain) on the liabilities.

Duration matching does not immunize a portfolio against nonparallel shifts in the zero curve. This is a weakness of the approach. In practice, short-term rates are usually more volatile than, and are not perfectly correlated with, long-term rates. Sometimes it even happens that short- and long-term rates move in opposite directions to each other. Duration matching is therefore only a first step and

---

[6] For a more detailed discussion of Equation (9.5), see R.J. Rendleman, "Duration-Based Hedging with Treasury Bond Futures," *Journal of Fixed Income* 9, 1 (June 1999): 84–91.

The asset-liability management (ALM) committees of banks now monitor their exposure to interest rates very carefully. Matching the durations of assets and liabilities is sometimes a first step, but this does not protect a bank against non-parallel shifts in the yield curve. A popular approach is known as *GAP management*. This involves dividing the zero-coupon yield curve into segments, known as *buckets*. The first bucket might be 0 to 1 month, the second 1 to 3 months, and so on. The ALM committee then investigates the effect on the value of the bank's portfolio of the zero rates corresponding to one bucket changing while those corresponding to all other buckets stay the same.

If there is a mismatch, corrective action is usually taken. This can involve changing deposit and lending rates in the way described in Chapter 7. Alternatively, tools such as swaps, FRAs, bond futures, Eurodollar futures, and other interest rate derivatives can be used.

The Eurodollar futures contract is a contract on the 3-month rate on the third Wednesday of the delivery month. Eurodollar futures are frequently used to estimate LIBOR forward rates for the purpose of constructing a LIBOR zero curve. When long-dated contracts are used in this way, it is important to make what is termed a convexity adjustment to allow for the marking to market in the futures contract.

The concept of duration is important in hedging interest rate risk. It enables a hedger to assess the sensitivity of a bond portfolio to small parallel shifts in the yield curve. It also enables the hedger to assess the sensitivity of an interest rate futures price to small changes in the yield curve. The number of futures contracts necessary to protect the bond portfolio against small parallel shifts in the yield curve can therefore be calculated.

The key assumption underlying duration-based hedging is that all interest rates change by the same amount. This means that only parallel shifts in the term structure are allowed for. In practice, short-term interest rates are generally more volatile than are long-term interest rates, and hedge performance is liable to be poor if the duration of the bond underlying the futures contract differs markedly from the duration of the asset being hedged.

financial institutions have developed other tools to help them manage their interest rate exposure. See Box 9-3.

SUMMARY

Two very popular interest rate contracts are the Treasury bond and Eurodollar futures contracts that trade in the United States. In the Treasury bond futures contracts, the party with the short position has a number of interesting delivery options:

1. Delivery can be made on any day during the delivery month.

2. There are a number of alternative bonds that can be delivered.

3. On any day during the delivery month, the notice of intention to deliver at the 2:00 p.m. settlement price can be made any time up to 8:00 p.m.

These options all tend to reduce the futures price.

Further Reading

Burghardt, G., and W. Hoskins. "The Convexity Bias in Eurodollar Futures," *Risk*, 8, 3 (1995): 63−70.

Duffie, D. "Debt Management and Interest Rate Risk," in W. Beaver and G. Parker (eds.), *Risk Management: Challenges and Solutions*. New York: McGraw-Hill, 1994.

Fabozzi, F. J. *Duration, Convexity, and Other Bond Risk Measures*. Frank Fabozzi Assoc., 1999.

Grinblatt, M., and N. Jegadeesh. "The Relative Price of Eurodollar Futures and Forward Contracts," *Journal of Finance*, 51, 4 (September 1996): 1499−1522.

10

Swaps

Learning Objectives

Candidates, after completing this reading, should be able to:

- Explain the mechanics of a plain vanilla interest rate swap and compute its cash flows.
- Explain how a plain vanilla interest rate swap can be used to transform an asset or a liability and calculate the resulting cash flows.
- Explain the role of financial intermediaries in the swaps market.
- Describe the role of the confirmation in a swap transaction.
- Describe the comparative advantage argument for the existence of interest rate swaps and explain some of the criticisms of this argument.
- Explain how the discount rates in a plain vanilla interest rate swap are computed.
- Calculate the value of a plain vanilla interest rate swap based on two simultaneous bond positions.

- Calculate the value of a plain vanilla interest rate swap from a sequence of forward rate agreements (FRAs).
- Explain the mechanics of a currency swap and compute its cash flows.
- Explain how a currency swap can be used to transform an asset or liability and calculate the resulting cash flows.
- Calculate the value of a currency swap based on two simultaneous bond positions.
- Calculate the value of a currency swap based on a sequence of FRAs.
- Describe the credit risk exposure in a swap position.
- Identify and describe other types of swaps, including commodity, volatility, and exotic swaps.

Excerpt is Chapter 7 of Options, Futures, and Other Derivatives, *Eighth Edition, by John Hull.*

The first swap contracts were negotiated in the early 1980s. Since then the market has seen phenomenal growth. Swaps now occupy a position of central importance in derivatives markets.

A swap is an over-the-counter agreement between two companies to exchange cash flows in the future. The agreement defines the dates when the cash flows are to be paid and the way in which they are to be calculated. Usually the calculation of the cash flows involves the future value of an interest rate, an exchange rate, or other market variable.

A forward contract can be viewed as a simple example of a swap. Suppose it is March 1, 2012, and a company enters into a forward contract to buy 100 ounces of gold for $1,200 per ounce in 1 year. The company can sell the gold in 1 year as soon as it is received. The forward contract is therefore equivalent to a swap where the company agrees that on March 1, 2013, it will pay $120,000 and receive $100S$, where S is the market price of 1 ounce of gold on that date.

Whereas a forward contract is equivalent to the exchange of cash flows on just one future date, swaps typically lead to cash flow exchanges on several future dates. In this chapter we examine how swaps are designed, how they are used, and how they are valued. Most of this chapter focuses on two popular swaps: plain vanilla interest rate swaps and fixed-for-fixed currency swaps.

MECHANICS OF INTEREST RATE SWAPS

The most common type of swap is a "plain vanilla" interest rate swap. In this swap a company agrees to pay cash flows equal to interest at a predetermined fixed rate on a notional principal for a predetermined number of years. In return, it receives interest at a floating rate on the same notional principal for the same period of time.

LIBOR

The floating rate in most interest rate swap agreements is the London Interbank Offered Rate (LIBOR). We introduced this in Chapter 7. It is the rate of interest at which a bank is prepared to deposit money with other banks that have a AA credit rating. One-month, three-month,

six-month, and 12-month LIBOR are quoted in all major currencies.

Just as prime is often the reference rate of interest for floating-rate loans in the domestic financial market, LIBOR is a reference rate of interest for loans in international financial markets. To understand how it is used, consider a 5-year bond with a rate of interest specified as 6-month LIBOR plus 0.5% per annum. The life of the bond is divided into 10 periods, each 6 months in length. For each period, the rate of interest is set at 0.5% per annum above the 6-month LIBOR rate at the beginning of the period. Interest is paid at the end of the period.

Illustration

Consider a hypothetical 3-year swap initiated on March 5, 2012, between Microsoft and Intel. We suppose Microsoft agrees to pay Intel an interest rate of 5% per annum on a principal of $100 million, and in return Intel agrees to pay Microsoft the 6-month LIBOR rate on the same principal. Microsoft is the *fixed-rate payer*; Intel is the *floating-rate payer*. We assume the agreement specifies that payments are to be exchanged every 6 months and that the 5% interest rate is quoted with semiannual compounding. This swap is represented diagrammatically in Figure 10-1.

The first exchange of payments would take place on September 5, 2012, 6 months after the initiation of the agreement. Microsoft would pay Intel $2.5 million. This is the interest on the $100 million principal for 6 months at 5%. Intel would pay Microsoft interest on the $100 million principal at the 6-month LIBOR rate prevailing 6 months prior to September 5, 2012—that is, on March 5, 2012. Suppose that the 6-month LIBOR rate on March 5, 2012, is 4.2%. Intel pays Microsoft $0.5 \times 0.042 \times \$100 = \$2.1$ million.[1] Note that there is no uncertainty about this first exchange of payments because it is determined by the LIBOR rate at the time the contract is entered into.

The second exchange of payments would take place on March 5, 2013, a year after the initiation of the agreement. Microsoft would pay $2.5 million to Intel. Intel would pay interest on the $100 million principal to Microsoft at the 6-month LIBOR rate prevailing 6 months prior

---

[1] The calculations here are simplified in that they ignore day count conventions. This point is discussed in more detail later in the chapter.

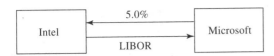

FIGURE 10-1 Interest rate swap between Microsoft and Intel.

to March 5, 2013—that is, on September 5, 2012. Suppose that the 6-month LIBOR rate on September 5, 2012, is 4.8%. Intel pays $0.5 \times 0.048 \times \$100 = \$2.4$ million to Microsoft.

In total, there are six exchanges of payment on the swap. The fixed payments are always $2.5 million. The floating-rate payments on a payment date are calculated using the 6-month LIBOR rate prevailing 6 months before the payment date. An interest rate swap is generally structured so that one side remits the difference between the two payments to the other side. In our example, Microsoft would pay Intel $0.4 million (= $2.5 million − $2.1 million) on September 5, 2012, and $0.1 million (= $2.5 million − $2.4 million) on March 5, 2013.

Table 10-1 provides a complete example of the payments made under the swap for one particular set of 6-month LIBOR rates. The table shows the swap cash flows from the perspective of Microsoft. Note that the $100 million principal is used only for the calculation of interest payments. The principal itself is not exchanged. For this reason it is termed the *notional principal*, or just the *notional*.

If the principal were exchanged at the end of the life of the swap, the nature of the deal would not be changed in any way. The principal is the same for both the fixed and floating payments. Exchanging $100 million for $100 million at the end of the life of the swap is a transaction that would have no financial value to either Microsoft or Intel. Table 10-2 shows the cash flows in Table 10-1 with a final exchange of principal added in. This provides an interesting way of viewing the swap. The cash flows in the third column of this table are the cash flows from a long position in a floating-rate bond. The cash flows in the fourth column of the table are the cash flows from a short position in a fixed-rate bond. The table shows that the swap can be regarded as the exchange of a fixed-rate bond for a floating-rate bond. Microsoft, whose position is described by Table 10-2, is long a floating-rate bond and short a fixed-rate bond. Intel is long a fixed-rate bond and short a floating-rate bond.

This characterization of the cash flows in the swap helps to explain why the floating rate in the swap is set 6 months before it is paid. On a floating-rate bond, interest is generally set at the beginning of the period to which it will apply and is paid at the end of the period. The calculation of the floating-rate payments in a "plain vanilla" interest rate swap such as the one in Table 10-2 reflects this.

Using the Swap to Transform a Liability

For Microsoft, the swap could be used to transform a floating-rate loan into a fixed-rate loan. Suppose that

TABLE 10-1 Cash Flows (millions of dollars) to Microsoft in a $100 Million 3-year Interest Rate Swap When a Fixed Rate of 5% Is Paid and LIBOR Is Received

Date	Six-month LIBOR Rate (%)	Floating Cash Flow Received	Fixed Cash Flow Paid	Net Cash Flow
Mar. 5, 2012	4.20			
Sept. 5, 2012	4.80	+2.10	−2.50	−0.40
Mar. 5, 2013	5.30	+2.40	−2.50	−0.10
Sept. 5, 2013	5.50	+2.65	−2.50	+0.15
Mar. 5, 2014	5.60	+2.75	−2.50	+0.25
Sept. 5, 2014	5.90	+2.80	−2.50	+0.30
Mar. 5, 2015		+2.95	−2.50	+0.45

TABLE 10-2 Cash Flows (millions of dollars) from Table 10-1 When There Is a Final Exchange of Principal

Date	Six-month LIBOR Rate (%)	Floating Cash Flow Received	Fixed Cash Flow Paid	Net Cash Flow
Mar. 5, 2012	4.20			
Sept. 5, 2012	4.80	+2.10	−2.50	−0.40
Mar. 5, 2013	5.30	+2.40	−2.50	−0.10
Sept. 5, 2013	5.50	+2.65	−2.50	+0.15
Mar. 5, 2014	5.60	+2.75	−2.50	+0.25
Sept. 5, 2014	5.90	+2.80	−2.50	+0.30
Mar. 5, 2015		+102.95	−102.50	+0.45

Microsoft has arranged to borrow $100 million at LIBOR plus 10 basis points. (One basis point is one-hundredth of 1%, so the rate is LIBOR plus 0.1%.) After Microsoft has entered into the swap, it has the following three sets of cash flows:

1. It pays LIBOR plus 0.1% to its outside lenders.
2. It receives LIBOR under the terms of the swap.
3. It pays 5% under the terms of the swap.

These three sets of cash flows net out to an interest rate payment of 5.1%. Thus, for Microsoft, the swap could have the effect of transforming borrowings at a floating rate of LIBOR plus 10 basis points into borrowings at a fixed rate of 5.1%.

For Intel, the swap could have the effect of transforming a fixed-rate loan into a floating-rate loan. Suppose that Intel has a 3-year $100 million loan outstanding on which it pays 5.2%. After it has entered into the swap, it has the following three sets of cash flows:

1. It pays 5.2% to its outside lenders.
2. It pays LIBOR under the terms of the swap.
3. It receives 5% under the terms of the swap.

These three sets of cash flows net out to an interest rate payment of LIBOR plus 0.2% (or LIBOR plus 20 basis points). Thus, for Intel, the swap could have the effect of transforming borrowings at a fixed rate of 5.2% into borrowings at a floating rate of LIBOR plus 20 basis points. These potential uses of the swap by Intel and Microsoft are illustrated in Figure 10-2.

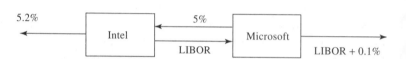

FIGURE 10-2 Microsoft and Intel use the swap to transform a liability.

Using the Swap to Transform an Asset

Swaps can also be used to transform the nature of an asset. Consider Microsoft in our example. The swap could have the effect of transforming an asset earning a fixed rate of interest into an asset earning a floating rate of interest. Suppose that Microsoft owns $100 million in bonds that will provide interest at 4.7% per annum over the next 3 years.

After Microsoft has entered into the swap, it has the following three sets of cash flows:

1. It receives 4.7% on the bonds.
2. It receives LIBOR under the terms of the swap.
3. It pays 5% under the terms of the swap.

These three sets of cash flows net out to an interest rate inflow of LIBOR minus 30 basis points. Thus, one possible use of the swap for Microsoft is to transform an asset earning 4.7% into an asset earning LIBOR minus 30 basis points.

Next, consider Intel. The swap could have the effect of transforming an asset earning a floating rate of interest into an asset earning a fixed rate of interest. Suppose that

Intel has an investment of $100 million that yields LIBOR minus 20 basis points. After it has entered into the swap, it has the following three sets of cash flows:

1. It receives LIBOR minus 20 basis points on its investment.

2. It pays LIBOR under the terms of the swap.

3. It receives 5% under the terms of the swap.

These three sets of cash flows net out to an interest rate inflow of 4.8%. Thus, one possible use of the swap for Intel is to transform an asset earning LIBOR minus 20 basis points into an asset earning 4.8%. These potential uses of the swap by Intel and Microsoft are illustrated in Figure 10-3.

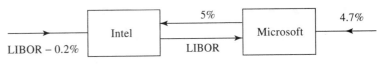

FIGURE 10-3 Microsoft and Intel use the swap to transform an asset.

FIGURE 10-4 Interest rate swap from Figure 10-2 when financial institution is involved.

Role of Financial Intermediary

Usually two nonfinancial companies such as Intel and Microsoft do not get in touch directly to arrange a swap in the way indicated in Figures 10-2 and 10-3. They each deal with a financial intermediary such as a bank or other financial institution. "Plain vanilla" fixed-for-floating swaps on US interest rates are usually structured so that the financial institution earns about 3 or 4 basis points (0.03% or 0.04%) on a pair of offsetting transactions.

Figure 10-4 shows what the role of the financial institution might be in the situation in Figure 10-2. The financial institution enters into two offsetting swap transactions with Intel and Microsoft. Assuming that both companies honor their obligations, the financial institution is certain to make a profit of 0.03% (3 basis points) per year multiplied by the notional principal of $100 million. This amounts to $30,000 per year for the 3-year period. Microsoft ends up borrowing at 5.115% (instead of 5.1%, as in Figure 10-2), and Intel ends up borrowing at LIBOR plus 21.5 basis points (instead of at LIBOR plus 20 basis points, as in Figure 10-2).

Figure 10-5 illustrates the role of the financial institution in the situation in Figure 10-3. The swap is the same as before and the financial institution is certain to make a profit of 3 basis points if neither company defaults. Microsoft ends up earning LIBOR minus 31.5 basis points

FIGURE 10-5 Interest rate swap from Figure 10-3 when financial institution is involved.

(instead of LIBOR minus 30 basis points, as in Figure 10-3), and Intel ends up earning 4.785% (instead of 4.8%, as in Figure 10-3).

Note that in each case the financial institution has two separate contracts: one with Intel and the other with Microsoft. In most instances, Intel will not even know that the financial institution has entered into an offsetting swap with Microsoft, and vice versa. If one of the companies defaults, the financial institution still has to honor its agreement with the other company. The 3-basis-point spread earned by the financial institution is partly to compensate it for the risk that one of the two companies will default on the swap payments.

Market Makers

In practice, it is unlikely that two companies will contact a financial institution at the same time and want to take opposite positions in exactly the same swap. For this reason, many large financial institutions act as market makers for swaps. This means that they are prepared to enter into a swap without having an offsetting swap with another counterparty.[2] Market makers must carefully

---

[2] This is sometimes referred to as *warehousing* swaps.

TABLE 10-3 Bid and Offer Fixed Rates in the Swap Market and Swap Rates (Percent per Annum)

Maturity (Years)	Bid	Offer	Swap Rate
2	6.03	6.06	6.045
3	6.21	6.24	6.225
4	6.35	6.39	6.370
5	6.47	6.51	6.490
7	6.65	6.68	6.665
10	6.83	6.87	6.850

quantify and hedge the risks they are taking. Bonds, forward rate agreements, and interest rate futures are examples of the instruments that can be used for hedging by swap market makers. Table 10-3 shows quotes for plain vanilla US dollar swaps that might be posted by a market maker.[3] As mentioned earlier, the bid–offer spread is 3 to 4 basis points. The average of the bid and offer fixed rates is known as the *swap rate*. This is shown in the final column of Table 10-3.

Consider a new swap where the fixed rate equals the current swap rate. We can reasonably assume that the value of this swap is zero. (Why else would a market maker choose bid–offer quotes centered on the swap rate?) In Table 10-2 we saw that a swap can be characterized as the difference between a fixed-rate bond and a floating-rate bond. Define:

B_{fix}: Value of fixed-rate bond underlying the swap we are considering

B_{fl}: Value of floating-rate bond underlying the swap we are considering

Since the swap is worth zero, it follows that

$$B_{fix} = B_{fl} \qquad \textbf{(10.1)}$$

We will use this result later in the chapter when discussing how the LIBOR/swap zero curve is determined.

---

[3] The standard swap in the United States is one where fixed payments made every 6 months are exchanged for floating LIBOR payments made every 3 months. In Table 10-1 we assumed that fixed and floating payments are exchanged every 6 months. The fixed rate should be almost exactly the same in both cases.

DAY COUNT ISSUES

We discussed day count conventions in Chapter 9. The day count conventions affect payments on a swap, and some of the numbers calculated in the examples we have given do not exactly reflect these day count conventions. Consider, for example, the 6-month LIBOR payments in Table 10-1. Because it is a US money market rate, 6-month LIBOR is quoted on an actual/360 basis. The first floating payment in Table 10-1, based on the LIBOR rate of 4.2%, is shown as $2.10 million. Because there are 184 days between March 5, 2012, and September 5, 2012, it should be

$$100 \times 0.042 \times \frac{184}{360} = \$2.1467 \text{ million}$$

In general, a LIBOR-based floating-rate cash flow on a swap payment date is calculated as $L R n / 360$, where L is the principal, R is the relevant LIBOR rate, and n is the number of days since the last payment date.

The fixed rate that is paid in a swap transaction is similarly quoted with a particular day count basis being specified. As a result, the fixed payments may not be exactly equal on each payment date. The fixed rate is usually quoted as actual/365 or 30/360. It is not therefore directly comparable with LIBOR because it applies to a full year. To make the rates approximately comparable, either the 6-month LIBOR rate must be multiplied by 365/360 or the fixed rate must be multiplied by 360/365.

For clarity of exposition, we will ignore day count issues in the calculations in the rest of this chapter.

CONFIRMATIONS

A *confirmation* is the legal agreement underlying a swap and is signed by representatives of the two parties. The drafting of confirmations has been facilitated by the work of the International Swaps and Derivatives Association (ISDA; www.isda.org) in New York. This organization has produced a number of Master Agreements that consist of clauses defining in some detail the terminology used in swap agreements, what happens in the event of default by either side, and so on. Master Agreements cover all outstanding transactions between two parties. In Box 10-1, we show a possible extract from the confirmation for the swap shown in Figure 10-4 between Microsoft and a financial institution (assumed here to be Goldman Sachs).

Trade date:	27-February-2012
Effective date:	5-March-2012
Business day convention (all dates):	Following business day
Holiday calendar:	US
Termination date:	5-March-2015
Fixed amounts	
Fixed-rate payer:	Microsoft
Fixed-rate notional principal:	USD 100 million
Fixed rate:	5.015% per annum
Fixed-rate day count convention:	Actual/365
Fixed-rate payment dates:	Each 5-March and 5-September, commencing 5-September-2012, up to and including 5-March-2015
Floating amounts	
Floating-rate payer:	Goldman Sachs
Floating-rate notional principal:	USD 100 million
Floating rate:	USD 6-month LIBOR
Floating-rate day count convention:	Actual/360
Floating-rate payment dates:	Each 5-March and 5-September, commencing 5-September-2012, up to and including 5-March-2015

The full confirmation might state that the provisions of an ISDA Master Agreement apply.

The confirmation specifies that the following business day convention is to be used and that the US calendar determines which days are business days and which days are holidays. This means that, if a payment date falls on a weekend or a US holiday, the payment is made on the next business day.[4]

THE COMPARATIVE-ADVANTAGE ARGUMENT

An explanation commonly put forward to explain the popularity of swaps concerns comparative advantages.

Consider the use of an interest rate swap to transform a liability. Some companies, it is argued, have a comparative advantage when borrowing in fixed-rate markets, whereas other companies have a comparative advantage in floating-rate markets. To obtain a new loan, it makes sense for a company to go to the market where it has a comparative advantage. As a result, the company may borrow fixed when it wants floating, or borrow floating when it wants fixed. The swap is used to transform a fixed-rate loan into a floating-rate loan, and vice versa.

Suppose that two companies, AAACorp and BBBCorp, both wish to borrow $10 million for 5 years and have been offered the rates shown in Table 10-4. AAACorp has a AAA credit rating; BBBCorp has a BBB credit rating.[5] We assume that BBBCorp wants to borrow at a fixed rate of interest, whereas AAACorp wants to borrow at a floating rate of

---

[4] Another business day convention that is sometimes specified is the *modified following* business day convention, which is the same as the following business day convention except that, when the next business day falls in a different month from the specified day, the payment is made on the immediately preceding business day. *Preceding* and *modified preceding* business day conventions are defined analogously.

[5] The credit ratings assigned to companies by S&P and Fitch (in order of decreasing creditworthiness) are AAA, AA, A, BBB, BB, B, CCC, CC, and C. The corresponding ratings assigned by Moody's are Aaa, Aa, A, Baa, Ba, B, Caa, Ca, and C, respectively.

TABLE 10-4 Borrowing Rates That Provide a Basis for the Comparative-Advantage Argument

	Fixed	Floating
AAACorp	4.0%	6-month LIBOR − 0.1%
BBBCorp	5.2%	6-month LIBOR + 0.6%

FIGURE 10-6 Swap agreement between AAACorp and BBBCorp when rates in Table 10-4 apply.

interest linked to 6-month LIBOR. Because it has a worse credit rating than AAACorp, BBBCorp pays a higher rate of interest than AAACorp in both fixed and floating markets.

A key feature of the rates offered to AAACorp and BBB-Corp is that the difference between the two fixed rates is greater than the difference between the two floating rates. BBBCorp pays 1.2% more than AAACorp in fixed-rate markets and only 0.7% more than AAACorp in floating-rate markets. BBBCorp appears to have a comparative advantage in floating-rate markets, whereas AAACorp appears to have a comparative advantage in fixed-rate markets.[6] It is this apparent anomaly that can lead to a swap being negotiated. AAACorp borrows fixed-rate funds at 4% per annum. BBBCorp borrows floating-rate funds at LIBOR plus 0.6% per annum. They then enter into a swap agreement to ensure that AAACorp ends up with floating-rate funds and BBBCorp ends up with fixed-rate funds.

To understand how this swap might work, we first assume that AAACorp and BBBCorp get in touch with each other directly. The sort of swap they might negotiate is shown in Figure 10-6. This is similar to our example in Figure 10-2. AAACorp agrees to pay BBBCorp interest at 6-month LIBOR

on $10 million. In return, BBBCorp agrees to pay AAACorp interest at a fixed rate of 4.35% per annum on $10 million.

AAACorp has three sets of interest rate cash flows:

1. It pays 4% per annum to outside lenders.
2. It receives 4.35% per annum from BBBCorp.
3. It pays LIBOR to BBBCorp.

The net effect of the three cash flows is that AAACorp pays LIBOR minus 0.35% per annum. This is 0.25% per annum less than it would pay if it went directly to floating-rate markets. BBBCorp also has three sets of interest rate cash flows:

1. It pays LIBOR + 0.6% per annum to outside lenders.
2. It receives LIBOR from AAACorp.
3. It pays 4.35% per annum to AAACorp.

The net effect of the three cash flows is that BBBCorp pays 4.95% per annum. This is 0.25% per annum less than it would pay if it went directly to fixed-rate markets.

In this example, the swap has been structured so that the net gain to both sides is the same, 0.25%. This need not be the case. However, the total apparent gain from this type of interest rate swap arrangement is always $a − b$, where a is the difference between the interest rates facing the two companies in fixed-rate markets, and b is the difference between the interest rates facing the two companies in floating-rate markets. In this case, $a = 1.2\%$ and $b = 0.7\%$, so that the total gain is 0.5%.

If AAACorp and BBBCorp did not deal directly with each other and used a financial institution, an arrangement such as that shown in Figure 10-7 might result. (This is similar to the example in Figure 10-4.) In this case, AAACorp ends up borrowing at LIBOR minus 0.33%, BBBCorp ends up borrowing at 4.97%, and the financial institution earns a spread of 4 basis points per year. The gain to AAACorp is 0.23%; the gain to BBBCorp is 0.23%; and the gain to the financial institution is 0.04%. The total gain to all three parties is 0.50% as before.

Criticism of the Argument

The comparative-advantage argument we have just outlined for explaining the attractiveness of interest rate swaps is open to question. Why in Table 10-4 should the spreads between the rates offered to AAACorp and

---

[6] Note that BBBCorp's comparative advantage in floating-rate markets does not imply that BBBCorp pays less than AAACorp in this market. It means that the extra amount that BBBCorp pays over the amount paid by AAACorp is less in this market. One of my students summarized the situation as follows: "AAACorp pays more less in fixed-rate markets; BBBCorp pays less more in floating-rate markets."

FIGURE 10-7 Swap agreement between AAACorp and BBBCorp when rates in Table 10-4 apply and a financial intermediary is involved.

BBBCorp be different in fixed and floating markets? Now that the swap market has been in existence for some time, we might reasonably expect these types of differences to have been arbitraged away.

The reason that spread differentials appear to exist is due to the nature of the contracts available to companies in fixed and floating markets. The 4.0% and 5.2% rates available to AAACorp and BBBCorp in fixed-rate markets are 5-year rates (e.g., the rates at which the companies can issue 5-year fixed-rate bonds). The LIBOR − 0.1% and LIBOR + 0.6% rates available to AAACorp and BBBCorp in floating-rate markets are 6-month rates. In the floating-rate market, the lender usually has the opportunity to review the floating rates every 6 months. If the creditworthiness of AAACorp or BBBCorp has declined, the lender has the option of increasing the spread over LIBOR that is charged. In extreme circumstances, the lender can refuse to roll over the loan at all. The providers of fixed-rate financing do not have the option to change the terms of the loan in this way.[7]

The spreads between the rates offered to AAACorp and BBBCorp are a reflection of the extent to which BBBCorp is more likely than AAACorp to default. During the next 6 months, there is very little chance that either AAACorp or BBBCorp will default. As we look further ahead, the probability of a default by a company with a relatively low credit rating (such as BBBCorp) is liable to increase faster than the probability of a default by a company with a relatively high credit rating (such as AAACorp). This is why the spread between the 5-year rates is greater than the spread between the 6-month rates.

After negotiating a floating-rate loan at LIBOR + 0.6% and entering into the swap shown in Figure 10-7, BBBCorp appears to obtain a fixed-rate loan at 4.97%. The arguments

just presented show that this is not really the case. In practice, the rate paid is 4.97% only if BBBCorp can continue to borrow floating-rate funds at a spread of 0.6% over LIBOR. If, for example, the credit rating of BBBCorp declines so that the floating-rate loan is rolled over at LIBOR + 1.6%, the rate paid by BBBCorp increases to 5.97%. The market expects that BBBCorp's spread over 6-month LIBOR will on average rise during the swap's life. BBBCorp's expected average borrowing rate when it enters into the swap is therefore greater than 4.97%.

The swap in Figure 10-7 locks in LIBOR − 0.33% for AAACorp for the whole of the next 5 years, not just for the next 6 months. This appears to be a good deal for AAACorp. The downside is that it is bearing the risk of a default by the financial institution. If it borrowed floating-rate funds in the usual way, it would not be bearing this risk.

THE NATURE OF SWAP RATES

At this stage it is appropriate to examine the nature of swap rates and the relationship between swap and LIBOR markets. We explained earlier that LIBOR is the rate of interest at which AA-rated banks borrow for periods between 1 and 12 months from other banks. Also, as indicated in Table 10-3, a swap rate is the average of (a) the fixed rate that a swap market maker is prepared to pay in exchange for receiving LIBOR (its bid rate) and (b) the fixed rate that it is prepared to receive in return for paying LIBOR (its offer rate).

Like LIBOR rates, swap rates are not risk-free lending rates. However, they are close to risk-free. A financial institution can earn the 5-year swap rate on a certain principal by doing the following:

1. Lend the principal for the first 6 months to a AA borrower and then relend it for successive 6-month periods to other AA borrowers; and

2. Enter into a swap to exchange the LIBOR income for the 5-year swap rate.

This shows that the 5-year swap rate is an interest rate with a credit risk corresponding to the situation where 10 consecutive 6-month LIBOR loans to AA companies are made. Similarly the 7-year swap rate is an interest rate

---

[7] If the floating-rate loans are structured so that the spread over LIBOR is guaranteed in advance regardless of changes in credit rating, the spread differentials disappear.

with a credit risk corresponding to the situation where 14 consecutive 6-month LIBOR loans to AA companies are made. Swap rates of other maturities can be interpreted analogously.

Note that 5-year swap rates are less than 5-year AA borrowing rates. It is much more attractive to lend money for successive 6-month periods to borrowers who are always AA at the beginning of the periods than to lend it to one borrower for the whole 5 years when all we can be sure of is that the borrower is AA at the beginning of the 5 years.

DETERMINING LIBOR/SWAP ZERO RATES

We explained in Chapter 7 that derivatives traders have traditionally used LIBOR rates as proxies for risk-free rates when valuing derivatives. One problem with LIBOR rates is that direct observations are possible only for maturities out to 12 months. As described earlier, one way of extending the LIBOR zero curve beyond 12 months is to use Eurodollar futures. Typically Eurodollar futures are used to produce a LIBOR zero curve out to 2 years—and sometimes out to as far as 5 years. Traders then use swap rates to extend the LIBOR zero curve further. The resulting zero curve is sometimes referred to as the LIBOR zero curve and sometimes as the swap zero curve. To avoid any confusion, we will refer to it as the LIBOR/swap zero curve. We will now describe how swap rates are used in the determination of the LIBOR/swap zero curve.

The first point to note is that the value of a newly issued floating-rate bond that pays 6-month LIBOR is always equal to its principal value (or par value) when the LIBOR/swap zero curve is used for discounting.[8] The reason is that the bond provides a rate of interest of LIBOR, and LIBOR is the discount rate. The interest on the bond exactly matches the discount rate, and as a result the bond is fairly priced at par.

In Equation (10.1), we showed that for a newly issued swap where the fixed rate equals the swap rate, $B_{fix} = B_{fl}$. We have just argued that B_{fl} equals the notional principal. It follows that B_{fix} also equals the swap's notional principal. Swap rates therefore define a set of par yield bonds.

---

[8] The same is of course true of a newly issued bond that pays 1-month, 3-month, or 12-month LIBOR.

For example, from the swap rates in Table 10-3, we can deduce that the 2-year LIBOR/swap par yield is 6.045%, the 3-year LIBOR/swap par yield is 6.225%, and so on.[9]

In Chapter 7 we showed how the bootstrap method can be used to determine the Treasury zero curve from Treasury bond prices. It can be used with swap rates in a similar way to extend the LIBOR/swap zero curve.

Example 10.1

Suppose that the 6-month, 12-month, and 18-month LIBOR/swap zero rates have been determined as 4%, 4.5%, and 4.8% with continuous compounding and that the 2-year swap rate (for a swap where payments are made semiannually) is 5%. This 5% swap rate means that a bond with a principal of $100 and a semiannual coupon of 5% per annum sells for par. It follows that, if R is the 2-year zero rate, then

$$2.5e^{-0.04 \times 0.5} + 2.5e^{-0.045 \times 1.0} + 2.5e^{-0.048 \times 1.5} + 102.5e^{-2R} = 100$$

Solving this, we obtain $R = 4.953\%$. (Note that this calculation is simplified in that it does not take the swap's day count conventions and holiday calendars into account. See the "Day Count Issues" section.)

VALUATION OF INTEREST RATE SWAPS

We now move on to discuss the valuation of interest rate swaps. An interest rate swap is worth close to zero when it is first initiated. After it has been in existence for some time, its value may be positive or negative. There are two valuation approaches. The first regards the swap as the difference between two bonds; the second regards it as a portfolio of FRAs.

Valuation in Terms of Bond Prices

Principal payments are not exchanged in an interest rate swap. However, as illustrated in Table 10-2, we can assume that principal payments are both received and paid at

---

[9] Analysts frequently interpolate between swap rates before calculating the zero curve, so that they have swap rates for maturities at 6-month intervals. For example, for the data in Table 10-3 the 2.5-year swap rate would be assumed to be 6.135%; the 7.5-year swap rate would be assumed to be 6.696%; and so on.

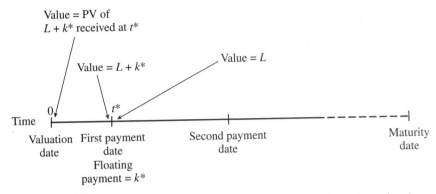

Value = PV of
L + k* received at t*

Value = L + k*

Value = L

Time

0

t*

Valuation
date

First payment
date
Floating
payment = k*

Second payment
date

Maturity
date

FIGURE 10-8 Valuation of floating-rate bond when bond principal is L and next payment is k* at t*.

the end of the swap without changing its value. By doing this, we find that, from the point of view of the floating-rate payer, a swap can be regarded as a long position in a fixed-rate bond and a short position in a floating-rate bond, so that

$$V_{swap} = B_{fix} - B_{fl}$$

where V_{swap} is the value of the swap, B_{fl} is the value of the floating-rate bond (corresponding to payments that are made), and B_{fix} is the value of the fixed-rate bond (corresponding to payments that are received). Similarly, from the point of view of the fixed-rate payer, a swap is a long position in a floating-rate bond and a short position in a fixed-rate bond, so that the value of the swap is

$$V_{swap} = B_{fl} - B_{fix}$$

The value of the fixed rate bond, B_{fix}, can be determined as described earlier. To value the floating-rate bond, we note that the bond is worth the notional principal immediately after an interest payment. This is because at this time the

bond is a "fair deal" where the borrower pays LIBOR for each subsequent accrual period.

Suppose that the notional principal is L, the next exchange of payments is at time t*, and the floating payment that will be made at time t* (which was determined at the last payment date) is k*. Immediately after the payment $B_{fl} = L$ as just explained. It follows that immediately before the payment $B_{fl} = L + k^*$. The floating-rate bond can therefore be regarded as an instrument providing a single cash flow of L + k* at time t*. Discounting this, the value of the floating-rate bond today is $(L + k^*)e^{-r^*t^*}$, where r^* is the LIBOR/swap zero rate for a maturity of t*. This argument is illustrated in Figure 10-8.

Example 10.2

Suppose that a financial institution has agreed to pay 6-month LIBOR and receive 8% per annum (with semiannual compounding) on a notional principal of $100 million. The swap has a remaining life of 1.25 years. The LIBOR rates with continuous compounding for 3-month, 9-month, and 15-month maturities are 10%, 10.5%, and 11%, respectively. The 6-month LIBOR rate at the last payment date was 10.2% (with semiannual compounding).

The calculations for valuing the swap in terms of bonds are summarized in Table 10-5. The fixed-rate bond has cash flows of 4, 4, and 104 on the three payment dates. The discount factors for these cash flows are, respectively, $e^{-0.1 \times 0.25}$; $e^{-0.105 \times 0.75}$; and $e^{-0.11 \times 1.25}$ and are shown in the fourth column of Table 10-5. The table shows that the value of the fixed-rate bond (in millions of dollars) is 98.238.

TABLE 10-5 Valuing a Swap in Terms of Bonds ($ millions). Here, B_{fix} is fixed-rate bond underlying the swap, and B_{fl} is floating-rate bond underlying the swap.

Time	B_{fix} Cash Flow	B_{fl} Cash Flow	Discount Factor	Present Value B_{fix} Cash Flow	Present Value B_{fl} Cash Flow
0.25	4.0	105.100	0.9753	3.901	102.505
0.75	4.0		0.9243	3.697	
1.25	104.0		0.8715	90.640	
Total:				98.238	102.505

In this example, L = $100 million, $k^* = 0.5 \times 0.102 \times 100$ = $5.1 million, and $t^* = 0.25$, so that the floating-rate bond can be valued as though it produces a cash flow of $105.1 million in 3 months. The table shows that the value of the floating bond (in millions of dollars) is $105.100 \times 0.9753 = 102.505$.

The value of the swap is the difference between the two bond prices:

$$V_{swap} = 98.238 - 102.505 = -4.267$$

or −4.267 million dollars.

If the financial institution had been in the opposite position of paying fixed and receiving floating, the value of the swap would be +$4.267 million. Note that these calculations do not take account of day count conventions and holiday calendars.

Valuation in Terms of FRAs

A swap can be characterized as a portfolio of forward rate agreements. Consider the swap between Microsoft and Intel in Figure 10-1. The swap is a 3-year deal entered into on March 5, 2012, with semiannual payments. The first exchange of payments is known at the time the swap is negotiated. The other five exchanges can be regarded as FRAs. The exchange on March 5, 2013, is an FRA where interest at 5% is exchanged for interest at the 6-month rate observed in the market on September 5, 2012; the exchange on September 5, 2013, is an FRA where interest at 5% is exchanged for interest at the 6-month rate observed in the market on March 5, 2013; and so on.

As shown in Chapter 7, an FRA can be valued by assuming that forward interest rates are realized. Because it is

nothing more than a portfolio of forward rate agreements, a plain vanilla interest rate swap can also be valued by making the assumption that forward interest rates are realized. The procedure is as follows:

1. Use the LIBOR/swap zero curve to calculate forward rates for each of the LIBOR rates that will determine swap cash flows.

2. Calculate swap cash flows on the assumption that the LIBOR rates will equal the forward rates.

3. Discount these swap cash flows (using the LIBOR/swap zero curve) to obtain the swap value.

Example 10.3

Consider again the situation in Example 10.2. Under the terms of the swap, a financial institution has agreed to pay 6-month LIBOR and receive 8% per annum (with semiannual compounding) on a notional principal of $100 million. The swap has a remaining life of 1.25 years. The LIBOR rates with continuous compounding for 3-month, 9-month, and 15-month maturities are 10%, 10.5%, and 11%, respectively. The 6-month LIBOR rate at the last payment date was 10.2% (with semiannual compounding).

The calculations are summarized in Table 10-6. The first row of the table shows the cash flows that will be exchanged in 3 months. These have already been determined. The fixed rate of 8% will lead to a cash inflow of $100 \times 0.08 \times 0.5 = \$4$ million. The floating rate of 10.2% (which was set 3 months ago) will lead to a cash outflow of $100 \times 0.102 \times 0.5 = \$5.1$ million. The second row of the table shows the cash flows that will be exchanged in 9 months assuming that forward rates are realized. The

| **TABLE 10-6** | Valuing Swap in Terms of FRAs ($ millions). Floating cash flows are calculated by assuming that forward rates will be realized. |

Time	Fixed Cash Flow	Floating Cash Flow	Net Cash Flow	Discount Factor	Present Value of Net Cash Flow
0.25	4.0	−5.100	−1.100	0.9753	−1.073
0.75	4.0	−5.522	−1.522	0.9243	−1.407
1.25	4.0	−6.051	−2.051	0.8715	−1.787
Total:					−4.267

cash inflow is $4.0 million as before. To calculate the cash outflow, we must first calculate the forward rate corresponding to the period between 3 and 9 months. From Equation (7.5), this is

$$\frac{0.105 \times 0.75 - 0.10 \times 0.25}{0.5} = 0.1075$$

or 10.75% with continuous compounding. From Equation (7.4), the forward rate becomes 11.044% with semi-annual compounding. The cash outflow is therefore $100 \times 0.11044 \times 0.5 = \$5.522$ million. The third row similarly shows the cash flows that will be exchanged in 15 months assuming that forward rates are realized. The discount factors for the three payment dates are, respectively,

$$e^{-0.1 \times 0.25} \qquad e^{-0.105 \times 0.75} \qquad e^{-0.11 \times 1.25}$$

The present value of the exchange in three months is −$1.073 million. The values of the FRAs corresponding to the exchanges in 9 months and 15 months are −$1.407 and −$1.787 million, respectively. The total value of the swap is −$4.267 million. This is in agreement with the value we calculated in Example 10.2 by decomposing the swap into bonds.

A swap is worth close to zero initially. This means that at the outset of a swap the sum of the values of the FRAs underlying the swap is close to zero. It does not mean that the value of each individual FRA is close to zero. In general, some FRAs will have positive values whereas others have negative values.

Consider the FRAs underlying the swap between Microsoft and Intel in Figure 10-1:

Value of FRA to Microsoft > 0 when forward interest rate > 5.0%

Value of FRA to Microsoft = 0 when forward interest rate = 5.0%

Value of FRA to Microsoft < 0 when forward interest rate < 5.0%

Suppose that the term structure of interest rates is upward-sloping at the time the swap is negotiated. This means that the forward interest rates increase as the maturity of the FRA increases. Since the sum of the values of the FRAs is close to zero, the forward interest rate must be less than 5.0% for the early payment dates and greater than 5.0% for the later payment dates. The value to Microsoft of the FRAs corresponding to early payment dates is therefore negative, whereas the value of the FRAs

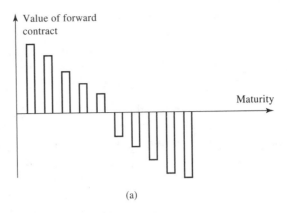

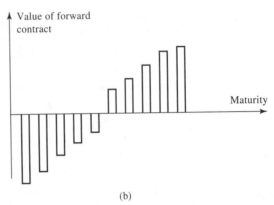

FIGURE 10-9 Valuing of forward rate agreements underlying a swap as a function of maturity. In (a) the term structure of interest rates is upward-sloping and we receive fixed, or it is downward-sloping and we receive floating; in (b) the term structure of interest rates is upward-sloping and we receive floating, or it is downward-sloping and we receive fixed.

corresponding to later payment dates is positive. If the term structure of interest rates is downward-sloping at the time the swap is negotiated, the reverse is true. The impact of the shape of the term structure of interest rates on the values of the forward contracts underlying a swap is illustrated in Figure 10-9.

OVERNIGHT INDEXED SWAPS

Before leaving interest rate swaps, we discuss overnight indexed swaps. Since their introduction in the 1990s, they have become popular in all the major currencies. Their use arises from the fact that banks satisfy their liquidity needs at the end of each day by borrowing from and lending at an overnight rate. This rate is often a rate targeted by the central bank to influence monetary policy. In the United States, the rate is called the Fed Funds rate.

An overnight indexed swap (OIS) is a swap where a fixed rate for a period (e.g., 1 month, 3 months, 1 year, or 2 years) is exchanged for the geometric average of the overnight rates during the period. If during a certain period a bank borrows funds at the overnight rate (rolling the loan forward each day), then its effective interest rate is the geometric average of the overnight interest rates. Similarly, if it lends money at the overnight interest rate every day, the effective rate of interest that it earns is the geometric average of the overnight interest rates. An OIS therefore allows overnight borrowing or lending to be swapped for borrowing or lending at a fixed rate. The fixed rate in an OIS is referred to as the overnight indexed swap rate.

A bank (Bank A) can engage in the following transactions:

1. Borrow $100 million in the overnight market for 3 months, rolling the loan forward each night

2. Lend the $100 million for 3 months at LIBOR to another bank (Bank B)

3. Use an OIS to exchange the overnight borrowings for fixed-rate borrowings.

This will lead to Bank A receiving the 3-month LIBOR rate and paying the 3-month overnight indexed swap rate. We might therefore expect the 3-month overnight indexed swap rate to equal the 3-month LIBOR rate. However, it is generally lower. This is because Bank A requires some compensation for the risk it is taking that Bank B will default on the LIBOR loan.

The excess of the 3-month LIBOR rate over the 3-month overnight indexed swap rate is known as the LIBOR-OIS spread. It is used as a measure of stress in financial markets. In normal market conditions, it is about 10 basis points. However, it rose sharply during the 2007–2009 credit crisis because banks became less willing to lend to each other. In October 2008, the spread spiked to an all time high of 364 basis points. By a year later, it had returned to more normal levels. It rose to over 30 basis points in June 2010 as a result of concerns about the financial health of Greece and a few other European countries.

The OIS rate is increasingly being regarded as a better proxy for the risk-free rate than LIBOR.

CURRENCY SWAPS

Another popular type of swap is known as a *currency swap*. In its simplest form, this involves exchanging principal and interest payments in one currency for principal and interest payments in another.

A currency swap agreement requires the principal to be specified in each of the two currencies. The principal amounts are usually exchanged at the beginning and at the end of the life of the swap. Usually the principal amounts are chosen to be approximately equivalent using the exchange rate at the swap's initiation. When they are exchanged at the end of the life of the swap, their values may be quite different.

Illustration

Consider a hypothetical 5-year currency swap agreement between IBM and British Petroleum entered into on February 1, 2011. We suppose that IBM pays a fixed rate of interest of 5% in sterling and receives a fixed rate of interest of 6% in dollars from British Petroleum. Interest rate payments are made once a year and the principal amounts are $18 million and £10 million. This is termed a *fixed- for-fixed* currency swap because the interest rate in each currency is at a fixed rate. The swap is shown in Figure 10-10. Initially, the principal amounts flow in the opposite direction to the arrows in Figure 10-10. The interest payments during the life of the swap and the final principal payment flow in the same direction as the arrows. Thus, at the outset of the swap, IBM pays $18 million and receives £10 million. Each year during the life of the swap contract, IBM receives $1.08 million (= 6% of $18 million) and pays £0.50 million (= 5% of £10 million). At the end of the life of the swap, it pays a principal of £10 million and receives a principal of $18 million. These cash flows are shown in Table 10-7.

Use of a Currency Swap to Transform Liabilities and Assets

A swap such as the one just considered can be used to transform borrowings in one currency to borrowings

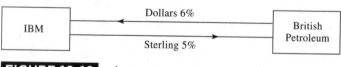

FIGURE 10-10 A currency swap.

TABLE 10-7 Cash Flows to IBM in Currency Swap

Date	Dollar Cash Flow (millions)	Sterling Cash Flow (millions)
February 1, 2011	−18.00	+10.00
February 1, 2012	+1.08	−0.50
February 1, 2013	+1.08	−0.50
February 1, 2014	+1.08	−0.50
February 1, 2015	+1.08	−0.50
February 1, 2016	+19.08	−10.50

TABLE 10-8 Borrowing Rates Providing Basis for Currency Swap

	USD*	AUD*
General Electric	5.0%	7.6%
Qantas Airways	7.0%	8.0%

*Quoted rates have been adjusted to reflect the differential impact of taxes.

in another. Suppose that IBM can issue $18 million of US-dollar-denominated bonds at 6% interest. The swap has the effect of transforming this transaction into one where IBM has borrowed £10 million at 5% interest. The initial exchange of principal converts the proceeds of the bond issue from US dollars to sterling. The subsequent exchanges in the swap have the effect of swapping the interest and principal payments from dollars to sterling.

The swap can also be used to transform the nature of assets. Suppose that IBM can invest £10 million in the UK to yield 5% per annum for the next 5 years, but feels that the US dollar will strengthen against sterling and prefers a US-dollar-denominated investment. The swap has the effect of transforming the UK investment into a $18 million investment in the US yielding 6%.

Comparative Advantage

Currency swaps can be motivated by comparative advantage. To illustrate this, we consider another hypothetical example. Suppose the 5-year fixed-rate borrowing costs to General Electric and Qantas Airways in US dollars (USD) and Australian dollars (AUD) are as shown in Table 10-8. The data in the table suggest that Australian rates are higher than USD interest rates, and also that General Electric is more creditworthy than Qantas Airways, because it is offered a more favorable rate of interest in both currencies. From the viewpoint of a swap trader, the interesting aspect of Table 10-8 is that the spreads between the rates paid by General Electric and Qantas Airways in the two markets are not the same. Qantas Airways pays 2% more than General Electric in the US dollar market and only 0.4% more than General Electric in the AUD market.

This situation is analogous to that in Table 10-4. General Electric has a comparative advantage in the USD market, whereas Qantas Airways has a comparative advantage in the AUD market. In Table 10-4, where a plain vanilla interest rate swap was considered, we argued that comparative advantages are largely illusory. Here we are comparing the rates offered in two different currencies, and it is more likely that the comparative advantages are genuine. One possible source of comparative advantage is tax. General Electric's position might be such that USD borrowings lead to lower taxes on its worldwide income than AUD borrowings. Qantas Airways' position might be the reverse. (Note that we assume that the interest rates shown in Table 10-8 have been adjusted to reflect these types of tax advantages.)

We suppose that General Electric wants to borrow 20 million AUD and Qantas Airways wants to borrow 15 million USD and that the current exchange rate (USD per AUD) is 0.7500. This creates a perfect situation for a currency swap. General Electric and Qantas Airways each borrow in the market where they have a comparative advantage; that is, General Electric borrows USD whereas Qantas Airways borrows AUD. They then use a currency swap to transform General Electric's loan into an AUD loan and Qantas Airways' loan into a USD loan.

As already mentioned, the difference between the USD interest rates is 2%, whereas the difference between the AUD interest rates is 0.4%. By analogy with the interest rate swap case, we expect the total gain to all parties to be 2.0 − 0.4 = 1.6% per annum.

There are several ways in which the swap can be arranged. Figure 10-11 shows one way swaps might be entered into with a financial institution. General Electric borrows USD and Qantas Airways borrows AUD. The effect of the swap is to transform the USD interest rate of 5% per annum to an AUD interest rate of 6.9% per annum for General Electric. As a result, General Electric is 0.7% per annum better off than it would be if it went directly to AUD markets. Similarly, Qantas exchanges an AUD loan at 8% per annum for a USD loan at 6.3% per annum and ends up 0.7% per annum better off than it would be if it went directly to USD markets. The financial institution gains 1.3% per annum on its USD cash flows and loses 1.1% per annum on its AUD flows. If we ignore the difference between the two currencies, the financial institution makes a net gain of 0.2% per annum. As predicted, the total gain to all parties is 1.6% per annum.

Each year the financial institution makes a gain of USD 195,000 (= 1.3% of 15 million) and incurs a loss of AUD 220,000 (= 1.1% of 20 million). The financial institution can avoid any foreign exchange risk by buying AUD 220,000 per annum in the forward market for each year of the life of the swap, thus locking in a net gain in USD.

It is possible to redesign the swap so that the financial institution makes a 0.2% spread in USD. Figures 10-12 and 10-13 present two alternatives. These alternatives are unlikely to be used in practice because they do not lead to General Electric and Qantas being free of foreign exchange risk.[10] In Figure 10-12, Qantas bears some foreign exchange risk because it pays 1.1% per annum in AUD and pays 5.2% per annum in USD. In Figure 10-13, General Electric bears some foreign exchange risk because it receives 1.1% per annum in USD and pays 8% per annum in AUD.

VALUATION OF CURRENCY SWAPS

Like interest rate swaps, fixed-for-fixed currency swaps can be decomposed into either the difference between two bonds or a portfolio of forward contracts.

---

[10] Usually it makes sense for the financial institution to bear the foreign exchange risk, because it is in the best position to hedge the risk.

FIGURE 10-11 A currency swap motivated by comparative advantage.

FIGURE 10-12 Alternative arrangement for currency swap: Qantas Airways bears some foreign exchange risk.

FIGURE 10-13 Alternative arrangement for currency swap: General Electric bears some foreign exchange risk.

Valuation in Terms of Bond Prices

If we define V_{swap} as the value in US dollars of an outstanding swap where dollars are received and a foreign currency is paid, then

$$V_{swap} = B_D - S_0 B_F$$

where B_F is the value, measured in the foreign currency, of the bond defined by the foreign cash flows on the swap and B_D is the value of the bond defined by the domestic cash flows on the swap, and S_0 is the spot exchange rate (expressed as number of dollars per unit of foreign currency). The value of a swap can therefore be determined from LIBOR rates in the two currencies, the term structure of interest rates in the domestic currency, and the spot exchange rate.

Similarly, the value of a swap where the foreign currency is received and dollars are paid is

$$V_{swap} = S_0 B_F - B_D$$

Example 10.4

Suppose that the term structure of LIBOR/swap interest rates is flat in both Japan and the United States. The Japanese rate is 4% per annum and the US rate is 9% per annum (both with continuous compounding). Some time

TABLE 10-9 Valuation of Currency Swap in Terms of Bonds (all amounts in millions)

Time	Cash Flows on Dollar Bond ($)	Present Value ($)	Cash Flows on Yen Bond (Yen)	Present Value (Yen)
1	0.8	0.7311	60	57.65
2	0.8	0.6682	60	55.39
3	0.8	0.6107	60	53.22
3	10.0	7.6338	1,200	1,064.30
Total:		9.6439		1,230.55

ago a financial institution has entered into a currency swap in which it receives 5% per annum in yen and pays 8% per annum in dollars once a year. The principals in the two currencies are $10 million and 1,200 million yen. The swap will last for another 3 years, and the current exchange rate is 110 yen = $1.

The calculations are summarized in Table 10-9. In this case the cash flows from the dollar bond underlying the swap are as shown in the second column. The present value of the cash flows using the dollar discount rate of 9% are shown in the third column. The cash flows from the yen bond underlying the swap are shown in the fourth column of the table. The present value of the cash flows using the yen discount rate of 4% are shown in the final column of the table.

The value of the dollar bond, B_D, is 9.6439 million dollars. The value of the yen bond is 1230.55 million yen. The value of the swap in dollars is therefore

$$\frac{1,230.55}{110} - 9.6439 = 1.5430 \text{ million}$$

Valuation as Portfolio of Forward Contracts

Each exchange of payments in a fixed-for-fixed currency swap is a forward foreign exchange contract. In Chapter 8, forward foreign exchange contracts were valued by assuming that forward exchange rates are realized. The same assumption can therefore be made for a currency swap.

Example 10.5

Consider again the situation in Example 10.4. The LIBOR/ swap term structure of interest rates is flat in both Japan and the United States. The Japanese rate is 4% per annum and the US rate is 9% per annum (both with continuous compounding). Some time ago a financial institution has entered into a currency swap in which it receives 5% per annum in yen and pays 8% per annum in dollars once a year. The principals in the two currencies are $10 million and 1,200 million yen. The swap will last for another 3 years, and the current exchange rate is 110 yen = $1.

The calculations are summarized in Table 10-10. The financial institution pays $0.08 \times 10 = \$0.8$ million dollars and receives $1,200 \times 0.05 = 60$ million yen each year. In addition, the dollar principal of $10 million is paid and the yen principal of 1,200 is received at the end of year 3. The current spot rate is 0.009091 dollar per yen. In this case $r = 9\%$ and $r_f = 4\%$, so that, from Equation (8.9), the 1-year forward rate is

$$0.009091 \, e^{(0.09-0.04)\times1} = 0.009557$$

The 2- and 3-year forward rates in Table 10-10 are calculated similarly. The forward contracts underlying the swap can be valued by assuming that the forward rates are realized. If the 1-year forward rate is realized, the yen cash flow in year 1 is worth $60 \times 0.009557 = 0.5734$ million dollars and the net cash flow at the end of year 1 is $0.8 - 0.5734 = -0.2266$ million dollars. This has a present value of

$$-0.2266 \, e^{-0.09\times1} = -0.2071$$

million dollars. This is the value of forward contract corresponding to the exchange of cash flows at the end of year 1. The value of the other forward contracts are calculated similarly. As shown in Table 10-10, the total value of the forward contracts is $1.5430 million. This agrees with the value calculated for the swap in Example 10.4 by decomposing it into bonds.

TABLE 10-10 Valuation of Currency Swap as a Portfolio of Forward Contracts (all amounts in millions)

Time	Dollar Cash Flow	Yen Cash Flow	Forward Exchange Rate	Dollar Value of Yen Cash Flow	Net Cash Flow ($)	Present Value
1	−0.8	60	0.009557	0.5734	−0.2266	−0.2071
2	−0.8	60	0.010047	0.6028	−0.1972	−0.1647
3	−0.8	60	0.010562	0.6337	−0.1663	−0.1269
3	−10.0	1200	0.010562	12.6746	+2.6746	2.0417
Total:						1.5430

The value of a currency swap is normally close to zero initially. If the two principals are worth the same at the start of the swap, the value of the swap is also close to zero immediately after the initial exchange of principal. However, as in the case of interest rate swaps, this does not mean that each of the individual forward contracts underlying the swap has a value close to zero. It can be shown that, when interest rates in two currencies are significantly different, the payer of the currency with the high interest rate is in the position where the forward contracts corresponding to the early exchanges of cash flows have negative values, and the forward contract corresponding to final exchange of principals has a positive value. The payer of the currency with the low interest rate is in the opposite position; that is, the forward contracts corresponding to the early exchanges of cash flows have positive values, while that corresponding to the final exchange has a negative value. These results are important when the credit risk in the swap is being evaluated.

CREDIT RISK

Contracts such as swaps that are private arrangements between two companies entail credit risks. Consider a financial institution that has entered into offsetting contracts with two companies (see Figure 10-4, 10-5, or 10-7). If neither party defaults, the financial institution remains fully hedged. A decline in the value of one contract will always be offset by an increase in the value of the other contract. However, there is a chance that one party will get into financial difficulties and default. The financial institution then still has to honor the contract it has with the other party.

Suppose that, some time after the initiation of the contracts in Figure 10-4, the contract with Microsoft has a positive value to the financial institution, whereas the contract with Intel has a negative value. If Microsoft defaults, the financial institution is liable to lose the whole of the positive value it has in this contract. To maintain a hedged position, it would have to find a third party willing to take Microsoft's position. To induce the third party to take the position, the financial institution would have to pay the third party an amount roughly equal to the value of its contract with Microsoft prior to the default.

A financial institution clearly has credit-risk exposure from a swap when the value of the swap to the financial institution is positive. What happens when this value is negative and the counterparty gets into financial difficulties? In theory, the financial institution could realize a windfall gain, because a default would lead to it getting rid of a liability. In practice, it is likely that the counterparty would choose to sell the contract to a third party or rearrange its affairs in some way so that its positive value in the contract is not lost. The most realistic assumption for the financial institution is therefore as follows. If the counterparty goes bankrupt, there will be a loss if the value of the swap to the financial institution is positive, and there will be no effect on the financial institution's position if the value of the swap to the financial institution is negative. This situation is summarized in Figure 10-14.

In swaps, it is sometimes the case that the early exchanges of cash flows have positive values and the later exchanges have negative values. (This would be true in Figure 10-9a and in a currency swap where the interest paid is lower than the interest received.) These swaps are likely to have negative values for most of their lives

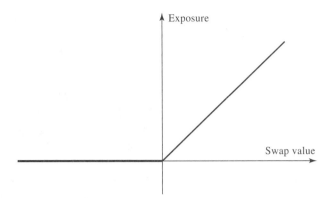

FIGURE 10-14 The credit exposure in a swap.

and therefore entail less credit risk than swaps where the reverse is true.

Potential losses from defaults on a swap are much less than the potential losses from defaults on a loan with the same principal. This is because the value of the swap is usually only a small fraction of the value of the loan. Potential losses from defaults on a currency swap are greater than on an interest rate swap. The reason is that, because principal amounts in two different currencies are exchanged at the end of the life of a currency swap, a currency swap is liable to have a greater value at the time of a default than an interest rate swap.

It is important to distinguish between the credit risk and market risk to a financial institution in any contract. As discussed earlier, the credit risk arises from the possibility of a default by the counterparty when the value of the contract to the financial institution is positive. The market risk arises from the possibility that market variables such as interest rates and exchange rates will move in such a way that the value of a contract to the financial institution becomes negative. Market risks can be hedged relatively easily by entering into offsetting contracts; credit risks are less easy to hedge.

One of the more bizarre stories in swap markets is outlined in Box 10-2. It concerns the British Local Authority Hammersmith and Fulham and shows that, in addition to bearing market risk and credit risk, banks trading swaps also sometimes bear legal risk.

Clearing Houses

As explained in Box 5-3, regulators are concerned about the potential for credit risk in the over-the-counter market to cause systemic risk. The volume of trading between financial institutions is huge. A default by one financial institution can lead to losses by other financial institutions. As a result, some of these financial institutions may also default, creating yet more losses for other financial institutions, more defaults, and so on. It was concerns about systemic risk that led governments to bail out financial institutions during the crisis that started in July 2007. To reduce systemic risk, governments have, since the crisis, introduced legislation requiring that clearing houses be

---

BOX 10-2 The Hammersmith and Fulham Story

Between 1987 to 1989 the London Borough of Hammersmith and Fulham in the UK entered into about 600 interest rate swaps and related instruments with a total notional principal of about 6 billion pounds. The transactions appear to have been entered into for speculative rather than hedging purposes. The two employees of Hammersmith and Fulham responsible for the trades had only a sketchy understanding of the risks they were taking and how the products they were trading worked.

By 1989, because of movements in sterling interest rates, Hammersmith and Fulham had lost several hundred million pounds on the swaps. To the banks on the other side of the transactions, the swaps were worth several hundred million pounds. The banks were concerned about credit risk. They had entered into offsetting swaps to hedge their interest rate risks. If Hammersmith and

Fulham defaulted, the banks would still have to honor their obligations on the offsetting swaps and would take a huge loss.

What happened was something a little different from a default. Hammersmith and Fulham's auditor asked to have the transactions declared void because Hammersmith and Fulham did not have the authority to enter into the transactions. The British courts agreed. The case was appealed and went all the way to the House of Lords, Britain's highest court. The final decision was that Hammersmith and Fulham did not have the authority to enter into the swaps, but that they ought to have the authority to do so in the future for risk-management purposes. Needless to say, banks were furious that their contracts were overturned in this way by the courts.

used for many swaps and other derivatives. The way this works was discussed in Chapter 5. The clearing house acts as an intermediary between the two sides in a transaction. It requires an initial margin and variation margins in the same way that these are required for futures contracts.

OTHER TYPES OF SWAPS

In this chapter, we have covered interest rate swaps where LIBOR is exchanged for a fixed rate of interest and currency swaps where a fixed rate of interest in one currency is exchanged for a fixed rate of interest in another currency. Many other types of swaps are traded.

Variations on the Standard Interest Rate Swap

In fixed-for-floating interest rate swaps, LIBOR is the most common reference floating interest rate. In the examples in this chapter, the tenor (i.e., payment frequency) of LIBOR has been 6 months, but swaps where the tenor of LIBOR is 1 month, 3 months, and 12 months trade regularly. The tenor on the floating side does not have to match the tenor on the fixed side. (Indeed, as pointed out in footnote 3, the standard interest rate swap in the United States is one where there are quarterly LIBOR payments and semiannual fixed payments.) LIBOR is the most common floating rate, but others such as the commercial paper (CP) rate are occasionally used. Sometimes floating-for-floating interest rates swaps are negotiated. For example, the 3-month CP rate plus 10 basis points might be exchanged for 3-month LIBOR with both being applied to the same principal. (This deal would allow a company to hedge its exposure when assets and liabilities are subject to different floating rates.)

The principal in a swap agreement can be varied throughout the term of the swap to meet the needs of a counterparty. In an *amortizing swap*, the principal reduces in a predetermined way. (This might be designed to correspond to the amortization schedule on a loan.) In a *step-up swap*, the principal increases in a predetermined way. (This might be designed to correspond to drawdowns on a loan agreement.) Deferred swaps or *forward swaps*, where the parties do not begin to exchange interest payments until some future date, can also be arranged. Sometimes swaps are negotiated where the principal to which the fixed payments are applied is different from the principal to which the floating payments are applied.

A *constant maturity swap* (CMS swap) is an agreement to exchange a LIBOR rate for a swap rate. An example would be an agreement to exchange 6-month LIBOR applied to a certain principal for the 10-year swap rate applied to the same principal every 6 months for the next 5 years. A *constant maturity Treasury swap* (CMT swap) is a similar agreement to exchange a LIBOR rate for a particular Treasury rate (e.g., the 10-year Treasury rate).

In a *compounding swap*, interest on one or both sides is compounded forward to the end of the life of the swap according to preagreed rules and there is only one payment date at the end of the life of the swap. In a *LIBOR-in arrears swap*, the LIBOR rate observed on a payment date is used to calculate the payment on that date. (As explained earlier, in a standard deal the LIBOR rate observed on one payment date is used to determine the payment on the next payment date.) In an *accrual swap*, the interest on one side of the swap accrues only when the floating reference rate is in a certain range.

Other Currency Swaps

In this chapter we have considered fixed-for-fixed currency swaps. Another type of swap is a fixed-for-floating currency swap, whereby a floating rate (usually LIBOR) in one currency is exchanged for a fixed rate in another currency. This is a combination of a fixed-for-floating interest rate swap and a fixed-for-fixed currency swap and is known as a *cross-currency interest rate swap*. A further type of currency swap is a *floating-for-floating currency swap*, where a floating rate in one currency is exchanged for a floating rate in another currency.

Sometimes a rate observed in one currency is applied to a principal amount in another currency. One such deal might be where 3-month LIBOR observed in the United States is exchanged for 3-month LIBOR in Britain, with both rates being applied to a principal of 10 million British pounds. This type of swap is referred to as a *diff swap or a quanto*.

Equity Swaps

An *equity swap* is an agreement to exchange the total return (dividends and capital gains) realized on an equity index for either a fixed or a floating rate of interest. For example, the total return on the S&P 500 in successive 6-month periods might be exchanged for LIBOR, with both being applied to the same principal. Equity swaps can be used by portfolio managers to convert returns from a fixed or floating investment to the returns from investing in an equity index, and vice versa.

Options

Sometimes there are options embedded in a swap agreement. For example, in an *extendable swap*, one party has the option to extend the life of the swap beyond the specified period. In a *puttable swap*, one party has the option to terminate the swap early. Options on swaps, or *swaptions*, are also available. These provide one party with the right at a future time to enter into a swap where a predetermined fixed rate is exchanged for floating.

Commodity Swaps, Volatility Swaps, and Other Exotic Instruments

Commodity swaps are in essence a series of forward contracts on a commodity with different maturity dates and the same delivery prices. In a *volatility swap* there are a series of time periods. At the end of each period, one side pays a preagreed volatility, while the other side pays the historical volatility realized during the period. Both volatilities are multiplied by the same notional principal in calculating payments.

Swaps are limited only by the imagination of financial engineers and the desire of corporate treasurers and fund managers for exotic structures.

SUMMARY

The two most common types of swaps are interest rate swaps and currency swaps. In an interest rate swap, one party agrees to pay the other party interest at a fixed rate on a notional principal for a number of years. In return, it receives interest at a floating rate on the same notional principal for the same period of time. In a currency swap, one party agrees to pay interest on a principal amount in one currency. In return, it receives interest on a principal amount in another currency.

Principal amounts are not usually exchanged in an interest rate swap. In a currency swap, principal amounts are usually exchanged at both the beginning and the end of the

life of the swap. For a party paying interest in the foreign currency, the foreign principal is received, and the domestic principal is paid at the beginning of the swap's life. At the end of the swap's life, the foreign principal is paid and the domestic principal is received.

An interest rate swap can be used to transform a floating-rate loan into a fixed-rate loan, or vice versa. It can also be used to transform a floating-rate investment to a fixed-rate investment, or vice versa. A currency swap can be used to transform a loan in one currency into a loan in another currency. It can also be used to transform an investment denominated in one currency into an investment denominated in another currency.

There are two ways of valuing interest rate and currency swaps. In the first, the swap is decomposed into a long position in one bond and a short position in another bond. In the second it is regarded as a portfolio of forward contracts.

When a financial institution enters into a pair of offsetting swaps with different counterparties, it is exposed to credit risk. If one of the counterparties defaults when the financial institution has positive value in its swap with that counterparty, the financial institution loses money because it still has to honor its swap agreement with the other counterparty.

Further Reading

Baz, J., and M. Pascutti. "Alternative Swap Contracts Analysis and Pricing," *Journal of Derivatives*, (Winter 1996): 7–21.

Brown, K. C, and D. J. Smith. *Interest Rate and Currency Swaps: A Tutorial*. Association for Investment Management and Research, 1996.

Cooper, I., and A. Mello. "The Default Risk in Interest Rate Swaps," *Journal of Finance*, 46, 2 (1991): 597–620.

Dattatreya, R. E., and K. Hotta. *Advanced Interest Rate and Currency Swaps: State-of-the-Art Products, Strategies, and Risk Management Applications*. Irwin, 1993.

Flavell, R. *Swaps and Other Instruments*. Chichester: Wiley, 2002.

Gupta, A., and M. G. Subrahmanyam. "An Empirical Examination of the Convexity Bias in the Pricing of Interest Rate Swaps," *Journal of Financial Economics*, 55, 2 (2000): 239–79.

Litzenberger, R. H. "Swaps: Plain and Fanciful," *Journal of Finance*, 47, 3 (1992): 831–50.

Minton, B. A. "An Empirical Examination of the Basic Valuation Models for Interest Rate Swaps," *Journal of Financial Economics*, 44, 2 (1997): 251–77.

Sun, T., S. Sundaresan, and C. Wang. "Interest Rate Swaps: An Empirical Investigation," *Journal of Financial Economics*, 34, 1 (1993): 77–99.

Titman, S. "Interest Rate Swaps and Corporate Financing Choices," *Journal of Finance*, 47, 4 (1992): 1503–16.

Properties of Stock Options

■ Learning Objectives

Candidates, after completing this reading, should be able to:

- ■ Identify the six factors that affect an option's price and describe how these six factors affect the price for both European and American options.
- ■ Identify and compute upper and lower bounds for option prices.

- ■ Explain put-call parity and apply it to the valuation of European and American stock options.
- ■ Explain the early exercise features of American call and put options.

Excerpt is Chapter 10 of Options, Futures, and Other Derivatives, *Eighth Edition, by John Hull.*

In this chapter, we look at the factors affecting stock option prices. We use a number of different arbitrage arguments to explore the relationships between European option prices, American option prices, and the underlying stock price. The most important of these relationships is put-call parity, which is a relationship between the price of a European call option, the price of a European put option, and the underlying stock price.

The chapter examines whether American options should be exercised early. It shows that it is never optimal to exercise an American call option on a non-dividend-paying stock prior to the option's expiration, but that under some circumstances the early exercise of an American put option on such a stock is optimal. When there are dividends, it can be optimal to exercise either calls or puts early.

FACTORS AFFECTING OPTION PRICES

There are six factors affecting the price of a stock option:

1. The current stock price, S_0
2. The strike price, K
3. The time to expiration, T
4. The volatility of the stock price, σ
5. The risk-free interest rate, r
6. The dividends that are expected to be paid.

In this section, we consider what happens to option prices when there is a change to one of these factors, with all the other factors remaining fixed. The results are summarized in Table 11-1.

Figures 11-1 and 11-2 show how European call and put prices depend on the first five factors in the situation where $S_0 = 50$, $K = 50$, $r = 5\%$ per annum, $\sigma = 30\%$ per annum, $T = 1$ year, and there are no dividends. In this case the call price is 7.116 and the put price is 4.677.

Stock Price and Strike Price

If a call option is exercised at some future time, the payoff will be the amount by which the stock price exceeds the strike price. Call options therefore become more valuable as the stock price increases and less valuable as the strike price increases. For a put option, the payoff on exercise is the amount by which the strike price exceeds the stock price. Put options therefore behave in the opposite way from call options: they become less valuable as the stock price increases and more valuable as the strike price increases. Figure 11-1a–d illustrate the way in which put and call prices depend on the stock price and strike price.

Time to Expiration

Now consider the effect of the expiration date. Both put and call American options become more valuable (or at least do not decrease in value) as the time to expiration increases. Consider two American options that differ only as far as the expiration date is concerned. The owner of the long-life option has all the exercise opportunities

TABLE 11-1   Summary of the Effect on the Price of a Stock Option of Increasing One Variable While Keeping All Others Fixed*

Variable	European Call	European Put	American Call	American Put
Current stock price	+	−	+	−
Strike price	−	+	−	+
Time to expiration	?	?	+	+
Volatility	+	+	+	+
Risk-free rate	+	−	+	−
Amount of future dividends	−	+	−	+

* + indicates that an increase in the variable causes the option price to increase;

− indicates that an increase in the variable causes the option price to decrease;

? indicates that the relationship is uncertain.

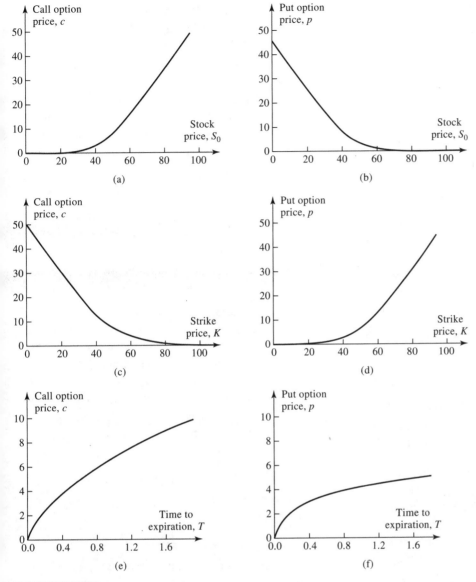

FIGURE 11-1 Effect of changes in stock price, strike price, and expiration date on option prices when $S_0 = 50$, $K = 50$, $r = 5\%$, $\sigma = 30\%$, and $T = 1$.

in 6 weeks. The dividend will cause the stock price to decline, so that the short-life option could be worth more than the long-life option.[1]

Volatility

Roughly speaking, the *volatility* of a stock price is a measure of how uncertain we are about future stock price movements. As volatility increases, the chance that the stock will do very well or very poorly increases. For the owner of a stock, these two outcomes tend to offset each other. However, this is not so for the owner of a call or put. The owner of a call benefits from price increases but has limited downside risk in the event of price decreases because the most the owner can lose is the price of the option. Similarly, the owner of a put benefits from price decreases, but has limited downside risk in the event of price increases. The values of both calls and puts therefore increase as volatility increases (see Figure 11-2a, b).

Risk-Free Interest Rate

The risk-free interest rate affects the price of an option in a less clear-cut way. As interest rates in the economy increase, the expected return required by investors from the stock tends to increase. In addition, the present value of any future cash flow received by the holder of the option decreases. The combined impact of these two effects is to increase the value of call options and decrease the value of put options (see Figure 11-2c, d).

It is important to emphasize that we are assuming that interest rates change while all other variables stay the same. In particular we are assuming in Table 11-1 that

open to the owner of the short-life option—and more. The long-life option must therefore always be worth at least as much as the short-life option.

Although European put and call options usually become more valuable as the time to expiration increases (see Figure 11-1e, f), this is not always the case. Consider two European call options on a stock: one with an expiration date in 1 month, the other with an expiration date in 2 months. Suppose that a very large dividend is expected

---

[1] We assume that, when the life of the option is changed, the dividends on the stock and their timing remain unchanged.

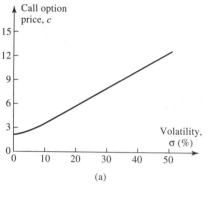

(a)

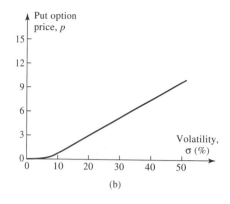

(b)

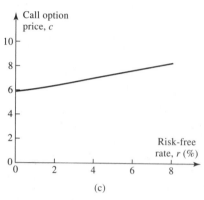

(c)

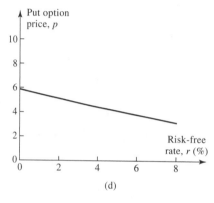

(d)

FIGURE 11-2 Effect of changes in volatility and risk-free interest rate on option prices when $S_0 = 50$, $K = 50$, $r = 5\%$, $\sigma = 30\%$, and $T = 1$.

ASSUMPTIONS AND NOTATION

In this chapter, we will make assumptions similar to those made when deriving forward and futures prices in Chapter 8. We assume that there are some market participants, such as large investment banks, for which the following statements are true:

1. There are no transactions costs.

2. All trading profits (net of trading losses) are subject to the same tax rate.

3. Borrowing and lending are possible at the risk-free interest rate.

We assume that these market participants are prepared to take advantage of arbitrage opportunities as they arise. As discussed in Chapters 4 and 8, this means that any available arbitrage opportunities disappear very quickly. For the purposes of our analysis, it is therefore reasonable to assume that there are no arbitrage opportunities.

We will use the following notation:

S_0: Current stock price

K: Strike price of option

T: Time to expiration of option

S_T: Stock price on the expiration date

r: Continuously compounded risk-free rate of interest for an investment maturing in time T

C: Value of American call option to buy one share

P: Value of American put option to sell one share

c: Value of European call option to buy one share

p: Value of European put option to sell one share

It should be noted that r is the nominal rate of interest, not the real rate of interest. We can assume that $r > 0$. Otherwise, a risk-free investment would provide no advantages over cash. (Indeed, if $r < 0$, cash would be preferable to a risk-free investment.)

interest rates change while the stock price remains the same. In practice, when interest rates rise (fall), stock prices tend to fall (rise). The combined effect of an interest rate increase and the accompanying stock price decrease can be to decrease the value of a call option and increase the value of a put option. Similarly, the combined effect of an interest rate decrease and the accompanying stock price increase can be to increase the value of a call option and decrease the value of a put option.

Amount of Future Dividends

Dividends have the effect of reducing the stock price on the ex-dividend date. This is bad news for the value of call options and good news for the value of put options. Consider a dividend whose ex-dividend date is during the life of an option. The value of the option is negatively related to the size of the dividend if the option is a call and positively related to the size of the dividend if the option is a put.

UPPER AND LOWER BOUNDS FOR OPTION PRICES

In this section we derive upper and lower bounds for option prices. These bounds do not depend on any particular assumptions about the factors mentioned earlier (except $r > 0$). If an option price is above the upper bound or below the lower bound, then there are profitable opportunities for arbitrageurs.

Upper Bounds

An American or European call option gives the holder the right to buy one share of a stock for a certain price. No matter what happens, the option can never be worth more than the stock. Hence, the stock price is an upper bound to the option price:

$$c \leq S_0 \quad \text{and} \quad C \leq S_0 \tag{11.1}$$

If these relationships were not true, an arbitrageur could easily make a riskless profit by buying the stock and selling the call option.

An American put option gives the holder the right to sell one share of a stock for K. No matter how low the stock price becomes, the option can never be worth more than K. Hence,

$$P \leq K \tag{11.2}$$

For European options, we know that at maturity the option cannot be worth more than K. It follows that it cannot be worth more than the present value of K today:

$$p \leq Ke^{-rT} \tag{11.3}$$

If this were not true, an arbitrageur could make a riskless profit by writing the option and investing the proceeds of the sale at the risk-free interest rate.

Lower Bound for Calls on Non-Dividend-Paying Stocks

A lower bound for the price of a European call option on a non-dividend-paying stock is

$$S_0 - Ke^{-rT}$$

We first look at a numerical example and then consider a more formal argument.

Suppose that $S_0 = \$20$, $K = \$18$, $r = 10\%$ per annum, and $T = 1$ year. In this case,

$$S_0 - Ke^{-rT} = 20 - 18e^{-0.1} = 3.71$$

or \$3.71. Consider the situation where the European call price is \$3.00, which is less than the theoretical minimum of \$3.71. An arbitrageur can short the stock and buy the call to provide a cash inflow of \$20.00 − \$3.00 = \$17.00. If invested for 1 year at 10% per annum, the \$17.00 grows to $17e^{0.1} = \$18.79$. At the end of the year, the option expires. If the stock price is greater than \$18.00, the arbitrageur exercises the option for \$18.00, closes out the short position, and makes a profit of

$$\$18.79 - \$18.00 = \$0.79$$

If the stock price is less than \$18.00, the stock is bought in the market and the short position is closed out. The arbitrageur then makes an even greater profit. For example, if the stock price is \$17.00, the arbitrageur's profit is

$$\$18.79 - \$17.00 = \$1.79$$

For a more formal argument, we consider the following two portfolios:

Portfolio A: one European call option plus a zero-coupon bond that provides a payoff of K at time T

Portfolio B: one share of the stock.

In portfolio A, the zero-coupon bond will be worth K at time T. If $S_T > K$, the call option is exercised at maturity and portfolio A is worth S_T. If $S_T < K$, the call option expires worthless and the portfolio is worth K. Hence, at time T, portfolio A is worth

$$\max(S_T, K)$$

Portfolio B is worth S_T at time T. Hence, portfolio A is always worth as much as, and can be worth more than, portfolio B at the option's maturity. It follows that in the absence of arbitrage opportunities this must also be true today. The zero-coupon bond is worth Ke^{-rT} today. Hence,

$$c + Ke^{-rT} \geq S_0$$

or

$$c \geq S_0 - Ke^{-rT}$$

Because the worst that can happen to a call option is that it expires worthless, its value cannot be negative. This means that $c \geq 0$ and therefore

$$c \geq \max(S_0 - Ke^{-rT}, 0) \qquad \textbf{(11.4)}$$

Example 11.1

Consider a European call option on a non-dividend-paying stock when the stock price is $51, the strike price is $50, the time to maturity is 6 months, and the risk-free interest rate is 12% per annum. In this case, $S_0 = 51$, $K = 50$, $T = 0.5$, and $r = 0.12$. From Equation (11.4), a lower bound for the option price is $S_0 - Ke^{-rT}$, or

$$51 - 50e^{-0.12 \times 0.5} = \$3.91$$

Lower Bound for European Puts on Non-Dividend-Paying Stocks

For a European put option on a non-dividend-paying stock, a lower bound for the price is

$$Ke^{-rT} - S_0$$

Again, we first consider a numerical example and then look at a more formal argument. Suppose that $S_0 = \$37$, $K = \$40$, $r = 5\%$ per annum, and $T = 0.5$ years. In this case,

$$Ke^{-rT} - S_0 = 40e^{-0.05 \times 0.5} - 37 = \$2.01$$

Consider the situation where the European put price is $1.00, which is less than the theoretical minimum of $2.01. An arbitrageur can borrow $38.00 for 6 months to buy both the put and the stock. At the end of the 6 months, the arbitrageur will be required to repay $38e^{0.05 \times 0.5} = \$38.96$. If the stock price is below $40.00, the arbitrageur exercises the option to sell the stock for $40.00, repays the loan, and makes a profit of

$$\$40.00 - \$38.96 = \$1.04$$

If the stock price is greater than $40.00, the arbitrageur discards the option, sells the stock, and repays the loan for an even greater profit. For example, if the stock price is $42.00, the arbitrageur's profit is

$$\$42.00 - \$38.96 = \$3.04$$

For a more formal argument, we consider the following two portfolios:

Portfolio C: one European put option plus one share
Portfolio D: a zero-coupon bond paying off K at time T.

If $S_T < K$, then the option in portfolio C is exercised at option maturity and the portfolio becomes worth K. If $S_T > K$, then the put option expires worthless and the portfolio is worth S_T at this time. Hence, portfolio C is worth

$$\max(S_T, K)$$

in time T. Portfolio D is worth K in time T. Hence, portfolio C is always worth as much as, and can sometimes be worth more than, portfolio D in time T. It follows that in the absence of arbitrage opportunities portfolio C must be worth at least as much as portfolio D today. Hence,

$$p + S_0 \geq Ke^{-rT}$$

or

$$p \geq Ke^{-rT} - S_0$$

Because the worst that can happen to a put option is that it expires worthless, its value cannot be negative. This means that

$$p \geq \max(Ke^{-rT} - S_0, 0) \qquad \textbf{(11.5)}$$

Example 11.2

Consider a European put option on a non-dividend-paying stock when the stock price is $38, the strike price is $40, the time to maturity is 3 months, and the risk-free rate of interest is 10% per annum. In this case $S_0 = 38$, $K = 40$, $T = 0.25$, and $r = 0.10$. From Equation (11.5), a lower bound for the option price is $Ke^{-rT} - S_0$, or

$$40e^{-0.1 \times 0.25} - 38 = \$1.01$$

PUT-CALL PARITY

We now derive an important relationship between the prices of European put and call options that have the same strike price and time to maturity. Consider the following two portfolios that were used in the previous section:

Portfolio A: one European call option plus a zero-coupon bond that provides a payoff of K at time T

Portfolio C: one European put option plus one share of the stock.

We continue to assume that the stock pays no dividends. The call and put options have the same strike price K and the same time to maturity T.

As discussed in the previous section, the zero-coupon bond in portfolio A will be worth K at time T. If the stock price S_T at time T proves to be above K, then the call option in portfolio A will be exercised. This means that portfolio A is worth $(S_T - K) + K = S_T$ at time T in these circumstances. If S_T proves to be less than K, then the call option in portfolio A will expire worthless and the portfolio will be worth K at time T.

In portfolio C, the share will be worth S_T at time T. If S_T proves to be below K, then the put option in portfolio C will be exercised. This means that portfolio C is worth $(K - S_T) + S_T = K$ at time T in these circumstances. If S_T proves to be greater than K, then the put option in portfolio C will expire worthless and the portfolio will be worth S_T at time T.

The situation is summarized in Table 11-2. If $S_T > K$, both portfolios are worth S_T at time T; if $S_T < K$, both portfolios are worth K at time T. In other words, both are worth

$$\max(S_T, K)$$

when the options expire at time T. Because they are European, the options cannot be exercised prior to time T. Since the portfolios have identical values at time T, they must have identical values today. If this were not the case, an arbitrageur could buy the less expensive portfolio and sell the more expensive one. Because the portfolios are guaranteed to cancel each other out at time T, this trading strategy would lock in an arbitrage profit equal to the difference in the values of the two portfolios.

The components of portfolio A are worth c and Ke^{-rT} today, and the components of portfolio C are worth p and S_0 today. Hence,

$$c + Ke^{-rT} = p + S_0 \tag{11.6}$$

This relationship is known as *put–call parity*. It shows that the value of a European call with a certain exercise price and exercise date can be deduced from the value of a European put with the same exercise price and exercise date, and vice versa.

To illustrate the arbitrage opportunities when Equation (11.6) does not hold, suppose that the stock price is $31, the exercise price is $30, the risk-free interest rate is 10% per annum, the price of a three-month European call option is $3, and the price of a 3-month European put option is $2.25. In this case,

$$c + Ke^{-rT} = 3 + 30e^{-0.1 \times 3/12} = \$32.26$$
$$p + S_0 = 2.25 + 31 = \$33.25$$

TABLE 11-2 Values of Portfolio A and Portfolio C at Time T

		$S_T > K$	$S_T < K$
Portfolio A	Call option	$S_T - K$	0
	Zero-coupon bond	K	K
	Total	S_T	K
Portfolio C	Put option	0	$K - S_T$
	Share	S_T	S_T
	Total	S_T	K

Portfolio C is overpriced relative to portfolio A. An arbitrageur can buy the securities in portfolio A and short the securities in portfolio C. The strategy involves buying the call and shorting both the put and the stock, generating a positive cash flow of

$$-3 + 2.25 + 31 = \$30.25$$

up front. When invested at the risk-free interest rate, this amount grows to

$$30.25e^{0.1 \times 0.25} = \$31.02$$

in three months. If the stock price at expiration of the option is greater than $30, the call will be exercised. If it is less than $30, the put will be exercised. In either case, the arbitrageur ends up buying one share for $30. This share can be used to close out the short position. The net profit is therefore

$$\$31.02 - \$30.00 = \$1.02$$

For an alternative situation, suppose that the call price is $3 and the put price is $1. In this case,

$$c + Ke^{-rT} = 3 + 30e^{-0.1 \times 3/12} = \$32.26$$
$$p + S_0 = 1 + 31 = \$32.00$$

Portfolio A is overpriced relative to portfolio C. An arbitrageur can short the securities in portfolio A and buy the securities in portfolio C to lock in a profit. The strategy involves shorting the call and buying both the put and the stock with an initial investment of

$$\$31 + \$1 - \$3 = \$29$$

When the investment is financed at the risk-free interest rate, a repayment of $29e^{0.1 \times 0.25} = \$29.73$ is required at the end of the three months. As in the previous case, either the call or the put will be exercised. The short call

TABLE 11-3 Arbitrage Opportunities When Put–Call Parity Does Not Hold. Stock price = $31; interest rate = 10%; call price = $3. Both put and call have a strike price of $30 and 3 months to maturity.	
Three-month Put Price = $2.25	**Three-month Put Price = $1**
Action now: Buy call for $3 Short put to realize $2.25 Short the stock to realize $31 Invest $30.25 for 3 months	*Action now:* Borrow $29 for 3 months Short call to realize $3 Buy put for $1 Buy the stock for $31
Action in 3 months if $S_T > 30$: Receive $31.02 from investment Exercise call to buy stock for $30 Net profit = $1.02	*Action in 3 months if $S_T > 30$:* Call exercised: sell stock for $30 Use $29.73 to repay loan Net profit = $0.27
Action in 3 months if $S_T < 30$: Receive $31.02 from investment Put exercised: buy stock for $30 Net profit = $1.02	*Action in 3 months if $S_T < 30$:* Exercise put to sell stock for $30 Use $29.73 to repay loan Net profit = $0.27

and long put option position therefore leads to the stock being sold for $30.00. The net profit is therefore

$$\$30.00 - \$29.73 = \$0.27$$

These examples are illustrated in Table 11-3. Box 11-1 shows how options and put-call parity can help us understand the positions of the debt holders and equity holders in a company.

American Options

Put-call parity holds only for European options. However, it is possible to derive some results for American option prices. It can be shown (see Exercise 18) that, when there are no dividends,

$$S_0 - K \le C - P \le S_0 - Ke^{-rT} \qquad \textbf{(11.7)}$$

Example 11.3

An American call option on a non-dividend-paying stock with strike price $20.00 and maturity in 5 months is worth $1.50. Suppose that the current stock price is $19.00 and the risk-free interest rate is 10% per annum. From Equation (11.7), we have

$$19 - 20 \le C - P \le 19 - 20e^{-0.1 \times 5/12}$$

or

$$1 \ge P - C \ge 0.18$$

showing that $P - C$ lies between $1.00 and $0.18. With C at $1.50, P must lie between $1.68 and $2.50. In other words, upper and lower bounds for the price of an American put with the same strike price and expiration date as the American call are $2.50 and $1.68.

CALLS ON A NON-DIVIDEND-PAYING STOCK

In this section, we first show that it is never optimal to exercise an American call option on a non-dividend-paying stock before the expiration date.

To illustrate the general nature of the argument, consider an American call option on a non-dividend-paying stock with one month to expiration when the stock price is $70 and the strike price is $40. The option is deep in the money, and the investor who owns the option might well be tempted to exercise it immediately. However, if the investor plans to hold the stock obtained by exercising the option for more than one month, this is not the best strategy. A better course of action is to keep the option and exercise it at the end of the month. The $40 strike price is then paid out one month later than it would be if the option were exercised immediately, so that interest is earned on the $40 for one month. Because the stock pays no dividends, no income from the stock is sacrificed. A further advantage of waiting rather than exercising immediately is that there is some chance (however remote) that the stock price will fall below $40 in one month. In this case the investor will not exercise in one month and will be glad that the decision to exercise early was not taken!

The pioneers of option pricing were Fischer Black, Myron Scholes, and Robert Merton. In the early 1970s they showed that options can be used to characterize the capital structure of a company. Today this analysis is widely used by financial institutions to assess a company's credit risk.

To illustrate the analysis, consider a company that has assets that are financed with zero-coupon bonds and equity. Suppose that the bonds mature in five years at which time a principal payment of K is required. The company pays no dividends. If the assets are worth more than K in five years, the equity holders choose to repay the bond holders. If the assets are worth less than K, the equity holders choose to declare bankruptcy and the bond holders end up owning the company.

The value of the equity in five years is therefore $\max(A_T - K, 0)$, where A_T is the value of the company's assets at that time. This shows that the equity holders have a five-year European call option on the assets of the company with a strike price of K. What about the bondholders? They get $\min(A_T, K)$ in five years. This is

the same as $K - \max(K - A_T, 0)$. This shows that today the bonds are worth the present value of K minus the value of a five-year European put option on the assets with a strike price of K.

To summarize, if c and p are the values, respectively, of the call and put options on the company's assets, then

$$\text{Value of equity} = c$$

$$\text{Value of debt} = PV(K) - p$$

Denote the value of the assets of the company today by A_0. The value of the assets must equal the total value of the instruments used to finance the assets. This means that it must equal the sum of the value of the equity and the value of the debt, so that

$$A_0 = c + [PV(K) - p]$$

Rearranging this equation, we have

$$c + PV(K) = p + A_0$$

This is the put-call parity result in Equation (11.6) for call and put options on the assets of the company.

This argument shows that there are no advantages to exercising early if the investor plans to keep the stock for the remaining life of the option (one month, in this case). What if the investor thinks the stock is currently overpriced and is wondering whether to exercise the option and sell the stock? In this case, the investor is better off selling the option than exercising it.[2] The option will be bought by another investor who does want to hold the stock. Such investors must exist. Otherwise the current stock price would not be $70. The price obtained for the option will be greater than its intrinsic value of $30, for the reasons mentioned earlier.

For a more formal argument, we can use Equation (11.4):

$$c \geq S_0 - Ke^{-rT}$$

Because the owner of an American call has all the exercise opportunities open to the owner of the corresponding European call, we must have $C \geq c$. Hence,

$$C \geq S_0 - Ke^{-rT}$$

Given $r > 0$, it follows that $C > S_0 - K$ when $T > 0$. This means that C is always greater than the option's intrinsic value prior to maturity. If it were optimal to exercise at a particular time prior to maturity, C would equal the option's intrinsic value at that time. It follows that it can never be optimal to exercise early.

To summarize, there are two reasons an American call on a non-dividend-paying stock should not be exercised early. One relates to the insurance that it provides. A call option, when held instead of the stock itself, in effect insures the holder against the stock price falling below the strike price. Once the option has been exercised and the strike price has been exchanged for the stock price, this insurance vanishes. The other reason concerns the time value of money. From the perspective of the option holder, the later the strike price is paid out the better.

Bounds

Because American call options are never exercised early when there are no dividends, they are equivalent to

---

[2] As an alternative strategy, the investor can keep the option and short the stock to lock in a better profit than $10.

European call options, so that $C = c$. From Equations (11.1) and (11.4), it follows that upper and lower bounds are given by

$$\max(S_0 - Ke^{-rT}, 0) \leq c, C \leq S_0$$

These bounds are illustrated in Figure 11-3.

The general way in which the call price varies with the stock price, S_0, is shown in Figure 11-4. As r or T or the stock price volatility increases, the line relating the call price to the stock price moves in the direction indicated by the arrows.

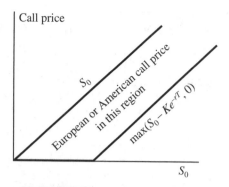

FIGURE 11-3 Bounds for European and American call options when there are no dividends.

PUTS ON A NON-DIVIDEND-PAYING STOCK

It can be optimal to exercise an American put option on a non-dividend-paying stock early. Indeed, at any given time during its life, a put option should always be exercised early if it is sufficiently deep in the money.

To illustrate, consider an extreme situation. Suppose that the strike price is $10 and the stock price is virtually zero. By exercising immediately, an investor makes an immediate gain of $10. If the investor waits, the gain from exercise might be less than $10, but it cannot be more than $10, because negative stock prices are impossible. Furthermore, receiving $10 now is preferable to receiving $10 in the future. It follows that the option should be exercised immediately.

Like a call option, a put option can be viewed as providing insurance. A put option, when held in conjunction with the stock, insures the holder against the stock price falling below a certain level. However, a put option is different from a call option in that it may be optimal for an investor to forgo this insurance and exercise early in order to realize the strike price immediately. In general, the early exercise of a put option becomes more attractive as S_0 decreases, as r increases, and as the volatility decreases.

Bounds

From Equations (11.3) and (11.5), upper and lower bounds for a European put option when there are no dividends are given by

$$\max(Ke^{-rT} - S_0, 0) \leq p \leq Ke^{-rT}$$

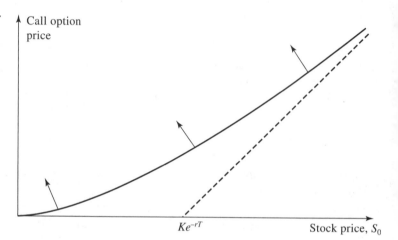

FIGURE 11-4 Variation of price of an American or European call option on a non-dividend-paying stock with the stock price. Curve moves in the direction of the arrows when there is an increase in the interest rate, or stock price volatility.

For an American put option on a non-dividend-paying stock, the condition

$$P \geq \max(K - S_0, 0)$$

must apply because the option can be exercised at any time. This is a stronger condition than the one for a European put option in Equation (11.5). Using the result in Equation (11.2), bounds for an American put option on a non-dividend-paying stock are

$$\max(K - S_0, 0) \leq P \leq K$$

Figure 11-5 illustrates the bounds.

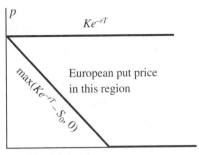

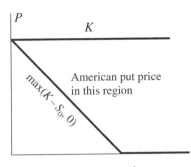

FIGURE 11-5 Bounds for European and American put options when there are no dividends.

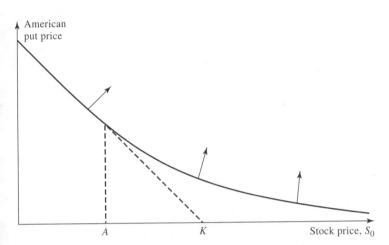

FIGURE 11-6 Variation of price of a American put option with the stock price. Curve moves in the direction of the arrows when the time to maturity or stock price volatility increases or when the interest rate decreases.

Figure 11-6 shows the general way in which the price of an American put option varies with S_0. As we argued earlier, provided that $r > 0$, it is always optimal to exercise an American put immediately when the stock price is sufficiently low. When early exercise is optimal, the value of the option is $K - S_0$. The curve representing the value of the put therefore merges into the put's intrinsic value, $K - S_0$, for a sufficiently small value of S_0. In Figure 11-6, this value of S_0 is shown as point A. The line relating the put price to the stock price moves in the direction indicated by the arrows when r decreases, when the volatility increases, and when T increases.

Because there are some circumstances when it is desirable to exercise an American put option early, it follows that an American put option is always worth more than the corresponding European put option. Furthermore, because an American put is sometimes worth its intrinsic value (see Figure 11-6), it follows that a European put option must sometimes be worth less than its intrinsic value. This means that the curve representing the relationship between the put price and the stock price for a European option must be below the corresponding curve for an American option.

Figure 11-7 shows the variation of the European put price with the stock price. Note that point B in Figure 11-7, at which the price of the option is equal to its intrinsic value, must represent a higher value of the stock price than point A in Figure 11-6 because the curve in Figure 11-7 is below that in Figure 11-6. Point E in Figure 11-7 is where $S_0 = 0$ and the European put price is Ke^{-rT}.

EFFECT OF DIVIDENDS

The results produced so far in this chapter have assumed that we are dealing with options on a non-dividend-paying stock. In this section, we examine the impact of dividends. We assume that the dividends that will be paid during the life of the option are known. Most exchange-traded stock options have a life of less than one year, so this assumption is not too unreasonable in many situations. We will use D to denote the present value of the dividends during the life of the option. In the calculation of D, a dividend is assumed to occur at the time of its ex-dividend date.

Lower Bound for Calls and Puts

We can redefine portfolios A and B as follows:

    Portfolio A: one European call option plus an amount of cash equal to $D + Ke^{-rT}$

    Portfolio B: one share

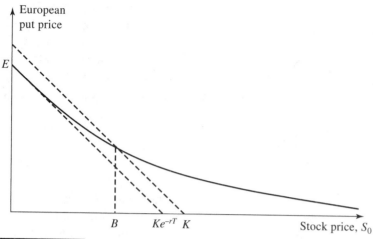

FIGURE 11-7 Variation of price of a European put option with the stock price.

A similar argument to the one used to derive Equation (11.4) shows that

$$c \geq \max(S_0 - D - Ke^{-rT}, 0) \qquad \textbf{(11.8)}$$

We can also redefine portfolios C and D as follows:

Portfolio C: one European put option plus one share

Portfolio D: an amount of cash equal to $D + Ke^{-rT}$

A similar argument to the one used to derive Equation (11.5) shows that

$$p \geq \max(D + Ke^{-rT} - S_0, 0) \qquad \textbf{(11.9)}$$

Early Exercise

When dividends are expected, we can no longer assert that an American call option will not be exercised early. Sometimes it is optimal to exercise an American call immediately prior to an ex-dividend date. It is never optimal to exercise a call at other times.

Put-Call Parity

Comparing the value at option maturity of the redefined portfolios A and C shows that, with dividends, the put-call parity result in Equation (11.6) becomes

$$c + D + Ke^{-rT} = p + S_0 \qquad \textbf{(11.10)}$$

Dividends cause Equation (11.7) to be modified (see Problem 11.19) to

$$S_0 - D - K \leq C - P \leq S_0 - Ke^{-rT} \qquad \textbf{(11.11)}$$

SUMMARY

There are six factors affecting the value of a stock option: the current stock price, the strike price, the expiration date, the stock price volatility, the risk-free interest rate, and the dividends expected during the life of the option. The value of a call generally increases as the current stock price, the time to expiration, the volatility, and the risk-free interest rate increase. The value of a call decreases as the strike price and expected dividends increase. The value of a put generally increases as the strike price, the time to expiration, the volatility, and the expected dividends increase. The value of a put decreases as the current stock price and the risk-free interest rate increase.

It is possible to reach some conclusions about the value of stock options without making any assumptions about the volatility of stock prices. For example, the price of a call option on a stock must always be worth less than the price of the stock itself. Similarly, the price of a put option on a stock must always be worth less than the option's strike price.

A European call option on a non-dividend-paying stock must be worth more than

$$\max(S_0 - Ke^{-rT}, 0)$$

where S_0 is the stock price, K is the strike price, r is the risk-free interest rate, and T is the time to expiration. A European put option on a non-dividend-paying stock must be worth more than

$$\max(Ke^{-rT} - S_0, 0)$$

When dividends with present value D will be paid, the lower bound for a European call option becomes

$$\max(S_0 - D - Ke^{-rT}, 0)$$

and the lower bound for a European put option becomes

$$\max(Ke^{-rT} + D - S_0, 0)$$

Put-call parity is a relationship between the price, c, of a European call option on a stock and the price, p, of a European put option on a stock. For a non-dividend-paying stock, it is

$$c + Ke^{-rT} = p + S_0$$

For a dividend-paying stock, the put-call parity relationship is

$$c + D + Ke^{-rT} = p + S_0$$

Put-call parity does not hold for American options. However, it is possible to use arbitrage arguments to obtain upper and lower bounds for the difference between the price of an American call and the price of an American put.

Further Reading

Black, F., and M. Scholes. "The Pricing of Options and Corporate Liabilities," *Journal of Political Economy*, 81 (May/June 1973): 637–59.

Broadie, M., and J. Detemple. "American Option Valuation: New Bounds, Approximations, and a Comparison of Existing Methods," *Review of Financial Studies*, 9, 4 (1996): 1211–50.

Merton, R. C. "On the Pricing of Corporate Debt: The Risk Structure of Interest Rates," *Journal of Finance*, 29, 2 (1974): 449–70.

Merton, R. C. "Theory of Rational Option Pricing," *Bell Journal of Economics and Management Science*, 4 (Spring 1973): 141–83.

Merton, R. C. "The Relationship between Put and Call Prices: Comment," *Journal of Finance*, 28 (March 1973): 183–84.

Stoll, H. R. "The Relationship between Put and Call Option Prices," *Journal of Finance*, 24 (December 1969): 801–24.

Trading Strategies Involving Options

12

■ Learning Objectives

Candidates, after completing this reading, should be able to:

- Explain the motivation to initiate a covered call or a protective put strategy.
- Describe the use and calculate the payoffs of various spread strategies.

- Describe the use and explain the payoff functions of combination strategies.

Excerpt is Chapter 11 of Options, Futures, and Other Derivatives, *Eighth Edition, by John Hull.*

We discussed the profit pattern from an investment in a single option. In this chapter, we look at what can be achieved when an option is traded in conjunction with other assets. In particular, we examine the properties of portfolios consisting of positions in (a) an option and a zero-coupon bond, (b) an option and the asset underlying the option, and (c) two or more options on the same underlying asset.

PRINCIPAL-PROTECTED NOTES

Options are often used to create what are termed *principal-protected notes* for the retail market. These are products that appeal to conservative investors. The return earned by the investor depends on the performance of a stock, a stock index, or other risky asset, but the initial principal amount invested is not at risk. An example will illustrate how a simple principal-protected note can be created.

Example 12.1

Suppose that the 3-year interest rate is 6% with continuous compounding. This means that $1,000e^{-0.06\times3} = \$835.27$ will grow to $1,000 in 3 years. The difference between $1,000 and $835.27 is $164.73. Suppose that a stock portfolio is worth $1,000 and provides a dividend yield of 1.5% per annum. Suppose further that a 3-year at-the-money European call option on the stock portfolio can be purchased for less than $164.73. (From DerivaGem, it can be verified that this will be the case if the volatility of the value of the portfolio is less than about 15%.) A bank can offer clients a $1,000 investment opportunity consisting of:

1. A 3-year zero-coupon bond with a principal of $1,000

2. A 3-year at-the-money European call option on the stock portfolio.

If the value of the portfolio increases, the investor gets whatever $1,000 invested in the portfolio would have grown to. (This is because the zero-coupon bond pays off $1,000, and this equals the strike price of the option.) If the value of the portfolio goes down, the option has no value, but payoff from the zero-coupon bond ensures that the investor receives the original $1,000 principal invested.

The attraction of a principal-protected note is that an investor is able to take a risky position without risking any principal. The worst that can happen is that the investor loses the chance to earn interest, or other income such as dividends, on the initial investment for the life of the note.

There are many variations on the product we have described. An investor who thinks that the price of an asset will decline can buy a principal-protected note consisting of a zero-coupon bond plus a put option. The investor's payoff in 3 years is then $1,000 plus the payoff (if any) from the put option.

Is a principal-protected note a good deal from the retail investor's perspective? A bank will always build in a profit for itself when it creates a principal-protected note. This means that, in Example 12.1, the zero-coupon bond plus the call option will always cost the bank less than $1,000. In addition, investors are taking the risk that the bank will not be in a position to make the payoff on the principal-protected note at maturity. (Some retail investors lost money on principal-protected notes created by Lehman Brothers when it failed in 2008.) In some situations, therefore, an investor will be better off if he or she buys the underlying option in the usual way and invests the remaining principal in a risk-free investment. However, this is not always the case. The investor is likely to face wider bid–offer spreads on the option than the bank and is likely to earn lower interest rates than the bank. It is therefore possible that the bank can add value for the investor while making a profit itself.

Now let us look at the principal-protected notes from the perspective of the bank. The economic viability of the structure in Example 12.1 depends critically on the level of interest rates and the volatility of the portfolio. If the interest rate is 3% instead of 6%, the bank has only $1,000 - 1,000e^{-0.03\times3} = \$86.07$ with which to buy the call option. If interest rates are 6%, but the volatility is 25% instead of 15%, the price of the option would be about $221. In either of these circumstances, the product described in Example 12.1 cannot be profitably created by the bank. However, there are a number of ways the bank can still create a viable 3-year product. For example, the strike price of the option can be increased so that the value of the portfolio has to rise by, say, 15% before the investor makes a gain; the investor's return could be capped; the return of the investor could depend on the average price of the asset instead of the final price; a knockout barrier could be specified. The derivatives involved in some of these alternatives will be discussed later in the book. (Capping the option corresponds to the creation of a bull spread for the investor and will be discussed later in this chapter.)

One way in which a bank can sometimes create a profitable principal-protected note when interest rates are low or volatilities are high is by increasing its life. Consider the situation in Example 12.1 when (a) the interest rate is 3% rather than 6% and (b) the stock portfolio has a volatility of 15% and provides a dividend yield of 1.5%. DerivaGem shows that a 3-year at-the-money European option costs about $119. This is more than the funds available to purchase it (1,000 − 1,000$e^{-0.03 \times 3}$ = $86.07). A 10-year at-the-money option costs about $217. This is less than the funds available to purchase it (1,000 − 1,000$e^{-0.03 \times 10}$ = $259.18), making the structure profitable. When the life is increased to 20 years, the option cost is about $281, which is much less than the funds available to purchase it (1,000 − 1,000$e^{-0.03 \times 20}$ = $451.19), so that the structure is even more profitable.

A critical variable for the bank in our example is the dividend yield. The higher it is, the more profitable the product is for the bank. If the dividend yield were zero, the principal-protected note in Example 12.1 cannot be profitable for the bank no matter how long it lasts. (This follows from Equation (11.4).)

TRADING AN OPTION AND THE UNDERLYING ASSET

For convenience, we will assume that the asset underlying the options considered in the rest of the chapter is a stock. Similar trading strategies can be developed for other underlying assets. We will also follow the usual practice of calculating the profit from a trading strategy as the final payoff minus the initial cost without discounting.

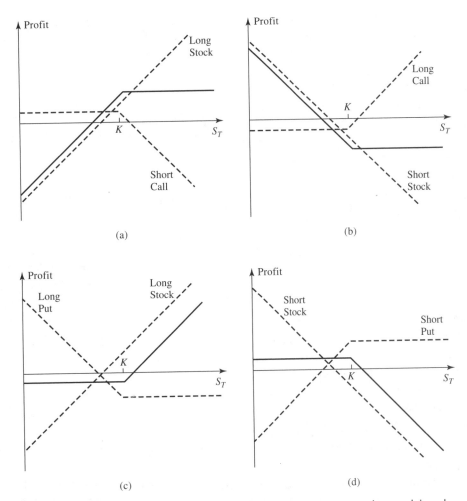

FIGURE 12-1 Profit patterns (a) long position in a stock combined with short position in a call; (b) short position in a stock combined with long position in a call; (c) long position in a put combined with long position in a stock; (d) short position in a put combined with short position in a stock.

There are a number of different trading strategies involving a single option on a stock and the stock itself. The profits from these are illustrated in Figure 12-1. In this figure and in other figures throughout this chapter, the dashed line shows the relationship between profit and the stock price for the individual securities constituting the portfolio, whereas the solid line shows the relationship between profit and the stock price for the whole portfolio.

In Figure 12-1a, the portfolio consists of a long position in a stock plus a short position in a European call option. This is known as *writing a covered call*. The long stock position "covers" or protects the investor from the payoff on the short call that becomes necessary if there is a sharp rise in the stock price. In Figure 12-1b, a short position in a stock is combined with a long position in a call option. This is the reverse of writing a covered call. In Figure 12-1c, the investment strategy involves buying a European put option on a stock and the stock itself. The approach is referred to as a *protective put* strategy. In Figure 12-1d, a short position in a put option is combined with a short position in the stock. This is the reverse of a protective put.

The profit patterns in Figures 12-1a, b, c, d have the same general shape as the profit patterns for short put, long put, long call, and short call, respectively. Put-call parity provides a way of understanding why this is so. From Chapter 11, the put–call parity relationship is

$$p + S_0 = c + Ke^{-rT} + D \qquad \text{(12.1)}$$

where p is the price of a European put, S_0 is the stock price, c is the price of a European call, K is the strike price of both call and put, r is the risk-free interest rate, T is the time to maturity of both call and put, and D is the present value of the dividends anticipated during the life of the options.

Equation (12.1) shows that a long position in a European put combined with a long position in the stock is equivalent to a long European call position plus a certain amount ($= Ke^{-rT} + D$) of cash. This explains why the profit pattern in Figure 12-1c is similar to the profit pattern from a long call position. The position in Figure 12-1d is the reverse of that in Figure 12-1c and therefore leads to a profit pattern similar to that from a short call position.

Equation (12.1) can be rearranged to become

$$S_0 - c = Ke^{-rT} + D - p$$

This shows that a long position in a stock combined with a short position in a European call is equivalent to a short European put position plus a certain amount ($= Ke^{-rT} + D$) of cash. This equality explains why the profit pattern in Figure 12-1a is similar to the profit pattern from a short put position. The position in Figure 12-1b is the reverse of that in Figure 12-1a and therefore leads to a profit pattern similar to that from a long put position.

SPREADS

A spread trading strategy involves taking a position in two or more options of the same type (i.e., two or more calls or two or more puts).

Bull Spreads

One of the most popular types of spreads is a *bull spread*. This can be created by buying a European call option on a stock with a certain strike price and selling a European call option on the same stock with a higher strike price. Both options have the same expiration date. The strategy is illustrated in Figure 12-2. The profits from the two option positions taken separately are shown by the dashed lines. The profit from the whole strategy is the sum of the profits given by the dashed lines and is indicated by the solid line. Because a call price always decreases as the strike price increases, the value of the option sold is always less than the value of the option bought. A bull spread, when created from calls, therefore requires an initial investment.

Suppose that K_1 is the strike price of the call option bought, K_2 is the strike price of the call option sold, and S_T is the stock price on the expiration date of the options. Table 12-1 shows the total payoff that will be realized from a bull spread in different circumstances. If the stock price does well and is greater than the higher strike price, the payoff is the difference between the two strike prices, or $K_2 - K_1$. If the stock price on the expiration date lies between the two strike prices, the payoff is $S_T - K_1$. If the stock price on the expiration date is below the lower

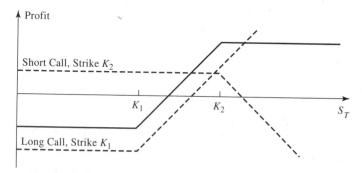

FIGURE 12-2 Profit from bull spread created using call options.

strike price, the payoff is zero. The profit in Figure 12-2 is calculated by subtracting the initial investment from the payoff.

A bull spread strategy limits the investor's upside as well as downside risk. The strategy can be described by saying that the investor has a call option with a strike price equal to K_1 and has chosen to give up some upside potential by selling a call option with strike price K_2 ($K_2 > K_1$). In return for giving up the upside potential, the investor gets the price of the option with strike price K_2. Three types of bull spreads can be distinguished:

1. Both calls are initially out of the money.

2. One call is initially in the money; the other call is initially out of the money.

3. Both calls are initially in the money.

The most aggressive bull spreads are those of type 1. They cost very little to set up and have a small probability of giving a relatively high payoff (= $K_2 - K_1$). As we move from type 1 to type 2 and from type 2 to type 3, the spreads become more conservative.

Example 12.2

An investor buys for $3 a 3-month European call with a strike price of $30 and sells for $1 a 3-month European call with a strike price of $35. The payoff from this bull spread strategy is $5 if the stock price is above $35, and zero if it is below $30. If the stock price is between $30 and $35, the payoff is the amount by which the stock price exceeds $30. The cost of the strategy is $3 − $1 = $2. So the profit is:

Stock Price Range	Profit
$S_T \leq 30$	−2
$30 < S_T < 35$	$S_T - 32$
$S_T \geq 35$	3

Bull spreads can also be created by buying a European put with a low strike price and selling a European put with a high strike price, as illustrated in Figure 12-3. Unlike bull spreads created from calls, those created from puts involve a positive up-front cash flow to the investor (ignoring margin requirements) and a payoff that is either negative or zero.

TABLE 12-1 Payoff from a Bull Spread Created Using Calls

Stock Price Range	Payoff from Long Call Option	Payoff from Short Call Option	Total Payoff
$S_T \leq K_1$	0	0	0
$K_1 < S_T < K_2$	$S_T - K_1$	0	$S_T - K_1$
$S_T \geq K_2$	$S_T - K_1$	$-(S_T - K_2)$	$K_2 - K_1$

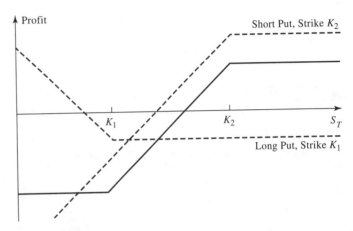

FIGURE 12-3 Profit from bull spread created using put options.

Bear Spreads

An investor who enters into a bull spread is hoping that the stock price will increase. By contrast, an investor who enters into a *bear spread* is hoping that the stock price will decline. Bear spreads can be created by buying a European put with one strike price and selling a European put with another strike price. The strike price of the option purchased is greater than the strike price of the option sold. (This is in contrast to a bull spread, where the strike price of the option purchased is always less than the strike price of the option sold.) In Figure 12-4, the profit from the spread is shown by the solid line. A bear spread created from puts involves an initial cash outflow because the price of the put sold is less than the price of the put purchased. In essence, the investor has bought a put with a certain strike price and chosen to give up some of the profit potential by selling a put with a lower strike price. In return for the profit given up, the investor gets the price of the option sold.

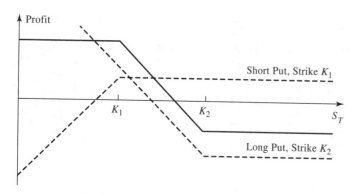

FIGURE 12-4 Profit from bear spread created using put options.

TABLE 12-2 Payoff from a Bear Spread Created with Put Options

Stock Price Range	Payoff from Long Put Option	Payoff from Short Put Option	Total Payoff
$S_T \leq K_1$	$K_2 - S_T$	$-(K_1 - S_T)$	$K_2 - K_1$
$K_1 < S_T < K_2$	$K_2 - S_T$	0	$K_2 - S_T$
$S_T \geq K_2$	0	0	0

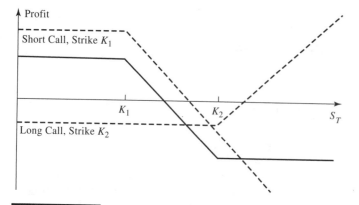

FIGURE 12-5 Profit from bear spread created using call options.

Assume that the strike prices are K_1 and K_2, with $K_1 < K_2$. Table 12-2 shows the payoff that will be realized from a bear spread in different circumstances. If the stock price is greater than K_2, the payoff is zero. If the stock price is less than K_1, the payoff is $K_2 - K_1$. If the stock price is between K_1 and K_2, the payoff is $K_2 - S_T$. The profit is calculated by subtracting the initial cost from the payoff.

Example 12.3

An investor buys for $3 a 3-month European put with a strike price of $35 and sells for $1 a 3-month European put with a strike price of $30. The payoff from this bear spread strategy is zero if the stock price is above $35, and $5 if it is below $30. If the stock price is between $30 and $35, the payoff is $35 - S_T$. The options cost $3 − $1 = $2 up front. So the profit is:

Stock Price Range	Profit
$S_T \leq 30$	$+3$
$30 < S_T < 35$	$33 - S_T$
$S_T \geq 35$	-2

Like bull spreads, bear spreads limit both the upside profit potential and the downside risk. Bear spreads can be created using calls instead of puts. The investor buys a call with a high strike price and sells a call with a low strike price, as illustrated in Figure 12-5. Bear spreads created with calls involve an initial cash inflow (ignoring margin requirements).

Box Spreads

A box spread is a combination of a bull call spread with strike prices K_1 and K_2 and a bear put spread with the same two strike prices. As shown in Table 12-3, the payoff from a box spread is always $K_2 - K_1$. The value of a box spread is therefore always the present value of this payoff or $(K_2 - K_1)e^{-rT}$. If it has a different value there is an arbitrage opportunity. If the market price of the box spread is too low, it is profitable to buy the box. This involves buying a call with strike price K_1, buying a put with strike price K_2, selling a call with strike price K_2, and selling a put with strike price K_1. If the market price of the box spread is too high, it is profitable to sell the box. This involves buying a call with strike price K_2, buying a put with strike price K_1, selling a call with strike price K_1, and selling a put with strike price K_2.

It is important to realize that a box-spread arbitrage only works with European options. Many of the options that trade on exchanges are American. As shown in Box 12-1, inexperienced traders who treat American options as European are liable to lose money.

Suppose that a stock has a price of $50 and a volatility of 30%. No dividends are expected and the risk-free rate is 8%. A trader offers you the chance to sell on the CBOE a 2-month box spread where the strike prices are $55 and $60 for $5.10. Should you do the trade?

The trade certainly sounds attractive. In this case $K_1 = 55$, $K_2 = 60$, and the payoff is certain to be $5 in 2 months. By selling the box spread for $5.10 and investing the funds for 2 months you would have more than enough funds to meet the $5 payoff in 2 months. The theoretical value of the box spread today is $5 \times e^{-0.08 \times 2/12} = \$4.93$.

Unfortunately there is a snag. CBOE stock options are American and the $5 payoff from the box spread is calculated on the assumption that the options comprising the box are European. Option prices for this example (calculated using DerivaGem) are shown in the table. A bull call spread where the strike prices are $55 and $60 costs $0.96 - 0.26 = \$0.70$. (This is the same for both European and American options because the price of a European call is the same as the price of an

American call when there are no dividends.) A bear put spread with the same strike prices costs $9.46 - 5.23 = \$4.23$ if the options are European and $10.00 - 5.44 = \$4.56$ if they are American. The combined value of both spreads if they are created with European options is $0.70 + 4.23 = \$4.93$. This is the theoretical box spread price calculated above. The combined value of buying both spreads if they are American is $0.70 + 4.56 = \$5.26$. Selling a box spread created with American options for $5.10 would not be a good trade. You would realize this almost immediately as the trade involves selling a $60 strike put and this would be exercised against you almost as soon as you sold it!

Option Type	Strike Price	European Option Price	American Option Price
Call	60	0.26	0.26
Call	55	0.96	0.96
Put	60	9.46	10.00
Put	55	5.23	5.44

Butterfly Spreads

A *butterfly spread* involves positions in options with three different strike prices. It can be created by buying a European call option with a relatively low strike price K_1, buying a European call option with a relatively high strike price K_3, and selling two European call options with a strike price K_2 that is halfway between K_1 and K_3. Generally, K_2 is close to the current stock price. The pattern of profits from the strategy is shown in Figure 12-6. A butterfly spread leads to a profit if the stock price stays close to K_2, but gives rise to a small loss if there is a significant stock price move in either direction. It is therefore an appropriate strategy for an investor who feels that large stock price moves are unlikely. The strategy requires a small investment initially. The payoff from a butterfly spread is shown in Table 12-4.

Suppose that a certain stock is currently worth $61. Consider an investor who feels that a significant price move in the next 6 months is unlikely. Suppose that the market prices of 6-month European calls are as follows:

TABLE 12-3 Payoff from a Box Spread

Stock Price Range	Payoff from Bull Call Spread	Payoff from Bear Put Spread	Total Payoff
$S_T \leq K_1$	0	$K_2 - K_1$	$K_2 - K_1$
$K_1 < S_T < K_2$	$S_T - K_1$	$K_2 - S_T$	$K_2 - K_1$
$S_T \geq K_2$	$K_2 - K_1$	0	$K_2 - K_1$

Strike Price ($)	Call Price ($)
55	10
60	7
65	5

The investor could create a butterfly spread by buying one call with a $55 strike price, buying one call with a $65 strike price, and selling two calls with a $60 strike price. It costs $10 + \$5 - (2 \times \$7) = \$1$ to create the spread. If the stock price in 6 months is greater than $65 or less than $55, the total payoff is zero, and the investor incurs a net loss of $1. If the stock price is between $56 and $64, a profit is made. The maximum profit, $4, occurs when the stock price in 6 months is $60.

TABLE 12-4 Payoff from a Butterfly Spread

Stock Price Range	Payoff from First Long Call	Payoff from Second Long Call	Payoff from Short Calls	Total Payoff*
$S_T \leq K_1$	0	0	0	0
$K_1 < S_T \leq K_2$	$S_T - K_1$	0	0	$S_T - K_1$
$K_2 < S_T < K_3$	$S_T - K_1$	0	$-2(S_T - K_2)$	$K_3 - S_T$
$S_T \geq K_3$	$S_T - K_1$	$S_T - K_3$	$-2(S_T - K_2)$	0

*These payoffs are calculated using the relationship $K_2 = 0.5(K_1 + K_3)$.

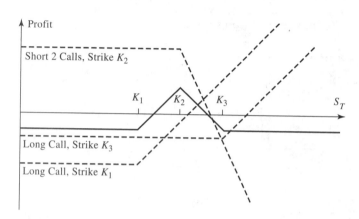

FIGURE 12-6 Profit from butterfly spread using call options.

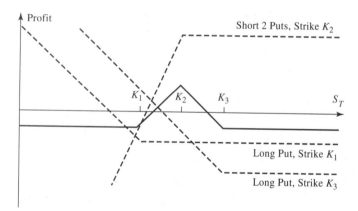

FIGURE 12-7 Profit from butterfly spread using put options.

Butterfly spreads can be created using put options. The investor buys two European puts, one with a low strike price and one with a high strike price, and sells two European puts with an intermediate strike price, as illustrated in Figure 12-7. The butterfly spread in the example considered above would be created by buying one put with a strike price of $55, another with a strike price of $65, and selling two puts with a strike price of $60. The use of put options results in exactly the same spread as the use of call options. Put–call parity can be used to show that the initial investment is the same in both cases.

A butterfly spread can be sold or shorted by following the reverse strategy. Options are sold with strike prices of K_1 and K_3, and two options with the middle strike price K_2 are purchased. This strategy produces a modest profit if there is a significant movement in the stock price.

Calendar Spreads

Up to now we have assumed that the options used to create a spread all expire at the same time. We now move on to *calendar spreads* in which the options have the same strike price and different expiration dates.

A calendar spread can be created by selling a European call option with a certain strike price and buying a longer-maturity European call option with the same strike price. The longer the maturity of an option, the more expensive it usually is. A calendar spread therefore usually requires an initial investment. Profit diagrams for calendar spreads are usually produced so that they show the profit when the short-maturity option expires on the assumption that the long-maturity option is closed out at that time. The profit pattern for a calendar spread produced from call options is shown in Figure 12-8. The pattern is similar to the profit from the butterfly spread in Figure 12-6. The investor makes a profit if the stock price at the expiration of the short-maturity option is close to the strike price of the short-maturity option.

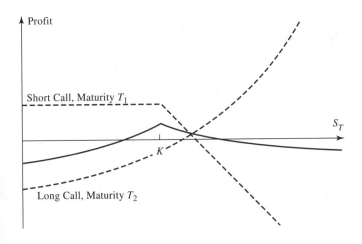

FIGURE 12-8 Profit from calendar spread created using two call options, calculated at the time when the short-maturity call option expires.

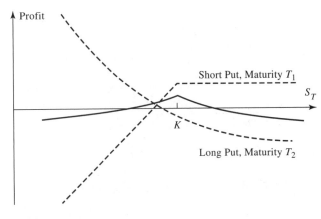

FIGURE 12-9 Profit from a calendar spread created using two put options, calculated at the time when the short-maturity put option expires.

However, a loss is incurred when the stock price is significantly above or significantly below this strike price.

To understand the profit pattern from a calendar spread, first consider what happens if the stock price is very low when the short-maturity option expires. The short-maturity option is worthless and the value of the long-maturity option is close to zero. The investor therefore incurs a loss that is close to the cost of setting up the spread initially. Consider next what happens if the stock price, S_T, is very high when the short-maturity option expires. The short-maturity option costs the investor $S_T - K$, and the long-maturity option is worth close to $S_T - K$, where K is the strike price of the options. Again, the investor makes a net loss that is close to the cost of setting up the spread initially. If S_T is close to K, the short-maturity option costs the investor either a small amount or nothing at all. However, the long-maturity option is still quite valuable. In this case a significant net profit is made.

In a *neutral calendar spread*, a strike price close to the current stock price is chosen. A *bullish calendar spread* involves a higher strike price, whereas a *bearish calendar spread* involves a lower strike price.

Calendar spreads can be created with put options as well as call options. The investor buys a long-maturity put option and sells a short-maturity put option. As shown in

Figure 12-9, the profit pattern is similar to that obtained from using calls.

A *reverse calendar spread* is the opposite to that in Figures 12-8 and 12-9. The investor buys a short-maturity option and sells a long-maturity option. A small profit arises if the stock price at the expiration of the short-maturity option is well above or well below the strike price of the short-maturity option. However, a significant loss results if it is close to the strike price.

Diagonal Spreads

Bull, bear, and calendar spreads can all be created from a long position in one call and a short position in another call. In the case of bull and bear spreads, the calls have different strike prices and the same expiration date. In the case of calendar spreads, the calls have the same strike price and different expiration dates.

In a *diagonal spread* both the expiration date and the strike price of the calls are different. This increases the range of profit patterns that are possible.

COMBINATIONS

A *combination* is an option trading strategy that involves taking a position in both calls and puts on the same stock. We will consider straddles, strips, straps, and strangles.

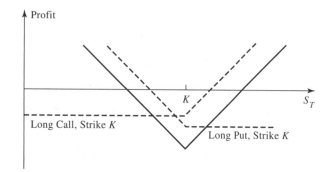

FIGURE 12-10   Profit from a straddle.

TABLE 12-5   Payoff from a Straddle

Range of Stock Price	Payoff from Call	Payoff from Put	Total Payoff
$S_T \leqslant K$	0	$K - S_T$	$K - S_T$
$S_T > K$	$S_T - K$	0	$S_T - K$

Straddle

One popular combination is a *straddle*, which involves buying a European call and put with the same strike price and expiration date. The profit pattern is shown in Figure 12-10. The strike price is denoted by K. If the stock price is close to this strike price at expiration of the options, the straddle leads to a loss. However, if there is a sufficiently large move in either direction, a significant profit will result. The payoff from a straddle is calculated in Table 12-5.

A straddle is appropriate when an investor is expecting a large move in a stock price but does not know in which direction the move will be. Consider an investor who feels that the price of a certain stock, currently valued at $69 by the market, will move significantly in the next 3 months. The investor could create a straddle by buying both a put and a call with a strike price of $70 and an expiration date in 3 months. Suppose that the call costs $4 and the put costs $3. If the stock price stays at $69, it is easy to see that the strategy costs the investor $6. (An up-front investment of $7 is required, the call expires worthless, and the put expires worth $1.) If the stock price moves to $70, a loss of $7 is experienced. (This is the worst that can happen.) However, if the stock price jumps up to $90, a profit of $13 is made; if the stock moves down to $55, a profit of $8 is made; and so

on. As discussed in Box 12-2 an investor should carefully consider whether the jump that he or she anticipates is already reflected in option prices before putting on a straddle trade.

The straddle in Figure 12-10 is sometimes referred to as a *bottom straddle* or *straddle purchase*. A *top straddle* or *straddle write* is the reverse position. It is created by selling a call and a put with the same exercise price and expiration date. It is a highly risky strategy. If the stock price on the expiration date is close to the strike price, a significant profit results. However, the loss arising from a large move is unlimited.

Strips and Straps

A *strip* consists of a long position in one European call and two European puts with the same strike price and expiration date. A *strap* consists of a long position in two European calls and one European put with the same strike price and expiration date. The profit patterns from strips and straps are shown in Figure 12-11. In a strip the investor is betting that there will be a big stock price move and considers a decrease in the stock price to be more likely than an increase. In a strap the investor is also betting that there will be a big stock price move. However, in this case, an increase in the stock price is considered to be more likely than a decrease.

Strangles

In a *strangle*, sometimes called a *bottom vertical combination*, an investor buys a European put and a European call with the same expiration date and different strike prices. The profit pattern that is obtained is shown in Figure 12-12. The call strike price, K_2, is higher than the put strike price, K_1. The payoff function for a strangle is calculated in Table 12-6.

A strangle is a similar strategy to a straddle. The investor is betting that there will be a large price move, but is uncertain whether it will be an increase or a decrease. Comparing Figures 12-12 and 12-10, we see that the stock price has to move farther in a strangle than in a straddle for the investor to make a profit. However, the downside risk if the stock price ends up at a central value is less with a strangle.

The profit pattern obtained with a strangle depends on how close together the strike prices are. The farther they are apart, the less the downside risk and the farther the stock price has to move for a profit to be realized.

The sale of a strangle is sometimes referred to as a *top vertical combination*. It can be appropriate for an investor who feels that large stock price moves are unlikely. However, as with sale of a straddle, it is a risky strategy involving unlimited potential loss to the investor.

OTHER PAYOFFS

This chapter has demonstrated just a few of the ways in which options can be used to produce an interesting relationship between profit and stock price. If European options expiring at time T were available with every single possible strike price, any payoff function at time T could in theory be obtained. The easiest illustration of this involves butterfly spreads. Recall that a butterfly spread is created by buying options with strike prices K_1 and K_3 and selling two options with strike price K_2, where $K_1 < K_2 < K_3$ and $K_3 - K_2 = K_2 - K_1$. Figure 12-13 shows the payoff from

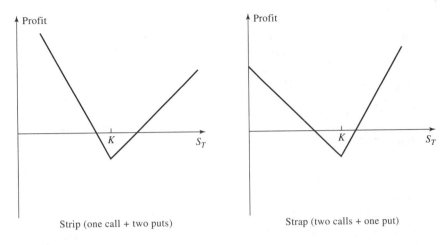

Strip (one call + two puts)   Strap (two calls + one put)

FIGURE 12-11   Profit from a strip and a strap.

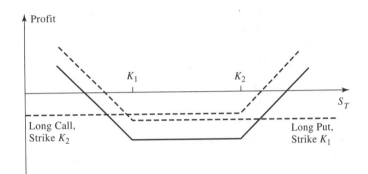

FIGURE 12-12   Profit from a strangle.

TABLE 12-6   Payoff from a Strangle

Range of Stock Price	Payoff from Call	Payoff from Put	Total Payoff
$S_T \leq K_1$	0	$K_1 - S_T$	$K_1 - S_T$
$K_1 < S_T < K_2$	0	0	0
$S_T \geq K_2$	$S_T - K_2$	0	$S_T - K_2$

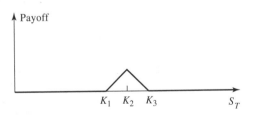

FIGURE 12-13   "Spike payoff" from a butterfly spread that can be used as a building block to create other payoffs.

a butterfly spread. The pattern could be described as a spike. As K_1 and K_3 move closer together, the spike becomes smaller. Through the judicious combination of a large number of very small spikes, any payoff function can be approximated.

SUMMARY

Principal-protected notes can be created from a zero-coupon bond and a European call option. They are attractive to some investors because the issuer of the product guarantees that the purchaser will be receive his or her principal back regardless of the performance of the asset underlying the option.

A number of common trading strategies involve a single option and the underlying stock. For example, writing a covered call involves buying the stock and selling a call option on the stock; a protective put involves buying a put option and buying the stock. The former is similar to selling a put option; the latter is similar to buying a call option.

Spreads involve either taking a position in two or more calls or taking a position in two or more puts. A bull spread can be created by buying a call (put) with a low strike price and selling a call (put) with a high strike price. A bear spread can be created by buying a put (call) with a high strike price and selling a put (call) with a low strike price. A butterfly spread involves buying calls (puts) with a low and high strike price and selling two calls (puts) with some intermediate strike price. A calendar spread involves selling a call (put) with a short time to expiration and buying a call (put) with a longer time to expiration. A diagonal spread involves a long position in one option and a short position in another option such that both the strike price and the expiration date are different.

Combinations involve taking a position in both calls and puts on the same stock. A straddle combination involves taking a long position in a call and a long position in a put with the same strike price and expiration date. A strip consists of a long position in one call and two puts with the same strike price and expiration date. A strap consists of a long position in two calls and one put with the same strike price and expiration date. A strangle consists of a long position in a call and a put with different strike prices and the same expiration date. There are many other ways in which options can be used to produce interesting payoffs. It is not surprising that option trading has steadily increased in popularity and continues to fascinate investors.

Further Reading

Bharadwaj, A. and J. B. Wiggins. "Box Spread and Put–Call Parity Tests for the S&P Index LEAPS Markets," *Journal of Derivatives*, 8, 4 (Summer 2001): 62–71.

Chaput, J. S. and L. H. Ederington, "Option Spread and Combination Trading," *Journal of Derivatives*, 10, 4 (Summer 2003): 70–88.

McMillan, L. G. *McMillan on Options*, 2nd edn. Hoboken, NJ: Wiley, 2004.

Rendleman, R. J. "Covered Call Writing from an Expected Utility Perspective," *Journal of Derivatives*, 8, 3 (Spring 2001): 63–75.

Ronn, A. G. and E. I. Ronn. "The Box–Spread Arbitrage Conditions," *Review of Financial Studies*, 2, 1 (1989): 91–108.

Commodity Forwards and Futures

Learning Objectives

Candidates, after completing this reading, should be able to:

- Define commodity terminology such as storage costs, carry markets, lease rate, and convenience yield.
- Explain the basic equilibrium formula for pricing commodity forwards.
- Describe an arbitrage transaction in commodity forwards, and compute the potential arbitrage profit.
- Define the lease rate and explain how it determines the no-arbitrage values for commodity forwards and futures.
- Define carry markets, and explain the impact of storage costs and convenience yields on commodity forward prices and no-arbitrage bounds.
- Compute the forward price of a commodity with storage costs.
- Compare the lease rate with the convenience yield.

- Identify factors that impact gold, corn, electricity, natural gas, and oil forward prices.
- Define and compute a commodity spread.
- Explain how basis risk can occur when hedging commodity price exposure.
- Evaluate the differences between a strip hedge and a stack hedge and explain how these differences impact risk management.
- Describe examples of cross-hedging, specifically the process of hedging jet fuel with crude oil and using weather derivatives.
- Explain how to create a synthetic commodity position, and use it to explain the relationship between the forward price and the expected future spot price.

Excerpt is Chapter 6 of Derivatives Markets, *Third Edition, by Robert McDonald.*

Tolstoy observed that happy families are all alike; each unhappy family is unhappy in its own way. An analogous idea in financial markets is that financial forwards are all alike; each commodity, however, has unique economic characteristics that determine forward pricing in that market. In this chapter we will see the extent to which commodity forwards on different assets differ from each other, and also how they differ from financial forwards and futures. We first discuss the pricing of commodity contracts, and then examine specific contracts, including gold, corn, natural gas, and oil. Finally, we discuss hedging.

You might wonder about the definition of a commodity. Gerard Debreu, who won the Nobel Prize in economics, said this (Debreu, 1959, p. 28):

> A commodity is characterized by its physical properties, the date at which it will be available, and the location at which it will be available. The price of a commodity is the amount which has to be paid *now* for the (future) availability of one unit of that commodity.

Notice that with this definition, corn in July and corn in September, for example, are different commodities: They are available on different dates. With a financial asset, such as a stock, we think of the stock as being fundamentally the same asset over time.[1] The same is not necessarily true of a commodity, since it can be costly or impossible to transform a commodity on one date into a commodity on another date. This observation will be important.

In our discussion of forward pricing for financial assets we relied heavily on the fact that the price of a financial asset today is the present value of the asset at time T, less the value of dividends to be received between now and time T. It follows that the difference between the forward price and spot price of a financial asset reflects the costs and benefits of delaying payment for, and receipt of, the asset. Specifically, the forward price on a financial asset is given by

$$F_{0,T} = S_0 e^{(r-\delta)T} \qquad \textbf{(13.1)}$$

where S_0 is the spot price of the asset, r is the continuously compounded interest rate, and δ is the continuous dividend yield on the asset. We will explore the extent to which Equation (13.1) also holds for commodities.

---

[1] When there are dividends, however, a share of stock received on different dates can be materially different.

INTRODUCTION TO COMMODITY FORWARDS

This section provides an overview of some issues that arise in discussing commodity forward and futures contracts. We begin by looking at some commodity futures prices. We then discuss some terms and concepts that will be important for commodities.

Examples of Commodity Futures Prices

For many commodities there are futures contracts available that expire at different dates in the future. Table 13-1 provides illustrative examples: we can examine these prices to see what issues might arise with commodity forward pricing.

First, consider corn. From May to July, the corn futures price rises from 646.50 to 653.75. This is a 2-month increase of $653.75/646.50 - 1 = 1.12\%$, an annual rate of approximately 7%. As a reference interest rate, 3-month LIBOR on March 17, 2011, was 0.31%, or about 0.077% for 3 months. Assuming that $\delta \geq 0$, this futures price is greater than that implied by Equation (13.1). A discussion would suggest an arbitrage strategy: Buy May corn and sell July corn. However, storing corn for 2 months will be costly, a consideration that did not arise with financial futures. Another issue arises with the December price: The price of corn falls 74.5 cents between July and December. It seems unlikely that this could be explained by a dividend. An alternative, intuitive explanation would be that the fall harvest causes the price of corn to drop, and hence the December futures price is low. But how is this explanation consistent with our results about no-arbitrage pricing of financial forwards?

If you examine the other commodities, you will see similar patterns for soybeans, gasoline, and oil. Only gold, with the forward price rising at approximately $0.70 per month (about 0.6% annually), has behavior resembling that of a financial contract.

The prices in Table 13-1 suggest that commodities are different than financial contracts. The challenge is to reconcile the patterns with our understanding of financial forwards, in which explicit expectations of future prices (and harvests!) do not enter the forward price formula.

There are *many* more commodities with traded futures than just those in Table 13-1. You might think that a futures contract could be written on anything, but it is an interesting bit of trivia, discussed in the box below, that Federal law in the United States prohibits trading on two commodities.

Differences Between Commodities and Financial Assets

In discussing the commodity prices in Table 13-1, we invoked considerations that did not arise with financial assets, but that will arise repeatedly when we discuss commodities. Among these are:

Storage costs. The cost of storing a physical item such as corn or copper can be large relative to its value. Moreover. some commodities deteriorate over time. which is also a cost of storage. By comparison, financial securities are inexpensive to store. Consequently. we did not mention storage costs when discussing financial assets.

Carry markets. A commodity for which the forward price compensates a commodity owner

TABLE 13-1 Futures Prices for Various Commodities, March 17, 2011

Expiration Month	Corn (cents/ bushel)	Soybeans (cents/ bushel)	Gasoline (cents/ gallon)	Oil (Brent) (dollars/ barrel)	Gold (dollars/ ounce)
April	—	—	2.9506	—	1404.20
May	646.50	1335.25	2.9563	114.90	1404.90
June	—	—	2.9491	114.65	1405.60
July	653.75	1343.50	2.9361	114.38	—
August	—	—	2.8172	114.11	1406.90
September	613.00	1321.00	2.8958	113.79	—
October	—	—	2.7775	113.49	1408.20
November	—	1302.25	2.7522	113.17	—
December	579.25	—	2.6444	112.85	1409.70

Data from CME Group.

BOX 13-1 Forbidden Futures

In the United States, futures contracts on two items are explicitly prohibited by statute: onions and box office receipts for movies. Title 7, Chapter 1, §13-1 of the United States Code is titled "Violations, prohibition against dealings in onion futures; punishment" and states

(a) No contract for the sale of onions for future delivery shall be made on or subject to the rules of any board of trade in the United States. The terms used in this section shall have the same meaning as when used in this chapter.

(b) Any person who shall violate the provisions of this section shall be deemed guilty of a misdemeanor and upon conviction thereof be fined not more than $5,000.

Along similar lines, Title VII of the Dodd-Frank Wall Street Reform and Consumer Protection Act of 2010 bans trading in "motion picture box office receipts (or any index, measure, value, or data related to such receipts), and all services, rights, and interests . . . in which contracts for future delivery are presently or in the future dealt in."

These bans exist because of lobbying by special interests. The onion futures ban was passed in 1959 when Michigan onion growers lobbied their new congressman,

Gerald Ford, to ban such trading, believing that it depressed prices. Today, some regret the law:

Onion prices soared 400% between October 2006 and April 2007, when weather reduced crops, according to the U.S. Department of Agriculture, only to crash 96% by March 2008 on overproduction and then rebound 300% by this past April.

The volatility has been so extreme that the son of one of the original onion growers who lobbied Congress for the trading ban now thinks the onion market would operate more smoothly if a futures contract were in place.

"There probably has been more volatility since the ban," says Bob Debruyn of Debruyn Produce, a Michigan-based grower and wholesaler. "I would think that a futures market for onions would make some sense today, even though my father was very much involved in getting rid of it."

Source: Fortune magazine on-line, June 27, 2008.

Similarly, futures on movie box office receipts had been approved early in 2010 by the Commodity Futures Trading Commission. After lobbying by Hollywood interests, the ban on such trading was inserted into the Dodd-Frank financial reform bill.

for costs of storage is called a **carry market**. (In such a market. the return on a cash-and-carry, net of all costs, is the risk-free rate.) Storage of a commodity is an economic decision that varies across commodities and that can vary over time for a given commodity. Some commodities are at times stored for later use (we will see that this is the case for natural gas and corn), others are more typically used as they are produced (oil, copper). By contrast, financial markets are always carry markets: Assets are always "stored" (owned), and forward prices always compensate owners for storage.

Lease rate. The short-seller of an item may have to compensate the owner of the item for lending. In the case of financial assets, short-sellers have to compensate lenders for missed dividends or other payments accruing to the asset. For commodities, a short-seller may have to make a payment, called a lease payment, to the commodity lender. The lease payment typically would nor correspond to dividends in the usual sense of the word.

Convenience yield. The owner of a commodity in a commodity-related business may receive nonmonetary benefits from physical possession of the commodity. Such benefits may be reflected in forward prices and are generically referred to as a **convenience yield**.

We will discuss all of these concepts in more depth later in the chapter. For now, the important thing to keep in mind is that commodities differ in important respects from financial assets.

Commodity Terminology

There are many terms that are particular to commodities and thus often unfamiliar even to those well acquainted with financial markets. These terms deal with the properties of the forward curve and the physical characteristics of commodities.

Table 13-1 illustrates two terms often used by commodity traders in talking about forward curves: **contango** and **backwardation**. If the forward curve is upward sloping—i.e.. forward prices more distant in time are higher—then we say the market is in contango. We observe this pattern with near-term corn and soybeans, and with gold. If the forward curve is downward sloping, we say the market is in backwardation. We observe this with medium-term corn and soybeans, with gasoline (after 2 months), and with crude oil.

Commodities can be broadly classified as **extractive** and **renewable**. Extractive commodities occur naturally in the ground and are obtained by mining and drilling. Examples include metals (silver, gold, and copper) and hydrocarbons, including oil and natural gas. Renewable commodities are obtained through agriculture and include grains (corn, soybeans, wheat), livestock (cattle, pork bellies), dairy (cheese, milk), and lumber.

Commodities can be further classified as **primary** and **secondary**. Primary commodities are unprocessed: corn, soybeans, oil, and gold are all primary. Secondary commodities have been processed. In Table 13-1, gasoline is a secondary commodity.

Finally, commodities are measured in uncommon units for which you may not know precise definitions. Table 13-1 has several examples. A **barrel** of oil is 42 gallons. A **bushel** is a dry measure containing approximately 2150 cubic inches. The ounce used to weigh precious metals, such as gold, is a **troy ounce**, which is approximately 9.7% greater in weight than the customary avoirdupois ounce.[2]

Entire books are devoted to commodities (e.g., see Geman, 2005). Our goal here is to understand the *logic* of forward pricing for commodities and where it differs from the logic of forward pricing for financial assets. We will see that understanding a forward curve generally requires that we understand something about the underlying commodity.

EQUILIBRIUM PRICING OF COMMODITY FORWARDS

In this section we present definitions relating the prepaid forward price, forward price, and present value of a future commodity price.

---

[2] A troy ounce is 480 grains and the more familiar avoirdupois ounce is 437.5 grains. Twelve troy ounces make 1 troy pound, which weighs approximately 0.37 kg.

The prepaid forward price for a commodity is the price today to receive a unit of the commodity on a future date. The prepaid forward price is therefore by definition the present value of the commodity on the future date. Hence, the prepaid forward price is

$$F_{0,T}^P = e^{-\alpha T}E_0[S_T] \tag{13.2}$$

where α is the discount rate for the commodity.

The forward price is the future value of the prepaid forward price, with the future value computed using the risk-free rate:

$$F_{0,T} = e^{rT}F_{0,T}^P \tag{13.3}$$

Substituting Equation (13.2) into Equation (13.3), we see that the commodity forward price is the expected spot price, discounted at the risk premium (this is the same as Equation (8.9)):

$$F_{0,T} = E_0(S_T)e^{-(\alpha-r)T} \tag{13.4}$$

We can rewrite Equation (13.4) to obtain

$$e^{-rT}F_{0,T} = E_0(S_T)e^{-\alpha T} \tag{13.5}$$

Equation (13.5) deserves emphasis: *The time-T forward price discounted at the risk-free rate is the present value of a unit of commodity received at time T.* This equation implies that, for example, an industrial producer who buys oil can calculate the present value of future oil costs by discounting oil forward prices at the risk-free rate. This calculation does not depend upon whether the producer hedges. We will see an example of this calculation later in the chapter.

PRICING COMMODITY FORWARDS BY ARBITRAGE

We now investigate no-arbitrage pricing for commodity forward contracts. We begin by using copper as an example. Copper is durable and can be stored, but it is typically not stored except as needed for production. The primary goal in this section will be to understand the issues that distinguish forward pricing for commodities from forward pricing for financial assets.

Figure 13-1 shows specifications for the CME Group copper contract and Figure 13-2 shows forward curves for copper on four dates. The copper forward curve lacks drama: For three of the four curves, the forward price in 1 year is

approximately equal to the forward price in the current month. For the fourth curve, the 1-year price is below the current price (the curve exhibits backwardation).

We saw that for non-dividend-paying financial assets. the forward price rises at the interest rate. How can the

Underlying	High-grade (Grade 1) copper
Where traded	CME Group/COMEX
Size	25,000 pounds
Months	24 consecutive months
Trading ends	Third-to-last business day of the maturing month
Delivery	Exchange-designated warehouse within the United States

FIGURE 13-1 Specifications for the CME Group/ COMEX high-grade copper contract.

Data from Datastream.

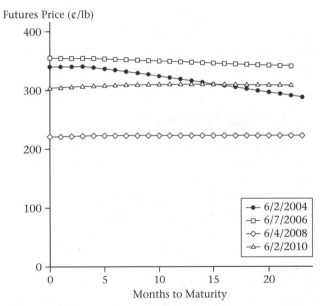

FIGURE 13-2 Forward curves for four dates for the CME Group high-grade copper futures contract.

Data from Datastream.

forward price of copper on a future date equal the current forward price? At an intuitive level, it is reasonable to expect the price of copper in 1 year to equal the price today. Suppose, for example, that the extraction and other costs of copper production are $3/pound and are expected to remain $3. If demand is not expected to change, or if it is easy for producers to alter production, it would be reasonable to expect that on average the price of copper would remain at $3. The question is how to reconcile this intuition with the behavior of forward prices for financial assets.

While it is reasonable to think that the price of copper will be expected to remain the same over the next year, it is important to recognize that a constant price would *not* be a reasonable assumption about the price of a non-dividend-paying stock. Investors must expect that a stock will on average pay a positive return, or no one would own it. In equilibrium, stocks and other financial assets must be held by investors, or *stored*. The stock price appreciates on average so that investors will willingly store the stock. There is no such requirement for copper, which can be extracted and then used in production. The equilibrium condition for copper relates to extraction, not to storage above ground. This distinction between a storage and production equilibrium is a central concept in our discussion of commodities. At the outset, then, there is an obvious difference between copper and a financial asset. It is not necessarily obvious, however, what bearing this difference has on pricing forward contracts.

An Apparent Arbitrage

Suppose that you observe that both the current price and 1-year forward price for copper are $3.00 and that the effective annual interest rate is 10%. For the reasons we have just discussed, market participants could rationally believe that the copper price in 1 year will be $3.00. From our discussion of financial forwards, however, you might think that the forward price should be 1.10 × $3.00 = $3.30, the future value of the current copper price. The $3.00 forward price would therefore create an arbitrage opportunity.[3] If the forward price were $3.00 you could buy copper

---

[3] We will discuss arbitrage in this section focusing on the forward price relative to the spot price. However, the difference between any forward prices at different dates must also reflect no-arbitrage conditions. So you can apply the discussions in this section to any two points on the forward curve.

TABLE 13-2 Apparent Reverse Cash-and-Carry Arbitrage for Copper If the Copper Forward Price Is $F_{0,1} < \$3.30$. These calculations *appear* to demonstrate that there is an arbitrage opportunity if the copper forward price is below $3.30. S_1 is the spot price of copper in 1 year, and $F_{0,1}$ is the copper forward price. There is a logical error in the table.

Transaction	Cash Flows	
	Time 0	Time 1
Long forward @ $F_{0,1}$	0	$S_1 - F_{0,1}$
Short-sell copper	+$3.00	$- S_1$
Lend short-sale proceeds @ 10%	−$3.00	+$3.30
Total	0	$\$3.30 - F_{0,1}$

forward and short sell copper today. Table 13-2 depicts the cash flows in this reverse cash-and-carry arbitrage. The result seems to show that there is an arbitrage opportunity for any copper forward price below $3.30. If the copper forward price is $3.00, it seems that you make a profit of $0.30 per pound of copper.

We seem to be stuck. Common sense suggests that a forward price of $3.00 would be reasonable, but the transactions in Table 13-2 imply that any forward price less than $3.30 leads to an arbitrage opportunity, where we would earn $3.30 − $F_{0,1}$ per pound of copper.

If you are puzzled, you should stop and think before proceeding. There is a problem with Table 13-2.

The arbitrage assumes that you can short-sell copper by borrowing it today and returning it in a year. However, in order for you to short-sell for a year, there must be an investor willing to lend copper for that period. The lender must both be holding the asset and willing to give up physical possession for the period of the short-sale. A lender in this case will think: "I have spent $3.00 for copper. Copper that I lend will be returned in 1 year. If copper at that time sells for $3.00, then I have earned zero interest on my $3.00 investment. If I hedge by selling copper forward for $3.00, I will for certain earn zero interest, having bought copper for $3.00 and then selling it for $3.00 a year later." Conversely, from the perspective of the short-seller, borrowing a pound of copper for a year is an arbitrage because it is an interest-free loan of $3.00. The borrower benefits and the lender loses, so *no one will lend copper without charging an additional fee*. While it is straightforward to borrow a financial asset, borrowing copper appears to be a different matter.

To summarize: The apparent arbitrage in Table 13-2 has nothing to do with mispriced forward contracts on copper. The issue is that the copper loan is equivalent to an interest-free loan, and thus generates an arbitrage profit.

Short-Selling and the Lease Rate

How do we correct the arbitrage analysis in Table 13-2? We have to recognize that the copper lender has invested $3.00 in copper and must expect to earn a satisfactory return on that investment. *The copper lender will require us to make a lease payment so that the commodity loan is a fair deal*. The actual payment the lender requires will depend on the forward price. The lender will recognize that it is possible to use the forward market to lock in a selling price for the copper in 1 year, and will reason that copper bought for $3.00 today can be sold for $F_{0,1}$ in 1 year. A copper borrower must therefore be prepared to make an extra payment—a lease payment—of

$$\text{Lease payment} = 1.1 \times \$3.00 - F_{0,1}$$

With the lender requiring this extra payment, we can correct the analysis in Table 13-2. Table 13-3 incorporates the lease payment and shows that the apparent arbitrage vanishes.

We can also interpret a lease payment in terms of discounted cash flow. Let α denote the equilibrium discount rate for an asset with the same risk as the commodity. The lender is buying the commodity for S_0. One unit returned at time T is worth S_T, with a present value of $E_0(S_T)e^{-\alpha T}$. If there is a proportional continuous lease payment of δ_l, the NPV of buying the commodity and lending it is

$$\text{NPV} = E_0(S_T)e^{-\alpha T}e^{\delta_l T} - S_0 \qquad \text{(13.6)}$$

The lease rate that makes NPV zero is then

$$\delta_l = \alpha - \frac{1}{T}\ln\left[E_0(S_T) / S_0\right]$$

The lease rate is the difference between the discount rate for the commodity and the expected price appreciation.

TABLE 13-3 Reverse Cash-and-Carry Arbitrage for Copper. This table demonstrates that there is no arbitrage opportunity if the commodity lender requires an appropriate lease payment.

Transaction	Cash Flows	
	Time 0	Time 1
Long forward @ $F_{0,1}$	0	$S_1 - F_{0,1}$
Short-sell copper	+$3.00	$- S_1$
Lease payment	0	$-(\$3.30 - F_{0,1})$
Lend short-sale proceeds @ 10%	-$3.00	+$3.30
Total	0	0

From substituting Equation (13.5) into this expression, an equivalent way to write the continuous lease rate is

$$\delta_l = r - \frac{1}{T}\ln\left[F_{0,T} / S_0\right] \qquad \text{(13.7)}$$

It is important to be clear about the reason a lease payment is required for a commodity and not for a financial asset. For a non-dividend-paying financial asset, the price is the present value of the future price, so that $S_0 = E_0(S_T)e^{-\alpha T}$. This implies that the lease payment is zero. For most commodities, the current price is not the present value of the expected future price, so there is no presumption that the lease rate would be zero.

No-Arbitrage Pricing Incorporating Storage Costs

We now consider the effects of storage costs. Storage is not always feasible (for example, fresh strawberries are perishable), and when technically feasible, storage for commodities is almost always costly. If storage is feasible, how do storage costs affect forward pricing? The intuitive answer is that if it is optimal to store the commodity, then the forward price must be high enough so that the returns on a cash-and-carry compensate for both financing and storage costs. However, if storage is not optimal, storage costs are irrelevant. We will examine both cash-and-carry and reverse cash-and-carry arbitrages to see how they are affected by storage costs.

Cash-and-Carry Arbitrage. Put yourself in the position of a commodity merchant who owns one unit of the commodity, and ask whether you would be willing to store it until time T. You face the choice of selling it today, receiving S_0, or selling it at time T. If you guarantee your selling price by selling forward, you will receive $F_{0,T}$:

It is common sense that *you will store only if the present value of selling at time T is at least as great as that of selling today*. Denote the future value of storage costs for one unit of the commodity from time 0 to T as $\lambda(0, T)$. Table 13-4 summarizes the cash flows for a cash-and-carry with storage costs. The table shows that the cash-and-carry arbitrage is not profitable if

$$F_{0,1} < (1+R)S_0 + \lambda(0,1) \qquad \textbf{(13.8)}$$

If inequality (13.8) is violated, storage will occur because the forward premium is great enough that sale proceeds in the future compensate for the financial costs of storage (RS_0) and the physical costs of storage ($\lambda(0, 1)$). If there is to be both storage and no arbitrage, then Equation (13.8) holds with equality. An implication of Equation (13.8) is that when costly storage occurs, the forward curve can rise faster than the interest rate. We can view storage costs as a negative dividend: Instead of receiving cash flow for holding the asset, you have to pay to hold the asset. If there is storage, storage costs increase the upper bound for the forward price. Storage costs can include depreciation of the commodity, which is less a problem for metals such as copper than for commodities such as strawberries and electricity.

In the special case where continuous storage costs of λ are paid continuously and are proportional to the value of the commodity, storage cost is like a continuous negative dividend. If storage occurs and there is no arbitrage, we have[4]

$$F_{0,T} = S_0 e^{(r+\lambda)T} \qquad \textbf{(13.9)}$$

This would be the forward price in a carry market, where the commodity is stored.

Example 13.1

Suppose that the November price of corn is $2.50/bushel, the effective monthly interest rate is 1%, and storage costs per bushel are $0.05/month. Assuming that corn is stored from November to February, the February forward price must compensate owners for interest and storage. The future value of storage costs is

$$\$0.05 + (\$0.05 \times 1.01) + (\$0.05 \times 1.01^2)$$
$$= (\$0.05/.01) \times [1 + 0.01)^3 - 1]$$
$$= \$0.1515$$

Thus, the February forward price will be

$$2.50 \times (1.01)^3 + 0.1515 = 2.7273$$

Exercise 9 asks you to verify that this is a no-arbitrage price.

Keep in mind that just because a commodity *can* be stored does not mean that it *should* (or will) be stored. Copper is typically not stored for long periods, because storage is not economically necessary: A constant new supply of copper is available to meet demand. Thus, Equation (13.8) describes the forward price *when storage occurs*. We now consider a reverse cash-and-carry arbitrage to see what happens when the forward price is lower than in Equation (13.8).

Reverse Cash-and-Carry Arbitrage. Suppose an arbitrageur buys the commodity forward and short-sells it. We have seen that the commodity lender likely requires

---

[4] You might be puzzled by the different ways of representing quantities such as costs and dividends. In some cases we have used discrete values; in others, we have used continuous approximations. All of these represent the same conceptual amount (a present or future value of a cost of cash flow). You should be familiar with different ways of writing the formulas.

TABLE 13-4 Cash-and-Carry for Copper for 1 Year, Assuming That There Is a 1-year Storage Cost of $\lambda(0, 1)$ Payable at Time 1, and an Effective Interest Rate of R

Transaction	Cash Flows	
	Time 0	**Time 1**
Buy copper	$-S_0$	S_1
Pay storage cost	0	$-\lambda(0, 1)$
Short forward	0	$F_{0,1} - S_1$
Borrow @ R	$+S_0$	$-(1 + R)S_0$
Total	0	$F_{0,1} - [(1 + R)S_0 + \lambda(0, 1)]$

a lease payment and that the payment *should* be equal to $(1 + R)S_0 - F_{0,1}$. The results of this transaction are in Table 13-5. Note first that storage costs do not affect profit because neither the arbitrageur nor the lender is actually storing the commodity. The reverse cash-and-carry is profitable if the lender requires a lease payment below $(1 + R)S_0 - F_{0,1}$. Otherwise, arbitrage is not profitable. If the commodity lender uses the forward price to determine the lease rate, then the resulting circularity guarantees that profit is zero. This is evident in Table 13-5, where profit is zero if $L = (1 + R)S_0 - F_{0,1}$.

This analysis has the important implication that the ability to engage in a reverse cash-and-carry arbitrage does not put a lower bound on the forward price. We conclude that a forward price that is too high can give rise to arbitrage, but a forward price that is too low need not.

Of course there are economic pressures inducing the forward price to reach the "correct" level. If the forward price is too low, there will be an incentive for arbitrageurs to buy the commodity forward. If it is too high, there is an incentive for traders to sell the commodity, whether or not arbitrage is feasible. Leasing and storage costs complicate arbitrage, however.

Convenience Yields

The discussion of commodities has so far ignored business reasons for holding commodities. For example, if you are a food producer for whom corn is an essential input, you will hold corn in inventory. If you hold too much corn,

you can sell the excess. However, if you hold too little, you may run out of corn, halting production and idling workers and machines. The physical inventory of corn in this case has value: It provides insurance that you can keep producing in case there is a disruption in the supply of corn.

In this situation, corn holdings provide an extra nonmonetary return called the convenience yield.[5] You will be willing to store corn with a lower rate of return than if you did not earn the convenience yield. What are the implications of the convenience yield for the forward price?

The convenience yield is only relevant when the commodity is stored. In order to store the commodity, an owner will require that the forward price compensate for the financial and physical costs of storing, but the owner will accept a lower forward price to the extent there is a convenience yield. Specifically, if the continuously compounded convenience yield is c, proportional to the value of the commodity, the owner will earn an acceptable return from storage if the forward price is

$$F_{0,T} \geq S_0 e^{(r + \lambda - c)T}$$

Because we saw that low commodity forward prices cannot easily be arbitraged, this price would not yield an arbitrage opportunity.

What is the commodity lease rate in this case? An owner lending the commodity saves λ and loses c from not storing the commodity. Hence, the commodity borrower would need to pay $\delta_l = c - \lambda$ in order to compensate the lender for convenience yield less storage cost.

The difficulty with the convenience yield in practice is that convenience is hard to observe. The concept of the convenience yield serves two purposes. First, it explains patterns in storage—for example, why a commercial user might store a commodity when the average investor will not. Second, it provides an additional parameter to better explain the forward curve. You might object that we can invoke the convenience yield to explain *any* forward curve, and therefore the concept of the

---

[5] The term *convenience yield* is defined differently by different authors. Convenience yield generally means a return to physical ownership of the commodity. In practice it is sometimes used to mean what we call the lease rate. In this book, the two concepts are distinct, and commodities need not have a convenience yield. The lease rate of a commodity can be inferred from the forward price using Equation (13.7).

TABLE 13-5 Reverse Cash-and-Carry for Copper for 1 Year, Assuming That the Commodity Lender Requires a Lease Payment of L		
	Cash Flows	
Transaction	**Time 0**	**Time 1**
Short-sell copper	S_0	$-S_1$
Lease payment	0	$-L$
Long forward	0	$S_1 - F_{0,1}$
Invest @ R	$-S_0$	$(1 + R)S_0$
Total	0	$[(1 + R)S_0 - F_{0,1}] - L$

convenience yield is vacuous. While convenience yield can be tautological, it is a meaningful economic concept and it would be just as arbitrary to assume that there is never convenience. Moreover. the upper bound in Equation (13.8) depends on storage costs but not the convenience yield. Thus, the convenience yield only explains anomalously low forward prices, and only when there is storage.

Summary

Much of the discussion in this section was aimed at explaining the differences between commodities and financial assets. The main conclusions are intuitive:

- The forward price, $F_{0,T}$, should not exceed $S_0 e^{(r+\lambda)T}$. If the forward price were greater, you could undertake a simple cash-and-carry and earn a profit after paying both storage costs and interest on the position. Storage costs here includes deterioration of the commodity, so fragile commodities could have large (or infinite) storage costs.

- In a carry market, the forward price should equal $S_0 e^{(r-c+\lambda)T}$. A user who buys and stores the commodity will then be compensated for interest and physical storage costs less a convenience yield.

- In any kind of market, a reverse cash-and-carry arbitrage (attempting to arbitrage too low a forward price) will be difficult, because the terms at which a lender will lend the commodity will likely reflect the forward price, making profitable arbitrage difficult.

GOLD

Of all commodities, gold is most like a financial asset. Gold is durable, nonreactive, noncorrosive, relatively inexpensive to store (compared to its value), widely held, and actively produced through gold mining. Because of transportation costs and purity concerns, gold often trades in certificate form, as a claim to physical gold at a specific location. There are exchange-traded gold futures, specifications for which are in Figure 13-3.

Figure 13-4 graphs futures prices for all available gold futures contracts—the forward curve—for four different dates. The forward curves all show the forward price steadily increasing with time to maturity.

Underlying	Refined gold bearing approved refiner stamp
Where traded	CME Group/NYMEX
Size	100 troy ounces
Months	February, April, August, October, out 2 years. June, December, out 5 years
Trading ends	Third-to-last business day of maturity month
Delivery	Any business day of the delivery month

FIGURE 13-3 Specifications for the CME Group gold futures contract.

Data from Datastream.

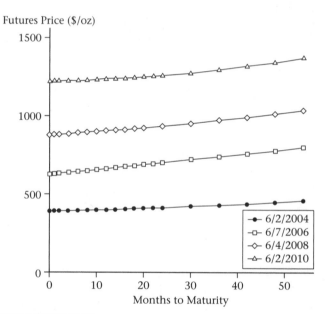

FIGURE 13-4 The forward curve for gold on four dates, from NYMEX gold futures prices.

Data from Datastream.

Gold Leasing

From our discussion in the previous section, the forward price implies a lease rate for gold. Short sales and loans of gold are in fact common in the gold market. On the lending side, large gold holders (including some central banks) put gold on deposit with brokers, in order that it may be loaned to short-sellers. The gold lenders earn the lease rate.

The lease rate for gold, silver, and other commodities is typically reported using Equation (13.7), with LIBOR as the interest rate. In recent years the lease rate has often been negative, especially for periods of 6 months or less.

As an example of the lease rate computation, consider gold prices on June 2, 2010. The June, December, and June 2011 futures settlement prices that day were 1220.6, 1226.8, and 1234.3. The return from buying June gold and selling December gold would have been

$$\text{Return}_{6\,\text{months}} = \frac{1226.8}{1220.6} - 1 = 0.00508$$

At the same time. June LIBOR was 99.432 and September LIBOR was 99.2, so the implied 6-month interest rate was $(1 + 0.00568/4) \times (1 + 0.008/4)$, a 6-month interest rate of 0.00342. Because the (nonannualized) implied 6-month gold appreciation rate exceeds (nonannualized) 6-month LIBOR, the lease rate is negative. The annualized lease rate in this calculation is

$$2 \times (0.00342 - 0.00508) = -0.003313$$

The negative lease rate seems to imply that gold owners would pay to lend gold. With significant demand in recent years for gold storage, the negative lease rate could be measuring increased marginal storage costs. It is also possible that LIBOR is not the correct interest rate to use in computing the lease rate. Whatever the reason for negative lease rates, gold in recent years has been trading at close to full carry.

Evaluation of Gold Production

Suppose we wish to compute the present value of future production for a proposed gold mine. As discussed earlier, the present value of a unit of commodity received in the future is simply the present value of the forward price, with discounting performed at the risk-free rate. We can thus use the forward curve for gold to compute the value of an operating gold mine.

Suppose that at times t_i, $i = 1, \ldots, n$, we expect to extract n_{t_i} ounces of gold by paying a per-unit extraction cost of $x(t_i)$. We have a set of n forward prices, F_{0,t_i}. If the continuously compounded annual risk-free rate from time 0 to t_i is $r(0, t_i)$, the value of the gold mine is

$$\text{PV gold production} = \sum_{i=1}^{n} n_{t_i} \left[F_{0,t_i} - x(t_i) \right] e^{-r(0,t_i)t_i} \quad \textbf{(13.10)}$$

This equation assumes that the gold mine is certain to operate the entire time and that the quantity of production is known. Only price is uncertain. Note that in Equation (13.10), by computing the present value of the forward price, we compute the prepaid forward price.

Example 13.2

Suppose we have a mining project that will produce 1 ounce of gold every year for 6 years. The cost of this project is $1100 today, the marginal cost per ounce at the time of extraction is $100, and the continuously compounded interest rate is 6%.

We observe the gold forward prices in the second column of Table 13-6, with implied prepaid forward prices in the third column. Using Equation (13.10), we can use these prices to perform the necessary present value calculations.

$$\text{Net present value} = \sum_{i=1}^{6} \left[F_{0,i} - 100 \right] e^{-0.06 \times i} \quad \textbf{(13.11)}$$

$$- \$1100 = \$119.56$$

TABLE 13-6 Gold Forward and Prepaid Forward Prices on 1 Day for Gold Delivered at 1-year Intervals, out to 6 Years. The continuously compounded interest rate is 6% and the lease rate is assumed to be a constant 1.5%.

Expiration Year	Forward Price ($)	Prepaid Forward Price ($)
1	313.81	295.53
2	328.25	291.13
3	343.36	286.80
4	359.17	282.53
5	375.70	278.32
6	392.99	274.18

CORN

Important grain futures in the United States include corn, soybeans, and wheat. In this section we discuss corn as an example of an agricultural product. Corn is harvested primarily in the fall, from September through November. The United States is a leading corn producer, generally exporting rather than importing corn. Figure 13-5 presents specifications for the CME Group corn futures contract.

Given seasonality in production, what should the forward curve for corn look like? Corn is produced at one time of the year, but consumed throughout the year. In order to be consumed when it is not being produced, corn must be stored.

As discussed, storage is an economic decision in which there is a trade-off between selling today and selling tomorrow. If we can sell corn today for $2/bu and in 2 months for $2.25/bu, the storage decision entails comparing the price we can get today with the present value of the price we can get in 2 months. In addition to interest, we need to include storage costs in our analysis.

An equilibrium with some current selling and some storage requires that corn prices be expected to rise at the interest rate plus storage costs, which implies that there will be an upward trend in the price between harvests. While corn is being stored, the forward price should behave as in Equation (13.9), rising at interest plus storage costs.

In a typical year, once the harvest begins, storage is no longer necessary; if supply and demand remain constant from year to year, the harvest price will be the same every year. Those storing corn will plan to deplete inventory as harvest approaches and to replenish inventory from the new harvest. The corn price will fall at harvest, only to begin rising again after the harvest.

The behavior of the corn forward price, graphed in Figure 13-6, largely conforms with this description. In three of the four forward curves, the forward price of corn rises to reward storage between harvests, and it falls at harvest. An important caveat is that the supply of corn varies from year to year. When there is an unusually large crop, producers will expect corn to be stored not just over the current year but into the next year as well. If there is a large harvest, therefore, we might see the forward curve rise continuously until year 2. This might explain the low price and steady rise in 2006.

Although corn prices vary throughout the year, farmers will plant in anticipation of receiving the harvest price. It is therefore the harvest price that guides production decisions. The price during the rest of the year should approximately equal the harvest price plus storage, less convenience.

Underlying	#2 Yellow, with #1 Yellow deliverable at a $0.015 premium and #3 Yellow at a $0.015 discount
Where traded	CME Group/CBOT
Size	5000 bushels (~127 metric tons)
Months	March, May, July, September, and December, out 2 years
Trading ends	Business day prior to the 15th day of the month
Delivery	Second business day following the last trading day of the delivery month

FIGURE 13-5 Specifications for the CME Group/CBOT corn futures contract.

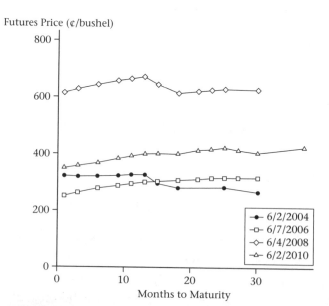

FIGURE 13-6 Forward curves for corn for four years.

Data from Datastream.

ENERGY MARKETS

One of the most important and heavily traded commodity sectors is energy. This sector includes oil, oil products (heating oil and gasoline), natural gas, and electricity. These products represent different points on the spectrum of storage costs and carry.

Electricity

The forward market for electricity illustrates forward pricing when storage is often not possible, or at least quite costly. Electricity is produced in different ways: from fuels such as coal and natural gas, or from nuclear power, hydroelectric power, wind power, or solar power. Once it is produced, electricity is transmitted over the power grid to end-users.

There are several economic characteristics of electricity that are important to understand. First, it is difficult to store; hence it must be consumed when it is produced or else it is wasted.[6] Second, at any point in time the maximum supply of electricity is fixed. You can produce less but not more. Third, demand for electricity varies substantially by season, by day of week, and by time of day.

_____

[6] There are costly ways to store electricity. Three examples are _pumped storage hydroelectricity_ (pump water into an uphill reservoir when prices are low, and release the water to flow over turbines when electricity is expensive); _night wind storage_ (refrigerated warehouses are cooled to low temperature when electricity is cheap and the temperature is allowed to rise when electricity is expensive); _compressed air energy storage_ (use wind power to compress air, then use the compressed air to drive turbines when electricity is expensive). All three of these methods entail losses.

Because carry is limited and costly. the electricity price at any time is set by demand and supply at that time.

To illustrate the effects of nonstorability, Table 13-7 displays 1-day-ahead hourly prices for 1 megawatt-hour of electricity in New York City. The 1-day-ahead forward price is $32.22 at 2 A.M. and $63.51 at 7 P.M. Ideally one would buy 2 A.M. electricity, store it, and sell it at 7 P.M., but there is no way to do so costlessly.

Notice two things. First, the swings in Table 13-7 could not occur with financial assets, which are stored. The 3 A.M. and 3 P.M. forward prices for a stock will be almost identical; if they were not, it would be possible to arbitrage the difference. Second, whereas the forward price for a stock is largely redundant in the sense that it reflects information about the current stock price, interest, and the dividend yield, the forward prices in Table 13-7 provide **price discovery**, revealing otherwise unobtainable information about the future price of the commodity. The prices in Table 13-7 are best interpreted using Equation (13.4).

Just as intraday arbitrage is difficult, there is no costless way to buy winter electricity and sell it in the summer, so there are seasonal variations as well as intraday variations. Peak-load power plants operate only when prices are high, temporarily increasing the supply of electricity. However, expectations about supply, storage, and peak-load power generation should already be reflected in the forward price.

Natural Gas

Natural gas is a market in which seasonality and storage costs are important. The natural gas futures contract, introduced in 1990, has become one of the most heavily

TABLE 13-7 Day-Ahead Price, by Hour, for 1 Megawatt-Hour of Electricity in New York City, March 21, 2011

Time	Price	Time	Price	Time	Price	Time	Price
0000	$36.77	0600	$44.89	1200	$53.84	1800	$56.18
0100	$34.43	0700	$58.05	1300	$51.36	1900	$63.51
0200	$32.22	0800	$52.90	1400	$50.01	2000	$54.99
0300	$32.23	0900	$54.06	1500	$49.55	2100	$47.01
0400	$32.82	1000	$55.06	1600	$49.71	2200	$40.26
0500	$35.84	1100	$55.30	1700	$51.66	2300	$37.29

Data from Bloomberg.

Underlying	Natural gas delivered at Sabine Pipe Lines Co.'s Henry Hub, Louisiana
Where traded	New York Mercantile Exchange
Size	10,000 million British thermal units (MMBtu)
Months	72 consecutive months
Trading ends	Third-to-last business day of month prior to maturity month
Delivery	As uniformly as possible over the delivery month

FIGURE 13-7 Specifications for the NYMEX Henry Hub natural gas contract.

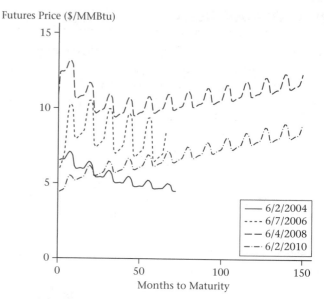

FIGURE 13-8 Forward curves for natural gas for four years. Prices are dollars per MMBtu, from CME Group/NYMEX.

Data from Datastream.

traded futures contracts in the United States. The asset underlying one contract is 10,000 MMBtu, delivered over one month at a specific location (different gas contracts call for delivery at different locations). Figure 13-7 details the specifications for the Henry Hub contract.

Natural gas has several interesting characteristics. First, gas is costly to transport internationally, so prices and forward curves vary regionally. Second, once a given well has begun production, gas is costly to store. Third, demand for gas in the United States is highly seasonal, with peak demand arising from heating in winter months. Thus, there is a relatively steady stream of production with variable demand, which leads to large and predictable price swings. Whereas corn has seasonal production and relatively constant demand, gas has relatively constant supply and seasonal demand.

Figure 13-8 displays strips of gas futures prices for the first Wednesday in June for 4 years between 2004 and 2010. In all curves, seasonality is evident, with high winter prices and low summer prices. The 2004 and 2006 strips show seasonal cycles combined with a downward trend in prices, suggesting that the market considered prices in that year as anomalously high. For the other years, the long-term trend is upward.

Gas storage is costly and demand for gas is highest in the winter. The steady rise of the forward curve (contango) during the fall months suggests that storage occurs just before the heaviest demand. In the June 2006 forward

curve, the October, November, and December 2006 prices were $7.059, $8.329, and $9.599. The interest rate at that time was about 5.5%, or 0.5%/month. Interest costs would thus contribute at most a few cents to contango. Considering the October and November prices, in a carry market, storage cost would have to satisfy Equation (13.8):

$$8.329 = 7.059e^{0.005} + \lambda$$

This calculation implies an estimated expected marginal storage cost of $\lambda = \$1.235$ in November 2006. The technologies for storing gas range from pumping it into underground storage facilities to freezing it and storing it offshore in liquified natural gas tankers. By examining Figure 13-8 you will find different imputed storage costs in each year, but this is to be expected if marginal storage costs vary with the quantity stored.

Because of the expense in transporting gas internationally, the seasonal behavior of the forward curve can vary in different parts of the world. In tropical areas where gas is used for cooking and electricity generation, the forward curve is relatively flat because demand is relatively flat. In the Southern hemisphere, where seasons are reversed from the Northern hemisphere, the forward

Underlying	Specific domestic crudes delivered at Cushing, Oklahoma
Where traded	New York Mercantile Exchange
Size	1000 U.S. barrels (42,000 gallons)
Months	30 consecutive months plus long-dated futures out 7 years
Trading ends	Third-to-last business day preceding the 25th calendar day of month prior to maturity month
Delivery	As uniformly as possible over the delivery month

FIGURE 13-9 Specifications for the NYMEX light sweet crude oil contract.

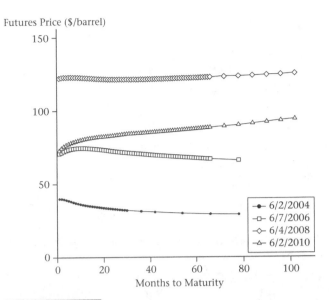

FIGURE 13-10 Multi-year strips of NYMEX crude oil futures prices, $/barrel, for four different dates.

Data from Datastream.

curve will peak in June and July rather than December and January.

Oil

Both oil and natural gas produce energy and are extracted from wells, but the different physical characteristics and uses of oil lead to a very different forward curve than that for gas. Oil is easier to transport than gas, with the result that oil trades in a global market. Oil is also easier to store than gas. Thus, seasonals in the price of crude oil are relatively unimportant. Specifications for the NYMEX light sweet crude oil contract (also known as West Texas Intermediate, or WTI) are shown in Figure 13-9.[7] The NYMEX forward curve on four dates is plotted in Figure 13-10.

On the four dates in the figure, near-term oil prices range from $40 to $125. At each price, the forward curves are relatively flat. In 2004, it appears that the market expected oil prices to decline. Obviously, that did not happen. In 2006 and 2008, the early part of the forward curve is steeply sloped, suggesting that there was a return to storage and a temporary surplus supply. During 2009, for example, there was substantial arbitrage activity with traders storing oil on tankers. This is discussed in Box 13-2.

---

[7] Oil is called "sweet" if it has a relatively low sulfur content, and "sour" if the sulfur content is high.

Although oil is a global market, the delivery point for the WTI oil contract is Cushing, Oklahoma, which is land-locked. Another important oil contract is the Brent crude oil contract, based on oil from the North Sea. Historically WTI and Brent traded within a few dollars of each other, and they are of similar quality. In early 2011, however, the price of Brent was at one point almost $20/barrel greater than the price of WTI. Though there is no one accepted explanation for this discrepancy, the difficulty of transporting oil from Cushing to ports undoubtedly plays a role, and the WTI contract in recent years has lost favor as a global oil benchmark. In particular, in 2009 Saudi Arabia dropped WTI from its export benchmarks. The WTI-Brent price discrepancy illustrates the importance of transportation costs even in an integrated global market.

Oil Distillate Spreads

Some commodities are inputs in the creation of other commodities, which gives rise to **commodity spreads**. Crude oil is refined to make petroleum products, in particular heating oil and gasoline. The refining process entails distillation, which separates crude oil into different components, including gasoline, kerosene, and heating oil. The split of oil into these different components can be complemented

From *The Wall Street Journal:* The huge floating stock-pile of crude oil kept on tankers amid a global supply glut is showing signs of shrinking, as traders struggle to make profits from the once highly lucrative storage play.

The volume being stored at sea has nearly halved from a peak of about 90 million barrels in April last year, according to ship broker ICAP, and [is] expected to fall even further. . . .

The phenomenon of floating storage took off early last year. Oil on the spot market traded at a big discount to forward-dated contracts, in a condition known as contango. Traders took advantage of that by buying crude and putting it into storage on tankers for sale at a higher price at a future date. Profits from the trade more than covered the costs of storage.

At its peak in April last year, there were about 90 million barrels of crude oil in floating storage on huge tankers known as very large crude carriers, or VLCCs, according to ICAP.

But the spread between prompt crude-oil prices and forward prices has narrowed in recent weeks, while freight rates have increased, reducing the incentive to store oil for future delivery.

Contango has narrowed to around 40 cents a barrel, and "to cover your freight and other costs you need at least 90 cents," said Torbjorn Kjus, an oil analyst at DnB NOR Markets.

J.P. Morgan has said prices could even go into backwardation at the end of the second quarter, where spot prices are higher than those in forward contracts. This would be the first time the spread has been in positive territory since July last year.

ICAP said there were currently 21 trading VLCCs offshore with some 43 million barrels of crude. Seven of these are expected to discharge in February and one more in March. So far, it appeared those discharged cargoes wouldn't be replaced by new ones. . . .

Source: Chazan (2010)

---

by a process known as "cracking"; hence, the difference in price between crude oil and equivalent amounts of heating oil and gasoline is called the **crack spread**.[8]

Oil can be processed in different ways, producing different mixes of outputs. The spread terminology identities the number of gallons of oil as input, and the number of gallons of gasoline and heating oil as outputs. Traders will speak of "5-3-2," "3-2-1," and "2-1-1" crack spreads. The 5-3-2 spread, for example, reflects the profit from taking 5 gallons of oil as input, and producing 3 gallons of gasoline and 2 gallons of heating oil. A petroleum refiner producing gasoline and heating oil could use a futures crack spread to lock in both the cost of oil and output prices. This strategy would entail going long oil futures and short the appropriate quantities of gasoline and heating oil futures. Of course there are other inputs to production and it is possible to produce other outputs, such as jet fuel, so the crack spread is not a perfect hedge.

Example 13.3

A refiner in June 2010 planning for July production could have purchased July oil for $72.86/barrel and sold August gasoline and heating oil for $2.0279/gallon and $2.0252/gallon. The 3-2-1 crack spread is the gross margin from buying 3 gallons of oil and selling 2 gallons of gasoline and 1 of heating oil. Using these prices, the spread is

$$2 \times \$2.0279 + \$2.0252 - 3 \times \$72.86/42 = \$0.8767$$

or $0.8767/3 = $0.29221/gallon.

There are crack spread swaps and options. Most commonly these are based on the difference between the price of heating oil and crude oil, and the price of gasoline and heating oil, both in a 1:1 ratio.

---

[8] Spreads are also important in agriculture. Soybeans, for example, can be crushed to produce soybean meal and soybean oil (and a small amount of waste). A trader with a position in soybeans and an opposite position in equivalent quantities of soybean meal and soybean oil has a **crush spread** and is said to be "trading the crush."

HEDGING STRATEGIES

In this section we discuss some issues when using commodity futures and forwards to hedge commodity price exposure. First, since commodities are heterogeneous and often costly to transport and store, it is common to hedge a risk with a commodity contract that is imperfectly correlated with the risk being hedged. This gives rise to *basis risk*: The price of the commodity underlying the futures contract may move differently than the price of the commodity you are hedging. For example, because of transportation cost and time, the price of natural gas in California may differ from that in Louisiana, which is the location underlying the principal natural gas futures contract (see again Figure 13-7). Second, in some cases one commodity may be used to hedge another. As an example of this we discuss the use of crude oil to hedge jet fuel. Finally, weather derivatives provide another example of an instrument that can be used to cross-hedge. We discuss degree-day index contracts as an example of such derivatives.

Basis Risk

Exchange-traded commodity futures contracts call for delivery of the underlying commodity at specific locations and specific dates. The actual commodity to be bought or sold may reside at a different location and the desired delivery date may not match that of the futures contract. Additionally, the *grade* of the deliverable under the futures contract may not match the grade that is being delivered.

This general problem of the futures or forward contract not representing exactly what is being hedged is called *basis risk*. Basis risk is a generic problem with commodities because of storage and transportation costs and quality differences. Basis risk can also arise with financial futures, as for example when a company hedges its own borrowing cost with the Eurodollar contract.

We demonstrated how an individual stock could be hedged with an index futures contract. We saw that if we regressed the individual stock return on the index return, the resulting regression coefficient provided a hedge ratio that minimized the variance of the hedged position.

In the same way, suppose we wish to hedge oil delivered on the East Coast with the NYMEX oil contract, which calls for delivery of oil in Cushing, Oklahoma. The variance-minimizing hedge ratio would be the regression coefficient obtained by regressing the East Coast price on the Cushing price. Problems with this regression are that the relationship may not be stable over time or may be estimated imprecisely.

Another example of basis risk occurs when hedgers decide to hedge distant obligations with near-term futures. For example, an oil producer might have an obligation to deliver 100,000 barrels per month at a fixed price for a year. The natural way to hedge this obligation would be to buy 100,000 barrels per month, locking in the price and supply on a month-by month basis. This is called a **strip hedge**. We engage in a strip hedge when we hedge a stream of obligations by offsetting each individual obligation with a futures contract matching the maturity and quantity of the obligation. For the oil producer obligated to deliver every month at a fixed price, the hedge would entail buying the appropriate quantity each month, in effect taking a long position in the strip.

An alternative to a strip hedge is a **stack hedge**. With a stack hedge, we enter into futures contracts with a *single* maturity, with the number of contracts selected so that changes in the *present value* of the future obligations are offset by changes in the value of this "stack" of futures contracts. In the context of the oil producer with a monthly delivery obligation, a stack hedge would entail going long 1.2 million barrels using the near-term contract. (Actually, we would want to tail the position and go long fewer than 1.2 million barrels, but we will ignore this.) When the near-term contract matures, we reestablish the stack hedge by going long contracts in the new near month. This process of stacking futures contracts in the near-term contract and rolling over into the new near-term contract is called a **stack and roll**. If the new near-term futures price is below the expiring near-term price (i.e., there is backwardation), rolling is profitable.

There are at least two reasons for using a stack hedge. First, there is often more trading volume and liquidity in near-term contracts. With many commodities, bid-ask spreads widen with maturity. Thus, a stack hedge may have lower transaction costs than a strip hedge. Second, the manager may wish to speculate on the shape of the forward curve. You might decide that the forward curve looks unusually steep in the early months. If you undertake a stack hedge and the forward curve then flattens, you will have locked in all your oil at the relatively cheap near-term price, and implicitly made gains from not having locked in the relatively high strip prices. However, if the curve becomes steeper, it is possible to lose.

Box 13-3 recounts the story of Metallgesellschaft A. G. (MG), in which MG's large losses on a hedged position might have been caused, at least in part, by the use of a stack hedge.

Hedging Jet Fuel with Crude Oil

Jet fuel futures do not exist in the United States, but firms sometimes hedge jet fuel with crude oil futures along with futures for related petroleum products. In order to perform this hedge, it is necessary to understand the relationship between crude oil and jet fuel prices. If we own a quantity of jet fuel and hedge by holding H crude oil futures contracts, our mark-to-market profit depends on the change in the jet fuel price and the change in the futures price:

$$(P_t - P_{t-1}) + H(F_t - F_{t-1}) \qquad \textbf{(13.12)}$$

where P_t is the price of jet fuel and F_t the crude oil futures price. We can estimate H by regressing the change in the jet fuel price (denominated in dollars per gallon) on the change in the crude oil futures price (denominated in dollars per gallon, which is the barrel price divided by 42). We use the nearest to maturity oil futures contract. Running this regression using daily data for January 2006–March 2011 gives[9]

$$P_t - P_{t-1} = \underset{(0.0009)}{0.0004} + \underset{(0.0192)}{0.8379}\left(F_t^{\text{oil}} - F_{t-1}^{\text{oil}}\right) \quad R^2 = 0.596 \quad \textbf{(13.13)}$$

Standard errors are below coefficients. The coefficient on the futures price change tells us that, on average, when the crude futures price increases by \$0.01, a gallon of jet fuel increases by \$0.008379.[10] The R^2 of 0.596 implies a correlation coefficient of about 0.77, so there is considerable variation in the price of jet fuel not accounted for by the price of crude. Because jet fuel is but one product produced from crude oil, it makes sense to see if adding other oil products to the regression improves the accuracy of the hedge. Adding the near term futures prices for heating oil and gasoline, we obtain

$$P_t - P_{t-1} = \underset{(0.0001)}{0.0006} + \underset{(0.0278)}{0.0897}\left(F_t^{\text{oil}} - F_{t-1}^{\text{oil}}\right) \qquad \textbf{(13.14)}$$
$$+ \underset{(0.0277)}{0.8476}\left(F_t^{\text{heating oil}} - F_{t-1}^{\text{heating oil}}\right)$$
$$+ \underset{(0.0222)}{0.0069}\left(F_t^{\text{gasoline}} - F_{t-1}^{\text{gasoline}}\right) \quad R^2 = 0.786$$

The explanatory power of the regression is improved, with an implied correlation of 0.886 between the actual and predicted jet fuel price. The price of heating oil is more closely related to the price of jet fuel than is the price of crude oil.

Weather Derivatives

Many businesses have revenue that is sensitive to weather: Ski resorts are harmed by warm winters, soft drink manufacturers are harmed by a cold spring, summer, or fall, and makers of lawn sprinklers are harmed by wet summers. In all of these cases, firms could hedge their risk using **weather derivatives**—contracts that make payments based upon realized characteristics of weather—to cross-hedge their specific risk.

Weather can affect both the price and consumption of energy-related products. If a winter is colder than average, homeowners and businesses will consume extra electricity, heating oil, and natural gas, and the prices of these products will tend to be high as well. Conversely, during a warm winter, energy prices and quantities will be low. While it is possible to use futures markets to hedge prices of commodities such as natural gas, hedging the quantity is more difficult. Weather derivatives can provide an additional contract with a payoff correlated with the quantity of energy used.

---

[9] This regression omits 4 days: September 11, 12, 15, and 16, 2008. The reported price of jet fuel on those days—a stressful period during the financial crisis—increased by over \$1/gallon and then on September 17 returned to its previous price.

[10] Recall that we estimated a hedge ratio for stocks using a regression based on percentage changes. In that case, we had an economic reason (an asset pricing model) to believe that there was a stable relationship based upon rates of return. In this case, crude is used to produce jet fuel, so it makes sense that dollar changes in the price of crude would be related to dollar changes in the price of jet fuel.

Metallgesellschaft A. G.

In 1992, a U.S. subsidiary of the Gennan industrial firm Metallgesellschaft A. G. (MG) had offered customers fixed prices on over 150 million barrels of petroleum products, including gasoline, heating oil, and diesel fuel, over periods as long as 10 years. To hedge the resulting short exposure, MG entered into futures and swaps.

Much of MG's hedging was done using short-dated NYMEX crude oil and heating oil futures. Thus, MG was using stack hedging, rolling over the hedge each month.

During much of 1993, the near-term oil market was in contango (the forward curve was upward sloping). As a result of the market remaining in contango, MG systematically lost money when rolling its hedges and had to meet substantial margin calls. In December 1993, the supervisory board of MG decided to liquidate both its supply contracts and the futures positions used to hedge those contracts. In the end, MG sustained losses estimated at between $200 million and $1.3 billion.

The MG case was extremely complicated and has been the subject of pointed exchanges among academics—see in particular Culp and Miller (1995), Edwards and Canter (1995), and Mello and Parsons (1995). While the case is complicated, several issues stand out. First, was the stack and roll a reasonable strategy for MG to have undertaken? Second, should the position have been liquidated when and in the manner it was? (As it turned out, oil prices increased—which would have worked in MG's favor—following the liquidation.) Third, did MG encounter liquidity problems from having to finance losses on its hedging strategy? While the MG case has receded into history, hedgers still confront the issues raised by this case.

An example of a weather contract is the degree-day index futures contract traded at the CME Group. The contract is based on the premise that heating is used when temperatures are below 65 degrees and cooling is used when temperatures are above 65 degrees. Thus, a **heating degree-day** is the difference between 65 degrees Fahrenheit and the average daily temperature, if positive, or zero otherwise. A **cooling degree-day** is the difference between the average daily temperature and 65 degrees Fahrenheit, if positive, and zero otherwise. The monthly degree-day index is the sum of the daily degree-days over the month. The futures contract then settles based on the cumulative heating or cooling degree-days (the two are separate contracts) over the course of a month. The size of the contract is $100 times the degree-day index. Degree-day index contracts are available for major cities in the United States, Europe, and Japan. There are also puts and calls on these futures.

With city-specific degree-day index contracts, it is possible to create and hedge payoffs based on average temperatures, or using options, based on ranges of average temperatures. If Minneapolis is unusually cold but the rest of the country is normal, the heating degree-day contract for Minneapolis will make a large payment that will compensate the holder for the increased consumption of energy.

SYNTHETIC COMMODITIES

Just as it is possible to use stock index futures to create a synthetic stock index, it is also possible to use commodity futures to create synthetic commodities. We can create a synthetic commodity by combining a commodity forward contract and a zero-coupon bond. Enter into a long commodity forward contract at the price $F_{0,T}$ and buy a zero-coupon bond that pays $F_{0,T}$ at time T. Since the forward contract is costless, the cost of this investment strategy at time 0 is just the cost of the bond, which equals the prepaid forward price: $e^{-rT}F_{0,T}$. At time T, the strategy pays

$$\underbrace{S_T - F_{0,T}}_{\text{Forward contract payoff}} + \underbrace{F_{0,T}}_{\text{Bond payoff}} = S_T$$

where S_T is the time T price of the commodity. This investment strategy creates a *synthetic commodity*, which has the same value as a unit of the commodity at time T.

During the early 2000s, indexed commodity investing became popular. Commodity funds use futures contracts and Treasury bills or other bonds to create synthetic commodities and replicate published commodity indexes. Two important indexes are the S&P GSCI index (originally created by Goldman Sachs) and the Dow Jones UBS index (originally created by AIG). Masters (2008) estimates that money invested in commodity funds grew 20-fold between 2003 and 2008, from $13 billion to $260 billion.[11] During this same period, commodity prices rose significantly. Figure 13-11 shows the performance of two commodity indexes plotted with the S&P 500. The two indexes diverge sharply in 2009 because they weight commodities differently. The S&P GSCI index, for example, is world-production weighted and more heavily weights the petroleum sector. The DJ UBS index is designed to be more evenly weighted.[12]

You might wonder whether a commodity fund should use futures contracts to create synthetic commodities, or whether the fund should hold the physical commodity (where feasible). An important implication of the earlier discussion is that it is generally preferable to invest in synthetic commodities rather than physical commodities. To see this, we can compare the returns to owning the physical commodity and owning a synthetic commodity. As before, let $\lambda(0, T)$ denote the future value of storage costs.

To invest in the physical commodity for 1 year, we can buy the commodity and prepay storage costs. This costs $S_0 + \lambda(0, 1)/(1 + R)$ initially and one period later pays $S_1 + \lambda(0, 1) - \lambda(0, 1) = S_1$.

An investment in the synthetic commodity costs the present value of the forward price, $F_{0,1}/(1 + R)$, and pays S_1. The synthetic investment will be preferable if

$$F_{0,1} / (1 + R) < S_0 + \lambda(0, 1) / (1 + R)$$

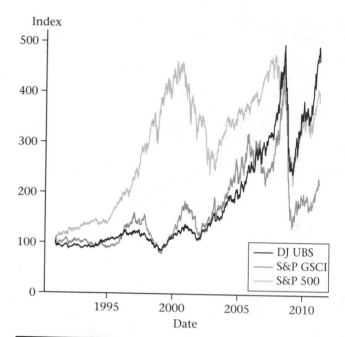

FIGURE 13-11 Value of S&P GSCI and DJ UBS indexes from 1991 to 2011, plotted against the S&P 500 index.

Source: Datastream.

or $F_{0,1} < S_0(1 + R) + \lambda(0, 1)$. Suppose, however, that $F_{0,1} > S_0(1 + R) + \lambda(0, 1)$. This is an arbitrage opportunity exploitable by buying the commodity, storing it, paying storage costs, and selling it forward. Thus, if there is no arbitrage, we expect that $F_{0,1} \leq S_0(1 + R) + \lambda(0, 1)$ and the synthetic commodity will be the less expensive way to obtain the commodity return. Moreover, there will be equality only in a carry market. So investors will be indifferent between physical and synthetic commodities in a carry market, and will prefer synthetic commodities at all other times.

SUMMARY

At a general level, commodity forward prices can be described by the same formula as financial forward prices:

$$F_{0, T} = S_0 e^{(r - \delta)T} \tag{13.15}$$

For financial assets, δ is the dividend yield. For commodities, δ is the commodity *lease rate*—the return that makes an investor willing to buy and then lend a commodity. Thus, for the commodity owner who lends the commodity, it is like a dividend. From the commodity

---

[11] Index investors have to periodically exchange an expiring futures contract for a new long position. This transaction is referred to as "rolling" the position. For large index investors, the dollar amount of this futures roll can be substantial. Mou (2010) provides evidence that price effects from the roll are predictable and that front-running it can be profitable.

[12] Historical commodity and futures data, necessary to estimate expected commodity returns, and thus to evaluate commodity investing as a strategy, are relatively hard to obtain. Bodie and Rosansky (1980) examine quarterly futures returns from 1950 to 1976, while Gorton and Rouwenhorst (2004) examine monthly futures returns from 1959 to 2004. Both studies construct portfolios of synthetic commodities—T-bills plus commodity futures— and find that these portfolios earn the same average return as stocks, are on average negatively correlated with stocks, and are positively correlated with inflation. These findings imply that a portfolio of stocks and synthetic commodities would have the same expected return and less risk than a diversified stock portfolio alone.

borrower's perspective, it is the cost of borrowing the commodity.

Different issues arise with commodity forwards than with financial forwards. For both commodities and financial assets, the forward price is the expected spot price discounted at the risk premium on the asset. (As with financial forwards, commodity forward prices are biased predictors of the future spot price when the commodity return contains a risk premium.) Storage of a commodity is an economic decision in which the investor compares the benefit from selling today with the benefit of selling in the future. When commodities are stored, the forward price must be sufficiently high so that a cash-and-carry compensates the investor for both financing and storage costs (this is called a carry market). When commodities are not stored, the forward price reflects the expected future spot price. Forward prices that are too high can be arbitraged with a cash-and-carry, while forward prices that are lower may not be arbitrageable, as the terms of a short sale should be based on the forward price. Some holders of a commodity receive a benefit from physical ownership. This benefit is called the commodity's *convenience yield*, and convenience can lower the forward price,

Forward curves provide information about individual commodities, each of which differs in the details. Forward curves for different commodities reflect different properties of storability, storage costs, production, demand, and seasonality. Electricity, gold, corn, natural gas, and oil all have distinct forward curves, reflecting the different characteristics of their physical markets.

These idiosyncracies will be reflected in the individual commodity lease rates.

It is possible to create synthetic commodities by combining commodity futures and default-free bonds. In general it is financially preferable to invest in a synthetic rather than a physical commodity. Synthetic commodity indexes have been popular investments in recent years.

Further Reading

Geman (2005) and Siegel and Siegel (1990) provide a detailed discussion of many commodity futures. There are numerous papers on commodities. Bodie and Rosansky (1980) and Gorton and Rouwenhorst (2004) examine the risk and return of commodities as an investment. Brennan (1991), Pindyck (1993b), and Pindyck (1994) examine the behavior of commodity prices. Schwartz (1997) compares the performance of different models of commodity price behavior. Jarrow and Oldfield (1981) discuss the effect of storage costs on pricing, and Routledge et. al. (2000) present a theoretical model of commodity forward curves. The websites of commodity exchanges are also useful resources, with information about particular contracts and sometimes about trading and hedging strategies.

Finally, Metallgesellschaft engendered a spirited debate. Papers written about that episode include Culp and Miller (1995), Edwards and Canter (1995), and Mello and Parsons (1995).

Fundamentals of Commodity Spot and Futures Markets
Instruments, Exchanges and Strategies

Learning Objectives

Candidates, after completing this reading, should be able to:

- Define the major risks involved with commodity spot transactions.
- Differentiate between ordinary and extraordinary transportation risks.
- Explain the major differences between spot, forward, and futures transactions, markets, and contracts.
- Describe the basic characteristics and differences between hedgers, speculators, and arbitrageurs.
- Describe an "arbitrage portfolio" and explain the conditions for a market to be arbitrage-free.
- Describe the structure of the futures market.

- Define basis risk and the variance of the basis.
- Assess the effectiveness of hedging a spot position with a specific futures contract, and compute and compare the effectiveness of different potential alternatives in hedging.
- Define and differentiate between an Exchange for Physical agreement and an Alternative Delivery Procedure.
- Explain how volume and open interest relate to liquidity and market depth.

Excerpt is Chapter 1 of Commodities and Commodity Derivatives: Modeling and Pricing for Agriculturals, Metals and Energy, *by Hélyette Geman.*

THE IMPORTANCE OF COMMODITY SPOT TRADING

Commodity price risk is an important element of the world physionomy at this date, as it has an impact on the economy of both developed and developing countries: in a rough approximation, one can state that the latter include most commodity producing countries, the former being originators, marketers and manufacturers. All parties are still involved in activities of spot trading with physical delivery while the formidable development of liquid derivative markets—forward, Futures contracts and options—has paved the way for risk management and optimal design of supply and demand contracts.

Every commodity is traded on a spot market. In the old days, buyers and sellers used to meet on the marketplace where transactions led to immediate delivery. In the 18th and 19th centuries, potato growers in the state of Maine started selling their crops at the time of planting in order to finance the production process. In a parallel manner, numerous forward transactions were taking place in Chicago for cereals and agricultural products and in London for metals. A need for standardization in terms of quantity, quality, delivery date emerged and led to the establishment of the New York Cotton Exchange (NYCE) in 1842 and the Chicago Board Of Trade (CBOT) in 1848. The clearing house, unique counterparty for buyers and sellers of Futures contracts was the effective signal that the Exchange was operating. As of today, some of these clearing houses are owned by independent shareholders, others are primarily owned by market participants as in the case of the London Metal Exchange (LME) and the International Petroleum Exchange (IPE). Different qualities of the same commodity may be traded on different exchanges. The most famous examples include: coffee which in its "arabica" variety is traded on the New York Coffee, Sugar and Cocoa Exchange (CSCE), while the "robusta" type is traded on the London International Financial Futures Exchange (LIFFE); and oil which is traded on the New York Mercantile Exchange (NYMEX) as Western Texas Intermediate (WTI) and on the IPE in its Brent variety.

Let us observe that the fact that any transaction on commodities may be physical (delivery of the commodity) or financial (a cash flow from one party to the other at maturity and no exchange of the underlying good) is in sharp contrast to bonds and stock markets where all trades are financial. However, physical and financial commodity markets are, as expected, strongly related. Price and volatility observed in "paper" transactions are correlated to the analogous quantities in the physical market, both because of the physical delivery that may take place at maturity of a Futures contract and the existence of spot forward relationships that will be discussed throughout the book.

Lastly, let us note that the last two decades have experienced dramatic changes in world commodity markets. Political upheavals in some countries, economic mutation, new environmental regulation, a huge rise in the consumption of commodities in countries such as China and other structural changes have contributed to increase the volatility of supply and prices. This has made hedging activities (through forwards, Futures and options) indispensable for many sectors of the economy, the airline industry in particular being an important example.

As mentioned before, we call spot trading any transaction where delivery either takes place immediately (which is rarely the case in practice) or if there is a minimum lag, due to technical constraints, between the trade and delivery. Beyond that minimal lag, the trade becomes a forward agreement between the two parties and is properly documented by a written contract which specifies, among other things, who among the buyer and seller is responsible for shipping, unloading the goods and other transportation-related issues.

Consider a standard situation where the seller is a producer (e.g., of copper) and the buyer a manufacturer: in general, they never meet and, even if they did, would rarely agree on prices, timing and so forth. Hence the existence of intermediaries who play the role of go-between, are prepared to take delivery of goods that may not resell immediately and organize the storage and shipping.

We can represent the different phases of the physical execution of a trade as:

Production entity

Customs

Producing country

Embarkment port

Disembarkment port

<----- Air freight ----->
         Shipping

Harbor storage

Storage in production location

Manufacturing plant

Customs

Country of consumption

Harbor storage

Storage in manufacturing location

The document that represents the ownership of the good is called a *bill of lading*. It is issued either by the captain of the transportation ship or by the transporter in charge. That transportation contract may eventually be traded. It can bear the label "shipped" or "to be shipped"; the latter terminology indicates that the merchandise has been embarked, leading to the qualification *clean on board*.

Responsibility for Commercial Execution

It may lie in the hands of the seller, or the buyer, or the intermediary (since, in practice, many intermediaries will play a role, in particular because of the lags in the timing of different operations).

The responsibility will take different forms:

- For the exporter, sale Free On Board (FOB).
- For the commercial intermediary, purchase FOB out of the dock or in warehouse.
- For the importer, purchase on the dock or in warehouse.

Note that the commercial responsibility may be fragmented in the course of contract execution. For instance, a manufacturer who buys metals under a FOB specification is responsible for organizing the shipping but the armator is in charge of managing the shipping and holds the corresponding risk.

Major Risks in Commodity Spot Transaction

Four major types of risk may be identified in commodity spot markets:

- *Price risk*, which will be discussed throughout the book and for which the first examples of hedging strategies are presented in the next section.
- *Transportation risk*, which is described below.
- *Delivery risk*, which concerns the quality of the commodity that is delivered and for which there is no financial hedge that may be put in place. The only coverage is provided by a very customized contract or by a solid long-term relationship with the originator.
- *Credit risk*, which is present all along until the final completion of the trade.

Risk Attached to the Transportation of Commodities

1. The first category of risks concerns the deterioration, partial or total, of goods during transportation. Two types of risks are usually recognized in this category:
   - "ordinary" risks;
   - "extraordinary" risks such as wars, riots and strikes.

   The expeditor of the goods or the FOB buyer directly holds the transportation risk, unless they purchase an insurance contract to be covered. Different companies specialized in freight insurance (such as the famous Lloyds of London) propose various types of contracts. We need to keep in mind that transportation risk is an important one as it includes the entire community—the tanker that sank in Alaska being a sad example. If no specific insurance coverage has been purchased, the company that bears the liability must put in place some kind of *self-insurance* process as do some major oil companies today.

2. Cost of transportation risk: All Futures exchanges around the world quote FOB prices. Consequently, if a trade (e.g., on sugar) is settled for delivery 12 months later with the CIF price as a reference, the seller needs to hedge his position not only against a decline in sugar prices by, say, selling Futures on the New York Coffee, Cocoa and Sugar Exchange, but also against

changes in the shipping cost. The latter risk will be hedged by entering into a Forward Freight Agreement (described later in this chapter). Consequently, the two components of the CIF price will get hedged in totally different exchanges.

FORWARD AND FUTURES CONTRACTS

A forward contract may be generically described as an agreement struck at date 0 between two parties to exchange at some fixed future date a given quantity of a commodity for an amount of dollars defined at date 0. A Futures contract has the same general features as a forward contract but is transacted through a Futures exchange. The clearing house standing behind that exchange essentially takes away any credit risk from the positions of the two participants engaged in the transaction. This default risk is almost reduced to zero through margin deposits or initial margins that need to be made before entering into any contract, as well as the daily margin calls required to keep a contract alive if its market value has declined from the previous day.

Futures contracts serve many purposes. Their first role has been to facilitate the trading of various commodities as financial instruments. But they have from the start been providing a hedging vehicle against *price risk*: a farmer selling his crops in January through a Futures contract maturing at time T of the harvest (say, September) for a price $F^T(0)$ defined on 1 January has secured at the beginning of the year this amount of revenue. Hence, he may allocate the proceeds to be received to the acquisition of new machinery or storage facilities and, more generally, design his investment plans for the year independently of any news of corn oversupply possibly occurring over the 9-month period.

It is noticeable in many markets, ranging from agricultural commodities to electricity, that Futures contracts are used as a substitute for the spot market by hedge funds, Commodity Trading Advisors (CTAs) or any class of investors wishing to take a position in commodities, both because it takes away the physical constraints of spot trading and provides the flexibility of short and long positions, hence the choice of positive or negative exposure to a rise in prices.

What follows describes in detail the mechanisms of forward and Futures contracts with their various characteristics as well as the way exchanges operate. The different classes of participants, the mechanism of *price discovery* and the crucial relationships, if they exist, between spot prices and Futures prices under some form of equilibrium assumptions are described in detail.

Forward Contracts

A forward contract is an agreement signed between two parties A and B at time 0, according to which party A has the obligation of delivering at a fixed future date T an underlying asset and party B the obligation of paying at that date an amount fixed at date 0, denoted $F^T(0)$ and called the forward price for date T for the asset. Note that this price is not a price in the sense of the price of a stock, but rather a reference value in the contractual transaction. If the underlying asset is traded in a liquid market, the no-arbitrage condition between spot and forward markets at maturity implies that:

$$S(T) = F^T(T)$$

If the value at date T of the Futures contract maturing at that date was different from the spot price, an arbitrage opportunity would be realized by buying in one market and selling immediately in the other.

Keeping in mind that the buyer of the forward contract may immediately sell at maturity in the spot market at the price S_T the commodity which was delivered to him against the payment of $F^T(0)$ dollars, the respective Profit and Loss (P&L) of party A (called long forward) and party B (called short forward) are depicted by the following graphs:

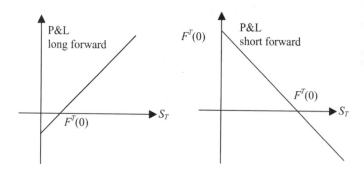

Obviously, the contract is a zero-sum game between the buyer and the seller. Note also that, by definition, both P&Ls are expressed in dollars at date T.

For practical purposes, party A represents an economic agent who wants to hedge against a possible rise in the price of the underlying asset between dates 0 and T and locks in at date 0 a purchase price equal to $F^T(0)$. Party B, conversely, fears a collapse of this price or expects to profit from a rise. The price $F^T(0)$ represents their estimation at date 0 of how much the underlying asset S will be worth at date T together with the risk premium they are willing to pay (or receive).

Should parties A and B enter into this T maturity contract at a future date t in the interval $(0; T)$, the price $F^T(t)$ on which they will agree is likely to be different from $F^T(0)$ and translates the changes between dates 0 and t in the expectations perceived by the market of the commodity future spot price $S(T)$.

Futures Contracts

They are analogous to forward contracts in terms of their definition but present some key differences from them:

- They are "standardized" in terms of their characteristics (maturity, quantity of the underlying commodity, quality or variety).

- They are traded on an exchange, such as NYMEX or the IPE; hence, they carry no counterparty risk since both the buyer and the seller of the Futures deal with the clearing house of the exchange which is in principle fully trustworthy.

- They require the payment of margin deposits in order to be able to start placing orders on the exchange.

- They are marked-to-market daily and the participants have to adjust their positions: for instance, if a participant has a long position in a Futures contract acquired at the price $F^T(0)$ and if the price $F^T(\text{day 1})$ is lower, then this participant has experienced a loss between days 0 and 1 equal to $F^T(\text{day 1}) - F^T(0)$. In order to keep his position, he has to adjust it by adding at the end of day 1 a cash amount equal to his loss.

Forward and Futures prices on the same underlying asset with the same time to expiry are different because of taxes, transaction costs and other important elements, such as the impact of credit risk on the one hand and stochastic interest rates on the other hand. In practice, they remain very close to each other since the fluctuations of the underlying commodity represent the most important explanatory factor. Except when stated otherwise, we will view the two prices as the same in a first-order approximation.

We can recap the similarities and differences between the fundamental types of transactions prevailing in commodity markets as depicted in the diagram below.

THE ACTORS IN FUTURES MARKETS

Hedgers

Futures markets were originally set up to meet the needs of hedgers, namely farmers who wanted to lock in advance a fixed price for their harvests. Commodity

Spot Trading	Forward Contracts	Futures Contracts
• *commercial contract* • flexible covenants	• *bilateral agreement* • flexible covenants	• *standardized instrument* • necessity of a physical delivery or termination of the position before maturity
• juridical commitments of the buyer and seller until execution of the contract	• replace spot transactions on many occasions (e.g., in the case of a non-storable commodity such as electricity)	• buyer and seller only refer to the clearing house
⟳	⟳	⟳
• long transaction	• form of contracting totally appropriate for commodities • credit risk fully present	• central clearing mechanism generating "market prices" • price transparency
• illiquid and discontinuous market • allows the transfer of goods in conditions suiting the demand	• flexibility regarding the optimal transfer of goods	• liquidity
		• low transaction costs

Futures are still widely used by producers and users of commodities for hedging purposes. Suppose that the date of analysis is January and company XYZ knows that it will have to buy on 25 September (date T) of the same year one million tons of fuel. In order to hedge against the possible increase in fuel price between January and the end of September, airline company XYZ will buy (equivalently, *enter a long position in*) Futures contracts written on fuel, maturity September and in an amount corresponding to the necessary quantity of fuel. By doing so, the airline company has locked in at the beginning of the year the price $F^T(0)$ it will pay in September and has done so with no cash flow payment at the beginning of the year.

Another possible hedge (as we will see later) would be to buy options—again in the appropriate quantity—written on the fuel as the underlying, with maturity T and strike price $k = F^T(0)$ for example.[1] In this case, the resulting cost of fuel in September for company XYZ will be either $F^T(0)$ or, strictly, less if the market spot price is very low. This alternative is strictly superior for the hedger at maturity, but at inception of the option contract in January company XYZ will have to pay the premium of the options involved in the hedge.

Returning to Futures contracts, *basic risk* refers to the risk remaining after the hedge has been put in place and essentially represents the difference between the Futures price—should the Futures position be closed prematurely—and the spot price. It also includes other components such as:

- The price of cleaning the local grade of the commodity into a grade deliverable in a Futures contract (or the premium for a superior grade).
- The price of transportation to or from the delivery point in the Futures contract.
- The physical cost of storage, including insurance, between the time of the harvest and the delivery date of the Futures contract.

Speculators

While hedgers want to avoid exposure to adverse movements of the price of a commodity which is part of their manufacturing process in the economy, speculators wish to get exposure to commodity price moves (i.e., take risks in order to make profits). Using the same example as before, a bank ABC which has no "natural" exposure to the price of fuel may decide to take a position either in a Futures contract on fuel or in an option written on fuel and, by doing so, will create for itself exposure to the fuel price; obviously, the nature of the position—long or short in either instrument—will be determined by the "view" that bank ABC has on the subsequent moves of the fuel price. It is in fact "betting" that this price will go up or will go down and counting on the corresponding profits the bank will generate. Unsurprisingly, commodities are becoming increasingly attractive to investors and hedge fund managers who view them as an *alternative asset class* allowing one to reduce the overall risk of a financial portfolio and enhance the return as well. Futures are the obvious instrument—because of their liquidity, because of the low transaction costs on the exchange, because of the absence of credit risk—to take positions reflecting an anticipation of a price rise by purchasing Futures or a decline by selling Futures. Most of the liquidity is generated by the combined activity of speculators and hedgers.

Arbitragers

Arbitragers represent a third important—but smaller in size—group of participants in futures and options markets. An arbitrage is a *riskless* profit realized by simultaneously entering into several transactions in two or more markets. Arbitrage opportunities are very desirable but not easy to uncover and they do not last for long. If a given instrument is underpriced, buying activity will cause the price to rise up to a value which is viewed by the market as the "fair" price and at which there will be no more excess demand.

In this book, as in the fundamental models of option pricing, the values of Futures and options contracts will be based on the assumption of no-arbitrage opportunities. Given the importance of this concept, we are going to propose several definitions of what is called in daily language "no free lunch."

Definition 1 A portfolio P is called an "arbitrage portfolio" if it satisfies simultaneously the following conditions:

$$\begin{cases} V_p(0) = 0 \\ V_p(H) \geq 0 \quad \text{in all states of the world at date } H \\ V_p(H) > 0 \quad \text{in some states of the world} \end{cases}$$

where H is a date later than date 0.

---

[1] For practical purposes, this will be the strike most often chosen when hedging with an option since everyone has the forward position in mind as the alternative hedge.

Definition 2 A market is said to be arbitrage-free if there exists no arbitrage opportunity; in other words, for any portfolio P:

$$\begin{cases} V_p(0) = 0 \\ \text{and} \qquad \Rightarrow V_p(H) = 0 \quad \text{in all states of the world} \\ V_p(H) \geq 0 \quad \text{in all states of the world} \\ \qquad \text{at date } H > 0 \end{cases}$$

In other words, if a portfolio *requires a null investment* and is *riskless* (there is no possible loss at the horizon H), then its terminal value at date H has to be zero. These are the various expressions of the no free lunch property: if you start with no money and *take no risk*, your final wealth will be zero. In the above statements, the assumption of "riskless" is crucial: if you have no money, you can always borrow from your banker and invest the proceeds in a hedge fund. Your final wealth may be quite large or very negative once you have repaid your loan, but rarely equal to zero.

Comments

For practical purposes, traders searching for arbitrage opportunities are realistically looking, in fact, for "quasi-riskless" strategies generating profits. Such a strategy should be as simple as possible and, hence, involve only spot and forward positions which have *linear payoffs and P&Ls* in the underlying price, making the nullification of risk possible by the resolution of a *single* equation in the price S of the underlying commodity. When we move to positions involving options, we will see that the convexity (or concavity) of the P&L (i.e., the gamma of the option), together with the sensitivity to volatility (i.e., the vega), make this "quasi-riskless" feature much more problematic. Hence, it is indeed in Futures markets that the fundamental concept of arbitrage finds its origin, since *fungibility* between the underlying commodity and the derivative is highest. This property will be lost, however, in the case of electricity because of the specificities of this commodity and this loss is certainly a significant part of the complexity of electricity markets. It allows us at the same time to measure the value of the spot–forward relationship when it exists, even if it holds in a temporal window because of some necessary assumptions on the convenience yield.

THE STRUCTURE OF FUTURES MARKETS

While some trading of Futures contracts may be traced back centuries ago in Europe and Japan, the modern form of Futures markets appeared in the 19th century in the American midwest. In fact, over the second half of the 19th century, more than 1,600 exchanges were established across the United States, often in the vicinity of harbors or railroad crossings. Most of them are gone today and there are only six exchanges in the United States where more that 600 million Futures contracts are traded every year (mostly softs in Chicago, energy in New York). The CBOT, established in 1848, was from the start an active exchange for agricultural commodities, especially corn and wheat. It set its General Rules in 1865. Shortly after, the New York Cotton Exchange organized cotton Futures trading. Futures trading in many other agricultural commodities followed.

The Grain Futures Act in 1922 defined the regulation of Futures exchanges; the Commodity Futures Trading Act of 1974 established the Commodity Futures Trading Commission (CFTC) as the new independent regulatory commission in charge of Futures markets. In the 1970s Futures contracts on stocks, equity indexes, bonds, foreign currencies as well as Futures on options were introduced. Active financial Futures markets have been introduced in different countries worldwide, such as Japan, the UK, France, Hong Kong and so on. Lower transaction costs, increased trading volume, expanded trading hours, electronic trading and international intermarket links contribute to make the Futures markets of today an efficient globalized trading network.

The classical structure of a Futures market is represented in the diagram below:

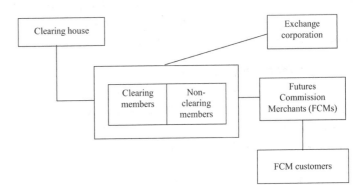

Most Futures exchanges are incorporated as membership associations and operated for the benefit of their members who are generally engaged in their own businesses related to Futures trading. The first purpose of an exchange is to provide an organized marketplace, with uniform rules and standardized contracts. Like any corporation, a Futures exchange has shareholders, a board of directors and executive officers. An exchange may operate markets for spot commodities, options and other financial securities in addition to Futures contracts and provide other services to the public (in particular, *price discovery*). An exchange funds its activities by membership dues and by transaction fees paid on the contracts traded on the exchange.

Exchange Members Although membership is limited to individuals, these individual members often act on behalf of firms, such as brokerage houses, investment banks, or commodity dealers and producers. The total number of members of an exchange is limited; memberships are available for sale on the floor of an exchange. The value of membership lies mainly in the possibility it grants for trading contracts directly on the floor of the exchange. Those members, nominees of members and other individuals who actually use floor-trading privileges are traders. Although floor brokers sometimes trade on their own accounts, their basic role is to allow the public at large to buy or sell contracts. Collectively, they meet a critical need for *liquidity*, namely the ability of the market to act as a reliable and efficient mechanism for quickly taking or offsetting contract positions.

Major Futures Exchanges

Chicago Board of Trade

CBOT used to be exclusively dedicated to agricultural commodities. Today, it trades Futures and options on corn, soybean, soy meal, wheat, rice as well as precious metals (gold and silver). Corn, soybean and wheat are, in this order, the most traded underlyings.

Chicago Mercantile Exchange

CME is the biggest Futures exchange in the US and the second in the world. It trades pork bellies, beef, dairy products and lumber. Founded in 1898 as a non-profit entity, it rapidly became a world platform for trading Futures.

New York Mercantile Exchange

NYMEX was founded in 1872 under the name "Butter and Cheese Exchange of New York." It merged in 1994 with the Commodity Exchange (COMEX), itself resulting from a merger in 1933 of four smaller commodity exchanges. Today, NYMEX is the biggest exchange for commodity Futures; in particular, crude oil (WTI), gas, copper, aluminum and precious metals.

Regarding energy commodities, NYMEX trades Futures and options on crude oil, natural gas, domestic fuel, unleaded gasoline and propane. Oil Futures contracts were introduced in 1983 and are the most active contracts in the world (see Tables 14-1 and 14-2).

Futures and options on gold, silver, copper and aluminium are traded on COMEX. The gold Futures contract, launched in 1974, is a world reference today.

New York Board of Trade

NYBOT regroups the two oldest commodity exchanges in New York: the Coffee, Sugar and Cocoa Exchange (CSCE) and the New York Cotton Exchange (NYCE). The first contracts on coffee, sugar and coca were respectively introduced in 1882, 1914 and 1925 on the CSCE; those on cotton and orange juice in 1870 and 1966 on the NYCE. NYBOT also controls the New York Futures Exchange (NYFE).

International Petroleum Exchange

IPE was founded in 1980 by a consortium of energy companies. The first contract, written on gas oil, was launched one year later. In June 1988, the successful Brent contract started trading and another on natural gas was quoted as of 1997.

London International Financial Futures Exchange

LIFFE was established in 1982 and started trading agricultural commodity Futures in 1996, after it merged with the London Commodity Exchange (LCE). Futures and options on cocoa, barley, robusta coffee, sugar and potatoes are traded on LIFFE.

London Metal Exchange

LME came to existence in 1877 to serve the needs created by the industrial revolution in the United Kingdom. It specializes in non-ferrous metals: aluminum (pure or alloy), copper, nickel, tin, lead and silver. LME is where metals are

TABLE 14-1 The Currently Most Active Commodity Futures Exchanges in the US and Worldwide

Traded Commodities	Exchange	Abbreviation
Wheat, corn, soybeans, silver	Chicago Board of Trade (One Chicago) www.cbt.com	CBOT
Hogs, pork bellies, lumber, gold, weather	Chicago Mercantile Exchange (One Chicago) www.cme.com	CME
Cotton, rice	Chicago Rice and Cotton Exchange	CRCE
Cocoa, sugar, coffee	Coffee, Sugar and Cocoa Exchange	CSCE
Wheat, corn syrup, orange juice	Minneapolis Grain Exchange www.mgex.com New York Cotton Exchange New York Mercantile Exchange www.nymex.com	MGE NYCE NYMEX
Oil, crude oil, heating gasoline, propane gas	New York Mercantile Exchange Hong Kong Futures Exchange www.hkfe.com Philadelphia Board of Trade International Petrol Exchange www.ipe.uk.com	NYMEX HKEX PBOT IPE
Metals	New York Mercantile Exchange London Metal Exchange www.lme.co.uk Commodity Exchange www.comex.com	NYMEX LME COMEX
Electricity	New York Mercantile Exchange (delisted in 2002) Minnesota Grain Exchange Nordic Power Exchange European Energy Exchange Amsterdam Power Exchange Paris Power Exchange	NYMEX MGEX NORDPOOL EEX APX POWERNEXT

traded: producers trade with speculators and hedgers, e.g., a company producing copper wires and wishing to hedge its revenues against a rise in the price of copper.

Le Marché à Terme International de France

Created in 1986 and first dedicated to bond Futures, MATIF introduced commodity Futures two years later. Today Futures on corn and Futures and options on colza and wheat are traded.

It is interesting to observe that most US Futures exchanges still function today as *open outcry trading*. Many exchanges around the world now operate with an electronic platform, as do some divisions of the NYMEX and the whole EUREX system existing in Europe and recently established in Chicago.

More precisely, energy trading is conducted on NYMEX in open outcry from 10.05 A.M. until 2.30 P.M. After hours Futures trading is conducted via the NYMEX access

Internet-based trading platform beginning at 3.15 P.M. on Mondays through Thursdays and concluding at 9.30 A.M. the following day. On Sundays, the session begins at 7 P.M.

On the metals front, CBOT unveiled in August 2004 details of a plan to challenge NYMEX's grip on trading of gold and silver Futures by offering them on an electronic basis on 6 October 2004. NYMEX announced in September that it would introduce on the same day a new system called "Neon" that will automatically send a customer's order to NYMEX gold and silver open outcry trading pits; currently, customers typically talk to floor clerks by phone. The Neon system should be extended to energy trading pits later. NYMEX—the largest energy futures and gold and silver Futures exchange—wants, however, to keep its practice of open outcry, which it views as a unique source of liquidity. It is interesting to observe how various exchanges are incorporating electronic trading while aiming at preserving their own specificity.

TABLE 14-2 Commodity Futures Contracts

Commodity Group	Commodity Type
Grains	Corn Oats Rice Wheat
Oil and meal	Soybean
Livestock	Pork Beef
Foodstuffs	Cocoa Coffee Orange juice Potatoes Sugar
Textiles	Cotton
Forest products	Lumber Pulp
Metals	Gold Silver Platinum Palladium Copper Aluminum
Energy	Crude oil Heating oil Gasoline Natural gas Propane gas Electricity

Returning to Futures contracts, trade can occur for delivery at different maturity dates in the future. The contract design also includes position limits, daily price limits and quotation conventions and attempts to reduce to the greatest extent any ambiguities as to the nature of a physically settled contract. Although an extremely small fraction of contracts purchased or sold are actually held until delivery, possible residual uncertainty as to the terms of the contract would reduce the quality of the hedge it provides and, in turn, its popularity. The details of delivery are fully specified by the exchange, namely: the quantity—number of bushels or tons per contract, number of cubic feet for natural gas; the type—robusta versus arabica for coffee; the location—which in general has nothing to do with the exchange (a NYMEX WTI contract is delivered at Cushing in Oklahoma). Sometimes, a choice is given to the seller with respect to one of these items, including the time window of delivery: this *option to deliver* (analogous to the one that exists for bond notional Futures regarding the specific bond that is delivered) has a positive value that can be computed in terms of the type of flexibility and this value is obviously negative for the buyer of the Futures contract.

Basis Risk

1. Understanding basis risk is fundamental to hedging. *Basis* is defined as:

$$\text{Basis}_{t,T} = \text{Spot price}_t - F^T(t)$$

is usually quoted as a premium or discount: the cash price as a premium or discount to the Future price.

The basis is said to be one dollar "over" Futures if the spot price is one dollar higher than the Futures price.

2. There are several types of basis risk:
   (a) In the case of a trading desk which needs to cut at date t (e.g., to avoid negative margin calls[2])—a position in Futures which was meant to hedge a position in the spot commodity—the basis risk is represented by the quantity defined above.

   (b) More generally, basis risk exists when Futures and spot prices do not change by the same amount over time and, possibly, will not converge at maturity *T*:
      —because the Futures contracts were written on an underlying similar but not identical to the source of risk, such as an airline company hedging exposure to a rise in jet fuel prices with NYMEX heating oil Futures contracts;
      —because of the optionalities left to the seller at maturity in the physical settlement of the Futures contract: grade of the commodity, location, chemical attributes.

Today, market participants analyze their risk in a mark-to-market perspective at date *t* (and not only at date *T*). Consequently, basis risk is often defined as the *variance of the basis*:

$$\sigma^2(S_t - F^T(t)) = \sigma^2(S_t) + \sigma^2(F^T(t)) - 2\rho\sigma(S_t)\sigma(F^T(t))$$

---

[2] One needs to keep in mind that the major bankruptcies of hedge funds occurred because of funds' inabilities to face the margin calls related to existing positions.

where ρ is the correlation coefficient between the Futures and spot price series.

This equation shows that basis risk is zero when variances between the Futures and spot prices are identical *and* the correlation coefficient ρ between spot and Futures prices is equal to one. In practice, the second condition is the most stringent one and the magnitude of basis risk depends mainly on the degree of correlation between cash and Futures prices.

Since hedgers are trying to eliminate price risk, the classical measure of the effectiveness of hedging a spot position with Futures contracts is defined by:

$$h = 1 - \frac{\sigma^2(\text{basis})}{\sigma^2(S_t)}$$

The closer *h* is to one, the more effective the hedge. To return to the airline example, if crude oil contracts and heating oil contracts are available to hedge its exposure to jet fuel price risk, it will choose the solution leading to the higher number *h*. Remembering that the position in the hedging of Futures may need to be cut at any time, one wants to be left with as small a basis as possible.

Returning to the different optionalities attached to delivery of the physical commodity, they have been the subject of a vast body of literature since both the seller and buyer of the Futures contract are quite aware of their financial value (see, e.g., Gay and Manaster, 1986).

Some commodity contracts, like most financial Futures, are based on cash delivery rather than physical delivery. In this case, the holder of a long contract receives at maturity the last marginal call, positive or negative, corresponding to the change of the Future price over the last trading day, since his gain or loss over the period has been incorporated daily in his account at the exchange.

In summary, a Future position may be terminated essentially in three ways:

1. By taking prior to maturity a symmetric position in an equal number of contracts in order to nullify the position and avoid the cumbersome and expensive procedure of physical delivery.

2. Roughly 1% of the Futures contracts go into physical delivery at maturity. The benefit of the existence of physical delivery is that it implies the convergence of spot and Futures prices at maturity of the contract; hence, the consistency in the moves of these two

quantities over time. The constraining part, however, is that the clearing house needs to fully specify the delivery location, the delivery period—which usually covers the delivery month for monthly Futures contracts on commodities, in contrast to financial Futures on bonds, for instance, which result in a unique delivery of the bond—as well as the delivery rate. Lastly, the grade of the commodity needs to be made clear as well as the optionalities left to the seller (respectively, buyer) in the delivery procedure. When the grade specification is left open, the seller will choose *the cheapest to deliver*; a vast literature exists on this issue in the case of bond Futures contracts.

3. By entering into an Exchange For Physical (EFP) agreement.

Exchange for Physical

An EFP is an agreement between a party holding a long Futures position and a party with an equal size short position to enter a bilateral contract specifying the terms of physical delivery (location and price). The two parties notify the clearing house of the quantity and price negotiated between them and both futures positions are then terminated under the terms of the EFP. In grain markets, this type of transaction is called "ex pit."

Alternative Delivery Procedure

An ADP is available to buyers and sellers who have been matched by the exchange subsequent to the termination of trading in the spot month contract. If buyer and seller agree to achieve delivery under terms different from those prescribed in the contract specifications, they may proceed on that basis after submitting a notice of their intention to the exchange.

SHIPPING AND FREIGHT: SPOT AND FORWARD MARKETS

The Current Issues in the Booming Freight Market

A recent jump in ocean-shipping rates to their highest levels in decades is adding upward pressure on already rising commodity prices that could increase further the cost of imported goods in the US, in China, in Europe and worldwide. The demand for sea-faring vessels is far outstripping supply and the cost of shipping iron ore, soybeans and other commodities used in the manufacture of a wide range of goods nearly tripled in 2003. The Baltic Dry Index (BDI), the key industry indicator published in London and representative of loose goods transportation (cereals, minerals, coal) kept rising sharply, showing no signs of relief on the horizon in terms of lower prices or additional supply of vessels. The Baltic Panama Index (BPI), essentially dedicated to cereals, follows the same pattern. A similar trend, at an even larger scale, is observed in the cost of oil tankers where the price of insurance for tankers coming from the Middle East adds to the other rising components.

China's surging economy is creating a huge demand for ships to import the basic raw materials the country needs to build infrastructure, supply its massive manufacturing sector and satisfy a growing consumer market. As more ships go to China, fewer are available to ferry goods between other parts of the world, causing a supply shortage and price rises. Compounding the problem, shrinking mining industries in the Americas and Europe have increased these regions' imports of coal. Besides these structural elements, events like the summer 2003 drought in Europe that boosted grain shipments from the US contribute to the price pressure.

Clarksons, a large London-based ship broker which has kept records on shipping rates for about 30 years, observed that the end of 2003 was the highest rate market of all times. Obviously, the impact on the world economy comes with some lag in the form of higher prices on goods made of steel, aluminum and other metals. For countries like China, the US and the European Community, which import more that they export, this may translate into inflationary pressure. The increase in the shipping cost is particularly clear for products like textiles and metals since they are heavier and bulkier (the situation being quite different for electronic equipment, for instance). In September 2003, copper was trading on the LME at $2.083 per ton, a 6-year high point. The cost for alumina, the basic ingredient to produce aluminum, nearly doubled in 2003 and cotton prices were trading at 5-year highs of about 84 cents a pound, in part because of increased demand from China and India.

The growing use of world freight is greatly explained by the rising demand in China which, for instance, in 2003 increased its imports of iron ore (the basic material to make steel) by nearly 40 million tons, or 33%. Meanwhile, imports by Europe of coal from China, Indonesia and Australia rose by 35%. On another register, Brazil—a major producer of soybeans—shipped greater quantities of them to China where they are used for animal feed and human food products, such as soybean oil.

Higher freight rates are mainly hitting bulk-shipping vessels, specialized carriers that transport commodities in their raw form and that account for about one-third of all commercial ocean-going trade. More that 30% of all bulk ships carry iron ore and coal.

The other classes of freight ships are: container vessels that carry semifinished and finished goods, such as electronic devices and appliances; and tankers that are used for oil and, more recently, natural gas. Although ships come in different sizes and shapes, the spot cost to rent a typical bulk to ferry coal or iron ore was about $75,000 a day at the end of 2003, according to traders and ship brokers—quite different from the $20,000 to $28,000 a day prevailing in January 2003. About 40% of goods are transported in ships hired on the spot market. As a comparison, companies that had bought forward contracts on freight back in 2001 or 2002 for "delivery" of freight in 2003 had locked in a forward price which was only around $30,000 a day.

At the same time, the shipbuilding business, centered in South Korea, Japan and China, is backed up with orders and the lead times for taking new deliveries are almost twice as long as normal. One of the reasons for the delays is the fact that the world's shipbuilders are busy building new oil tankers to satisfy the more stringent safety requirements called for by European regulators. Hence, previous orders for new container ships have pushed any new orders for bulk ships to the back of the line; a new ship that used to take 18 months to 2 years for completion now requires as much as 3 years for delivery.

Spot and Forward Freight Markets

Freight contracts can be transacted either in the spot market or in the Forward Freight Agreement (FFA) market, since Futures exchanges no longer trade them today. The Baltic International Freight Future Exchange (BIFFEX) offered Futures contracts between May 1985 and April 2002; the underlying asset was a basket index comprising

TABLE 14-3 Baltic Panama Index (BPI) Weighting

Routes	Route Description	Cargo	Weight in the BPI (%)
1	US Gulf of Mexico to ARA (Antwerp-Rotterdam-Amsterdam)	Light grain	10
2	Transatlantic round of 45–60 days	Time charter contracts	20
3	US Gulf to South Japan	Heavy grain, soybean, sorghum	12.5
4	Gibraltar to the Far East via Gulf of Mexico (duration 50–60 days)	Time charter contracts	12.5
5	US North Pacific port to South Japan	HSS	10
6	Transpacific round of 35–50 days	TCC	20
7	US West Coast or British Columbia to Japan/ South Korea	TCC	15

the seven routes of the BPI. This index, as it stands today, is presented in Table 14-3.

Since April 2002, only FFAs have been traded. They mostly trade on specific routes rather than on the entire index.

The aim of the introduction in 1992 of forward contracts, besides the BIFFEX Futures contracts, was to provide another way of hedging freight rate risk in the dry-bulk and wet-bulk sectors of the shipping industry. FFA contracts are principal-to-principal contracts to settle a freight or hire rate for a specified quantity of cargo or type of vessel for usually one (or a combination) of the major trade routes. The reason for the success of FFA contracts over BIFFEX ones is primarily related to the high basis risk remaining after hedging with a contract written on an index. Most market agents in the shipping industry operate in some defined regions of the world and, therefore, demand route-specific derivatives contracts.

Typically, a shipowner or a charterer feeling that the freight market in a given route and a specific vessel/cargo size might move against him would approach an approved broker to buy or sell FFA contracts. This broker would find another charterer or another broker with a client with opposite expectations in order to fix the FFA contract. The major FFA brokers are those on the panel of shipbrokers of the Forward Freight Agreement Brokers Association (FFABA) created in 1997. They include Clarksons

Securities Ltd, Lynch Flynn & Associates, Yamamizu Shipping. The city of London has established itself as the major FFA market.

Each member shipbroker of the FFABA submits to the Baltic Exchange its daily review of the rate on each constituent route of the Baltic indices. The Baltic Exchange excludes the highest and lowest assessments of the day and takes an arithmetic average of the remainder. The average rate of each route is then multiplied by the weighting factor to return the contribution of each route to the index; finally, by adding all the route contributions together, an overall average index is created (i.e., the daily BPI, see next page).

Currently, FFA contracts have the BHMI, BCI and BITR as underlying asset spot freight rates in routes of the BPI. As an example, consider a charterer who, on 10 June 2004, is interested in transporting Heavy grain, Soya and Sorghum (HSS) from the US Gulf to Japan under a voyage charter party two months later (31 August). In order to avoid adverse freight-rate movements between 10 June and 30 August (day of the spot fixture), the charterer will approach a broker and define the following contract specifications: route US Gulf–Japan; cargo size 80,000 tons HSS, contract date 31 August 2004. The broker will search for another broker with a client, typically a shipowner, having the same contract characteristics in mind, but with opposite expectations on evolution of the freight rate.

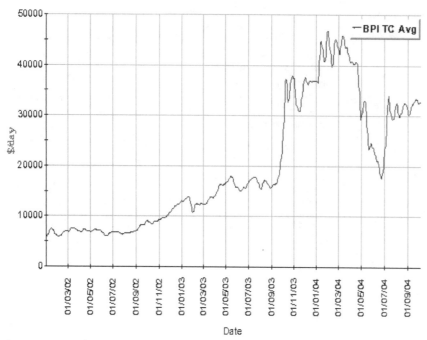

Source: Clarksons

The FFA market is a private market; hence, transactions and their nature are not made public. According to reliable sources, the total FFA volume went from 2,000 contracts in 2000 to 2,500 contracts in 2001 and more than 3,000 contracts in 2002. In practice, most of the trading concentrates in the nearby (1-month) and 2-month contracts, with much lower volumes in 3-month contracts. According to Kavussanos and Nomikos (2001), new information disseminates faster in the FFA market than in the spot market. Hence, it seems that FFA prices in all routes contain useful information about subsequent spot prices and can be used as price discovery vehicles for decision-making. Kavussanos and Nomikos (2001) investigate the relationship in daily returns and volatilities between spot and FFA price series on the major transatlantic and transpacific freight routes. Not only do they show that prices and volatilities in the spot and forward freight markets are "co-integrated" in the sense that they move together over long time periods,[3] but, by going through a lead–lag analysis, they also exhibit that it is the *forward market that leads the spot market*, as is the case in all commodity markets. They conclude that FFA prices in all routes contain information about future freight spot prices and, therefore, can be used as price discovery vehicles.

VOLUME, LIQUIDITY AND OPEN INTEREST IN FUTURES MARKETS

Table 14-4 displays the average daily volumes of Futures contracts traded on major exchanges in January 2004. Underlyings are divided into broad categories and ranked according to decreasing volumes. Unsurprisingly, oil products are by far the most traded: more than 200,000 transactions on crude oil take place every day on NYMEX and 100,000 on the IPE Brent. Gas immediately follows oil, showing the growing importance of this commodity. Agricultural products come after the energy group, starting with cereals. Among all commodities, corn has the second largest volume of trades after crude oil. Corn volume is higher than that for soybean, but not that of soybean and soybean complex. Outside cereals, it is coffee which has the highest volume. Aluminum and copper are the most traded among the industrial metals, while gold and silver are the most traded among the precious metals.

An important feature shared by all commodity Futures is that the highest liquidity is observed for short maturities, of the order of a few months. As an example, Figure 14-1 depicts the average daily volume observed in January 2004 on a Brent Future contract as a function of its maturity; volume gets divided by 10 when the time to maturity is 4 months instead of 1 month. This makes the establishment of reliable statistics difficult for the prices of Futures with medium-to long-term maturities.

Even though liquidity modeling is one of the topics on which financial theory needs more findings even in the context of classical instruments such as bonds and stocks, some qualitative concepts have emerged that can be extended to commodity markets:

- Liquidity may be measured by the size of the trade it takes to move the market.

- *Market depth* may be measured by the time it takes for an order of a standard size to be executed.

---

[3] Two processes (X_t) and (Y_t) are said to be co-integrated if there exists a linear combination $(aX_t + bY_t)_{t \geq 0}$ of the two processes that is a stationary process.

TABLE 14-4 Average Daily Volumes on Various Commodity Futures during January 2004

Exchange	CBOT	CME	NYMEX	COMEX	NYBOT	IPE	LME	MATIF
Energy								
Crude oil WTI			216,728					
Brent						97,801		
Natural gas			61,165			2,377		
Heating fuel			60,728					
Unleaded gasoline			50,320					
Gasoil						44,177		
PJM electricity index			322					
Propane			149					
Agriculturals								
Corn	101,286							161
Soybean	75,485							
Soymeal	32,435							
Wheat	32,844							373
Sugar					27,030			
Coffee					20,519			
Cotton					14,366			
Cocoa					9,194			
Oatmeals	1,687							
Rice	891							
Colza								647
Metals								
Aluminum				496			106,830	
Copper				11,239			85,235	
Zinc							44,211	
Lead							18,369	
Nickel							14,751	
Tin							5,061	
Gold				83,227				
Silver				20,266				
Platinum				860				
Palladium				806				
Agriculturals								
Beef		18,115						
Pork bellies		10,621						
Milk		893						
Lumber		896						

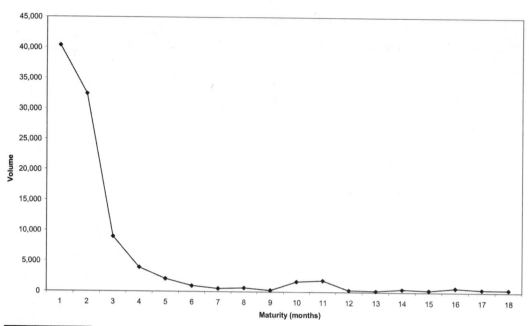

FIGURE 14-1   January 2004 average daily volume on the IPE Brent Future contract as a function of its maturity.

Open Interest in Futures Market

Open interest refers to the number of futures contracts outstanding at a particular moment, i.e., the number of contracts that have not been canceled by an offsetting trade. Official figures on open interest are released by the exchange in a daily manner for the day before. One needs to keep in mind that it represents the total number of contracts held by buyers *or* sold short by sellers since these two numbers are always equal. The size of the open interest reflects the determination of the two groups, longs and shorts, to hold to their positions. It is a major indicator for technical analysts who derive buy-and-sell rules from the combined effect of an upward or downward trend with a rising or falling open interest.

SUMMARY

Commodities and commodity markets have undergone dramatic changes over the last few years, with the deregulation of gas and electricity markets, the boom in South American production of soybean and the arrival of new actors in the coffee market. Countries like China are absorbing an increasing percentage of world commodity production and shifting up demand figures. Liquidity has increased in all Futures contracts, in particular for energy commodities which represent today the highest volume of traded Futures. This translates into higher volatility and price risk in all markets; hence, more hedging activities become necessary in all sectors of the economy, from the agrifood business to airline companies.

Foreign Exchange Risk

■ Learning Objectives

Candidates, after completing this reading, should be able to:

- Calculate a financial institution's overall foreign exchange exposure.
- Explain how a financial institution could alter its net position exposure to reduce foreign exchange risk.
- Calculate a financial institution's potential dollar gain or loss exposure to a particular currency.
- Identify and describe the different types of foreign exchange trading activities.
- Identify the sources of foreign exchange trading gains and losses.
- Calculate the potential gain or loss from a foreign currency denominated investment.

- Explain balance-sheet hedging with forwards.
- Describe how a non-arbitrage assumption in the foreign exchange markets leads to the interest rate parity theorem, and use this theorem to calculate forward foreign exchange rates.
- Explain why diversification in multicurrency asset-liability positions could reduce portfolio risk.
- Describe the relationship between nominal and real interest rates.

Excerpt is Chapter 15 of Financial Institutions Management: A Risk Management Approach, *Seventh Edition, by Anthony Saunders and Marcia Millon Cornett.*

The globalization of the U.S. financial services industry has meant that FIs are increasingly exposed to foreign exchange (FX) risk. FX risk can occur as a result of trading in foreign currencies, making foreign currency loans (such as a loan in pounds to a corporation), buying foreign-issued securities (U.K. pound–denominated gilt-edged bonds or German euro–government bonds), or issuing foreign currency–denominated debt (pound certificates of deposit) as a source of funds. Extreme foreign exchange risk at a single FI was evident in 2002 when a single trader at Allfirst Bank covered up $211 million in losses from foreign currency trading. After five years in which these losses were successfully hidden, the activities were discovered in 2002. More recently, in 2007 the dollar's considerable weakness boosted profits for internationally active firms. For example, IBM's third-quarter revenue rose 7 percent over the previous year, but would have been up just 3 percent if exchange rate shifts were not counted. In contrast, despite a global recession, Coca-Cola Co. announced a decline in, but better-than-expected, fourth-quarter 2008 net profit. Foreign exchange fluctuations reduced the company's fourth-quarter revenue by seven percentage points and reduced operating profit growth by nine percentage points. The company derives about 80 percent of profit from outside North America and had benefited in previous years from a weak dollar. Yet as the dollar strengthened during the financial crisis, Coke expected to reduce operating profit growth by between 10 percentage points and 12 percentage points.

This chapter looks at how FIs evaluate and measure the risks faced when their assets and liabilities are denominated in foreign (as well as in domestic) currencies and when they take major positions as traders in the spot and forward foreign currency markets.

FOREIGN EXCHANGE RATES AND TRANSACTIONS

Foreign Exchange Rates

A foreign exchange rate is the price at which one currency (e.g., the U.S. dollar) can be exchanged for another currency (e.g., the Swiss franc). Table 15-1 lists the exchange rates between the U.S. dollar and other currencies as of 4 PM eastern standard time on July 15, 2009. Foreign exchange rates are listed in two ways: U.S. dollars received for one unit of the foreign currency exchanged, or a **direct quote** (in US$), and foreign currency received for each U.S. dollar exchanged, or an **indirect quote** (per US$). For example, the exchange rate of U.S. dollars for Canadian dollars on July 15, 2009, was .8972 (US$/C$), or $0.8972 could be received for each Canadian dollar exchanged. Conversely, the exchange rate of Canadian dollars for U.S. dollars was 1.1146 (C$/US$), or 1.1146 Canadian dollars could be received for each U.S. dollar exchanged.

Foreign Exchange Transactions

There are two basic types of foreign exchange rates and foreign exchange transactions: spot and forward. **Spot foreign exchange transactions** involve the immediate exchange of currencies at the current (or spot) exchange rate—see Figure 15-1. Spot transactions can be conducted through the foreign exchange division of commercial banks or a nonbank foreign currency dealer. For example, a U.S. investor wanting to buy British pounds through a local bank on July 15, 2009, essentially has the dollars transferred from his or her bank account to the dollar account of a pound seller at a rate of $1 per .6089 pound (or $1.6422 per pound).[1] Simultaneously, pounds are transferred from the seller's account into an account designated by the U.S. investor. If the dollar depreciates in value relative to the pound (e.g., $1 per .6035 pound or $1.6570 per pound), the value of the pound investment, if converted back into U.S. dollars, increases. If the dollar appreciates in value relative to the pound (e.g., $1 per .6108 pound or $1.6372 per pound), the value of the pound investment, if converted back into U.S. dollars, decreases.

The appreciation of a country's currency (or a rise in its value relative to other currencies) means that the country's goods are more expensive for foreign buyers and that foreign goods are cheaper for foreign sellers (all else constant). Thus, when a country's currency appreciates, domestic manufacturers find it harder to sell their goods abroad and foreign manufacturers find it easier to sell their goods to domestic purchasers. Conversely, depreciation of a country's currency (or a fall in its value relative to other currencies) means the country's goods become

---

[1] In actual practice, settlement—exchange of currencies—occurs normally two days after a transaction.

TABLE 15-1 Foreign Currency Exchange Rates

Currencies

July 15, 2009

U.S. dollar foreign-exchange rates in late New York trading

Country/Currency	In US$	Per US$	US$ ys, YTD chg (%)	Country/Currency	In US$	Per US$	US$ ys, YTD chg (%)
Americas				**Czech. Rep.** koruna**	.05454	18.335	−4.6
Argentina peso*	.2627	3.8066	10.2	**Denmark** krone	.1895	5.2770	−1.0
Brazil real	.5170	1.9342	−16.4	**Euro area** euro	1.4107	.7089	−1.0
Canada dollar	.8972	1.1146	−8.4	**Hungary** forint	.005177	193.16	1.6
1-month forward	.8973	1.1145	−8.4	**Norway** krone	.1566	6.3857	−8.2
3-months forward	.8976	1.1141	−8.4	**Poland** zloty	.3296	3.0340	2.2
6-months forward	.8979	1.1137	−8.3	**Russia** ruble‡	.03140	31.847	4.3
Chile peso	.001861	537.35	−15.8	**Sweden** krona	.1288	7.7640	−0.8
Colombia peso	.0004954	2018.57	−10.2	**Switzerland** franc	.9306	1.0746	0.7
Ecuador US dollar	1	1	unch	1-month forward	.9309	1.0742	0.7
Mexico peso*	.0739	13.5373	−1.4	3-months forward	.9318	1.0732	0.7
Peru new sol	.3320	3.012	−3.9	6-months forward	.9335	1.0712	0.8
Uruguay peso†	.04320	23.15	−5.1	**Turkey** lira**	.6543	1.5284	−0.8
Venezuela b.fuerte	.465701	2.1473	unch	**U.K.** pound	1.6422	.6089	−11.1
				1-month forward	1.6421	.6090	−11.2
Asia-Pacific				3-months forward	1.6419	.6091	−11.3
Australian dollar	.8034	1.2447	−11.5	6-months forward	1.6419	.6091	−11.3
China yuan	.1464	6.8317	0.1	**Middle East/Africa**			
Hong Kong dollar	.1290	7.7502	unch	**Bahrain** dinar	2.6526	.3770	unch
India rupee	.02059	48.567	−0.1	**Egypt** pound*	.1791	5.5844	1.5
Indonesia rupiah	.0000988	10121	−7.2	**Israel** shekel	.2567	3.8956	3.1
Japan yen	.010599	94.35	4.0	**Jordan** dinar	1.4109	.7088	unch
1-month forward	.010603	94.31	4.0	**Kuwait** dinar	3.4781	.2875	4.1
3-months forward	.010611	94.24	4.1	**Lebanon** pound	.0006634	1507.39	unch
6-months forward	.010627	94.10	4.2	**Saudi Arabia** riyal	.2666	3.7509	−0.1
Malaysia ringgit	.2806	3.5638	3.2	**South Africa** rand	.1235	8.0972	−13.8
New Zealand dollar	.6499	1.5387	−9.8	**UAE** dirham	.2723	3.6724	unch
Pakistan rupee	.01217	82.169	3.9				
Philippines peso	.0209	47.939	1.0	**SDR**††	1.5540	.6435	−0.9
Singapore dollar	.6893	1.4507	1.3				
South Korea won	.0007859	1272.43	0.8				
Taiwan dollar	.03041	32.884	0.3				
Thailand baht	.02934	34.083	−2.0				
Vietnam dong	.0005616	17806	1.8				

Floating rate   †Financial   ‡Russian Central Bank rate   **Rebased as of Jan 1, 2005

††Special Drawing Rights (SDR); from the International Monetary Fund; based on exchange rates for U.S., British and Japanese currencies.

Note: Based on trading among banks of $1 million and more, as quoted at 4 p.m. ET by Reuters.

Source: The Wall Street Journal, July 16, 2009, p. C5. Reprinted by permission of *The Wall Street Journal.* © 2009 Dow Jones & Company Inc. All rights reserved worldwide. *www.wsj.com*

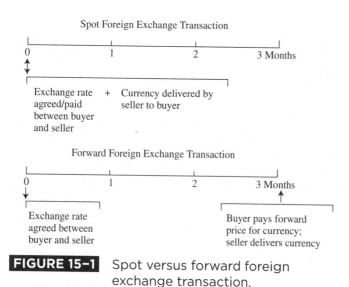

FIGURE 15–1 Spot versus forward foreign exchange transaction.

cheaper for foreign buyers and foreign goods become more expensive for foreign sellers. The Industry Perspectives box on the next page highlights how the financial crisis affected the appreciation and depreciation of the U.S. dollar and other major currencies.

A **forward foreign exchange transaction** is the exchange of currencies at a specified exchange rate (or forward exchange rate) at some specified date in the future, as illustrated in Figure 15-1. An example is an agreement today (at time 0) to exchange dollars for pounds at a given (forward) exchange rate three months in the future. Forward contracts are typically written for one-, three-, or six-month periods, but in practice they can be written over any given length of time.

Concept Question

1. What is the difference between a spot and a forward foreign exchange market transaction?

SOURCES OF FOREIGN EXCHANGE RISK EXPOSURE

The nation's largest commercial banks are major players in foreign currency trading and dealing, with large money center banks such as Citigroup and J.P. Morgan Chase also taking significant positions in foreign currency assets and liabilities. Table 15-2 shows the outstanding dollar value of U.S. banks' foreign assets and liabilities for the period 1994 to March 2009. The 2009 figure for foreign assets (claims) was $155.1 billion, with foreign liabilities of $205.8 billion. As you can see, both foreign currency liabilities and assets were growing until 1997 and then fell from 1998 through 2000. The financial crises in Asia and Russia in

TABLE 15-2 Liabilities to and Claims on Foreigners Reported by Banks in the United States, Payable in Foreign Currencies (in millions of dollars, end of period)

Item	1994	1995	1996	1997	1998	2000	2005	2009*
Banks' liabilities	$89,284	$109,713	$103,383	$117,524	$101,125	$76,120	$85,841	$205,830
Banks' claims	60,689	74,016	66,018	83,038	78,162	56,867	93,290	155,072
Deposits	19,661	22,696	22,467	28,661	45,985	22,907	43,868	70,659
Other claims	41,028	51,320	43,551	54,377	32,177	33,960	49,422	84,413
Claims of banks' domestic customers†	10,878	6,145	10,978	8,191	20,718	29,782	54,698	36,069

*2009 data are for end of March.

†Assets owned by customers of the reporting bank located in the United States that represent claims on foreigners held by reporting banks for the accounts of the domestic customers.

Note: Data on claims exclude foreign currencies held by U.S. monetary authorities.

TREASURY AND FEDERAL RESERVE FOREIGN EXCHANGE OPERATIONS: QUARTERLY REPORT

During the first quarter of 2009, the dollar's trade-weighted exchange value appreciated 4.8 percent, as measured by the Federal Reserve Board's major currencies index. The dollar appreciated 5.2 percent against the euro and 9.2 percent against the yen. These exchange rate movements occurred amid the backdrop of an historically low level of investor risk appetite, attributable to deteriorating global growth prospects and ongoing weakness in international equity markets . . . During the first two months of the quarter, the dollar's exchange value generally appreciated as a result of portfolio flows into dollar-denominated assets, reflecting heightened investor risk aversion. Sentiment toward the euro, in particular, waned in response to concerns over the region's growth prospects and European banks' exposures to eastern Europe . . . In contrast, the yen's depreciation accelerated as investors increasingly focused on the impact on the Japanese economy of slowing global growth and trade. Also contributing to the yen's depreciation was the improved risk appetite of Japanese investors, many of whom sought to increase their holdings of foreign investments as the quarter ended.

In January and February, the U.S. dollar outperformed most major currencies, including the euro and the yen. During this time, the dollar appreciated about 9.3 percent against the euro and about 7.6 percent against the yen . . . During the quarter, data continued to indicate that the U.S. economy was contracting at a significant pace . . . The dollar's gains were largely driven by similar factors as those observed since the global credit crisis sharply intensified during the fall of 2008. First, the dollar gained support as international investors revised downward their forecasts for growth in other industrialized and emerging market economies at a relatively faster pace than the growth outlook for the United States. In particular, dealers noted increased demand for dollars by U.S. institutional investors . . . as they scaled back their foreign investments and repatriated capital. Second, the deep liquidity and historically strong performance of U.S. Treasury securities during times of global stress also continued to attract "safe-haven" investor capital to the United States. Third, many analysts suggested that asset write-downs of U.S. credit and mortgage-related products by foreign investors continued to contribute to the dollar's appreciation. In recent years, many foreign investors had accumulated sizable holdings of U.S.-dollar-denominated credit- and mortgage-related investments. The declining value of some of these assets led many foreign investors to modify the amount of their outstanding foreign exchange hedges on these investments to reflect the reduced dollar amount they expected to exchange for their domestic currencies upon maturity. In practice, this led foreign investors, particularly European investors, to sell their domestic currencies in favor of the dollar. Finally, some analysts suggested that the dollar was supported by the relatively quick response of U.S. policymakers—compared with their counterparts in other countries—in lowering policy rates and implementing programs to support the financial sector and the economy . . .

Source: Federal Reserve Bank of New York, May 14, 2009, by Patricia Mosser, Senior Vice President and Acting Manager of the System Open Market Account.

1997 and 1998 and in Argentina in the early 2000s are likely reasons for the decrease in foreign assets and liabilities during this period. After this period, growth accelerated rapidly as the world economy recovered. While the growth of liability and asset claims on foreigners slowed during the financial crisis, levels remained stable as U.S. FIs were seen as some of the safest FIs during the crisis. Further, except for 2005, U.S. banks had more liabilities to than claims on (assets) foreigners. Thus, if the dollar depreciates relative to foreign currencies, more dollars (converted into foreign currencies) will be needed to pay off the liabilities and U.S. banks would experience a loss due to foreign exchange risk. The reverse was true in 2005.

Table 15-3 gives the categories of foreign currency positions (or investments) of all U.S. banks in major currencies as of March 2009. Columns (1) and (2) refer to the assets and liabilities denominated in foreign currencies that are held in the portfolios at U.S. banks. Columns (3) and (4) refer to trading in foreign currency markets (the **spot** market and **forward market for foreign exchange** in which contracts are bought—a long position—and sold—a short position—in each major currency). Foreign currency trading dominates direct portfolio investments. Even though the aggregate trading positions appear very large—for example, U.S. banks bought ¥463,587 billion—their overall or net exposure positions can be relatively small (e.g., the net position in yen was −¥728 billion).

TABLE 15-3 Monthly U.S. Bank Positions in Foreign Currencies and Foreign Assets and Liabilities, March 2009 (in currency of denomination)

	(1) Assets	(2) Liabilities	(3) FX Bought*	(4) FX Sold*	(5) Net Position†
Canadian dollars (millions of C$)	149,394	128,115	711,306	751,152	−18,567
Japanese yen (billions of ¥)	53,688	52,051	463,587	465,952	−728
Swiss francs (millions of SF)	64,812	67,732	1,030,042	1,037,312	−10,190
British pounds (millions of £)	462,479	331,262	1,051,157	1,066,555	115,819
Euros (millions of €)	1,783,672	1,771,541	4,907,000	4,891,317	27,814

*Includes spot, future, and forward contracts.

†Net position = (Assets − Liabilities) + (FX bought − FX sold).

Source: *Treasury Bulletin,* September 2009, pp. 89–99. *www.ustreas.gov*

An FIs' overall FX exposure in any given currency can be measured by the **net** position **exposure,** which is measured in local currency and reported in column (5) of Table 15-3 as:

$$\text{Net Exposure}_i = (\text{FX assets}_i - \text{FX liabilities}_i)$$
$$+ (\text{FX) bought}_i - \text{FX sold}_i)$$
$$= \text{Net foreign assets}_i + \text{Net FX bought}_i$$

where

$$i = i\text{th currency.}$$

Clearly, an FI could match its foreign currency assets to its liabilities in a given currency and match buys and sells in its trading book in that foreign currency to reduce its foreign exchange net exposure to zero and thus avoid FX risk. It could also offset an imbalance in its foreign asset–liability portfolio by an opposing imbalance in its trading book so that its net exposure position in that currency would be zero. Further, financial holding companies can aggregate their foreign exchange exposure even more. Financial holding companies might have a commercial bank, an insurance company, and a pension fund all under one umbrella that allows them to reduce their net foreign exchange exposure across all units. For example, at year-end 2008, Citigroup held over $4.2 trillion in foreign

exchange derivative securities off the balance sheet. Yet the company estimated the value-at-risk from its foreign exchange exposure was $118 million, or 0.003 percent.

Notice in Table 15-3 that U.S. banks had positive net FX exposures in two of the five major currencies in March 2009. A *positive* net exposure position implies a U.S. FI is overall **net long in a currency** (i.e., the FI has bought more foreign currency than it has sold) and faces the risk that the foreign currency will fall in value against the U.S. dollar, the domestic currency. A *negative* net exposure position implies that a U.S. FI is **net short in a foreign currency** (i.e., the FI has sold more foreign currency than it has purchased) and faces the *risk* that the foreign currency could rise in value against the dollar. Thus, failure to maintain a fully balanced position in any given currency exposes a U.S. FI to fluctuations in the FX rate of that currency against the dollar. Indeed, the greater the volatility of foreign exchange rates given any net exposure position, the greater the fluctuations in value of an FI's foreign exchange portfolio.

We have given the FX exposures for U.S. banks only, but most large nonbank FIs also have some FX exposure either through asset–liability holdings or currency trading. The absolute sizes of these exposures are smaller than those for major U.S. money center banks. The reasons for this are threefold: smaller asset sizes, prudent person concerns,[2] and regulations.[3] For example, U.S. pension funds invest approximately 5 percent of their asset portfolios in foreign securities, and U.S. life insurance companies generally hold less than 10 percent of their assets in foreign securities. Interestingly, U.S. FIs' holdings of overseas assets are less than those of FIs in Japan and Britain. For example, in Britain, pension funds have traditionally invested over 20 percent of their funds in foreign assets.

While the levels of claims and positions in foreign currencies held by financial institutions have increased consistently in recent years, the volume of foreign currency trading has decreased. For example, the Bank for International Settlements reported that average daily turnover in the global foreign exchange markets was $4 trillion in 2008, down from $1.2 trillion in 2003. The increased activity during this period was due to a number of factors, including the presence of trends and higher volatility in foreign exchange markets, which led to investments in currencies that experienced a persistent trend of appreciation (such as the euro). This volatility also resulted in an increase in hedging activity, which further increased currency trades. Also, interest rate differentials across countries resulted in investments in high interest rate currencies financed with short positions in low interest rate currencies. As cross-border investments increased, investors increasingly used foreign exchange markets as an asset class—that is, as an alternative investment to bonds and stocks.

Foreign Exchange Rate Volatility and FX Exposure

As discussed earlier, we can measure the potential size of an FI's FX exposure by analyzing the asset, liability, and currency trading mismatches on its balance sheet and the underlying volatility of exchange rate movements. Specifically, we can use the following equation:

Dollar loss/gain in currency i = [Net exposure in foreign currency i measured in U.S. dollars] × Shock (volatility) to the $/foreign currency i exchange rate

The larger the FI's net exposure in a foreign currency and the larger the foreign currency's exchange rate volatility,[4] the larger is the potential dollar loss or gain to an FI's earnings (i.e., the greater its daily earnings at risk [DEAR]). As we discuss in more detail later in the chapter, the underlying causes of FX volatility reflect fluctuations in the demand for and supply of a country's currency. That is, conceptually, an FX rate is like the price of any good and will appreciate in value relative to other currencies when demand is high or supply is low and will depreciate in value when demand is low or supply is high. For example, in October 1998 the dollar fell (depreciated) in value on one day from 121 yen/$ to 112 yen/$, or by over 7 percent. The major reason for this was the purchase of yen by hedge funds and the sale of dollars to repay Japanese banks for the yen loans they had borrowed at low interest rates earlier in 1998. While not as rapid a decline, in the early 2000s the dollar fell in value by almost 20 percent relative to the yen (from 134.0 in early 2002 to 107.8 in October 2003), much of which was due to an improving Japanese economy and intervention by Japan's Central Bank. A final example is the devaluation of the Argentinian peso in 2002 that resulted in a $595 million loss to Citigroup.

Concept Questions

1. How is the net foreign currency exposure of an FI measured?

2. If a bank is long in British pounds (£), does it gain or lose if the dollar appreciates in value against the pound?

3. A bank has £10 million in assets and £7 million in liabilities. It has also bought £52 million in foreign currency trading. What is its net exposure in pounds? (£55 million)

---

[2] Prudent person concerns are especially important for pension funds.

[3] For example, New York State restricts foreign asset holdings of New York–based life insurance companies to less than 10 percent of their assets.

[4] In the case of RiskMetrics the shock (or volatility) measure would equal 1.65 times the historic volatility (standard deviation) of the currency's exchange rate with the dollar. This shock, when multiplied by the net exposure in that currency (measured in dollars), provides an estimate of the loss exposure of the FI if tomorrow is that "1 bad day in 20."

FOREIGN CURRENCY TRADING

The FX markets of the world have become one of the largest of all financial markets. Trading turnover averaged as high as $4 trillion a day in recent years, 70 times the daily trading volume on the New York Stock Exchange. From 2007 to 2008, global FX trading volume increased by almost 15 percent. This growth, however, represented a drop from the 30 percent increases in FX trading volume seen in each of the two prior years. The volume drop was due mainly to hedge fund trading, which was a main driver of FX trading increases in 2006 and 2007. In these years, FX trading volume generated by hedge funds grew over 180 percent, and hedge fund trading business grew to 20 percent of global FX volume. From 2007 to 2008, hedge fund trading volumes fell 28 percent. For other market participants (e.g., commercial banks), however, continued levels of high volatility and an influx of investors seeking liquid markets and a plain vanilla asset class in the last quarter of 2008 produced a spike in trading that kept the FX market growing. Indeed, foreign exchange was one of the few sources of steady income for global banks during 2008.

London continues to be the largest FX trading market, followed by New York and Tokyo.[5] The top three banks operating in these markets are Deutsche Bank (21.0 percent of the market), UBS (14.6 percent), and Barclays (10.5 percent). Foreign exchange trading has been called the fairest market in the world because of its immense volume and the fact that no single institution can control the market's direction. Although professionals refer to global foreign exchange trading as a market, it is not really one in the traditional sense of the word. There is no central location where foreign exchange trading takes place. Moreover, the FX market is essentially a 24-hour market, moving among Tokyo, London, and New York throughout the day. Therefore, fluctuations in exchange rates and thus FX trading risk exposure continues into the night even when other FI operations are closed. This clearly adds to the risk from holding mismatched FX positions. Most of the volume is traded among the top international banks, which process currency transactions for everyone from

large corporations to governments around the world. Online foreign exchange trading is increasing. Electronic foreign exchange trading volume tripled from $700 billion in 2003 to over $2.1 trillion in 2008. The transnational nature of the electronic exchange of funds makes secure, Internet-based trading an ideal platform. Online trading portals—terminals where currency transactions are being executed—are a low-cost way of conducting spot and forward foreign exchange transactions.

FX Trading Activities

An FI's position in the FX markets generally reflects four trading activities:

1. The purchase and sale of foreign currencies to allow customers to partake in and complete international commercial trade transactions.

2. The purchase and sale of foreign currencies to allow customers (or the FI itself) to take positions in foreign real and financial investments.

3. The purchase and sale of foreign currencies for hedging purposes to offset customer (or FI) exposure in any given currency.

4. The purchase and sale of foreign currencies for speculative purposes through forecasting or anticipating future movements in FX rates.

In the first two activities, the FI normally acts as an *agent of* its customers for a fee but does not assume the FX risk itself. Citigroup is the dominant supplier of FX to retail customers in the United States and worldwide. As of 2008, the aggregate value of Citigroup's principal amount of foreign exchange contracts totaled $4.2 trillion. In the third activity, the FI acts defensively as a hedger to reduce FX exposure. For example, it may take a short (sell) position in the foreign exchange of a country to offset a long (buy) position in the foreign exchange of that same country. Thus, FX risk exposure essentially relates to **open positions** taken as a principal by the FI for speculative purposes, the fourth activity. An FI usually creates an open position by taking an unhedged position in a foreign currency in its FX trading with other FIs. The Federal Reserve estimates that 200 FIs are active market makers in foreign currencies in the U.S. foreign exchange market with about 30 commercial and investment banks making a market in the five major currencies. FIs can make speculative trades directly with other FIs or arrange them through specialist FX brokers. The Federal

---

[5] On a global basis, approximately 34 percent of trading in FX occurs in London, 17 percent in New York, and 6 percent in Tokyo. The remainder is spread throughout the world.

Reserve Bank of New York estimates that approximately 44 percent of speculative or open position trades are accomplished through specialized brokers who receive a fee for arranging trades between FIs. Speculative trades can be instituted through a variety of FX instruments. Spot currency trades are the most common, with FIs seeking to make a profit on the difference between buy and sell prices (i.e., on movements in the bid–ask prices over time). However, FIs can also take speculative positions in foreign exchange forward contracts, futures, and options.

Most profits or losses on foreign trading come from taking an open position or speculating in currencies. Revenues from market making—the bid–ask spread—or from acting as agents for retail or wholesale customers generally provide only a secondary or supplementary revenue source. Note the trading income from FX trading for some large U.S. banks in Table 15-4. As can be seen, total trading income has grown steadily over recent years. For just these 13 FIs, income from trading activities increased from $1,881.0 million in 1995 to $10,772.6 million in 2008, a 473 percent increase over the 13-year period. The dominant FX trading banks are Citigroup and J.P. Morgan Chase.

TABLE 15-4 Foreign Exchange Trading Income of Major U.S. Banks (in millions of dollars)

	1995	2000	2005	2008
Bank of America	$ 303.0	$ 524.0	$ 769.8	$ 1,772.8
Bank of New York Mellon	42.0	261.0	266.0	1,181.5
Citigroup	1,053.0	1,243.0	2,519.0	2,590.0
Fifth Third	0.0	0.0	51.7	105.6
HSBC North America	0.0	6.5	133.9	643.8
J. P. Morgan Chase	253.0	1,456.0	997.0	2,163.0
KeyCorp	8.0	19.6	38.6	63.0
Northern Trust	54.8	142.0	180.2	616.2
PNC	4.5	22.3	38.3	74.0
State Street B&TC	140.7	386.5	468.5	1,066.4
Suntrust	0.0	16.9	5.7	35.7
U.S. Bancorp	7.3	22.4	30.9	68.2
Wells Fargo	14.7	191.9	350.0	392.4
Total	$1,881.0	$4,292.1	$5,849.6	$10,772.6

Source: FDIC, *Statistics on Depository Institutions,* various dates. *www.fdic.gov*

Concept Questions

1. What are the four major FX trading activities?
2. In which trades do FIs normally act as agents, and in which trades as principals?
3. What is the source of most profits or losses on foreign exchange trading? What foreign currency activities provide a secondary source of revenue?

FOREIGN ASSET AND LIABILITY POSITIONS

The second dimension of an FI's FX exposure results from any mismatches between its foreign financial asset and foreign financial liability portfolios. As discussed earlier, an FI is long a foreign currency if its assets in that currency exceed its liabilities, while it is short a foreign currency if its liabilities in that currency exceed its assets. Foreign financial assets might include Swiss franc–denominated bonds, British pound–denominated gilt-edged securities, or peso-denominated Mexican bonds. Foreign financial liabilities might include issuing British pound CDs or a yen-denominated bond in the Euromarkets to raise yen funds. The globalization of financial markets has created an enormous range of possibilities for raising funds in currencies other than the home currency. This is important for FIs that wish to not only diversify their sources and uses of funds but also exploit imperfections in foreign banking markets that create opportunities for higher returns on assets or lower funding costs.

The Return and Risk of Foreign Investments

This section discusses the extra dimensions of return and risk from adding foreign currency assets and liabilities to an FI's portfolio. Like domestic assets and liabilities, profits (returns) result from the difference between contractual income from or costs paid on a security. With foreign assets and liabilities, however, profits (returns) are also affected by changes in foreign exchange rates.

Example 15.1

Calculating the Return of Foreign Exchange Transactions of a U.S. FI

Suppose that an FI has the following assets and liabilities:

Assets	Liabilities
$100 million U.S. loans (1 year) in dollars	$200 million U.S. CDs (1 year) in dollars
$100 million equivalent U.K. loans (1 year) (loans made in pounds)	

The U.S. FI is raising all of its $200 million liabilities in dollars (one-year CDs) but investing 50 percent in U.S. dollar assets (one-year maturity loans) and 50 percent in U.K. pound assets (one-year maturity loans).[6] In this example, the FI has matched the duration of its assets and liabilities ($D_A = D_L = 1$ year), but has mismatched the currency composition of its asset and liability portfolios. Suppose the promised one-year U.S. CD rate is 8 percent, to be paid in dollars at the end of the year, and that one-year, credit–free loans in the United States are yielding only 9 percent. The FI would have a positive spread of 1 percent from investing domestically. Suppose, however, that credit risk–free, one-year loans are yielding 15 percent in the United Kingdom.

To invest in the United Kingdom, the FI decides to take 50 percent of its $200 million in funds and make one-year maturity U.K. pound loans while keeping 50 percent of its funds to make U.S. dollar loans. To invest $100 million (of the $200 million in CDs issued) in one-year loans in

---

(a) Unhedged Foreign Exchange Transaction

FI lends $100 million for pounds at $1.6/£1   FI receives £62.5(1.15) for dollars at $?/£1

|————————————————|
0   1 year

(b) Foreign Exchange Transaction Hedged on the Balance Sheet

FI lends $100 million for pounds at $1   FI receives £62.5(1.15) for dollars at $?/£1

FI receives (from a CD) $100 million for pounds at $1.6/£1   FI pays £62.5(1.11) with dollars at $?/£1

|————————————————|
0   1 year

(c) Foreign Exchange Transaction Hedged with Forwards

FI lends $100 million for pounds at $1.6/£1

FI sells a 1-year pounds-for-dollars forward contract with a stated forward rate of $1.55/£1 and nominal value of £62.5 (1.15)   FI receives £62.5(1.15) from borrower and delivers funds to forward buyer receiving £62.5 × (1.15) × 1.55 guaranteed.

|————————————————|
0   1 year

FIGURE 15-2   Time line for a foreign exchange transaction.

the United Kingdom, the U.S. FI engages in the following transactions [illustrated in panel (a) of Figure 15-2].

1. At the beginning of the year, sells $100 million for pounds on the spot currency markets. If the exchange rate is $1.60 to £1, this translates into $100 million/1.6 = £62.5 million.

2. Takes the £62.5 million and makes one-year U.K. loans at a 15 percent interest rate.

3. At the end of the year, pound revenue from these loans will be £62.5(1.15) = £71.875 million.[7]

4. Repatriates these funds back to the United States at the end of the year. That is, the U.S. FI sells the £71.875 million in the foreign exchange market at the spot exchange rate that exists at that time, the end of the year spot rate.

Suppose the spot foreign exchange rate has not changed over the year; it remains fixed at $1.60/£1. Then the dollar proceeds from the U.K. investment will be:

£71.875 million × $1.60/£1 = $115 million

or, as a return,

$$\frac{\$115 \text{ million} - \$100 \text{ million}}{\$100 \text{ million}} = 15\%$$

---

[6] For simplicity, we ignore the leverage or net worth aspects of the FI's portfolio.

[7] No default risk is assumed.

Given this, the weighted return on the bank's portfolio of investments would be:

$$(.5)(.09) + (.5)(.15) = .12 \text{ or } 12\%$$

This exceeds the cost of the FI's CDs by 4 percent (12% − 8%).

Suppose, however, that at the end of the year the British pound had fallen in value relative to the dollar, or the U.S. dollar had appreciated in value relative to the pound. The returns on the U.K. loans could be far less than 15 percent even in the absence of interest rate or credit risk. For example, suppose the exchange rate had fallen from $1.60/£1 at the beginning of the year to $1.45/£1 at the end of the year when the FI needed to repatriate the principal and interest on the loan. At an exchange rate of $1.45/£1, the pound loan revenues at the end of the year translate into:

$$£71.875 \text{ million} \times \$1.45/£1 = \$104.22 \text{ million}$$

or as a return on the original dollar investment of:

$$\frac{\$104.22 - \$100}{\$100} = .0422 = 4.22\%$$

The weighted return on the FI's asset portfolio would be:

$$(.5)(.09) + (.5)(.0422) = .0661 \text{ or } 6.61\%$$

In this case, the FI actually has a loss or has a negative interest margin (6.61% − 8% = −1.39%) on its balance sheet investments.

The reason for the loss is that the depreciation of the pound from $1.60 to $1.45 has offset the attractive high yield on British pound loans relative to domestic U.S. loans. If the pound had instead appreciated (risen in value) against the dollar over the year—say, to $1.70/£1—then the U.S. FI would have generated a dollar return from its U.K. loans of:

$$£71.875 \times \$1.70 = \$122.188 \text{ million}$$

or a percentage return of 22.188 percent. Then the U.S. FI would receive a double benefit from investing in the United Kingdom: a high yield on the domestic British loans plus an appreciation in pounds over the one-year investment period.

Risk and Hedging

Since a manager cannot know in advance what the pound/dollar spot exchange rate will be at the end of the

year, a portfolio imbalance or investment strategy in which the FI is *net long* $100 million in pounds (or £62.5 million) is risky. As we discussed, the British loans would generate a return of 22.188 percent if the pound appreciated from $1.60/£1 to $1.70/£1, but would produce a return of only 4.22 percent if the pound depreciated in value against the dollar to $1.45/£1.

In principle, an FI manager can better control the scale of its FX exposure in two major ways: on-balance-sheet hedging and off-balance-sheet hedging. On-balance-sheet hedging involves making changes in the on-balance-sheet assets and liabilities to protect FI profits from FX risk. Off-balance-sheet hedging involves no on-balance-sheet changes, but rather involves taking a position in forward or other derivative securities to hedge FX risk.

On-Balance-Sheet Hedging

The following example illustrates how an FI manager can control FX exposure by making changes on the balance sheet.

Example 15.2

Hedging on the Balance Sheet

Suppose that instead of funding the $100 million investment in 15 percent British loans with U.S. CDs, the FI manager funds the British loans with $100 million equivalent one-year pound CDs at a rate of 11 percent [as illustrated in panel (b) of Figure 15-2]. Now the balance sheet of the bank would look like this:

Assets	Liabilities
$100 million U.S. loans (9%)	$100 million U.S. CDs (8%)
$100 million U.K. loans (15%) (loans made in pounds)	$100 million U.K. CDs (11%) (deposits raised in pounds)

In this situation, the FI has both a matched maturity and currency foreign asset–liability book. We might now consider the FI's profitability or spread between the return on assets and the cost of funds under two scenarios: first, when the pound depreciates in value against the dollar over the year from $1.60/£1 to $1.45/£1 and second, when the pound appreciates in value over the year from $1.60/£1 to $1.70/£1.

The Depreciating Pound

When the pound falls in value to $1.45/£1, the return on the British loan portfolio is 4.22 percent. Consider now what happens to the cost of $100 million in pound liabilities in dollar terms:

1. At the beginning of the year, the FI borrows $100 million equivalent in pound CDs for one year at a promised interest rate of 11 percent. At an exchange rate of $1.60£, this is a pound equivalent amount of borrowing of $100 million/1.6 = £62.5 million.

2. At the end of the year, the bank has to pay back the pound CD holders their principal and interest, £62.5 million(1.11) = £69.375 million.

3. If the pound had depreciated to $1.45/£1 over the year, the repayment in dollar terms would be £69.375 million × $1.45/£1 = $100.59 million, or a dollar cost of funds of 0.59 percent.

Thus, at the end of the year the following occurs:

Average return on assets:

$$(0.5)(0.09) + (0.5)(0.0422) = .0661 = 6.61\%$$

U.S. asset return + U.K. asset return = Overall return

Average cost of funds:

$$(0.5)(.08) + (0.5)(.0059) = .04295 = 4.295\%$$

U.S. cost of funds + U.K. cost of funds = Overall cost

Net return:

Average return on assets − Average cost of funds

$$6.61\% - 4.295\% = 2.315\%$$

The Appreciating Pound

When the pound appreciates over the year from $1.60/£1 to $1.70/£1, the return on British loans is equal to 22.188. Now consider the dollar cost of British one-year CDs at the end of the year when the U.S. FI has to pay the principal and interest to the CD holder:

$$£69.375 \text{ million} \times \$1.70/£1 = \$117.9375 \text{ million}$$

or a dollar cost of funds of 17.9375 percent. Thus, at the end of the year:

Average return on assets:

$$(0.5)(.09) + (0.5)(.22188) = .15594 \text{ or } 15.594\%$$

Average cost of funds:

$$(0.5)(.08) + (0.5)(.179375) = .12969 \text{ or } 12.969\%$$

Net return:

$$15.594 - 12.969 = 2.625\%$$

Note that even though the FI locked in a positive return when setting the net foreign exchange exposure on the balance sheet to zero, net return is still volatile. Thus, the FI is still exposed to foreign exchange risk. However, by directly matching its foreign asset and liability book, an FI can lock in a positive return or profit spread whichever direction exchange rates change over the investment period. For example, even if domestic U.S. banking is a relatively low profit activity (i.e., there is a low spread between the return on assets and the cost of funds), the FI could be quite profitable overall. Specifically, it could lock in a large positive spread—if it exists—between deposit rates and loan rates in foreign markets. In our example, a 4 percent positive spread existed between British one-year loan rates and deposit rates compared with only a 1 percent spread domestically.

Note that for such imbalances in domestic spreads and foreign spreads to continue over long periods of time, financial service firms would have to face significant barriers to entry in foreign markets. Specifically, if real and financial capital is free to move, FIs would increasingly withdraw from the U.S. market and reorient their operations toward the United Kingdom. Reduced competition would widen loan deposit interest spreads in the United States, and increased competition would contract U.K. spreads, until the profit opportunities from foreign activities disappears.[8]

---

[8] In the background of the previous example was the implicit assumption that the FI was also matching the durations of its foreign assets and liabilities. In our example, it was issuing one-year duration pound CDs to fund one-year duration pound loans. Suppose instead that it still had a matched book in size ($100 million) but funded the one-year 15 percent British loans with three-month 11 percent pound CDs.

$$D_{£A} - D_{£L} = 1 - .25 = .75 \text{ year}$$

Thus, pound assets have a longer duration than do pound liabilities.

If British interest rates were to change over the year, the market value of pound assets would change by more than the market value of pound liabilities. More importantly, the FI would no longer be locking in a fixed return by matching in the size of its foreign currency book since it would have to take into account its potential exposure to capital gains and losses on its pound assets and liabilities due to shocks to British interest rates. In essence, an FI is hedged against both foreign exchange rate risk and foreign interest rate risk only if it matches both the size and the durations of its foreign assets and liabilities in a specific currency.

Hedging with Forwards

Instead of matching its $100 million foreign asset position with $100 million of foreign liabilities, the FI might have chosen to remain unhedged on the balance sheet.[9] As a lower-cost alternative, it could hedge by taking a position in the forward market for foreign currencies—for example, the one-year forward market for selling pounds for dollars. However, here we introduce them to show how they can insulate the FX risk of the FI in our example. Any forward position taken would not appear on the balance sheet. It would appear as a contingent off-balance-sheet claim, which we described as an item below the bottom line. The role of the forward FX contract is to offset the uncertainty regarding the future spot rate on pounds at the end of the one-year investment horizon. Instead of waiting until the end of the year to transfer pounds back into dollars at an unknown spot rate, the FI can enter into a contract to sell forward its *expected* principal and interest earnings on the loan, at today's known **forward exchange rate** for dollars/pounds, with delivery of pound funds to the buyer of the forward contract taking place at the end of the year. Essentially, by selling the expected proceeds on the pound loan forward, at a known (forward FX) exchange rate today, the FI removes the future spot exchange rate uncertainty and thus the uncertainty relating to investment returns on the British loan.

Example 15.3

Hedging with Forwards

Consider the following transactional steps when the FI hedges its FX risk immediately by selling its expected one-year pound loan proceeds in the forward FX market [illustrated in panel (c) of Figure 15-2].

1. The U.S. FI sells $100 million for pounds at the *spot* exchange rate *today* and receives $100 million/1.6 = £62.5 million.

2. The FI then immediately lends the £62.5 million to a British customer at 15 percent for one year.

3. The FI also sells the expected principal and interest proceeds from the pound loan forward for dollars at today's forward rate for one-year delivery. Let the current forward one-year exchange rate between dollars

---

[9] An FI could also hedge its on-balance-sheet FX risk by taking off-balance-sheet positions in futures, swaps, and options on foreign currencies.

and pounds stand at $1.55/£1, or at a 5 cent discount to the spot pound; as a percentage discount:

$$(\$1.55 - \$1.60)/\$1.6 = -3.125\%$$

This means that the forward buyer of pounds promises to pay:

$$£62.5 \text{ million } (1.15) \times \$1.55/£ = £71.875 \text{ million}$$
$$\times \$1.55/£1 = \$111.406 \text{ million}$$

to the FI (the forward seller) in one year when the FI delivers the £71.875 million proceeds of the loan to the forward buyer.

4. In one year, the British borrower repays the loan to the FI plus interest in pounds (£71.875 million).

5. The FI delivers the £71.875 million to the buyer of the one-year forward contract and receives the promised $111.406 million.

Barring the pound borrower's default on the loan or the forward buyer's reneging on the forward contract, the FI knows from the very beginning of the investment period that it has locked in a guaranteed return on the British loan of:

$$\frac{\$111.406 - \$100}{\$100} = .11406 = 11.406\%$$

Specifically, this return is fully hedged against any dollar/pound exchange rate changes over the one-year holding period of the loan investment. Given this return on British loans, *the overall expected return* on the FI's asset portfolio is:

$$(.5)(.09) + (.5)(.11406) = .10203 \text{ or } 10.203\%$$

Since the cost of funds for the FI's $200 million U.S. CDs is an assumed 8 percent, it has been able to lock in a risk-free return spread over the year of 2.203 percent regardless of spot exchange rate fluctuations between the initial foreign (loan) investment and repatriation of the foreign loan proceeds one year later.

In the preceding example, it is profitable for the FI to increasingly drop domestic U.S. loans and invest in hedged foreign U.K. loans, since the hedged dollar return on foreign loans of 11.406 percent is so much higher than 9 percent domestic loans. As the FI seeks to invest more in British loans, it needs to buy more spot pounds. This drives up the spot price of pounds in dollar terms to more than $1.60/£1. In addition, the FI would need to sell more pounds forward (the proceeds of these pound loans) for dollars, driving the forward rate to below $1.55/£1. The outcome would widen the dollar forward–spot exchange rate spread on pounds, making forward hedged pounds investments less attractive than before. This process would continue until the U.S. cost of FI funds just equals the forward hedged return on British loans. That is, the FI could make no further profits by borrowing in U.S. dollars and making forward contract–hedged investments in U.K. loans (see also the discussion below on the interest rate parity theorem).

Multicurrency Foreign Asset–Liability Positions

So far, we have used a one-currency example of a matched or mismatched foreign asset–liability portfolio. Many FIs, including banks, mutual funds, and pension funds, hold multicurrency asset–liability positions. As for multicurrency trading portfolios, diversification across many asset and liability markets can potentially reduce the risk of portfolio returns and the cost of funds. To the extent that domestic and foreign interest rates or stock returns for equities do not move closely together over time, potential gains from asset–liability portfolio diversification can offset the risk of mismatching individual currency asset–liability positions.

Theoretically speaking, the one-period nominal interest rate (r_i) on fixed-income securities in any particular country has two major components. First, the **real interest rate** reflects underlying real sector demand and supply for funds in that currency. Second, the *expected inflation rate* reflects an extra amount of interest lenders demand from borrowers to compensate the lenders for the erosion in the principal (or real) value of the funds they lend due to inflation in goods prices expected over the period of the loan. Formally:[10]

$$r_i = rr_i + i_i^e$$

where

r_i = Nominal interest rate in country i

rr_i = Real interest rate in country i

i_i^e = Expected one-period inflation rate in country i

If real savings and investment demand and supply pressures, as well as inflationary expectations, are closely linked or economic integration across countries exists, we expect to find that nominal interest rates are highly correlated across financial markets. For example, if, as the result of a strong demand for investment funds, German real interest rates rise, there may be a capital outflow from other countries toward Germany. This may lead to rising real and nominal interest rates in other countries as policymakers and borrowers try to mitigate the size of their capital outflows. On the other hand, if the world capital market is not very well integrated, quite significant nominal and real interest deviations may exist before equilibrating international flows of funds materialize. Foreign asset or liability returns are likely to be relatively weakly correlated and significant diversification opportunities exist.

Table 15-5 lists the correlations among the returns in major equity and bond markets in the 2000s. Looking at correlations between foreign bond market returns and U.S. bond market returns, you can see that the correlations across bond markets vary from a high of .452 between Canada and the United States to a low of .068 between Canada and Germany. Further, these correlations are all positive.[11]

Concept Questions

1. The cost of one-year U.S. dollar CDs is 8 percent, one-year U.S. dollar loans yield 10 percent, and U.K. pound loans yield 15 percent. The dollar/pound spot exchange rate is $1.50/£1, and the one-year forward exchange rate is $1.48/£1. Are one-year U.S. dollar loans more or less attractive than U.K. pound loans?

2. What are two ways an FI manager can control FX exposure?

INTERACTION OF INTEREST RATES, INFLATION, AND EXCHANGE RATES

As global financial markets have become increasingly interlinked, so have interest rates, inflation, and foreign exchange rates. For example, higher domestic interest rates may attract foreign financial investment and impact

---

[10] This equation is often called the *Fisher equation* after the economist who first publicized this hypothesized relationship among nominal rates, real rates, and expected inflation. As shown, we ignore the small cross-product term between the real rate and the expected inflation rate.

[11] From the Fisher relationship, high correlations may be due to high correlations of real interest rates over time and/or inflation expectations.

TABLE 15-5 Correlations of Returns on Equity and Bonds in Local Currencies

	United States	United Kingdom	Germany	Canada
Equity Markets				
United States	1.000	.495	.432	.692
United Kingdom	.495	1.000	.562	.463
Germany	.432	.562	1.000	.399
Canada	.692	.463	.399	1.000
Bond Markets				
United States	1.000	.249	.221	.452
United Kingdom	.249	1.000	.656	.167
Germany	.221	.656	1.000	.068
Canada	.452	.167	.068	1.000

Source: L. Cappiello, R. F. Engle, and K. Sheppard, "Asymmetric Dynamics in the Correlations of Global Equity and Bond Returns," *Journal of Financial Econometrics*, Fall 2006.

the value of the domestic currency. In this section, we look at the effect that inflation in one country has on its foreign currency exchange rates—purchasing power parity (PPP). We also examine the links between domestic and foreign interest rates and spot and forward foreign exchange rates—interest rate parity (IRP).

Purchasing Power Parity

One factor affecting a country's foreign currency exchange rate with another country is the relative inflation rate in each country (which, as shown below, is directly related to the relative interest rates in these countries). Specifically:

$$r_{US} = i_{US} + rr_{US}$$

and

$$r_S = i_S + rr_S$$

where

r_{US} = Interest rate in the United States

r_S = Interest rate in Switzerland (or another foreign country)

i_{US} = Inflation rate in the United States

i_S = Inflation rate in Switzerland (or another foreign country)

rr_{US} = Real rate of interest in the United States

rr_S = Real rate of interest in Switzerland (or another foreign country)

Assuming real rates of interest (or rates of time preference) are equal across countries:

$$rr_{US} = rr_S$$

Then

$$r_{US} - r_S = i_{US} - i_S$$

The (nominal) interest rate spread between the United States and Switzerland reflects the difference in inflation rates between the two countries.

As relative inflation rates (and interest rates) change, foreign currency exchange rates that are not constrained by government regulation should also adjust to account for relative differences in the price levels (inflation rates) between the two countries. One theory that explains how this adjustment takes place is the theory of **purchasing power parity (PPP).** According to PPP, foreign currency exchange rates between two countries adjust to reflect changes in each country's price levels (or inflation rates and, implicitly, interest rates) as consumers and importers switch their demands for goods from relatively high inflation (interest) rate countries to low inflation (interest) rate countries. Specifically, the PPP theorem states that the change in the exchange rate between two countries' currencies is proportional to the difference in the inflation rates in the two countries. That is:

$$i_{Domestic} - i_{Foreign} = \Delta S_{Domestic/Foreign} / S_{Domestic/Foreign}$$

where

$S_{Domestic/Foreign}$ = Spot exchange rate of the domestic currency (e.g., U.S. dollars for Swiss Francs)

$\Delta S_{Domestic/Foreign}$ = Change in the one-period foreign exchange rate

Thus, according to PPP, the most important factor determining exchange rates is the fact that in open economies, differences in prices (and, by implication, price level changes with inflation) drive trade flows and thus demand for and supplies of currencies.

Example 15.4

Application of Purchasing Power Parity

Suppose that the current spot exchange rate of U.S. dollars for Russian rubles, $S_{US/R}$, is .17 (i.e., 0.17 dollar, or 17 cents, can be received for 1 ruble). The price of Russian-produced goods increases by 10 percent (i.e., inflation in Russia, i_R, is 10 percent), and the U.S. price index increases by 4 percent (i.e., inflation in the United States, i_{us}, is 4 percent). According to PPP, the 10 percent rise in the price of Russian goods relative to the 4 percent rise in the price of U.S. goods results in a depreciation of the Russian ruble (by 6 percent). Specifically, the exchange rate of Russian rubles to U.S. dollars should fall, so that:[12]

U.S. inflation rate – Russian inflation rate

$$= \frac{\text{Change in spot exchange rate of U.S. dollars for Russian rubles}}{\text{Initial spot exchange rate of U.S. dollars for Russian rubles}}$$

or

$$i_{us} - i_R = \Delta S_{US/R} / S_{US/R}$$

Plugging in the inflation and exchange rates, we get:

$$.04 - .10 = \Delta S_{US/R} / S_{US/R} = \Delta S_{US/R} / .17$$

or

$$-.06 = \Delta S_{US/R} / .17$$

and

$$\Delta S_{US/R} = -(.06) \times .17 = -.0102$$

Thus, it costs 1.02 cents less to receive a ruble (i.e., 1 ruble costs 15.98 cents: 17 cents – 1.02 cents), or .1598 of $1 can be received for 1 ruble. The Russian ruble depreciates in value by 6 percent against the U.S. dollar as a result of its higher inflation rate.[13]

Interest Rate Parity Theorem

We discussed above that foreign exchange spot market risk can be reduced by entering into forward foreign exchange contracts. In general, spot rates and forward rates for a given currency differ. For example, the spot exchange rate between the British pound and the U.S. dollar was 1.6422 on July 15, 2009, meaning that 1 pound could be exchanged on that day for 1.6422 U.S. dollars. The three-month forward rate between the two currencies, however, was 1.6419 on July 15, 2009. This forward exchange rate is determined by the spot exchange rate and the interest rate differential between the two countries. The specific relationship that links spot exchange rates, interest rates, and forward exchange rates is described as the **interest rate parity theorem** (IRPT). Intuitively, the IRPT implies that by hedging in the forward exchange rate market, an investor realizes the same returns whether investing domestically or in a foreign country. This is a so-called no-arbitrage relationship in the sense that the investor cannot make a risk-free return by taking offsetting positions in the domestic and foreign markets. That is, the hedged dollar return on foreign investments just equals the return on domestic investments. The eventual equality between the cost of domestic funds and the hedged return on foreign assets, or the IRPT, can be expressed as:

$$1 + r_{ust}^D = \frac{1}{S_t} \times [1 + r_{ukt}^L] \times F_t$$

Rate on U.S. investment = Hedged return on foreign (U.K.) investment

---

[12] This is the relative version of the PPP theorem. There are other versions of the theory (such as absolute PPP and the law of one price). However, the version shown here is the one most commonly used.

[13] A 6 percent fall in the ruble's value translates into a new exchange rate of .1598 dollars per ruble if the original exchange rate between dollars and rubles was .17.

where

$1 + r^D_{ust}$ = 1 plus the interest rate on U.S. CDs for the FI at time t

S_t = \$/£ spot exchange rate at time t

$1 + r^L_{ukt}$ = 1 plus the interest rate on U.K. CDs at time t

F_t = \$/£ forward exchange at time t

Example 15.5

An Application of Interest Rate Parity Theorem

Suppose r^D_{ust} = 8 percent and r^L_{ukt} = 11 percent, as in our preceding example. As the FI moves into more British CDs, suppose the spot exchange rate for buying pounds rises from \$1.60/£1 to \$1.63/£1. In equilibrium, the forward exchange rate would have to fall to \$1.5859/£1 to eliminate completely the attractiveness of British investments to the U.S. FI manager. That is:

$$(1.08) = \left(\frac{1}{1.63}\right)[1.11](1.5859)$$

This is a *no-arbitrage* relationship in the sense that the hedged dollar return on foreign investments just equals the FI's dollar cost of domestic CDs. Rearranging, the IRPT can be expressed as:

$$\frac{r^D_{ust} - r^L_{ukt}}{1 + r^L_{ukt}} \simeq \frac{F_t - S_t}{S_t}$$

$$\frac{.08 - .11}{1.11} \simeq \frac{1.5859 - 1.63}{1.63}$$

$$-.0270 \simeq -.0270$$

That is, the discounted spread between domestic and foreign interest rates is approximately equal to ($\simeq$) the percentage spread between forward and spot exchange rates.

Suppose that in the preceding example, the annual rate on U.S. time deposits is 8.1 percent (rather than 8 percent). In this case, it would be profitable for the investor to put excess funds in the U.S. rather than the U.K. deposits. In fact, the arbitrage opportunity that exists results in a flow of funds out of U.K. time deposits into U.S. time deposits. According to the IRPT, this flow of funds would quickly drive up the U.S. dollar–British pound exchange rate until the potential profit opportunities from U.S. deposits are eliminated. The implication of IRPT is that in a competitive market for deposits, loans, and foreign exchange, the potential profit opportunities from overseas investment for the FI manager are likely to be small and fleeting. Long-term violations of IRPT are likely to occur only if there are major imperfections in international deposit, loan, and other financial markets, including barriers to cross-border financial flows.

Concept Questions

1. What is purchasing power parity?
2. What is the interest rate parity condition? How does it relate to the existence or nonexistence of arbitrage opportunities?

SUMMARY

This chapter analyzed the sources of FX risk faced by modern FI managers. Such risks arise through mismatching foreign currency trading and/or foreign asset–liability positions in individual currencies. While such mismatches can be profitable if FX forecasts prove correct, unexpected outcomes and volatility can impose significant losses on an FI. They threaten its profitability and, ultimately, its solvency in a fashion similar to interest rate, off-balance-sheet, and technology risks. This chapter discussed possible ways to mitigate such risks, including direct hedging through matched foreign asset–liability books, hedging through forward contracts, and hedging through foreign asset and liability portfolio diversification.

Pertinent Web Sites

Bank for International Settlements **www.bis.org**

Board of Governors of the Federal Reserve **www.federalreserve.gov**

Citigroup **www.citigroup.com**

Federal Deposit Insurance Corporation **www.fdic.gov**

J.P. Morgan Chase **www.jpmorganchase.com**

U.S. Treasury **www.ustreas.gov**

The Wall Street Journal **www.wsj.com**

Chapter Notation

View Chapter Notation at the Web site to the textbook (**www.mhhe.com/saunders7e**).

Corporate Bonds

16

Learning Objectives

Candidates, after completing this reading, should be able to:

- Describe a bond indenture and explain the role of the corporate trustee in a bond indenture.
- Explain a bond's maturity date and how it impacts bond retirements.
- Describe the main types of interest payment classifications.
- Describe zero-coupon bonds and explain the relationship between original-issue-discount and reinvestment risk.
- Describe the following security types relevant for corporate bonds: mortgage bonds, collateral trust bonds, equipment trust certificates, subordinated and convertible debenture bonds, and guaranteed bonds.

- Describe the mechanisms by which corporate bonds can be retired before maturity.
- Describe and differentiate between credit default risk and credit spread risk.
- Describe event risk and explain what may cause it in corporate bonds.
- Define high-yield bonds and describe types of high-yield bond issuers and some of the payment features unique to high-yield bonds.
- Define and differentiate between an issuer default rate and a dollar default rate.
- Define recovery rates and describe the relationship between recovery rates and seniority.

Excerpt is Chapter 12 of The Handbook of Fixed Income Securities, *Eighth Edition, by Frank J. Fabozzi.*

In its simplest form, a corporate bond is a debt instrument that obligates the issuer to pay a specified percentage of the bond's par value on designated dates (the coupon payments) and to repay the bond's par or principal value at maturity. Failure to pay the interest and/or principal when due (and to meet other of the debt's provisions) in accordance with the instrument's terms constitutes legal default, and court proceedings can be instituted to enforce the contract. Bondholders as creditors have a prior legal claim over common and preferred shareholders as to both the corporation's income and assets for cash flows due them and may have a prior claim over other creditors if liens and mortgages are involved. This legal priority does not insulate bondholders from financial loss. Indeed, bondholders are fully exposed to the firm's prospects as to the ability to generate cash-flow sufficient to pay its obligations.

Corporate bonds usually are issued in denominations of $1,000 and multiples thereof. In common usage, a corporate bond is assumed to have a par value of $1,000 unless otherwise explicitly specified. A security dealer who says that she has five bonds to sell means five bonds each of $1,000 principal amount. If the promised rate of interest (coupon rate) is 6%, the annual amount of interest on each bond is $60, and the semiannual interest is $30.

Although there are technical differences between bonds, notes, and debentures, we will use Wall Street convention and call fixed income debt by the general term—bonds.

THE CORPORATE TRUSTEE

The promises of corporate bond issuers and the rights of investors who buy them are set forth in great detail in contracts generally called indentures. If bondholders were handed the complete indenture, some may have trouble understanding the legalese and have even greater difficulty in determining from time to time if the corporate issuer is keeping all the promises made. Further, it may be practically difficult and expensive for any one bondholder to try to enforce the indenture if those promises are not being kept. These problems are solved in part by bringing in a corporate trustee as a third party to the contract. The indenture is made out to the corporate trustee as a representative of the interests of bondholders; that is, the trustee acts in a fiduciary capacity for investors who own the bond issue.

A corporate trustee is a bank or trust company with a corporate trust department and officers who are experts in performing the functions of a trustee. The corporate trustee must, at the time of issue, authenticate the bonds issued; that is, keep track of all the bonds sold, and make sure that they do not exceed the principal amount authorized by the indenture. It must obtain and address various certifications and requests from issuers, attorneys, and bondholders about compliance with the covenants of the indenture. These covenants are many and technical, and they must be watched during the entire period that a bond issue is outstanding. We will describe some of these covenants in subsequent pages.

It is very important that corporate trustees be competent and financially responsible. To this end, there is a federal statute known as the Trust Indenture Act that generally requires a corporate trustee for corporate bond offerings in the amount of more than $5 million sold in interstate commerce. The indenture must include adequate requirements for performance of the trustee's duties on behalf of bondholders; there must be no conflict between the trustee's interest as a trustee and any other interest it may have, especially if it is also a creditor of the issuer; and there must be provision for reports by the trustee to bondholders. If a corporate issuer has breached an indenture promise, such as not to borrow additional secured debt, or fails to pay interest or principal, the trustee may declare a default and take such action as may be necessary to protect the rights of bondholders.

However, it must be emphasized that the trustee is paid by the debt issuer and can only do what the indenture provides. The indenture may contain a clause stating that the trustee undertakes to perform such duties and only such duties as are specifically set forth in the indenture, and no implied covenants or obligations shall be read into the indenture against the trustee. Trustees often are not required to take actions such as monitoring corporate balance sheets to determine issuer covenant compliance, and in fact, indentures often expressly allow a trustee to rely upon certifications and opinions from the issuer and its attorneys. The trustee is generally not bound to make investigations into the facts surrounding documents delivered to it, but it may do so if it sees fit. Also, the trustee is usually under no obligation to exercise the rights or powers under the indenture at the request of bondholders unless it has been offered reasonable security or indemnity.

The terms of bond issues set forth in bond indentures are always a compromise between the interests of the bond issuer and those of investors who buy bonds. The issuer always wants to pay the lowest possible rate of interest and wants its actions bound as little as possible with legal covenants. Bondholders want the highest possible interest rate, the best security, and a variety of covenants to restrict the issuer in one way or another. As we discuss the provisions of bond indentures, keep this opposition of interests in mind and see how compromises are worked out in practice.

SOME BOND FUNDAMENTALS

Bonds can be classified by a number of characteristics, which we will use for ease of organizing this section.

Bonds Classified by Issuer Type

The five broad categories of corporate bonds sold in the United States based on the type of issuer are public utilities, transportations, industrials, banks and finance companies, and international or Yankee issues. Finer breakdowns are often made by market participants to create homogeneous groupings. For example, public utilities are subdivided into telephone or communications, electric companies, gas distribution and transmission companies, and water companies. The transportation industry can be subdivided into airlines, railroads, and trucking companies. Like public utilities, transportation companies often have various degrees of regulation or control by state and/or federal government agencies. Industrials are a catchall class, but even here, finer degrees of distinction may be needed by analysts. The industrial grouping includes manufacturing and mining concerns, retailers, and service-related companies. Even the Yankee or international borrower sector can be more finely tuned. For example, one might classify the issuers into categories such as supranational borrowers (International Bank for Reconstruction and Development and the European Investment Bank), sovereign issuers (Canada, Australia, and the United Kingdom), and foreign municipalities and agencies.

Corporate Debt Maturity

A bond's maturity is the date on which the issuer's obligation to satisfy the terms of the indenture is fulfilled.

On that date, the principal is repaid with any premium and accrued interest that may be due. However, as we shall see later when discussing debt redemption, the final maturity date as stated in the issue's title may or may not be the date when the contract terminates. Many issues can be retired prior to maturity. The maturity structure of a particular corporation can be accessed using the Bloomberg function DDIS.

Interest Payment Characteristics

The three main interest payment classifications of domestically issued corporate bonds are straight-coupon bonds, zero-coupon bonds, and floating-rate, or variable rate, bonds.

However, before we get into interest-rate characteristics, let us briefly discuss bond types. We refer to the interest rate on a bond as the *coupon*. This is technically wrong because bonds issued today do not have coupons attached. Instead, bonds are represented by a certificate, similar to a stock certificate, with a brief description of the terms printed on both sides. These are called *registered bonds*. The principal amount of the bond is noted on the certificate, and the interest-paying agent or trustee has the responsibility of making payment by check to the registered holder on the due date. Years ago bonds were issued in *bearer* or coupon form, with coupons attached for each interest payment. However, the registered form is considered safer and entails less paperwork. As a matter of fact, the registered bond certificate is on its way out as more and more issues are sold in *book-entry* form. This means that only one master or global certificate is issued. It is held by a central securities depository that issues receipts denoting interests in this global certificate.

Straight-coupon bonds have an interest rate set for the life of the issue, however long or short that may be; they are also called *fixed-rate bonds*. Most fixed-rate bonds in the United States pay interest semiannually and at maturity. For example, consider the 4.75% Notes due 2013 issued by Goldman Sachs Group in July 2003. This bond carries a coupon rate of 4.75% and has a par amount of $1,000. Accordingly, this bond requires payments of $23.75 each January 15 and July 15, including the maturity date of July 15, 2013. On the maturity date, the bond's par amount is also paid. Bonds with annual coupon payments are uncommon in the U.S. capital markets but are the norm in continental Europe.

Interest on corporate bonds is based on a year of 360 days made up of twelve 30-day months. The corporate calendar day-count convention is referred to as 30/360.

Most fixed-rate corporate bonds pay interest in a standard fashion. However, there are some variations of which one should be aware. Most domestic bonds pay interest in U.S. dollars. However, starting in the early 1980s, issues were marketed with principal and interest payable in other currencies, such as the Australian, New Zealand, or Canadian dollar or the British pound. Generally, interest and principal payments are converted from the foreign currency to U.S. dollars by the paying agent unless it is otherwise notified. The bondholders bear any costs associated with the dollar conversion. Foreign currency issues provide investors with another way of diversifying a portfolio, but not without risk. The holder bears the currency, or exchange-rate, risk in addition to all the other risks associated with debt instruments.

There are a few issues of bonds that can participate in the fortunes of the issuer over and above the stated coupon rate. These are called *participating bonds* because they share in the profits of the issuer or the rise in certain assets over and above certain minimum levels. Another type of bond rarely encountered today is the *income bond*. These bonds promise to pay a stipulated interest rate, but the payment is contingent on sufficient earnings and is in accordance with the definition of available income for interest payments contained in the indenture. Repayment of principal is not contingent. Interest may be cumulative or noncumulative. If payments are cumulative, unpaid interest payments must be made up at some future date. If noncumulative, once the interest payment is past, it does not have to be repaid. Failure to pay interest on income bonds is not an act of default and is not a cause for bankruptcy. Income bonds have been issued by some financially troubled corporations emerging from reorganization proceedings.

Zero-coupon bonds are, just as the name implies, bonds without coupons or an interest rate. Essentially, zero-coupon bonds pay only the principal portion at some future date. These bonds are issued at discounts to par; the difference constitutes the return to the bondholder. The difference between the face amount and the offering price when first issued is called the *original-issue discount* (OID). The rate of return depends on the amount of the discount and the period over which it accretes to par. For

example, consider a zero-coupon bond issued by Xerox that matures September 30, 2023 and is priced at 55.835 as of mid-May 2011. In addition, this bond is putable starting on September 30, 2011 at 41.77. These embedded option features will be discussed in more detail shortly.

Zeros were first publicly issued in the corporate market in the spring of 1981 and were an immediate hit with investors. The rapture lasted only a couple of years because of changes in the income tax laws that made ownership more costly on an after-tax basis. Also, these changes reduced the tax advantages to issuers. However, tax-deferred investors, such as pension funds, could still take advantage of zero-coupon issues. One important risk is eliminated in a zero-coupon investment—the reinvestment risk. Because there is no coupon to reinvest, there isn't any reinvestment risk. Of course, although this is beneficial in declining-interest-rate markets, the reverse is true when interest rates are rising. The investor will not be able to reinvest an income stream at rising reinvestment rates. Investors tend to find zeros less attractive in lower-interest-rate markets because compounding is not as meaningful as when rates are higher. Also, the lower the rates are, the more likely it is that they will rise again, making a zero-coupon investment worth less in the eyes of potential holders.

In bankruptcy, a zero-coupon bond creditor can claim the original offering price plus the accretion that represents accrued and unpaid interest to the date of the bankruptcy filing, but not the principal amount of $1,000. Zero-coupon bonds have been sold at deep discounts, and the liability of the issuer at maturity may be substantial. The accretion of the discount on the corporation's books is not put away in a special fund for debt retirement purposes. There are no sinking funds on most of these issues. One hopes that corporate managers invest the proceeds properly and run the corporation for the benefit of all investors so that there will not be a cash crisis at maturity. The potentially large balloon repayment creates a cause for concern among investors. Thus it is most important to invest in higher-quality issues so as to reduce the risk of a potential problem. If one wants to speculate in lower-rated bonds, then that investment should throw off some cash return.

Finally, a variation of the zero-coupon bond is the *deferred-interest bond* (DIB), also known as a *zero-coupon bond*. These bonds generally have been subordinated issues of speculative-grade issuers, also known as *junk issuers*. Most of the issues are structured so that they do not pay cash interest for the first five years. At the end of the deferred-interest period, cash interest accrues and is paid semiannually until maturity, unless the bonds are redeemed earlier. The deferred-interest feature allows newly restructured, highly leveraged companies and others with less-than-satisfactory cash flows to defer the payment of cash interest over the early life of the bond. Barring anything untoward, when cash interest payments start, the company will be able to service the debt. If it has made excellent progress in restoring its financial health, the company may be able to redeem or refinance the debt rather than have high interest outlays.

An offshoot of the deferred-interest bond is the pay-in-kind (PIK) debenture. With PIKs, cash interest payments are deferred at the issuer's option until some future date. Instead of just accreting the original-issue discount as with DIBs or zeros, the issuer pays out the interest in additional pieces of the same security. The option to pay cash or in-kind interest payments rests with the issuer, but in many cases the issuer has little choice because provisions of other debt instruments often prohibit cash interest payments until certain indenture or loan tests are satisfied. The holder just gets more pieces of paper, but these at least can be sold in the market without giving up one's original investment; PIKs, DIBs, and zeros do not have provisions for the resale of the interest portion of the instrument. An investment in this type of bond, because it is issued by speculative grade companies, requires careful analysis of the issuer's cash-flow prospects and ability to survive.

SECURITY FOR BONDS

Investors who buy corporate bonds prefer some kind of security underlying the issue. Either real property (using a mortgage) or personal property may be pledged to offer security beyond that of the general credit standing of the issuer. In fact, the kind of security or the absence of a specific pledge of security is usually indicated by the title of a bond issue. However, the best security is a strong general credit that can repay the debt from earnings.

Mortgage Bond

A mortgage bond grants the bondholders a first-mortgage lien on substantially all its properties. This lien provides additional security for the bondholder. As a result, the

issuer is able to borrow at a lower rate of interest than if the debt were unsecured. A debenture issue (i.e., unsecured debt) of the same issuer almost surely would carry a higher coupon rate, other things equal. A *lien* is a legal right to sell mortgaged property to satisfy unpaid obligations to bondholders. In practice, foreclosure of a mortgage and sale of mortgaged property are unusual. If a default occurs, there is usually a financial reorganization on the part of the issuer, in which provision is made for settlement of the debt to bondholders. The mortgage lien is important, though, because it gives the mortgage bondholders a very strong bargaining position relative to other creditors in determining the terms of a reorganization.

Often first-mortgage bonds are issued in series with bonds of each series secured equally by the same first mortgage. Many companies, particularly public utilities, have a policy of financing part of their capital requirements continuously by long-term debt. They want some part of their total capitalization in the form of bonds because the cost of such capital is ordinarily less than that of capital raised by sale of stock. Thus, as a principal amount of debt is paid off, they issue another series of bonds under the same mortgage. As they expand and need a greater amount of debt capital, they can add new series of bonds. It is a lot easier and more advantageous to issue a series of bonds under one mortgage and one indenture than it is to create entirely new bond issues with different arrangements for security. This arrangement is called a *blanket mortgage*. When property is sold or released from the lien of the mortgage, additional property or cash may be substituted or bonds may be retired in order to provide adequate security for the debtholders.

When a bond indenture authorizes the issue of additional series of bonds with the same mortgage lien as those already issued, the indenture imposes certain conditions that must be met before an additional series may be issued. Bondholders do not want their security impaired; these conditions are for their benefit. It is common for a first-mortgage bond indenture to specify that property acquired by the issuer subsequent to the granting of the first-mortgage lien shall be subject to the first-mortgage lien. This is termed the *after-acquired clause*. Then the indenture usually permits the issue of additional bonds up to some specified percentage of the value of the after-acquired property, such as 60%. The other 40%, or whatever the percentage may be, must be financed in some other way. This is intended to ensure that there will be additional assets with a value significantly greater than the amount of additional bonds secured by the mortgage. Another customary kind of restriction on the issue of additional series is a requirement that earnings in an immediately preceding period must be equal to some number of times the amount of annual interest on all outstanding mortgage bonds including the new or proposed series (1.5, 2, or some other number). For this purpose, *earnings* usually are defined as earnings before income tax. Still another common provision is that additional bonds may be issued to the extent that earlier series of bonds have been paid off.

One seldom sees a bond issue with the term *second mortgage* in its title. The reason is that this term has a connotation of weakness. Sometimes companies get around that difficulty by using such words as *first and consolidated*, *first and refunding*, or *general and refunding mortgage bonds*. Usually this language means that a bond issue is secured by a first mortgage on some part of the issuer's property but by a second or even third lien on other parts of its assets. A general and refunding mortgage bond is generally secured by a lien on all the company's property *subject* to the prior lien of first-mortgage bonds, if any are still outstanding.

Collateral Trust Bonds

Some companies do not own fixed assets or other real property and so have nothing on which they can give a mortgage lien to secure bondholders. Instead, they own securities of other companies; they are *holding companies*, and the other companies are *subsidiaries*. To satisfy the desire of bondholders for security, they pledge stocks, notes, bonds, or whatever other kinds of obligations they own. These assets are termed *collateral* (or personal property), and bonds secured by such assets are *collateral trust bonds*. Some companies own both real property and securities. They may use real property to secure mortgage bonds and use securities for collateral trust bonds. As an example, consider the 10.375% Collateral Trust Bonds due 2018 issued by National Rural Utilities. According to the bond's prospectus, the securities deposited with the trustee include mortgage notes, cash, and other permitted investments.

The legal arrangement for collateral trust bonds is much the same as that for mortgage bonds. The issuer delivers to a corporate trustee under a bond indenture the securities pledged, and the trustee holds them for the benefit of the bondholders. When voting common stocks are included in the collateral, the indenture permits the issuer to vote the stocks so long as there is no default on its bonds. This is important to issuers of such bonds because usually the stocks are those of subsidiaries, and the issuer depends on the exercise of voting rights to control the subsidiaries.

Indentures usually provide that, in event of default, the rights to vote stocks included in the collateral are transferred to the trustee. Loss of the voting right would be a serious disadvantage to the issuer because it would mean loss of control of subsidiaries. The trustee also may sell the securities pledged for whatever prices they will bring in the market and apply the proceeds to payment of the claims of collateral trust bondholders. These rather drastic actions, however, usually are not taken immediately on an event of default. The corporate trustee's primary responsibility is to act in the best interests of bondholders, and their interests may be served for a time at least by giving the defaulting issuer a proxy to vote stocks held as collateral and thus preserve the holding company structure. It also may defer the sale of collateral when it seems likely that bondholders would fare better in a financial reorganization than they would by sale of collateral.

Collateral trust indentures contain a number of provisions designed to protect bondholders. Generally, the market or appraised value of the collateral must be maintained at some percentage of the amount of bonds outstanding. The percentage is greater than 100 so that there will be a margin of safety. If collateral value declines below the minimum percentage, additional collateral must be provided by the issuer. There is almost always provision for withdrawal of some collateral, provided other acceptable collateral is substituted.

Collateral trust bonds may be issued in series in much the same way that mortgage bonds are issued in series. The rules governing additional series of bonds require that adequate collateral must be pledged, and there may be restrictions on the use to which the proceeds of an additional series may be put. All series of bonds are issued under the same indenture and have the same claim on collateral.

Since 2005, an increasing percentage of high yield bond issues have been secured by some mix of mortgages and other collateral on a first, second, or even third lien basis. These secured high yield bonds have very customized provisions for issuing additional secured debt and there is some debate about whether the purported collateral for these kinds of bonds will provide greater recoveries in bankruptcy than traditional unsecured capital structures over an economic cycle.

Equipment Trust Certificates

The desire of borrowers to pay the lowest possible rate of interest on their obligations generally leads them to offer their best security and to grant lenders the strongest claim on it. Many years ago, the railway companies developed a way of financing purchase of cars and locomotives, called *rolling stock*, that enabled them to borrow at just about the lowest rates in the corporate bond market.

Railway rolling stock has for a long time been regarded by investors as excellent security for debt. This equipment is sufficiently standardized that it can be used by one railway as well as another. And it can be readily moved from the tracks of one railroad to those of another. There is generally a good market for lease or sale of cars and locomotives. The railroads have capitalized on these characteristics of rolling stock by developing a legal arrangement for giving investors a legal claim on it that is different from, and generally better than, a mortgage lien.

The legal arrangement is one that vests legal title to railway equipment in a trustee, which is better from the standpoint of investors than a first-mortgage lien on property. A railway company orders some cars and locomotives from a manufacturer. When the job is finished, the manufacturer transfers the legal title to the equipment to a trustee. The trustee leases it to the railroad that ordered it and at the same time sells *equipment trust certificates* (ETCs) in an amount equal to a large percentage of the purchase price, normally 80%. Money from the sale of certificates is paid to the manufacturer. The railway company makes an initial payment of rent equal to the balance of the purchase price, and the trustee gives that money to the manufacturer. Thus the manufacturer is paid off. The trustee collects lease rental money periodically from the railroad and uses it to pay interest and principal on the certificates. These interest payments are known as dividends. The amounts of lease rental payments are worked out carefully so that they are enough to pay the equipment trust certificates. At the end of some period of time,

such as 15 years, the certificates are paid off, the trustee sells the equipment to the railroad for some nominal price, and the lease is terminated.

Railroad ETCs usually are structured in serial form; that is, a certain amount becomes payable at specified dates until the final installment. For example, a $60 million ETC might mature $4 million on each June 15 from 2000 through 2014. Each of the 15 maturities may be priced separately to reflect the shape of the yield curve, investor preference for specific maturities, and supply-and-demand considerations. The advantage of a serial issue from the investor's point of view is that the repayment schedule matches the decline in the value of the equipment used as collateral. Hence principal repayment risk is reduced. From the issuer's side, serial maturities allow for the repayment of the debt periodically over the life of the issue, making less likely a crisis at maturity due to a large repayment coming due at one time.

The beauty of this arrangement from the viewpoint of investors is that the railroad does not legally own the rolling stock until all the certificates are paid. In case the railroad does not make the lease rental payments, there is no big legal hassle about foreclosing a lien. The trustee owns the property and can take it back because failure to pay the rent breaks the lease. The trustee can lease the equipment to another railroad and continue to make payments on the certificates from new lease rentals.

This description emphasizes the legal nature of the arrangement for securing the certificates. In practice, these certificates are regarded as obligations of the railway company that leased the equipment and are shown as liabilities on its balance sheet. In fact, the name of the railway appears in the title of the certificates. In the ordinary course of events, the trustee is just an intermediary who performs the function of holding title, acting as lessor, and collecting the money to pay the certificates. It is significant that even in the worst years of a depression, railways have paid their equipment trust certificates, although they did not pay bonds secured by mortgages. Although railroads have issued the largest amount of equipment trust certificates, airlines also have used this form of financing.

Debenture Bonds

While bondholders prefer to have security underlying their bonds, all else equal, most bonds issued are unsecured. These unsecured bonds are called *debentures*. With the exception of the utilities and structured products, nearly all other corporate bonds issued are unsecured.

Debentures are not secured by a specific pledge of designated property, but this does not mean that they have no claim on the property of issuers or on their earnings. Debenture bondholders have the claim of general creditors on all assets of the issuer not pledged specifically to secure other debt. And they even have a claim on pledged assets to the extent that these assets have value greater than necessary to satisfy secured creditors. In fact, if there are no pledged assets and no secured creditors, debenture bondholders have first claim on all assets along with other general creditors.

These unsecured bonds are sometimes issued by companies that are so strong financially and have such a high credit rating that to offer security would be superfluous. Such companies simply can turn a deaf ear to investors who want security and still sell their debentures at relatively low interest rates. But debentures sometimes are issued by companies that have already sold mortgage bonds and given liens on most of their property. These debentures rank below the mortgage bonds or collateral trust bonds in their claim on assets, and investors may regard them as relatively weak. This is the kind that bears the higher rates of interest.

Even though there is no pledge of security, the indentures for debenture bonds may contain a variety of provisions designed to afford some protection to investors. Sometimes the amount of a debenture bond issue is limited to the amount of the initial issue. This limit is to keep issuers from weakening the position of debenture holders by running up additional unsecured debt. Sometimes additional debentures may be issued a specified number of times in a recent accounting period, provided that the issuer has earned its bond interest on all existing debt plus the additional issue.

If a company has no secured debt, it is customary to provide that debentures will be secured equally with any secured bonds that may be issued in the future. This is known as the *negative-pledge clause*. Some provisions of debenture bond issues are intended to protect bondholders against other issuer actions when they might be too harmful to the creditworthiness of the issuer. For example, some provisions of debenture bond issues may require maintaining some level of net worth, restrict selling major assets, or limit paying dividends in some cases. However, the trend in recent years, at least with investment-grade companies, is away from indenture restrictions.

Subordinated and Convertible Debentures

Many corporations issue *subordinated debenture bonds*. The term *subordinated* means that such an issue ranks after secured debt, after debenture bonds, and often after some general creditors in its claim on assets and earnings. Owners of this kind of bond stand last in line among creditors when an issuer fails financially.

Because subordinated debentures are weaker in their claim on assets, issuers would have to offer a higher rate of interest unless they also offer some special inducement to buy the bonds. The inducement can be an option to convert bonds into stock of the issuer at the discretion of bondholders. If the issuer prospers and the market price of its stock rises substantially in the market, the bondholders can convert bonds to stock worth a great deal more than what they paid for the bonds. This conversion privilege also may be included in the provisions of debentures that are not subordinated.

The bonds may be convertible into the common stock of a corporation other than that of the issuer. Such issues are called *exchangeable bonds*. There are also issues indexed to a commodity's price or its cash equivalent at the time of maturity or redemption.

Guaranteed Bonds

Sometimes a corporation may guarantee the bonds of another corporation. Such bonds are referred to as *guaranteed bonds*. The guarantee, however, does not mean that these obligations are free of default risk. The safety of a guaranteed bond depends on the financial capability of the guarantor to satisfy the terms of the guarantee, as well as the financial capability of the issuer. The terms of the guarantee may call for the guarantor to guarantee the payment of interest and/or repayment of the principal. A guaranteed bond may have more than one corporate guarantor. Each guarantor may be responsible for not only its pro rata share but also the entire amount guaranteed by the other guarantors.

ALTERNATIVE MECHANISMS TO RETIRE DEBT BEFORE MATURITY

We can partition the alternative mechanisms to retire debt into two broad categories—namely, those mechanisms that must be included in the bond's indenture in order to be used and those mechanisms that can be used without being included in the bond's indenture. Among those debt retirement mechanisms included in a bond's indenture are the following: call and refunding provisions, sinking funds, maintenance and replacement funds, and redemption through sale of assets. Alternatively, some debt retirement mechanisms are not required to be included in the bond indenture (e.g., fixed-spread tender offers).

Call and Refunding Provisions

Many corporate bonds contain an embedded option that gives the issuer the right to buy the bonds back at a fixed price either in whole or in part prior to maturity. The feature is known as a *call provision*. The ability to retire debt before its scheduled maturity date is a valuable option for which bondholders will demand compensation ex-ante. All else equal, bondholders will pay a lower price for a callable bond than an otherwise identical option-free (i.e., straight) bond. The difference between the price of an option-free bond and the callable bond is the value of the embedded call option.

Conventional wisdom suggests that the most compelling reason for corporations to retire their debt prior to maturity is to take advantage of declining borrowing rates. If they are able to do so, firms will substitute new, lower-cost debt for older, higher-cost issues. However, firms retire their debt for other reasons as well. For example, firms retire their debt to eliminate restrictive covenants, to alter their capital structure, to increase shareholder value, or to improve financial/managerial flexibility. There are two types of call provisions included in corporate bonds—a fixed-price call and a make-whole call. We will discuss each in turn.

Fixed-Price Call Provision

With a standard fixed-price call provision, the bond issuer has the option to buy back some or all of the bond issue prior to maturity at a fixed price. The fixed price is termed the *call price*. Normally, the bond's indenture contains a call-price schedule that specifies when the bonds can be called and at what prices. The call prices generally start at a substantial premium over par and decline toward par over time such that in the final years of a bond's life, the call price is usually par.

In some corporate issues, bondholders are afforded some protection against a call in the early years of a bond's life. This protection usually takes one of two forms. First, some callable bonds possess a feature that prohibits a bond call for a certain number of years. Second, some callable bonds prohibit the bond from being refunded for a certain number of years. Such a bond is said to be *nonrefundable*. Prohibition of refunding precludes the redemption of a bond issue if the funds used to repurchase the bonds come from new bonds being issued with a lower coupon than the bonds being redeemed. However, a refunding prohibition does not prevent the redemption of bonds from funds obtained from other sources (e.g., asset sales, the issuance of equity, etc.). Call prohibition provides the bondholder with more protection than a bond that has a refunding prohibition that is otherwise callable.[1]

Make-Whole Call Provision

In contrast to a standard fixed-price call, a make-whole call price is calculated as the present value of the bond's remaining cash flows subject to a floor price equal to par value. The discount rate used to determine the present value is the yield on a comparable-maturity Treasury security plus a contractually specified *make-whole call premium*. For example, in November 2010, Coca-Cola sold $1 billion of 3.15% Notes due November 15, 2020. These notes are redeemable at any time either in whole or in part at the issuer's option. The redemption price is the greater of (1) 100% of the principal amount plus accrued interest or (2) the make whole redemption price, which is equal to the sum of the present value of the remaining coupon and principal payments discounted at the Treasury rate plus 10 basis points. The spread of 10 basis points is the aforementioned make-whole call premium. Thus the make-whole call price is essentially a floating call price that moves inversely with the level of interest rates.

---

[1] There are, of course, exceptions to a call prohibition, such as sinking funds and redemption of the debt under certain mandatory provisions.

The Treasury rate is calculated in one of two ways. One method is to use a constant-maturity Treasury (CMT) yield as the Treasury rate. CMT yields are published weekly by the Federal Reserve in its statistical release H.15. The maturity of the CMT yield will match the bond's remaining maturity (rounded to the nearest month). If there is no CMT yield that exactly corresponds with the bond's remaining maturity, a linear interpolation is employed using the yields of the two closest available CMT maturities. Once the CMT yield is determined, the discount rate for the bond's remaining cash flows is simply the CMT yield plus the make-whole call premium specified in the indenture.

Another method of determining the Treasury rate is to select a U.S. Treasury security having a maturity comparable with the remaining maturity of the make-whole call bond in question. This selection is made by a primary U.S. Treasury dealer designated in the bond's indenture. An average price for the selected Treasury security is calculated using the price quotations of multiple primary dealers. The average price is then used to calculate a bond-equivalent yield. This yield is then used as the Treasury rate.

Make-whole call provisions were first introduced in publicly traded corporate bonds in 1995. Bonds with make-whole call provisions are now issued routinely. Moreover, the make-whole call provision is growing in popularity while bonds with fixed-price call provisions are declining. Figure 16-1 presents a graph that shows the total par amount outstanding of corporate bonds issued in billions of dollars by type of bond (straight, fixed-price call, make-whole call) for years 1995 to 2009.[2] This sample of bonds contains all debentures issued on and after January 1, 1995, that might have certain characteristics.[3] These data suggest that the make-whole call provision is rapidly becoming the call feature of choice for corporate bonds.

The primary advantage from the firm's perspective of a make-whole call provision relative to a fixed-price call is a lower cost. Since the make-whole call price floats inversely with the level of Treasury rates, the issuer will not exercise the call to buy back the debt merely because its borrowing rates have declined. Simply put, the pure refunding motive is virtually eliminated. This feature will reduce the upfront compensation required by bondholders to hold make-whole call bonds versus fixed-price call bonds.

Sinking-Fund Provision

Term bonds may be paid off by operation of a *sinking fund*. These last two words are often misunderstood to mean that the issuer accumulates a fund in cash, or in assets readily sold for cash, that is used to pay bonds at maturity. It had that meaning many years ago, but too often the money supposed to be in a sinking fund was not all there when it was needed. In modem practice, there is no fund, and *sinking* means that money is applied periodically to redemption of bonds before maturity. Corporate bond indentures require the issuer to retire a specified portion of an issue each year. This kind of provision for repayment of corporate debt may be designed to liquidate all of a bond issue by the maturity date, or it may

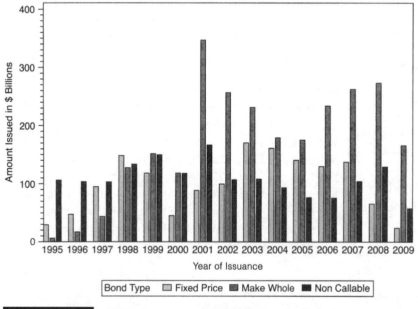

FIGURE 16-1 Total par amount of corporate bonds outstanding by type of call provision.

[2] Our data source is the Fixed Income Securities Database jointly published by LJS Global Information Services and Arthur Warga at the University of Houston.

[3] These characteristics include such things as the offering amount had to be at least $25 million and excluded medium-term notes and bonds with other embedded options (e.g., bonds that were potable or convertible). See Scott Brown and Eric Powers, "The Life Cycle of Make-Whole Call Provisions," *Working Paper,* March 2011.

be arranged to pay only a part of the total by the end of the term. As an example, consider a $150 million issue by Westvaco in June 1997. The bonds carry a 7.5% coupon and mature on June 15, 2027. The bonds' indenture provides for an annual sinking-fund payment of $7.5 million or $15 million to be determined on an annual basis.

The issuer may satisfy the sinking-fund requirement in one of two ways. A cash payment of the face amount of the bonds to be retired may be made by the corporate debtor to the trustee. The trustee then calls the bonds pro rata or by lot for redemption. Bonds have serial numbers, and numbers may be selected randomly for redemption. Owners of bonds called in this manner turn them in for redemption; *interest payments stop at the redemption date*. Alternatively, the issuer can deliver to the trustee bonds with a total face value equal to the amount that must be retired. The bonds are purchased by the *issuer* in the open market. This option is elected by the issuer when the bonds are selling below par. A few corporate bond indentures, however, prohibit the open-market purchase of the bonds by the issuer.

Many electric utility bond issues can satisfy the sinking-fund requirement by a third method. Instead of actually retiring bonds, the company may certify to the trustee that it has used unfunded property credits in lieu of the sinking fund. That is, it has made property and plant investments that have not been used for issuing bonded debt. For example, if the sinking-fund requirement is $1 million, it may give the trustee $1 million in cash to call bonds, it may deliver to the trustee $1 million of bonds it purchased in the open market, or it may certify that it made additions to its property and plant in the required amount, normally $1,667 of plant for each $1,000 sinking-fund requirement. In this case it could satisfy the sinking fund with certified property additions of $1,667,000.

The issuer is granted a special call price to satisfy any sinking-fund requirement. Usually, the sinking-fund call price is the par value if the bonds were originally sold at par. When issued at a price in excess of par, the sinking-fund call price generally starts at the issuance price and scales down to par as the issue approaches maturity.

There are two advantages of a sinking-fund requirement from the bondholder's perspective. First, default risk is reduced because of the orderly retirement of the issue before maturity. Second, if bond prices decline as a result of an increase in interest rates, price support may be provided by the issuer or its fiscal agent because it must enter the market on the buy side in order to satisfy the sinking-fund requirement. However, the disadvantage is that the bonds may be called at the special sinking-fund call price at a time when interest rates are lower than rates prevailing at the time of issuance. In that case, the bonds will be selling above par but may be retired by the issuer at the special call price that may be equal to par value.

Usually, the periodic payments required for sinking-fund purposes will be the same for each period. Gas company issues often have increasing sinking-fund requirements. However, a few indentures might permit variable periodic payments, where the periodic payments vary based on prescribed conditions set forth in the indenture. The most common condition is the level of earnings of the issuer. In such cases, the periodic payments vary directly with earnings. An issuer prefers such flexibility; however, an investor may prefer fixed periodic payments because of the greater default risk protection provided under this arrangement.

Many corporate bond indentures include a provision that grants the issuer the option to retire more than the amount stipulated for sinking-fund retirement. This option, referred to as an *accelerated sinking-fund provision*, effectively reduces the bondholder's call protection because, when interest rates decline, the issuer may find it economically advantageous to exercise this option at the special sinking-fund call price to retire a substantial portion of an outstanding issue.

Sinking fund provisions have fallen out of favor for most companies, but they used to be fairly common for public utilities, pipeline issuers, and some industrial issues. Finance issues almost never include a sinking fund provision. There can be a mandatory sinking fund where bonds have to be retired or, as mentioned earlier, a nonmandatory sinking fund in which it may use certain property credits for the sinking-fund requirement. If the sinking fund applies to a particular issue, it is called a *specific sinking fund.* There are also *nonspecific sinking funds* (also known as *funnel, tunnel, blanket*, or *aggregate sinking funds*), where the requirement is based on the total bonded debt outstanding of an issuer. Generally, it might require a sinking-fund payment of 1% of all bonds outstanding as of year-end. The issuer can apply the requirement to one particular issue or to any other issue or issues. Again, the blanket sinking fund may be mandatory (where bonds have to be retired) or nonmandatory (whereby it can use unfunded property additions).

Maintenance and Replacement Funds

Maintenance and replacement fund (M&R) provisions first appeared in bond indentures of electric utilities subject to regulation by the Securities and Exchange Commission (SEC) under the Public Holding Company Act of 1940. It remained in the indentures even when most of the utilities were no longer subject to regulation under the act. The original motivation for their inclusion is straightforward. Property is subject to economic depreciation, and the replacement fund ostensibly helps to maintain the integrity of the property securing the bonds. An M&R differs from a sinking fund in that the M&R only helps to maintain the value of the security backing the debt, whereas a sinking fund is designed to improve the security backing the debt. Although it is more complex, it is similar in spirit to a provision in a home mortgage requiring the homeowner to maintain the home in good repair.

An M&R requires a utility to determine annually the amounts necessary to satisfy the fund and any shortfall. The requirement is based on a formula that is usually some percentage (e.g., 15%) of adjusted gross operating revenues. The difference between what is required and the actual amount expended on maintenance is the shortfall. The shortfall is usually satisfied with unfunded property additions, but it also can be satisfied with cash. The cash can be used for the retirement of debt or withdrawn on the certification of unfunded property credits.

While the retirement of debt through M&R provisions is not as common as it once was, M&Rs are still relevant, so bond investors should be cognizant of their presence in an indenture. For example, in April 2000, PPL Electric Utilities Corporation redeemed all its outstanding 9.25% coupon series first-mortgage bonds due in 2019 using an M&R provision. The special redemption price was par. The company's stated purpose of the call was to reduce interest expense.

Redemption through the Sale of Assets and Other Means

Because mortgage bonds are secured by property, bondholders want the integrity of the collateral to be maintained. Bondholders would not want a company to sell a plant (which has been pledged as collateral) and then to use the proceeds for a distribution to shareholders. Therefore, release-of-property and substitution-of-property clauses are found in most secured bond indentures.

As an illustration, Texas–New Mexico Power Co. issued $130 million in first-mortgage bonds in January 1992 that carried a coupon rate of 11.25%. The bonds were callable beginning in January 1997 at a call price of 105. Following the sale of six of its utilities, Texas–New Mexico Power called the bonds at par in October 1995, well before the first call date. As justification for the call, Texas–New Mexico Power stated that it was forced to sell the six utilities by municipalities in northern Texas, and as a result, the bonds were callable under the eminent domain provision in the bond's indenture. The bondholders sued, stating that the bonds were redeemed in violation of the indenture. In April 1997, the court found for the bondholders, and they were awarded damages, as well as lost interest. In the judgment of the court, while the six utilities were under the threat of condemnation, no eminent domain proceedings were initiated.

Tender Offers

In addition to those methods specified in the indenture, firms have other tools for extinguishing debt prior to its stated maturity. At any time a firm may execute a tender offer and announce its desire to buy back specified debt issues. Firms employ tender offers to eliminate restrictive covenants or to refund debt. Usually the tender offer is for "any and all" of the targeted issue, but it also can be for a fixed dollar amount that is less than the outstanding face value. An offering circular is sent to the bondholders of record stating the price the firm is willing to pay and the window of time during which bondholders can sell their bonds back to the firm. If the firm perceives that participation is too low, the firm can increase the tender offer price and extend the tender offer window. When the tender offer expires, all participating bondholders tender their bonds and receive the same cash payment from the firm.

In recent years, tender offers have been executed using a fixed spread as opposed to a fixed price.[4] In a fixed-spread tender offer, the tender offer price is equal to the

---

[4] See Steven V. Mann and Eric A. Powers, "Determinants of Bond Tender Premiums and the Percentage Tendered," *Journal of Banking and Finance*, March 2007, pp. 547–566.

present value of the bond's remaining cash flows either to maturity or the next call date if the bond is callable. The present-value calculation occurs immediately after the tender offer expires. The discount rate used in the calculation is equal to the yield-to-maturity on a comparable-maturity Treasury or the associated CMT yield plus the specified fixed spread. Fixed-spread tender offers eliminate the exposure to interest-rate risk for both bondholders and the firm during the tender offer window.

CREDIT RISK

All corporate bonds are exposed to credit risk, which includes *credit default risk* and *credit-spread risk*.

Measuring Credit Default Risk

Any bond investment carries with it the uncertainty as to whether the issuer will make timely payments of interest and principal as prescribed by the bond's indenture. This risk is termed *credit default risk* and is the risk that a bond issuer will be unable to meet its financial obligations. Institutional investors have developed tools for analyzing information about both issuers and bond issues that assist them in accessing credit default risk. However, most individual bond investors and some institutional bond investors do not perform any elaborate credit analysis. Instead, they rely largely on bond ratings published by the major rating agencies that perform the credit analysis and publish their conclusions in the form of ratings. The three major nationally recognized statistical rating organizations (NRSROs) in the United States are Fitch Ratings, Moody's, and Standard & Poor's. These ratings are used by market participants as a factor in the valuation of securities on account of their independent and unbiased nature.

The ratings systems use similar symbols, as shown in Table 16-1. In addition to the generic rating category, Moody's employs a numerical modifier of 1, 2, or 3 to indicate the relative standing of a particular issue within a rating category. This modifier is called a *notch*. Both Standard & Poor's and Fitch use a plus (+) and a minus (−) to convey the same information. Bonds rated triple B or higher are referred to as *investment-grade bonds*. Bonds rated below triple B are referred to as *non-investment-grade bonds* or, more popularly, *high-yield bonds* or *junk bonds*.

Credit ratings can and do change over time. A *rating transition table*, also called a *rating migration table*, is a table that shows how ratings change over some specified time period. Table 16-2 presents a hypothetical rating transition table for a one-year time horizon. The ratings beside each of the rows are the ratings at the start of the year. The ratings at the head of each column are the ratings at the end of the year. Accordingly, the first cell in the table tells that 93.20% of the issues that were rated AAA at the beginning of the year still had that rating at the end. These tables are published periodically by the three rating agencies and can be used to access changes in credit default risk.

Measuring Credit-Spread Risk

The *credit-spread* is the difference between a corporate bond's yield and the yield on a comparable-maturity benchmark Treasury security.[5] Credit spreads are so named because the presumption is that the difference in yields is due primarily to the corporate bond's exposure to credit risk. This is misleading, however, because the risk profile of corporate bonds differs from Treasuries on other dimensions; namely, corporate bonds are less liquid and often have embedded options.

Credit-spread risk is the risk of financial loss or the underperformance of a portfolio resulting from changes in the level of credit spreads used in the marking to market of a fixed income product. Credit spreads are driven by both macro-economic forces and issue-specific factors. Macro-economic forces include such things as the level and slope of the Treasury yield curve, the business cycle, and consumer confidence. Correspondingly, the issue-specific factors include such things as the corporation's financial position and the future prospects of the firm and its industry.

One method used commonly to measure credit-spread risk is *spread duration*. Spread duration is the approximate percentage change in a bond's price for a 100 basis point change in the credit-spread assuming that the Treasury rate is unchanged. For example, if a bond has a spread duration of 3, this indicates that for a 100 basis

---

[5] The U.S. Treasury yield is a common but by no means the only choice for a benchmark to compute credit spreads. Other reasonable choices include the swap curve or the agency yield curve.

TABLE 16-1 Corporate Bond Credit Ratings

Fitch	Moody's	S&P	Summary Description
Investment Grade			
AAA	Aaa	AAA	Gilt edged, prime, maximum safety, lowest risk, and when sovereign borrower considered "default-free"
AA+	Aa1	AA+	
AA	Aa2	AA	High-grade, high credit quality
AA−	Aa3	AA−	
A+	A1	A+	
A	A2	A	Upper-medium grade
A−	A3	A−	
BBB+	Baa1	BBB+	
BBB	Baa2	BBB	Lower-medium grade
BBB−	Baa3	BBB−	
Speculative Grade			
BB+	Ba1	BB+	
BB	Ba2	BB	Low grade; speculative
BB−	Ba3	BB−	
B+	B1		
B	B	B	Highly speculative
B−	B3		
Predominantly Speculative, Substantial Risk or in Default			
CCC+		CCC+	
CCC	Caa	CCC	Substantial risk, in poor standing
CC	Ca	CC	May be in default, very speculative
C	C	C	Extremely speculative
		CI	Income bonds—no interest being paid
DDD			
DD			Default
D	D		

TABLE 16-2 Hypothetical One-Year Rating Transition Table

Rating at Start of Year	Rating at End of Year								
	AAA	AA	A	BBB	BB	B	CCC	D	Total
AAA	93.20	6.00	0.60	0.12	0.08	0.00	0.00	0.00	100
AA	1.60	92.75	5.07	0.36	0.11	0.07	0.03	0.01	100
A	0.18	2.65	91.91	4.80	0.37	0.02	0.02	0.05	100
BBB	0.04	0.30	5.20	87.70	5.70	0.70	0.16	0.20	100
BB	0.03	0.11	0.61	6.80	81.65	7.10	2.60	1.10	100
B	0.01	0.09	0.55	0.88	7.90	75.67	8.70	6.20	100
CCC	0.00	0.01	0.31	0.84	2.30	8.10	62.54	25.90	100

point change in the credit-spread, the bond's price should change be approximately 3%.

EVENT RISK

In recent years, one of the more talked-about topics among corporate bond investors is *event risk*. Over the last couple of decades, corporate bond indentures have become less restrictive, and corporate managements have been given a free rein to do as they please without regard to bondholders. Management's main concern or duty is to enhance shareholder wealth. As for the bondholder, all a company is required to do is to meet the terms of the bond indenture, including the payment of principal and interest. With few restrictions and the optimization of shareholder wealth of paramount importance for corporate managers, it is no wonder that bondholders became concerned when merger mania and other events swept the nation's boardrooms. Events such as decapitalizations, restructurings, recapitalizations, mergers, acquisitions, leveraged buyouts, and share repurchases, among other things, often caused substantial changes in a corporation's capital structure, namely, greatly increased leverage and decreased equity. Bondholders' protection was sharply reduced and debt quality ratings lowered, in many cases to speculative-grade categories. Along with greater risk came lower bond valuations. Shareholders were being enriched at the expense of bondholders. It is important to keep in mind the distinction between event risk and headline risk. Headline risk is the uncertainty engendered by the firm's media coverage that causes investors to alter their perception of the firm's prospects. Headline risk is present regardless of the veracity of the media coverage.

In reaction to the increased activity of leveraged buyouts and strategic mergers and acquisitions, some companies incorporated "poison puts" in their indentures. These are designed to thwart unfriendly takeovers by making the target company unpalatable to the acquirer. The poison put provides that the bondholder can require the company to repurchase the debt under certain circumstances arising out of specific designated events such as a change in control. Poison puts may not deter a proposed acquisition but could make it more expensive. Many times, in addition to a designated event, a rating change to below investment grade must occur within a certain period for the put to be activated. Some issues provide for a higher interest rate instead of a put as a designated event remedy.

At times, event risk has caused some companies to include other special debt-retirement features in their indentures. An example is the *maintenance of net worth clause* included in the indentures of some lower-rated bond issues. In this case, an issuer covenants to maintain its net worth above a stipulated level, and if it fails to do so, it must begin to retire its debt at par. Usually the redemptions affect only part of the issue and continue periodically until the net worth recovers to an amount above the stated figure or the debt is retired. In other cases, the company is required only to *offer to redeem* a required amount. An offer to redeem is not mandatory on the bondholders' part; only those holders who want their bonds redeemed need do so. In a number of instances in which the issuer is required to call bonds, the bondholders may elect not to have bonds redeemed. This is not much different from an offer to redeem. It may protect bondholders from the redemption of the high-coupon debt at lower interest rates. However, if a company's net worth declines to a level low enough to activate such a call, it probably would be prudent to have one's bonds redeemed.

Protecting the value of debt investments against the added risk caused by corporate management activity is not an easy job. Investors should analyze the issuer's fundamentals carefully to determine if the company may be a candidate for restructuring. Attention to news and equity investment reports can make the task easier. Also, the indenture should be reviewed to see if there are any protective covenant features. However, there may be loopholes that can be exploited by sharp legal minds. Of course, large portfolios can reduce risk with broad diversification among industry lines, but price declines do not always affect only the issue at risk; they also can spread across the board and take the innocent down with them. This happened in the fall of 1988 with the leveraged buyout of RJR Nabisco, Inc. The whole industrial bond market suffered as buyers and traders withdrew from the market, new issues were postponed, and secondary market activity came to a standstill. The impact of the initial leveraged buyout bid announcement on yield spreads for RJR Nabisco's debt to a benchmark Treasury increased from about 100 to 350 basis points. The RJR Nabisco transaction showed that size was not an obstacle. Therefore, other large firms that investors previously thought were unlikely candidates for a leveraged buyout were fair game. The spillover effect caused yield spreads to widen for other major corporations. This phenomenon was repeated in the mid-2000s with the buyout of large, investment grade public companies such as Alltel, First Data, and Hilton Hotels.

HIGH-YIELD BONDS

As noted, high-yield bonds are those rated below investment grade by the ratings agencies. These issues are also known as *junk bonds*. Despite the negative connotation of the term *junk*, not all bonds in the high-yield sector are on the verge of default or bankruptcy. Many of these issues are on the fringe of the investment-grade sector.

Types of Issuers

Several types of issuers fall into the less-than-investment-grade high-yield category. These categories are discussed below.

Original Issuers

Original issuers include young, growing concerns lacking the stronger balance sheet and income statement profile of many established corporations but often with lots of promise. Also called *venture-capital situations* or *growth or emerging market companies,* the debt is often sold with a story projecting future financial strength. From this we get the term *story bond.* There are also the established operating firms with financials neither measuring up to the strengths of investment grade corporations nor possessing the weaknesses of companies on the verge of bankruptcy. Subordinated debt of investment-grade issuers may be included here. A bond rated at the bottom rung of the investment-grade category (Baa and BBB) or at the top end of the speculative-grade category (Ba and BB) is referred to as a "businessman's risk."

Fallen Angels

"Fallen angels" are companies with investment-grade-rated debt that have come on hard times with deteriorating balance sheet and income statement financial parameters. They may be in default or near bankruptcy. In these cases, investors are interested in the workout value of the debt in a reorganization or liquidation, whether within or outside the bankruptcy courts. Some refer to these issues as "special situations." Over the years, they have fallen on hard times; some have recovered, and others have not.

Restructurings and Leveraged Buyouts

These are companies that have deliberately increased their debt burden with a view toward maximizing shareholder value. The shareholders may be the existing public group to which the company pays a special extraordinary dividend, with the funds coming from borrowings and the sale of assets. Cash is paid out, net worth decreased, and leverage increased, and ratings drop on existing debt. Newly issued debt gets junk-bond status because of the company's weakened financial condition.

In a leveraged buyout (LBO), a new and private shareholder group owns and manages the company. The debt issue's purpose may be to retire other debt from commercial and investment banks and institutional investors incurred to finance the LBO. The debt to be retired is called *bridge financing* because it provides a bridge between the initial LBO activity and the more permanent financing. One example is Ann Taylor, Inc.'s 1989 debt financing for bridge loan repayment. The proceeds of BCI Holding Corporation's 1986 public debt financing and bank borrowings were used to make the required payments to the common shareholders of Beatrice Companies, pay issuance expenses, and retire certain Beatrice debt and for working capital.

Unique Features of Some Issues

Often actions taken by management that result in the assignment of a non investment-grade bond rating result in a heavy interest-payment burden. This places severe cash-flow constraints on the firm. To reduce this burden, firms involved with heavy debt burdens have issued bonds with *deferred coupon structures* that permit the issuer to avoid using cash to make interest payments for a period of three to seven years. There are three types of deferred-coupon structures: (1) deferred-interest bonds, (2) step-up bonds, and (3) payment in-kind bonds.

Deferred-interest bonds are the most common type of deferred-coupon structure. These bonds sell at a deep discount and do not pay interest for an initial period, typically from three to seven years. (Because no interest is paid for the initial period, these bonds are sometimes referred to as "zero-coupon bonds.") *Step-up bonds* do pay coupon interest, but the coupon rate is low for an initial period and then increases ("steps up") to a higher coupon rate. Finally, *payment-in-kind (PIK) bonds* give the issuers an option to pay cash at a coupon payment date or give the bondholder a similar bond (i.e., a bond with the same coupon rate and a par value equal to the amount of the coupon payment that would have been paid). The period during which the issuer can make this choice varies from five to ten years.

Sometimes an issue will come to market with a structure allowing the issuer to reset the coupon rate so that the bond will trade at a predetermined price.[6] The coupon rate may reset annually or even more frequently, or reset only one time over the life of the bond. Generally, the coupon rate at the reset date will be the average of rates suggested by two investment banking firms. The new rate will then reflect (1) the level of interest rates at the reset date and (2) the credit-spread the market wants on the issue at the reset date. This structure is called an *extendible reset bond*.

Notice the difference between an extendible reset bond and a typical floating-rate issue. In a floating-rate issue, the coupon rate resets according to a fixed spread over the reference rate, with the index spread specified in the indenture. The amount of the index spread reflects market conditions at the time the issue is offered. The coupon rate on an extendible reset bond, in contrast, is reset based on market conditions (as suggested by several investment banking firms) at the time of the reset date. Moreover, the new coupon rate reflects the new level of interest rates and the new spread that investors seek.

The advantage to investors of extendible reset bonds is that the coupon rate will reset to the market rate—both the level of interest rates and the credit-spread—in principle keeping the issue at par value. In fact, experience with extendible reset bonds has not been favorable during periods of difficulties in the high-yield bond market. The sudden substantial increase in default risk has meant that the rise in the rate needed to keep the issue at par value was so large that it would have insured bankruptcy of the issuer. As a result, the rise in the coupon rate has been insufficient to keep the issue at the stipulated price.

---

[6] Most of the bonds have a coupon reset formula that requires the issuer to reset the coupon so that the bond will trade at a price of $101.

Some speculative-grade bond issues started to appear in 1992 granting the issuer a limited right to redeem a portion of the bonds during the noncall period if the proceeds are from an initial public stock offering. Called "clawback" provisions, they merit careful attention by inquiring bond investors. The provision appears in the vast majority of new speculative-grade bond issues, and sometimes allow even private sales of stock to be used for the clawback. The provision usually allows 35% of the issue to be retired during the first three years after issuance, at a price of par plus one year of coupon. Investors should be forewarned of claw backs because they can lose bonds at the point in time just when the issuer's finances have been strengthened through access to the equity market. Also, the redemption may reduce the amount of the outstanding bonds to a level at which their liquidity in the aftermarket may suffer.

DEFAULT RATES AND RECOVERY RATES

We now turn our attention to the various aspects of the historical performance of corporate issuers with respect to fulfilling their obligations to bondholders. Specifically, we will look at two aspects of this performance. First, we will look at the default rate of corporate borrowers. From an investment perspective, default rates by themselves are not of paramount significance; it is perfectly possible for a portfolio of bonds to suffer defaults and to outperform Treasuries at the same time, provided the yield spread of the portfolio is sufficiently high to offset the losses from default. Furthermore, because holders of defaulted bonds typically recover some percentage of the face amount of their investment, the *default loss rate* is substantially lower than the default rate. Therefore, it is important to look at default loss rates or, equivalently, *recovery rates*.

Default Rates

A default rate can be measured in different ways. A simple way to define a default rate is to use the issuer as the unit of study. A default rate is then measured as the number of issuers that default divided by the total number of issuers at the beginning of the year. This measure gives no recognition to the amount defaulted nor the total amount

of issuance. Moody's, for example, uses this default-rate statistic in its study of default rates.[7] The rationale for ignoring dollar amounts is that the credit decision of an investor does not increase with the size of the issuer. The second measure is to define the default rate as the par value of all bonds that defaulted in a given calendar year divided by the total par value of all bonds outstanding during the year. Edward Altman, who has performed extensive analyses of default rates for speculative-grade bonds, measures default rates in this way. We will distinguish between the default-rate statistic below by referring to the first as the *issuer default rate* and the second as the *dollar default rate*.

With either default-rate statistic, one can measure the default for a given year or an average annual default rate over a certain number of years. Researchers who have defined dollar default rates in terms of an average annual default rate over a certain number of years have measured it as

$$\frac{\text{Cumulative \$ value of all defaulted bonds}}{\left(\begin{array}{c}\text{Cumulative \$ value of all issuance}\\ \times \text{ weighted avg. no. of years outstanding}\end{array}\right)}$$

Alternatively, some researchers report a cumulative annual default rate. This is done by not normalizing by the number of years. For example, a cumulative annual dollar default rate is calculated as

$$\frac{\text{Cumulative \$ value of all defaulted bonds}}{\text{Cumulative \$ value of all issuance}}$$

There have been several excellent studies of corporate bond default rates. We will not review each of these studies because the findings are similar. Here we will look at a study by Moody's that covers the period 1970 to 1994.[8] Over this 25-year period, 640 of the 4,800 issuers in the study defaulted on more than $96 billion of publicly offered long-term debt. A *default* in the Moody's study is defined as "any missed or delayed disbursement of interest and/or principal." Issuer default rates are calculated.

---

[7] Moody's Investors Service, "Corporate Bond Defaults and Default Rates: 1970–1994," *Moody's Special Report,* January 1995, p. 13. Different issuers within an affiliated group of companies are counted separately.

[8] Moody's Investors Service, "Corporate Bond Defaults and Default Rates: 1970–1994."

The Moody's study found that the lower the credit rating, the greater is the probability of a corporate issuer defaulting.

There have been extensive studies focusing on default rates for speculative grade issuers. In their 2011 study, Altman and Kuehne find based on a sample of high-yield bonds outstanding over the period 1971–2010, default rates typically range between 2% and 5% with occasional spikes above 10% during periods of financial dislocation.[9]

Recovery Rates

There have been several studies that have focused on recovery rates or default loss rates for corporate debt. Measuring the amount recovered is not a simple task. The final distribution to claimants when a default occurs may consist of cash and securities. Often it is difficult to track what was received and then determine the present value of any noncash payments received.

While the empirical record is developing, we will state a few stylized facts about recovery rates and by implication default rates.[10]

- The average recovery rate of bonds across seniority levels is approximately 38%.
- The distribution of recovery rates is bimodal.
- Recovery rates are unrelated to the size of the bond issuance.
- Default rates and recovery rates are inversely correlated.
- Recovery rate is lower in an economic downturn and in a distressed industry.
- Tangible asset-intensive industries have higher recovery rates.

---

[9] Edward I. Altman and Brenda J. Kuehne, "Defaults and Returns in the High-Yield Bond and Distressed Market: The Year 2010 in Review and Outlook," Special Report, New York University Salomon Center, Leonard N. Stern School of Business, February 4, 2011.

[10] Dilip B. Madan, Gurdip S. Bakshi, and Frank Xiaoling Zhang. "Understanding the Role of Recovery in Default Risk Models: Empirical Comparisons and Implied Recovery Rates," FDIC CFR Working Paper No. 06; EFA 2004 Maastricht Meetings Paper No. 3584; FEDS Working Paper; AFA 20004 Meetings (September 2006). Available at SSRN: http://ssrn.com/abstract=285940 or doi:10.2139/ssrn.285940

MEDIUM-TERM NOTES

Medium-term notes (MTNs) are debt instruments that differ primarily in how they are sold to investors. Akin to a commercial paper program, they are offered continuously to institutional investors by an agent of the issuer. MTNs are registered with the Securities and Exchange Commission under Rule 415 ("shelf registration") which gives a corporation sufficient flexibility for issuing securities on a continuous basis. MTNs are also issued by non-U.S. corporations, federal agencies, supranational institutions, and sovereign governments.

One would suspect that MTNs would describe securities with intermediate maturities. However, it is a misnomer. MTNs are issued with maturities of 9 months to 30 years or even longer. For example, in 1993, Walt Disney Corporation issued bonds through its medium-term note program with a 100-year maturity a so-called century bond. MTNs can perhaps be more accurately described as highly flexible debt instruments that can easily be designed to respond to market opportunities and investor preferences.

As noted, MTNs differ in their primary distribution process. Most MTN programs have two to four agents. Through its agents, an issuer of MTNs posts offering rates over a range of maturities: for example, nine months to one year, one year to eighteen months, eighteen months to two years, and annually thereafter. Many issuers post rates as a yield spread over a Treasury security of comparable maturity.

Relatively attractive yield spreads are posted for maturities that the issuer desires to raise funds. The investment banks disseminate this offering rate information to their investor clients. When an investor expresses interest in an MTN offering, the agent contacts the issuer to obtain a confirmation of the terms of the transaction. Within a maturity range, the investor has the option of choosing the final maturity of the note sale, subject to agreement by the issuing company. The issuer will lower its posted rates once it raises the desired amount of funds at a given maturity.

Structured medium-term notes or simply *structured notes* are debt instruments coupled with a derivative position (options, forwards, futures, swaps, caps, and floors). For example, structured notes are often created with an underlying swap transaction. This "hedging swap" allows the issuer to create structured notes with interesting risk/return features desired by a swath of fixed income investors.

KEY POINTS

- A bond's indenture includes the promises of corporate bond issuers and the rights of investors. The terms of bond issues set forth in bond indentures are always a compromise between the interests of the bond issuer and those of investors who buy bonds.

- The classification of corporate bonds by type of issuer include public utilities, transportations, industrials, banks and finance companies, and international or Yankee issues.

- The three main interest payment classifications of domestically issued corporate bonds are straight-coupon bonds (fixed-rate bonds), zero-coupon bonds, and floating-rate bonds (variable-rate bonds).

- Either real property (using a mortgage) or personal property may be pledged to offer security beyond that of the general credit standing of the issuer. In fact, the kind of security or the absence of a specific pledge of security is usually indicated by the title of a bond issue. However, the best security is a strong general credit that can repay the debt from earnings.

- A mortgage bond grants the bondholders a first-mortgage lien on substantially all its properties and as a result the issuer is able to borrow at a lower rate of interest than if the debt were unsecured.

- Some companies do not own fixed assets or other real property and so have nothing tangible on which they can give a mortgage lien to secure bondholders. To satisfy the desire of bondholders for security, they pledge stocks, notes, bonds, or whatever other kinds of obligations they own and the resulting issues are referred to as collateral trust bonds.

- Debentures not secured by a specific pledge of designated property and therefore bondholders have the claim of general creditors on all assets of the issuer not pledged specifically to secure other debt. Moreover, debenture bondholders have a claim on pledged assets to the extent that these assets have value greater than necessary to satisfy secured creditors. In fact, if there are no pledged assets and no secured creditors, debenture bondholders have first claim on all assets along with other general creditors.

- Owners of subordinated debenture bonds stand last in line among creditors when an issuer fails financially.

- For a guaranteed bond there is a third party guaranteeing the debt but that does not mean a bond issue is free of default risk. The safety of a guaranteed bond depends on the financial capability of the guarantor to satisfy the terms of the guarantee, as well as the financial capability of the issuer.

- Debt retirement mechanisms included in a bond's indenture are call and refunding provisions, sinking funds, maintenance and replacement funds, redemption through sale of assets, and tender offers.

- All corporate bonds are exposed to credit risk, which includes credit default risk and credit-spread risk.

- Credit ratings can and do change over time and this information is captured in a rating transition table, also called a rating migration table.

- Credit-spread risk is the risk of financial loss or the underperformance of a portfolio resulting from changes in the level of credit spreads used in the marking to market of a fixed income product. One method used commonly to measure credit-spread risk is spread duration which is the approximate percentage change in a bond's price for a 100 basis point change in the credit-spread assuming that the Treasury rate is unchanged.

- The three types of issuers that comprise the less-than-investment-grade high-yield corporate bond category are original issuers, fallen angels, and restructuring and leveraged buyouts.

- Often actions taken by management that result in the assignment of a noninvestment-grade bond rating result in a heavy interest payment burden. To reduce this burden, firms involved with heavy debt burdens have issued bonds with deferred coupon structures that permit the issuer to avoid using cash to make interest payments for a period of three to seven years. There are three types of deferred-coupon structures: deferred-interest bonds, step-up bonds, and payment-in-kind bonds.

- From an investment perspective, default rates by themselves are not of paramount significance because a portfolio of bonds could suffer defaults and still outperform Treasuries at the same time. This can occur if the yield spread of the portfolio is sufficiently high to offset the losses from default. Furthermore, because holders of defaulted bonds typically recover some percentage of the face amount of their investment, the default loss rate is substantially lower than the default rate. Therefore, it is important to look at default loss rates or, equivalently, recovery rates.

- A default rate can be measured in term of the issuer default rate and the dollar default rate.

The Rating Agencies

■ Learning Objectives

Candidates, after completing this reading, should be able to:

- Describe the role of rating agencies in the financial markets.
- Explain market and regulatory forces that have played a role in the growth of the rating agencies.
- Describe a rating scale, define credit outlooks, and explain the difference between solicited and unsolicited ratings.
- Describe Standard and Poor's and Moody's rating scales and distinguish between investment and noninvestment grade ratings.
- Describe the difference between an issuer-pay and a subscriber-pay model and describe concerns regarding the issuer-pay model.

- Describe and contrast the process for rating corporate and sovereign debt and describe how the distributions of these ratings may differ.
- Describe the relationship between the rating agencies and regulators and identify key regulations that impact the rating agencies and the use of ratings in the market.
- Describe some of the trends and issues emerging from the recent credit crisis relevant to the rating agencies and the use of ratings in the market.

Excerpt is Chapter 6 of Managing Credit Risk: The Great Challenge for Global Financial Markets, *Second Edition, by John B. Caouette, Edward I. Altman, Paul Narayanan, and Robert W. J. Nimmo.*

> All that glitters is not gold;
> Often have you heard that told.
>
> —*William Shakespeare,* The Merchant of Venice *(II, vii)*

Rating agencies specialize in evaluating the creditworthiness of debt securities issued by corporate, financial, structured finance, municipal, and sovereign obligors, and by evaluating the general creditworthiness of the issuers themselves. It is the job of the agencies to inform investors about the likelihood that they will receive all the principal and interest payments as scheduled for a given security. In other words, what is the probability of repayment?

The agencies are tremendously influential around the world today, covering in excess of $34 trillion in securities around the world, and in excess of $750 billion in loans and their businesses are growing at double digit rates (Moody's Investors Service 2007). Jochen Sanio, president of Germany's financial regulator BaFin, said the rating agencies do a good job but they nevertheless have become "uncontrolled world powers" (Klein 2004).

In some markets—the United States for example—the capital markets have replaced banks as the primary source of debt capital; and ratings agencies have assumed enormous importance in the management of credit risk. The agencies make no recommendations about buying, selling, or holding a particular security or about suitability for a particular investor. Their ratings express nothing more than informed opinions about creditworthiness; although the agencies stress that the opinions are independent, objective, and produced through a transparent and high-quality analytic process. However, these ratings have achieved very widespread acceptance with investors who have confidence in their accuracy and like their convenience and low cost.

For borrowers credit ratings are critical because they affect their access to markets and the cost of their borrowings.

Increasingly regulators have permitted use of ratings from certain of the rating agencies, designated in the United States as *nationally recognized statistical rating organizations* (NRSROs) in evaluating the quality of loan and investment portfolios and the equity capital needed to support the risk in these portfolios. Examples of some of the primary regulatory uses in the United States of rating agency information are summarized in Table 17-1.

In the Basel II Agreement, finalized in June 2004, the Basel Committee of the Bank for International Settlements (BIS), whose membership consists of the major central banks in the world (including the United States, Japan, Germany, and the United Kingdom), has also raised the profile of the agencies, described as *external credit assessment institutions* (ECAIs), again highlighting their role in providing the basis for capital adequacy calculations.

AGENCIES AROUND THE WORLD

The three major U.S. rating agencies are Moody's Investors Service, Standard and Poor's (S&P), and Fitch Ratings. Moody's has been an independent, publicly owned company since 2000. Since 1966, S&P has been a subsidiary of McGraw-Hill Companies, Inc. which is a large, publicly owned publishing group. Fitch is majority owned by a French conglomerate FIMALAC SA, which has diverse global operations and whose shares are traded on the Paris Bourse, with some 64 percent owned by one individual. In addition, there are several other notable agencies in the United States and internationally (shown in Table 17-2), but the market shares on a revenue basis of the majors are highly concentrated, with S&P estimated to have 40 percent share, Moody's 39 percent, Fitch 15 percent, and A.M. Best 3 percent. Market shares can also be computed on a coverage basis, which tends to give a larger weighting to smaller agencies, and Fitch in particular, given the structure of fee levels between agencies. In this chapter, we focus mostly on the big three companies.

Ratings agencies developed in the United States when John Moody began initiating bond ratings in 1909 for U.S. railroads. Credit reporting agencies also developed in the United States during the middle of the nineteenth century, when two of the foremost were founded, namely R. G. Dun Company and John Bradstreet Company. They merged in 1933 to form Dun and Bradstreet, which, in 1962, acquired Moody's Investors Service, the company originally founded by John Moody. Moody's is the only pure play rating agency listed company. At the beginning of 2007, it had a market capitalization of US $19 billion, although by early December 2007 this had declined to US $10.3 billion as concerns about the future role and profitability of the agencies have risen.

Standard & Poor's grew out of the publishing venture established by Henry Varnum Poor to print financial and

TABLE 17-1 Uses of Ratings by the Regulators

Regulator	Examples
SEC	NRSRO ratings are included in a number of key SEC regulations including the Securities Act of 1933, the Exchange Act, and the Investment Company Act of 1940. For example: • Calculations of broker-dealer net capital requirements are based on the ratings of securities held. • The rating from an NRSRO may be included in the registration without obtaining the written consent of the NRSRO. • Exemption from certain reporting requirements on rated securities transactions. • Eligibility for investment by taxable money market funds, including aggregate risk limits, single risk limits, and downgrades linked to NRSRO ratings.
OTS/OCC/FDIC Federal Reserve	NRSRO ratings are used in a number of key federal and state banking regulations governing domestic banking and thrift institutions and foreign institutions operating in the United States. For example: • The assets with highest ratings qualify as liquid assets. • There is additional capacity to lend to highly rated borrowers which receive a favorable risk rating for capital purposes. • Eligibility for investment by FDIC-insured banks. • Capital calculations of state-chartered banks. • Eligibility and valuation of assets to be pledged by foreign banks whose deposits are insured by FDIC. • Investment eligibility of assets and valuation for capital determination, and margining requirements are based on agency ratings.
NAIC	Valuation of securities held for investment purposes, for reserve requirements and for capital adequacy.
DOL	Eligibility for pension fund investments.
States	Eligibility for investment by state-regulated entities such as insurance companies, public retirement funds, state chartered banks, and thrift institutions.
Other	Self-regulatory organizations such as the New York Stock Exchange (NYSE) and Nasdaq set margin requirements based on the type of security pledged to secure a loan.

operating information about U.S. railroads after the Civil War. Poor's Publishing Co. turned to bond ratings in 1916 and merged with Standard Statistics, another financial publishing and rating company in 1941.

The ratings agencies started out strongly and flourished into the 1930s. By the 1960s the agencies had become much less important as well as small and quite moribund. The U.S. bond markets were very safe, dominated by government debt and investment-grade corporates. Banks were the dominant medium-term corporate capital providers, and the markets in the rest of the world generated very little business.

However, starting from the 1970s, there were several major changes that together have caused the activity of the agencies to grow very strongly. Corporates began to diversify their funding bases and the volumes of debt issuance have exploded over the decades since, taking share from the banking system. Some major bankruptcies, notably Penn Central in 1970, shook the markets and heightened concerns about credit quality. In 1973, the first SEC securities rule was established that formally incorporated credit ratings into securities regulations and gave official status initially to a select group of four NRSROs. Over time, mergers reduced the number of NRSROs to three by 2002, after which two additional NRSROs were added. There are currently five NRSROs, namely S&P, Moody's, Fitch, A.M. Best and Dominion Bond Rating Services.

TABLE 17-2 Selected Ratings Agencies around the World

Agency Name	Year Founded	Market Orientation	Short-term Rating Symbols	Long-term Rating Symbols
A.M. Best	1999	Global	A-1+ to D	A++ to S
Canadian Bond Rating Service (S&P)	1972	Local	A-1 to A-4	A++ to D
Dominion Bond Rating Service (DBRS)	1976	Global	R-1 to U	AAA to C
Agence d'Évaluation Financière (S&P)	1986	Local	T-1 to T-4	AAA to D
Credit Rating Services of India Ltd.	1988	Local	P-1 to P-5	AAA to D
Egan Jones Rating	1995	Local	A-1+ to D	AAA to D
European Rating Agency	—	Local	S-1 to S-4	AAA to D
Japan Bond Research Institute	1979	Local	—	—
Japan Credit Rating Agency	1985	Local	J-1 to J-5	Aaa to D
Mikuni & Co.	1975	Local	N/A	AAA to D
Nippon Investors Service	1985	Local	A-1 to D	AAA to D
Korean Investors Service	1985	Local	A-1 to D	AAA to D
Fitch Ratings	1922	Global	F1+ to D	AAA to D
Moody's Investors Service	1909	Global	P-1 to P-3	Aaa to C
Standard & Poor's	1916	Global	A-1+ to D	AAA to D

Over time the agencies innovated with their business model and in the 1970s switched their revenue base from subscription-paying investors to fee-paying issuers. They also greatly broadened their services to cover the entire spectrum of instruments and obligors, including asset-backed securities, commercial paper, municipal bonds, counterparty risk, the claims-paying ability of insurance companies, and credit risks of all kinds (Moody's Investors Service 2007).

GROWTH IN ISSUES RATED

The importance of the ratings agencies is reflected in the rapid increase in the number of ratings that they provide. In 2005, for example, Moody's rated a total of 5,423 corporate bond issuers—substantially above the 2,522 in 1990 and 885 in 1960 (see Figure 17-1). The breadth of their ratings is wide, with Moody's following over 100 sovereigns, 11,000 corporates, 25,000 public finance issuers, and 70,000 structured finance issuers' obligations. Structured finance for all the agencies has been a major source of growth. In 2005, Moody's earned 41 percent of its revenue from these issuers, rating $2.4 trillion in issuance up from $632 billion in 2005.

In rating long-term debt, each agency uses a system of alphanumeric letter grades that locate an issuer or issue on a spectrum of credit quality from the very highest (AAA/Aaa meaning an extremely strong capacity to meet financial commitments) to the very lowest (C/D meaning there has been a payment default). Each letter grade has three notches (Fitch and S&P use + and − modifiers, Moody's uses numerical modifiers 1, 2, 3) within it (see Table 17-3).

The lower the grade the greater the risk that principal and interest payments will not be made. All debt rated BBB/Baa or above is considered to be of investment-grade quality, while issues rated BB/Ba or below are viewed as speculative or noninvestment grade. The agencies each use a different grading system for short-term debt obligations.

Since the credit quality of an obligor can change dramatically over time, ratings are subject to revision. As a part of their commitment to transparency, agencies update and publish their credit outlook for most issuers on a continuing basis. When they issue ratings, they indicate whether the rating outlook is *positive*, meaning the rating may be raised, *negative*, meaning the rating may be lowered, *stable* indicating a neutral outlook for rating changes, or *developing/evolving*, meaning it may change up or down. To do so they maintain contact with issuers they have rated and review not only their periodic earnings releases but also other relevant financial and economic data. When there is an important development whose rating impact has not yet been determined, an agency notifies both the issuer and the market of this fact—S&P by placing the issue on its Credit Watch, Moody's doing the same on its Rating Review WatchList and Fitch through a news release and posting on its web site.

The switch in payment arrangements from subscribers to issuers remains a point of some controversy, raising concerns about the independence of the agencies. It certainly has not changed the willingness of the regulators to incorporate ratings from NRSROs into their prudential oversight of financial institutions, which they are doing with more frequency.

In truth, although they are paid for their services, the agencies generally behave more like academic research centers than businesses. Analysts are engaged in pure analysis and their position is far from that of a bank lending officer or an investment banker who are always constrained by budgets. The International Organization of Securities Commissions (IOSCO) published a *Code of Conduct Fundamentals for Rating Agencies* in December 2005, which codifies guidelines for the agencies and is designed to promote sound practices.

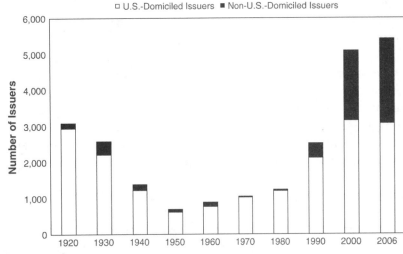

FIGURE 17-1 Moody's-rated corporate bond issuers, 1920–2006.

Source: Moody's Investors Service (2007).

TABLE 17-3 Long-Term Senior Debt Rating Symbols

Investment Grade Ratings	
Rating	**Interpretation**
AAA/Aaa	Highest quality; extremely strong, highly unlikely to be affected by foreseeable events.
AA/Aa	Very high quality; capacity for repayment is not significantly vulnerable to forseeable events.
A/A	Strong payment capacity; more likely to be affected by changes in economic circumstances.
BBB/Baa	Adequate payment capacity; a negative change in environment may affect capacity for repayment.
Below Investment Grade Ratings	
Rating	**Interpretation**
BB/Ba	Considered speculative with possibility of developing credit risks.
B/B	Considered very speculative with significant credit risk.
CCC/Caa	Considered highly speculative with substantial credit risk.
CC/Ca	Maybe in default or wildly speculative.
C/C/D	In bankruptcy or default.

Note: Summary from the main rating agencies. Consult each agency for specific details on their grades.

Policies vary from agency to agency regarding which securities they will rate. Both S&P and Moody's, for example, will rate nearly every taxable security in the U.S. market that has been registered with the SEC—whether or not that issuer has requested a rating. Agencies may also assign ratings at their own initiative, often described as unsolicited or agency-initiated ratings. Generally, such ratings represent only a small minority of the larger agencies' coverage, and the agencies maintain that such ratings are assigned on the same basis as compensated ratings. Disclosure of unsolicited ratings varies. Both Moody's and Fitch disclose agency-initiated ratings in press releases accompanying the initial rating assignment, and both have some form of regular disclosure regarding issuer participation in the rating process. S&P discloses uncompensated ratings in each press release, but does not otherwise indicate the level of issuer participation. Where ratings are either initiated by the agency, or maintained by the agency without compensation, each of the large agencies offers to meet with the issuer concerned and provides issuers with the same opportunity to appeal their ratings afforded to other issuers if they feel that factual errors have been made or material new information has not been considered.

THE RATING PROCESS

In evaluating credits issuers and obligations, the rating agencies use many of the same tools normally applied by equity analysts; but their approach is focused on a longer time horizon than short-term earnings and performance forecasts. Moody's indicates that they are looking at a variety of horizons depending on the maturity of the instruments being rated and the nature of the issuer. Equity analysts approach their work understandably from the perspective of shareholders, while the agencies are looking out for the interests of bondholders, other creditors and counterparties, and, in the case of insurance companies, policyholders. Figure 17-2 illustrates that there are a variety of approaches to debt ratings, some of which are designed to provide very sensitive short-term indicators and others, like the agency ratings, which are designed to evaluate inherent creditworthiness over the longer term.

The agencies are not uniformly transparent in the details of their ratings processes but appear to follow broadly similar approaches. For example, S&P explains that in rating an industrial bond it focuses on the following areas:

- Business risk
- Industry characteristics
- Competitive positioning
- Management
- Financial risk
- Financial characteristics
- Financial policies
- Profitability
- Capitalization
- Cash flow protection
- Financial flexibility

Of these characteristics, S&P claims that the industry risk—their analysis of the strength and stability of the industry in which the firm operates—probably receives the highest weight in the rating decision. Moody's has refined its approach to an industry by industry basis. At both S&P and Moody's, the industry risk analysis often sets an upper limit on the rating attainable by any firm in that industry. Similarly internationally, ratings are normally limited to the sovereign rating ceiling of the nation in which the issuer is domiciled.

In analyzing an issuer's financial strength, Moody's and S&P computes a number of financial ratios and tracks them over time. These include measures of debt coverage leverage, and cash flow. They both emphasize the qualitative such that, while quantification is integral to their rating analysis, it is only a part of their overall approach. While split ratings do occur between the two agencies, in the great majority of cases they agree with each other,

Pure point-in-time	Merton-type model	IRB system	Rating agency proxies	Rating agencies	Pure through-the-cycle

SHORT TIME HORIZON
HIGH RATING VOLATILITY

LONG TIME HORIZON
LOW RATING VOLATILITY

FIGURE 17-2 Point-in-time versus through-the-cycle credit assessments.

Source: Gonzalez, et. al. 2004, 17.

TABLE 17-4 Comparison of Sovereign Foreign Currency Ratings

	Share of Total		Rated Same by Moody's and Standard & Poor's
	Sovereigns Moody's (%)	Sovereigns S&P (%)	Sovereigns (%)
Broad rating categories			
AA/Aa or above	36	34	83
Other investment grade	33	32	79
Below investment grade	31	33	76

Note: The table was obtained by selecting sovereign ratings for 87 countries that are rated by both Moody's and Standard and Poor's.

Source: Credit Suisse (2007) and author compilation.

at least to the equivalent letter if not to the notch. Long-term cumulative default rates between these two agencies are likewise quite similar.

With respect to sovereign ratings issued by the agencies, ratings are similar in the investment grade categories, but less so in the below investment-grade area. A comparison of differences is shown in Table 17-4. While agencies need only consider relatively finite factors in the case of corporate ratings, with sovereigns there are a host of other qualitative factors to consider such as the stability of political institutions, social and economic coherence, and integration into the world's economic system. These factors lead to the greater dispersion around quantitative estimates in sovereign ratings.

The internal rating process at the agencies is rigorous. Ratings are produced by teams of analysts, with relevant expertise, led by a senior experienced analyst who coordinates with the issuer. They review public and nonpublic documentation that can be of a varied nature—financial, contractual, technical as well the documentation relating to a specific debt issue involved.

Accounting practices and differences are reviewed and stripped away. The team meets with an issuer's management to review in depth key factors affecting the rating, including operating and financial plans and management policies. The purpose of the analysis is to focus on the level and predictability of underlying cash flows. The greater the predictability and the more generous the

cushion these cash flows provide, the higher the rating will be, even when exposed to testing against reasonably adverse scenarios. Once this is complete the lead analyst presents the proposed rating to the ratings committee consisting of other senior analysts in the agency. One of the purposes of these cross-group agency reviews is to ensure to the greatest extent possible that each rating category has the same meaning across the entire universe of rated entities and issuers. In other words, that an AA or Aa are of the same credit quality. Once the rating is issued, the agency establishes a surveillance procedure, one part of which is a formal annual meeting with management—who are expected to notify the agency at this meeting and, on an ongoing basis, of any material developments. Agencies reserve the right to change ratings at any time. Normally, however, prospective changes are well signaled to the issuer and to the market through each agency's publications.

The subjective elements in the rating process are desirable and necessary but they do introduce a level of unpredictability into the ratings. For the most part, the agencies have performed their roles well, although in the last 10 years there have been some headline misses with several large U.S. corporate issuers, most notably Enron Corporation and WorldCom Inc., and some Asian countries in the regional crisis of 1998–1999. They take seriously the proposition that all that glitters in an issuer's view of the future is not gold and are parsimonious in their assignment of ratings. All three agencies publish historical data comparing their ratings to the actual occurrence of defaults to allow back testing of their performance.

RATINGS PERFORMANCE

Ratings are used to communicate opinions about the creditworthiness of issuers and obligations. The rating itself contains a lot of pieces of information, including information about the probability of default and the loss

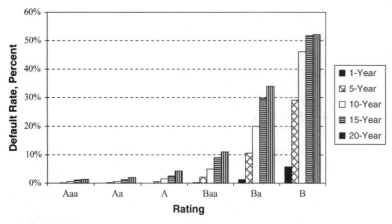

FIGURE 17-3 Corporate default rates based on 1970–2005 experience.

Source: Moody's Investors Service (2005).

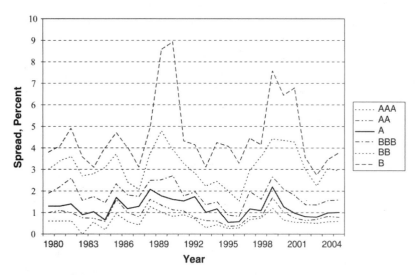

FIGURE 17-4 Bond yield spreads over 30-year treasury bonds.

Source: Bloomberg and author compilation.

severity in the event of default. The track record has been good. As Figure 17-3 demonstrates for corporate bonds, default rates are indeed consistently inversely related to credit ratings over both short and long periods of time. From 1970–2005, the one year default rate of Aaa bonds was zero but it was more than 5 percent for B-rated bonds. Likewise, for each of the given time horizons, the most abrupt increase in default probability occurred between Baa and Ba ratings—the dividing line between

investment grade and noninvestment grade bonds. This distinction, in other words, makes good statistical sense.

The market place tends to corroborate the accuracy of the agencies' work. The riskier a fixed income security, the higher the yield investors will require before they buy it. As Figure 17-4 shows, bond yields are indeed closely correlated to with ratings. (Table 17-5 lists the data for this figure.) Although the actual yield differential between triple-A- and double-A-rated bonds may vary widely over time the relationship remains constant: Investors consistently believe that triple-A-rated bonds are more secure than double-A-rated bonds.

The achievements of the agencies are all the more impressive given the types of credits that they evaluate. The agencies are able to state with confidence that Black & Decker and Best Buy are both BBB credits and that the United States government and Automatic Data Processing are both AAA. At each rating level, the quality of the credit is the same. Thanks to a combination of methodology, technology, and culture the agencies have succeeded in giving investors a relatively reliable guide to credit risk.

As shown in Figure 17-5, default rates can fluctuate over time quite widely with business cycles, but the rating categories still retain their relative quality rankings.

Moody's has published extensive information about the sensitivity of their ratings as predictors of default (Moody's Investors Service 2006a). As shown in Figure 17-6, the distribution of ratings one year prior to default measured over a 20-year period indicates a tight grouping around the low speculative grade level as should be the case. Figure 17-7 provides another perspective on how well ratings discriminate between defaulters and nondefaulters over a similar time frame. Over 90 percent of all rated companies that have defaulted since 1983 were rated Ba3 or worse at the beginning of the year in which they defaulted, and almost 80 percent of them were rated Ba3 or worse at the beginning of the fifth year before they defaulted.

TABLE 17-5 Data for Figure 17-4

Year	AAA	AA	A	BBB	BB	B
1980	0.60	1.00	1.30	1.90	3.00	3.80
1981	0.60	1.10	1.30	2.20	3.40	4.10
1982	0.60	1.00	1.40	2.60	3.60	4.90
1983	0.00	0.75	0.90	1.57	2.70	3.60
1984	0.55	0.73	1.04	1.75	2.80	3.10
1985	0.20	0.58	0.65	1.46	3.10	4.00
1986	0.95	1.59	1.70	2.33	3.70	4.70
1987	0.58	1.02	1.18	1.82	2.43	4.03
1988	0.42	0.79	1.29	1.75	2.07	3.12
1989	1.28	1.61	2.08	2.49	3.76	4.95
1990	1.02	1.34	1.77	2.52	4.78	8.57
1991	0.82	1.13	1.61	2.71	3.92	8.93
1992	0.90	1.08	1.54	1.77	3.29	4.34
1993	0.70	0.76	1.74	1.96	2.82	4.15
1994	0.29	0.62	1.01	1.37	2.23	3.12
1995	0.43	0.60	1.17	1.49	2.45	4.25
1996	0.25	0.35	0.54	0.88	2.00	4.08
1997	0.28	0.39	0.57	0.83	1.53	3.30
1998	0.67	0.81	1.17	1.99	2.97	4.46
1999	0.74	0.81	1.09	1.62	3.59	4.15
2000	1.20	1.67	2.19	2.64	4.42	7.57
2001	0.65	1.03	1.27	2.10	4.36	6.45
2002	0.55	0.75	0.98	1.81	4.28	6.79
2003	0.53	0.63	0.81	1.37	2.99	3.53
2004	0.50	0.68	0.79	1.36	2.25	2.75
2005	0.57	0.83	0.99	1.56	3.05	3.45
2006	0.59	0.78	1.01	1.59	2.94	3.79

Source: Bloomberg and author compilation.

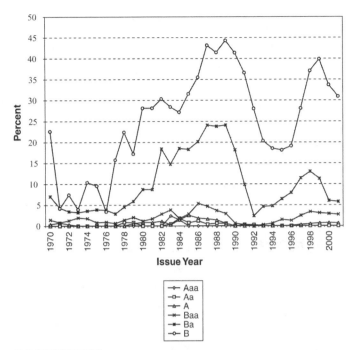

FIGURE 17-5 Trends in five-year default rates by original credit rating.

Source: Moody's Investors Service (2005).

Another important consideration with ratings is the extent to which they actually change within relatively short periods of time. Investors expect some movement but if the ratings are indeed long-term in nature the extent of these changes should be relatively modest. Table 17-6 shows the one year average rating transition matrix over an extended period of time. Higher ratings have generally been less likely to be revised than lower ratings over a one-year period. For example the ratings of 89 percent of the Aaa-rated issuers did not change within one year. By contrast, in the B category, only 78 percent of those issuers ended the year in the same category. Also, for issuers in the middle of the ratings scale, Ba and Baa, they are almost equally as likely to move up or down a grade within a one-year time period (Moody's Investors Service 2006).

RATINGS AND REGULATORS

The relationship between regulators and ratings agencies is deep and often ambiguous. The regulators are attracted

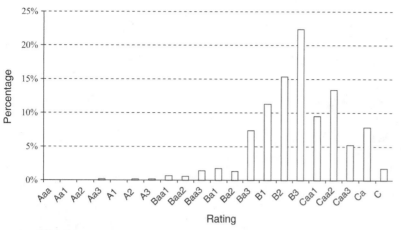

FIGURE 17-6 Distribution of ratings one year prior to default, 1983–2005.

Source: Moody's Investors Service (2006).

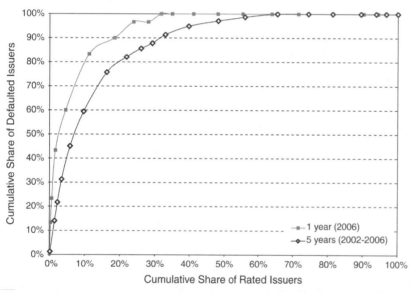

FIGURE 17-7 Cumulative accuracy profile: One year vs. five years.

Source: Moody's Investors Service (2002).

ratings of a few of the agencies (the NRSROs in the United States and the so-called ECAIs under the Basel II Capital Requirements Directive), this creates an important competitive advantage.

Congress passed the Credit Rating Agency Reform Act of 2006 to establish a new registration process setting a clear path to being designated an NSRO, and amending the Securities Exchange Act of 1934. The legislation also provides SEC oversight to ensure that registered rating agencies continue to issue credible and reliable ratings and to protect against conflicts of interest and misuse of nonpublic information.

As the Committee of European Banking Supervisors (CEBS) noted, "ECAI recognition for capital purposes does not in any way constitute a form of regulation of ECAIs or a form of licensing of rating agencies to do business in Europe" (CEBS 2005). The regulators do apply certain criteria as shown in Table 17-7.

In general, there are undoubted benefits from this close relationship that has been developed by the regulators with the rating agencies for the financial markets, which is really an extension of the benefits that ratings bring to the markets themselves—namely improving efficiency through providing information reliably, conveniently, and at low cost. The trust placed in the agencies is generally warranted and the agencies are acutely aware of the value of their reputation for quality and objectivity. It is far preferable that the agencies, however oligopolistic they may be, perform this role of providing creditworthiness opinions than having a government regulator try to do it. There are many complexities, however, in the rating process and by tying regulations closely into ratings there is a danger of magnifying some of these complexities. For example, even though the doors in the United States and Europe have been opened to allow further competition the top three agencies are still dominant and will remain so for the foreseeable future. Also, in the process of adopting rating levels in regulations, especially in Basel II, there is a danger of oversimplifying the ratings

to the high quality, the independence, and very widespread acceptance of the rating agency opinions on credit quality. On the other hand, they are concerned about putting so much reliance on the agencies over whose activities they have no control. For the agencies, the use of their opinions by the regulators is an important validation of their work. Also, because the regulators only accept the

TABLE 17-6 One-Year Average Rating Transition Matrix, 1983–2005

Beginning of Year Rating	End of Year Rating								
	Aaa	**Aa**	**A**	**Baa**	**Ba**	**B**	**Caa-C**	**Default**	**WR**
Aaa	89.54	7.14	0.41	0.00	0.02	0.00	0.00	0.00	2.89
Aa	1.25	88.82	5.72	0.25	0.04	0.02	0.00	0.01	3.89
A	0.05	2.63	87.35	5.29	0.59	0.13	0.02	0.02	3.92
Baa	0.04	0.22	4.92	83.95	4.81	0.99	0.32	0.21	4.53
Ba	0.01	0.06	0.54	6.10	75.53	7.93	0.72	1.15	7.98
B	0.01	0.05	0.16	0.41	4.66	73.56	6.63	5.76	8.75
Caa-C	0.00	0.04	0.03	0.22	0.60	5.47	59.46	10.41	23.78

Beginning of Year Rating	End of Year Rating								
	Aaa	**Aa**	**A**	**Baa**	**Ba**	**B**	**Caa-C**	**Default**	**WR**
Aaa	89.54%	7.14%	0.41%	0.00%	0.02%	0.00%	0.00%	0.00%	2.89%
Aa	1.25%	88.82%	5.72%	0.25%	0.04%	0.02%	0.00%	0.01%	3.89%
A	0.05%	2.63%	87.35%	5.29%	0.59%	0.13%	0.02%	0.02%	3.92%
Baa	0.04%	0.22%	4.92%	83.95%	4.81%	0.99%	0.32%	0.21%	4.53%
Ba	0.01%	0.06%	0.54%	6.10%	75.53%	7.93%	0.72%	1.15%	7.98%
B	0.01%	0.05%	0.16%	0.41%	4.66%	73.56%	6.63%	5.76%	8.75%
Caa-C	0.00%	0.04%	0.03%	0.22%	0.60%	5.47%	59.46%	10.41%	23.78%

Source: Moody's Investors Service (2006).

TABLE 17-7 Basel II ECAI Eligibility Criteria

Objectivity	The methodology for assigning credit assessments must be rigorous, systematic, and subject to some form of validation based on historical experience. Moreover, assessments must be subject to ongoing review and responsive to changes in financial condition. Before being recognized by supervisors, an assessment methodology for each market segment, including rigorous back testing, must have been established for at least one year and preferably three years.
Independence	An ECAI should be independent and should not be subject to political or economic pressures that may influence the rating. The assessment process should be as free as possible from any constraints that could arise in situations where the composition of the board of directors or the shareholder structure of the assessment institution may be seen as creating a conflict of interest.
International access and transparency	The individual assessments should be available to both domestic and foreign institutions with legitimate interests and at equivalent terms. In addition, the general methodology used by the ECAI should be publicly available.
Disclosure	An ECAI should disclose the following information: its assessment methodologies, including the definition of default, the time horizon, and the meaning of each rating; the actual default rates experienced in each assessment category; and the transitions of the assessments (e.g., the likelihood of AA ratings becoming A over time).
Resources	An ECAI should have sufficient resources to carry out high quality credit assessments. These resources should allow for substantial ongoing contact with senior and operational levels within the entities assessed in order to add value to the credit assessments. Such assessments should be based on methodologies combining qualitative and quantitative approaches.
Credibility	To some extent, credibility is derived from the criteria above. In addition, the reliance on an ECAI's external credit assessments by independent parties (investors, insurers, trading partners) is evidence of the credibility of the assessments of an ECAI. The credibility of an ECAI is also underpinned by the existence of internal procedures to prevent the misuse of confidential information. In order to be eligible for recognition, an ECAI does not have to assess firms in more than one country.

Source: Bank for International Settlements (2004).

process and not sufficiently recognizing the magnitude of the difference between the various rating grades for purposes of capital adequacy. The treatment of split ratings (where agencies' opinions on the same issuer) differ is another similar technicality to consider. Finally, there is a tension between the Basel II assumption of essentially a cardinal scale, and the ordinal scales actually employed by the agencies. Basel II's assumption of specific percentage default rates will eventually conflict with the agencies' won assignment of ordinally ranked ratings whose actual default frequency varies widely over the cycle. Agencies with such heavy reliance on their ratings will begin to make them considerably shorter term in outlook and thereby make them much more procyclical. This could have the effect of increasing the volatility of ratings movements and hence the volatility of capital requirements at the most critical parts of the credit cycle.

EMERGING TRENDS

The more power and influence the rating agencies have acquired the more controversial they have become. By and large market participants, both issuers and investors, are satisfied with the products produced by the agencies. They understand clearly that agency opinions are not intended to be the sole source of information to be used in making credit decisions. They expect there will be transparency in the process so that it will be clear how ratings are derived and what considerations might lead to their being changed. They also expect greater forensic activity from the agencies, to dig into nonpublic information and be more active in questioning key aspects of an issuer's performance. Market participants themselves use financial data and securities prices to track issuer performance but they expect that the agencies will base their views on fundamental credit measures to give a more stable view of intrinsic financial capacity.

We can expect the regulators and lawmakers to be increasingly involved in rating agency activities, and we saw the beginnings of this trend with the Congressional hearings after the collapse of Enron. When other corporate collapses or credit crises occur we can expect there will be more enquiries of the same kind. Oftentimes these hearings are enlivened with criticisms from other rating agencies who are outside those officially recognized by regulators.

The academic community faces many obstacle in generating valuable research on ratings. The ultimate test of a rating—default—is an extremely low frequency event. The rated universes of all three agencies, while adequate for capital markets users, are extremely small in statistical terms. Even a modestly sized commercial bank will likely have more statistically robust data pools for both default frequency and loss severity. Topics for study by both academics and regulators have nonetheless included: Whether widely available market-sensitive data does as good or better a job as the agencies in predicting financial distress, the conflict of interest inherent in having issuers pay the agencies for ratings. Cases, especially in emerging markets, where financial crises were not preceded by ratings downgrades. The question remains, given the unsuitability of agency ratings to capture all elements of credit performance, bank regulators and supervisors should remain cautious about excessive reliance on these ratings for regulatory purposes.

At this writing, the U.S. credit markets are in turmoil caused by concerns over defaults and credit losses arising from lending to subprime borrowers in the housing market. Several substantial U.S. mortgage originators have filed for bankruptcy and the largest full-service mortgage lender, Countrywide, has seen its market value significantly reduced. These concerns have spread into other markets, principally Europe, and into other borrower and product areas causing severe contractions in liquidity and abrupt and significant increases in credit spreads. Structured finance portfolios have been particularly affected because subprime loans have been securitized to an unusually high degree and because subprime loans have also been mixed in with other debt types in CDOs to obtain more beneficial rating outcomes.

The rating agencies are once again in the spotlight and facing heavy criticism for the enabling role they have played in the growth of the structured finance market (Lagard 2007). As a result of the current problems, the agencies have been actively recalibrating the default and loss assumptions in their rating models as well as their correlation assumptions for different asset classes in CDOs.

The agencies are defending themselves by insisting that they have provided transparency in their rating approaches; that they have given plenty of early notice of problems; and have defended the independence of their ratings. They acknowledge issues however, particularly with the quality of the information they were using and the fact that they probably needed to heed other factors than just "pure ability to pay," most importantly liquidity (Clarkson 2007).

It is too early to say what the effects of this credit crunch will be on the agencies, but we expect it will subject them to more intensive review and criticism than either the Asian crisis or Enron and Worldcom. IOSCO announced the formation of a task force in November 2007 to examine the role of the ratings agencies in the subprime crisis and to review the adequacy of their Credit Rating Agency Code of Conduct, referred to earlier in this chapter. Its report will be published in May 2008.

Credit rating agencies are going to remain a major influence in the capital markets and, if anything, their domination will grow stronger. Even though their performance has not been without blemish it is clear that global financial markets need their essential information services. In its October 2007 Financial Stability Report, the Bank of England produced a balanced assessment of the role of the agencies. It noted their vital contributions to investors in the credit markets, principally transparency, independence, and affordability. It summarized the lessons learned so far from the market turmoil and provided the agencies with suggestions to improve the information content of their ratings. These ideas are being evaluated by the agencies and may well provide the basis for the next phase of their evolution.

References

Bank for International Settlements (BIS). 2004, June. *Basel II: International Convergence of Capital Measurement and Capital Standards, Part 2: The First Pillar—Minimum Capital Requirements*. Basel.

Bank of England. 2007, October. Financial Stability Report Number 22. London.

Clarkson, B. 2007. "Market Insight: Transparency and Trust." *Financial Times*, 17 September.

Committee of European Banking Supervisors (CEBS). 2005. Consultation Paper on the recognition of External Credit Assessment Institutions, 29 June.

Credit Suisse. 2007. *Country Ratings*. entry.credit-suisse.ch/csfs/p/cb/en/tradefinance/landinfo/lio_laenderratings.jsp (27 December).

Gonzalez, F., F. Haas, R. Johannes, M. Persson, L. Toledo, R. Violi, M. Wieland, and C. Zins. 2004. *Market Dynamics Associated with Credit Ratings: A Literature Review*. Occasional Paper Series, No. 16. Frankfurt am Main: European Central Bank.

Klein, A. 2004. "Credit Rate's Power Leads to Abuses, Some Borrowers Say." *Washington Post*, 24 November.

Lagard, C. 2007. "Securitisation Must Lose the Excesses of Youth." *Financial Times*, 8 October.

Levich, R. M., G. Majnoni, and C. M. Reinhart, eds. 2002. *Ratings, Rating Agencies and the Global Financial System*. Norwell Mass.: Kluwer.

Moody's Investors Service. 2002, May. *Special Comment: Understanding Moody's Corporate Bond Ratings and Rating Process*. New York.

——. 2003, April. *Measuring the Performance of Corporate Bond Ratings,* New York.

——. 2006 *Exhibit taken from Moody's Default and Recovery Rates of Corporate Bond Issuers 1920–2005*. New York.

——. 2006a. *Default and Recovery Rates of Corporate Bond Issuers 1920–2005*. New York.

——. 2006b, January. *Special Comment: Default and Recovery Rates of Corporate Bond Issuers, 1920–2005*. New York.

——. 2006c. *Annual Report 2006*. New York.

——. 2007. Investor Day presentation, 5 June.

U.S. Senate. 2002. Committee on Government Affairs. *Rating the Raters: Enron and the Credit Rating Agencies*, 20 March.

Further Reading

Sandage, S. A. 2005. Chapters 4 through 6 in *Born Losers: A History of Failure in America*. Cambridge, Mass.: Harvard University Press.

SAMPLE EXAM QUESTIONS—FINANCIAL MARKETS AND PRODUCTS

1. A stock index is valued at USD 750 and pays a continuous dividend at the rate of 2% per annum. The 6-month futures contract on that index is trading at USD 757. The risk-free rate is 3.50% continuously compounded. There are no transaction costs or taxes. Is the futures contract priced so that there is an arbitrage opportunity? If yes, which of the following numbers comes closest to the arbitrage profit you could realize by taking a position in one futures contract?

   A. 4.18

   B. 1.35

   C. 12.60

   D. There is no arbitrage opportunity.

2. On Nov. 1, Jimmy Walton, a fund manager of a USD 60 million U.S. medium-to-large cap equity portfolio, considers locking up the profit from the recent rally. The S&P 500 index and its futures with the multiplier of 250 are trading at 900 and 910, respectively. Instead of selling off his holdings, he would rather hedge two-thirds of his market exposure over the remaining two months. Given that the correlation between Jimmy's portfolio and the S&P 500 index futures is 0.89 and the volatilities of the equity fund and the futures are 0.51 and 0.48 per year respectively, what position should he take to achieve his objective?

   A. Sell 250 futures contracts of S&P 500

   B. Sell 169 futures contracts of S&P 500

   C. Sell 167 futures contracts of S&P 500

   D. Sell 148 futures contracts of S&P 500

3. The following statement is made by S&P about the creditworthiness of company XYZ:

   "Strong capacity to meet financial commitments, but somewhat susceptible to adverse economic conditions and changes in circumstances."

   What is the rating assigned by S&P to company XYZ?

   A. AAA

   B. A

   C. B

   D. C

4. Company XYZ operates in the U.S. On April 1, 2009, it has a net trade receivable of EUR 5,000,000 from an export contract to Germany. The company expects to receive this amount on Oct. 1, 2009. The CFO of XYZ wants to protect the value of this receivable. On April 1, 2009, the EUR spot rate is 1.34, and the 6-month EUR forward rate is 1.33. The CFO can lock in an exchange rate by taking a position in the forward contract. Alternatively, he can sell a 6-month EUR 5,000,000 call option with strike price of 1.34. The CFO thinks that selling an option is better than taking a forward position because if the EUR goes up, XYZ can take delivery of the USD at 1.34, which is better than the outright forward rate of 1.33. If the EUR goes down, the contract will not be exercised. So, XYZ will pocket the premium obtained from selling the call option.

   What can be concluded about the CFO's analysis?

   A. CFO's analysis is correct. The company is better off whichever way the EUR rate goes.

   B. CFO's analysis is not correct. The company will suffer if the EUR goes up sharply.

   C. CFO's analysis is not correct. The company will suffer if the EUR moves within a narrow range.

   D. CFO's analysis is not correct. The company will suffer if the EUR goes down sharply.

5. An investor with a long position in a futures contract wants to issue instructions to close out the position. A market-if-touched order would be used if the investor wants to:

   A. Execute at the best available price once a trade occurs at the specified or better price.

   B. Execute at the best available price once a bid/offer occurs at the specified or worse price.

   C. Allow a broker to delay execution of the order to get a better price.

   D. Execute the order immediately or not at all.

6. Below is a table of term structure of swap rates:

Maturity in Years	Swap Rate
1	2.50%
2	3.00%
3	3.50%
4	4.00%
5	4.50%

   The 2-year forward swap rate starting in three years is closest to:

   A. 3.50%

   B. 4.50%

   C. 5.51%

   D. 6.02%

7. Three months ago a company entered in a one-year forward contract to buy 100 ounces of gold. At the time, the one-year forward price was USD 1,000 per ounce. The nine-month forward price of gold is now USD 1,050 per ounce. The continuously-compounded risk-free rate is 4% per year for all maturities, and there are no storage costs. Which of the following is closest to the value of the contract?

   A. USD 5,000

   B. USD 4,852

   C. USD 7,955

   D. USD 1,897

8. Calculate the impact of a 10 basis point increase in yield on the following bond portfolio:

Bond	Value (USD)	Modified Duration
1	4,000,000	7.5
2	2,000,000	1.6
3	3,000,000	6.0
4	1,000,000	1.3

    A. USD −41,000

    B. USD −52,500

    C. USD −410,000

    D. USD −525,000

9. An oil producer has an obligation under an agreement to supply one million barrels of oil at a fixed price. The producer wishes to hedge this liability using futures in order to address the possibility of an upward movement in oil prices. In comparing a strip hedge to a stack and roll hedge, which of the following statements is correct?

    A. A stack and roll hedge tends to involve fewer transactions.

    B. A strip hedge tends to have smaller bid-ask spreads.

    C. A stack and roll hedge tends to have greater liquidity.

    D. A strip hedge tends to realize gains and losses more frequently.

10. You wish to hedge an investment in zirconium using futures. Unfortunately, there are no futures that are based on this asset. To determine the best futures contract for you to hedge with, you run a regression of daily changes in the price of zirconium against daily changes in the prices of similar assets which do have futures contracts associated with them. Based on your results, futures tied to which asset would likely introduce the least basis risk into your hedging position?

Change in Price of Zirconium = $\alpha + \beta$ (Change in Price of Asset)			
Asset	α	β	R^2
A	1.25	1.03	0.62
B	0.67	1.57	0.81
C	0.01	0.86	0.35
D	4.56	2.30	0.45

    A. Asset A

    B. Asset B

    C. Asset C

    D. Asset D

11. As it relates to the bond indenture, the corporate trustee acts in a fiduciary capacity for:

    A. bond investors.

    B. bond issuers.

    C. bond underwriters.

    D. regulators.

12. As an asset manager, Sarah Peck wishes to reduce her exposure to fixed-income securities and increase her exposure to large-cap stocks. She enters into an equity swap with a dealer on the terms that she will pay the dealer a fixed rate of 5% and receive from him the return on the large-cap stock index. Assume that payments are made annually and that the notional principal is EUR 50 million. If the large-cap stock index had a value of 10,320 at the beginning of the year and a value of 11,219 at the end of the year, what is the net payment made at the end of the year, and which party makes the net payment?

Net Payment Made	Party Making Net Payment
A. EUR 1.86 million	Asset manager
B. EUR 2.50 million	Dealer
C. EUR 1.86 million	Dealer
D. EUR 2.50 million	Asset manager

13. The current stock price of a share is USD 100, and the continuously compounding risk-free rate is 12% per year. The maximum possible prices for a 3-month European call option, American call option, European put option, and American put option, all with strike price of USD 90, are:

    A. 100, 100, 87.34, 90

    B. 100, 100, 90, 90

    C. 97.04, 100, 90, 90

    D. 97.04, 97.04, 87.34, 87.34

14. Stock UGT is trading at USD 100. A 1-year European call option on UGT with a strike price of USD 80 is trading at USD 30. No dividends are being paid in the following year. What should be the lower bound for an American put option on UGT with a strike price of USD 80 in order to not have arbitrage opportunities? Assume a continuously-compounded risk-free rate of 4% per year.

    A. 6.1

    B. 7.7

    C. 5.7

    D. 6.9

15. Relative to coupon-bearing bonds of the same maturity, zero-coupon bonds are NOT subject to which type of risk?

    A. Interest rate risk

    B. Credit risk

    C. Reinvestment risk

    D. Liquidity risk

SAMPLE EXAM ANSWERS AND EXPLANATIONS—FINANCIAL MARKETS AND PRODUCTS

1. **Answer: B**

    Explanation: The formula for computing the forward price on a financial asset is:

    $$F_{0,T} = S_0 e^{(r-\delta)T}$$

    where S_0 is the spot price of the asset, r is the continuously compounded interest rate, and δ is the continuous dividend yield on the asset.

    The no-arbitrage futures price is computed as follows:

    $$750 e^{(0.035 - 0.02) \cdot 0.5} = 755.65$$

    Since the market price of the futures contract is higher than this price, there is an arbitrage opportunity. The futures contract could be sold and the index purchased.

2. **Answer: C**

    Explanation: The optimal hedge ratio is the product of the correlation coefficient between the change in the spot price and the change in futures price and the ratio of the volatility of the equity fund and the futures.

    Two-thirds of the equity fund is worth USD 40 million. The optimal hedge ratio computed:

    $$h = 0.89 * (0.51/0.48) = 0.945$$

    Computing the number of futures contracts:

    $$N = 0.945 * 40{,}000{,}000/(910 * 250) = 166.26 = 167, \text{ round up to nearest integer.}$$

3. **Answer: B**

    Explanation: The interpretation the statement refers to is a rating of A. The interpretations for each of the ratings are:

    AAA—Extremely strong capacity to meet financial commitments

    A—Strong capacity to meet financial commitments

    B—Very speculative with significant credit risk

    C—In bankruptcy or default

4. **Answer: D**

    Explanation: The CFO's analysis is incorrect because there is unlimited downside risk. The option premium received is a fixed amount, and if the EUR declines sharply, the value of the underlying receivable goes down as well. If instead the EUR moves in a narrow range, that would be good, but there is no guarantee of course that this will occur.

5. **Answer: A**

   Explanation: A market-if-touched order executes at the best available price once a trade occurs at the specified or better price. A stop order executes at the best available price once a bid/offer occurs at the specified or worse price. A discretionary order allows a broker to delay execution of the order to get a better price. A fill-or-kill order executes the order immediately or not at all.

6. **Answer: D**

   Explanation: Computing the 2-year forward swap rate starting in three years:

   $$6.02\% = [(1.045^5/(1.035^3))^{(1/2)}]$$

7. **Answer: B**

   Explanation: The forward price is computed as follows:

   $F_0 = 100 \times (F_0 - K)e^{-rT}$

   $F_0 = 1,050$

   $K = 1,000$

   $r = 0.04$

   $T = 0.75$

   $F = 100 \times (1050 - 1000)e^{-0.04 \cdot 0.75} = 4852$

8. **Answer: B**

   Explanation:

(A)	(B)	(C)	(D)	(E)
Bond	Value (USD)	Modified Duration	(B×C)	(D/B)
1	4,000,000	7.5	30,000,000	
2	2,000,000	1.6	3,200,000	
3	3,000,000	6.0	18,000,000	
4	1,000,000	1.3	1,300,000	
SUM	10,000,000		52,500,000	5.25

The portfolio modified duration is 5.25. This is obtained by multiplying the value of each bond by the modified duration(s), then taking the sum of these products, and dividing it by the value of the total bond portfolio.

The change in the value of the portfolio will be $-10,000,000 \times 5.25 \times 0.1\% = -52,500$

9. **Answer: C**

   Explanation: A strip hedge involves one-time buying of futures contracts to match the maturity of liabilities, whereas the stack and roll hedge involves multiple purchases over time. A strip hedge tends to have wider bid-ask spreads due to the use of longer maturity contracts. A strip hedge also tends to have lesser liquidity than a stack and roll hedge due to longer maturity contracts. Both a strip hedge and stack and roll hedge would realize gains/losses daily using futures.

10. **Answer: B**

    Explanation: Futures on an asset whose price changes are most closely correlated with the asset you are looking to hedge will have the least basis risk. This is determined by examining the R^2 of the regressions and choosing the highest one. R^2 is the most applicable statistic in the above chart to determine correlation with the price of zirconium.

11. **Answer: A**

    Explanation: The promises of corporate bond issuers and the rights of investors who buy them are set forth in great detail in contracts generally called *indentures.* The indenture is made out to the corporate trustee as a representative of the interests of bondholders; that is, the trustee acts in a fiduciary capacity for investors who own the bond issue.

12. **Answer: C**

    Explanation: Cash Flows for Peck:

    (Inflow at the return (%) on stock index − Outflow at 5%) * Notional principal

    Return on stock index = (11219/10320) − 1 = 0.0871 or 8.71%

    Net amount owed by the dealer to Peck = 50 M * (0.0871 − 0.05) = 50,000,000 * 0.0371 = EUR 1.86 million

13. **Answer: A**

    Explanation: For European and American call options, the maximum possible price is equal to current stock price. The option price can never be higher than the stock. The stock price is thus the "upper bound." For a European Put, the upper bound is the present value of strike price, while for American put, it is equal to the strike price.

14. **Answer: D**

   Explanation: The European call option is the same as an American call option since there are no dividends during the life of the options. American call and put prices satisfy the inequality.

   $S - K \leqslant C - P \leqslant S - Ke^{-rt}$, thus

   $Ke^{-rt} - S + C \leqslant P \leqslant K - S + C$, therefore:

   $6.86 \leqslant P \leqslant 10$.

   6.9 falls between 6.86 and 10.

15. **Answer: C**

   Explanation: Since zero-coupon bonds have no coupons, there is nothing to reinvest. However, they are subject to all of the other risks listed.

Index